HOSTAGES

GRIGORY SVIRSKY

HOSTAGES

THE PERSONAL TESTIMONY OF A SOVIET JEW

TRANSLATED FROM THE RUSSIAN
BY GORDON CLOUGH

ALFRED A. KNOPF   NEW YORK   1976

Translation Copyright © 1976 by The Bodley Head Ltd
and Alfred A. Knopf, Inc.
All rights reserved under International and Pan-American Copyright Conventions.
Published in the United States by Alfred A. Knopf, Inc., New York.
Distributed by Random House, Inc., New York.
Originally published in France as *Zalozhniki*
by Les Éditeurs Réunis, Paris.
Copyright © 1974 by Les Éditeurs Réunis.

Library of Congress Cataloging in Publication Data

Svirsky, Grigory, (Date)   Hostages.
Translation of Zalozhniki.
1. Jews in Russia—Persecutions. 2. Antisemitism—Russia.
3. Svirsky, Grigory, 1921–
4. Russia—Politics and government—1945–
5. World War, 1939–1945—Personal narratives, Jewish.
I. Title.
DS135.R92S9513   1976   301.45'19'24047024   [B]   75-36812
ISBN 0-394-49368-0

Manufactured in the United States of America
First American Edition

Once again we Communists appeal to all decent people
throughout the world to unite all their strengths against the
universally abhorred ideology and practice of racism.

> —From the basic document
> accepted by the International
> Conference of Workers' and
> Communist Parties, Moscow,
> June 17, 1969.

Our train leaves for Auschwitz—
today and every day.

> —Alexander Galich, Moscow, 1969.

CONTENTS

FOREWORD

TO AN EDITION
I NEVER EXPECTED TO SEE PUBLISHED

Jews fly out of Moscow. (So do non-Jews.) From Sheremetievo Airport. They fly out to Israel—all over the world. And meanwhile at military airports like Olsufievo, transport planes take off laden with weapons for killing Jews. That's reality. There is no end to the trail of blood and tragedy: Tel Aviv, Lod, Munich, London—nowhere left where Russian arms are not being used to slaughter Jews.

I have spent my entire life hoping for changes in Russia. Sometimes that hope defied all the available evidence; but there have been times when I have seen with my own eyes the green shoots of a plant that might have grown into the flower of equality. What I failed to realize was that the seeds from which those shoots had sprung had been sown on the stony ground of lawlessness.

I believed that changes would come to Russia, and I did what I could to bring those changes about. And Russian writers presented me with a whole collection of Don Quixotes, some cast in bronze, some carved in wood. I hoped for changes in Russia long before I began to think of Israel as a way of escape. I wrote this book hoping that there were still some vestiges of human conscience left, that there were still some traces of common sense. . . .

The shots fired in Czechoslovakia destroyed all that.

There are so many things in this book I would like to correct. In Russia I had to keep it under lock and key, and so its publication now is still something I find difficult to grasp. I would like to appear to my readers as wiser, more clear-sighted, as having had a much greater degree of inner freedom than I did when I was writing it. I would like to have sounded less cliché-ridden, less prone to a leaden journalese. In Russia, after all, you believe what journalists write—but then again, you do not.

But I'm afraid that once a song is sung there is no changing the words. As it was, so must it remain. I have no right to indulge in hindsight; I have no right to straighten out the twists and turns of the road that I (and not only I) have had to travel. It is the selfsame road that Russia's three million Jews have traveled with me. And within that Jewish community a feeling of being a worthy part of an ancient people is now, at last, beginning to awaken.

I would like to have been able to shed some of the load of my thoughts, my hopelessness, along that desperate, weary road. That is why I started this book and why, once started, I completed it, in spite of everything. It was no longer possible to keep silent about the painful side of life, as if it simply did not exist. That would have been unworthy of me as a man and as a writer, beneath contempt, even criminal. Yet, there is no point in trying to hide the fact that I would have liked to forget this part of my life—indeed, that is my dream. But it won't leave me.

People will say that this book is one-sided, that I have written only about the pain. But that is not relevant. You can find all the other aspects of life in many books on the subject, mine included; I have lived all those aspects enthusiastically for many years—but they are a long way from what I have tried to describe here.

I have been advised to change the names of the people in this book. Of course, it would be easy enough. But if I were to change the name of the poet Sergei Vasiliev to Vasilisa Prekrasnaya, for example, not one single informed reader in Russia would fail to recognize him. If I were to change the names, the story I have to tell would lose its documentary quality. And it must be—absolutely must be—documentary, the more so since it will be a long time before the book is finally published. . . .

The book, then, is strictly reportage. All the facts are true, all the names are genuine. Everything is based on written testimony. I have no time for rumors. I have written only about things *my own family has seen and experienced.*

PREFACE

A reception was held at the Writers' Union to mark the birthday of a famous novelist. There were respectful speeches about all he had accomplished. Proceedings were drawing to a close, and the congratulatory addresses in their fine bindings had piled up on the table.

The writer himself rose to speak. "At the end of the war I was in a village in Bulgaria, and I saw something quite extraordinary. There was a very fat man being chased around the village by soldiers. He was wrapped in a fishing net, and carrying a typewriter in his hands. It was terribly hot that day, and the fat man was staggering. He looked as if he might collapse at any moment. I wanted to do something, to help him—but finally I decided to wait until I could find out what it was all about. It turned out to be the local method of dealing with a thief. The man had robbed the local fish cooperative and escaped with a net and a typewriter, so he was being paraded around the village, carrying the things he had stolen. . . .

"When we writers reach the age when people hold receptions for us, it would be a good thing if we too were chased around our cities, up and down the main streets, carrying what we have stolen from the people. We should be forced to display all the things we should have written but never wrote, all the things we should have said but failed to say."

I was struck not merely by what this writer said, but by the way he said it. He was pale, he sounded choked, as if he were speaking not at a reception in his honor, but at the Last Judgment.

There was tragedy in his outstretched hands.

PART
ONE

1

Pauline's tram was almost at the factory when she heard a blast from the street loudspeakers. "Our troops have withdrawn from Krivoi Rog."

Suddenly the clanging and banging of the tramcar seemed muted, and the passengers jammed together inside swung and swayed with its motion silently, like a bell without a clapper. But the voice from the loudspeaker gabbled on (they always gabbled when they had to announce a retreat) ". . . withdrawn from Krivoi Rog."

The crowd swept her out of the car and carried her to the factory entrance. The timekeeper shouted something but all she could hear was ". . . withdrawn from Krivoi Rog."

The lactic acid laboratory was on the first floor of the factory. There was a rank stench of soured milk from the damp slippery tiles. Young laboratory assistants hurried by holding their breath. Pauline paced the first-floor landing. Her friends hurried on upstairs. "What's up? What's the matter with you?" She said nothing.

A week later she saw an announcement stuck on the university bulletin board. *All Ukrainian and Byelorussian speakers to report to the Komsomol Committee.* She rushed off to the Committee. They asked her if she'd agree to be parachuted into her homeland, provided permission were granted. "Of course."

They sent her to the Party offices. There the conversation was on a different, much more serious level. Men in impeccable military uniforms but without badges of rank questioned her for a long time, leafed through documents and medical reports. They told her to fill in a form.

Next she had to settle down to wait. But then they called her back. "We can't send you; the Germans are shooting every Jew they lay hands on." She caught her breath. So it was true. She dropped into a broad Ukrainian accent and asked: "Do you really think I look like a Jew?"

"No, you don't."

"All right. Just write 'Ukrainian' in my passport."

"But what if people give you away as a Jew?"

"Who'd do that?"

"Your neighbors might. There's always some bastard around."

"You must be out of your minds! That could never happen! Please let me go! I'd be useful, I know every inch of the country around there."

She went out onto the staircase—there was nowhere else to go—sat down on a step and burst into silent tears, biting her thumbnail. How could they think that? That anyone would give her away?

"Oh, Mama, Mama . . ." She could see her mother absolutely clearly, in her full skirt tucked up like a gypsy's, her feet bare. She was scrubbing the floor in expectation of Pauline's arrival. "You always said we were lucky, Mama!"

For as long as Pauline could remember, people at home had always said they were lucky. Whatever trouble came, their neighbors in the village and the peasants living outside would help them. Whenever there had been any danger, whenever Makhno or Petlyura or the Blues or the Greens or anyone else had descended on the village, someone had always crept up to the house, tapped on the window, and whispered, "Hide!"*

They used to hide in an empty stable, in the hay. Once they had only just buried themselves when Makhno's men brought their horses in for shelter. From that time on Mama had become superstitious, fatalistic: "No matter how the horses neighed and snorted and pawed the ground, they didn't give us away."

Once the neighbors dressed Mama in an old castoff dress and smeared her face with soot; and when Makhno's men galloped up, one of the neighbors barred the way in; she just said curtly, "We've got typhus here."

But they had taken her grandfather—either Denikin's† men or Petlyura's. They threw a rope over a branch, gathered all the local people together, and then hanged the dirty Yid.

The villagers fell to their knees and begged for his life. They took him down. For three whole days he couldn't speak. He just lay staring at the world out of round, bewildered eyes, as if it were all a dream, unreal.

* *Makhno:* Nestor Makhno (1889–1935), leader of Ukrainian peasant groups, more or less anarchist. Makhno became an anarchist after the 1905 revolution, which he took part in. *Petlyura:* Simon Petlyura (1879–1926), Ukrainian nationalist, in 1917–1920 one of the principal leaders of counterrevolution in the Ukraine. *Blues, Greens:* Names given to various detachments and groups, formed during the Civil War, falling between the Reds and Whites. The Greens in particular were gangs of peasants who fought Reds and Whites and were decimated by both. [Translator]

† *Denikin:* Anton Ivanovich Denikin (1872–1947), general in the Tsarist army, one of the main White commanders from 1917 to 1920. Commanded the Don volunteer army. [Translator]

There was another attack in 1934; all Mama's brothers who lived in Baku were suddenly arrested and brought back home to the Ukraine. The men who did it were looking for gold. They tore up all the floorboards in the house. (They'd been torn up twice before, once by Hetman Skoropadsky and once by Ataman Zelyony.*) They ripped open the feather mattresses. Where've you hidden your little hoard of gold? You'd better come clean. Mama's brother, Uncle Samuel, was short-tempered. He tore himself away from the two men who were holding him, and broke the investigator's teeth. Then they began systematically to kick Uncle Samuel. . . .

Once again the village begged that his life be spared. Everyone, young and old, came running, all talking at once: "We've known the Zabezhanskys all their lives." "They don't own a thing." "Gold? They don't have any gold —just look at the house they live in!" screamed one young woman, who'd had half her possessions taken. "I'll give them what you've left me."

That finally convinced them. Whatever you say, if people can't even manage to build a decent house, that must mean real poverty. They let the brothers go.

But Grandma died. She never got over the arrest of her children.

It was bad enough not to own your own house. But when you began to run short of food as well . . . The neighbors came to the rescue again, until they themselves began to swell up with hunger. That dreadful famine year of the Ukraine spared no one. Food ran out very early in the village of Shirokoye. The only place bread could be had was at the Inguletsk ore mines. The miners were given rations.

Every saleable possession the family had was taken off to market. Even the pillows went. Mama bartered her winter coat for grain, and braved the frosts in a sweater. The only thing that didn't go was a dark-green table-cloth that had been handed down from Great-grandma. It was the only family heirloom, and it was preserved like a holy relic.

That winter Father fell in the street in Krivoi Rog and was taken off to a hospital. Mother—skin turned yellow, feet all swollen—locked the children in the house and set out to hunt for bread, as far away as Minvody and Nikolayev.

Pauline had tried hard to avoid looking at the shelf where a bowl with the last few grains of precious wheat was concealed behind a curtain. The hours went by. She ground the last two handfuls of grain in the mortar and baked some flourcakes. That was the end of the food. They didn't dare open the door to anyone—there had already been incidents of cannibalism.

---

* *Skoropadsky:* Ukrainian overlord (Hetman) appointed to this post by the German command after they had broken up the Central Government on April 28, 1918. Before the Revolution he was a Tsarist general. *Zelyony:* Leader (Ataman) of Ukrainian White Guard detachments. [Translator]

But once two strangers did manage to get in through a window. Pauline had smashed the lock with a rolling pin and escaped out to the street. The neighbors came running and saved her.

How could they even think that people like that would betray her? . . . Betray her? Or perhaps her father? The thought of her father was like the memory of some great festival.

The neighbors could recall how her father had done his courting in Grandma's clay-walled cottage, in his threadbare greatcoat, limping on a crutch improvised from a long-handled paintbrush with its head wrapped in newspaper. Father had come back from the imperialist war with a German bullet in his shoulder, a soldier's knapsack on his back, and his boots held together with string.

Grandma asked suspiciously whether he could actually use his brush-crutch. Or had he just found it by the roadside? The soldier pointed his brush to the heavens. "Look up there at the sky, old woman. See that blue . . . it'll last forever. Never fades!"

The hoary old painter's joke angered her. She had her own special relationship with the heavens, and she wasn't pleased when any Tom, Dick, or Harry brandished a stick at the firmament in that way. And she wasn't all that old, either. . . . At that, Rosa, her daughter, who had been glancing out the window as if by pure chance, burst into shouts of laughter.

Father was a good man, as anyone around would tell you. When things were going well, he would give Mama at least half of everything he earned. The other half went to pay off family debts. But his face was stern. While Grandma lived with them at Shirokoye, he would sit at the table as if he were on parade. Even when he joked he never smiled. And Pauline could count every occasion that he had kissed her. But he never forgot things the children asked him for.

There were no pens, pencils, or exercise books to be had in the village store. Nothing of that kind. When he wasn't able to find things straightaway, he brought them later. Sometimes as much as six months afterward. Pauline might have forgotten, but Father always remembered. Once he went to Kharkov and came back with logarithm tables which she had asked for a couple of years earlier. And if he ever had to shout at the children, he felt so guilty that he couldn't look them in the eye.

Thinking about Father made Pauline feel better—a light, warm feeling.

After work she set off to the other end of the city to visit her Moscow uncle, as they called him respectfully back home in the Ukraine. He was packing a parcel for the family. His own people had been evacuated. The plywood packing case had iron corners. Her uncle, a man of some substance, moved slowly and methodically, wrapping winter clothes, canned meat, an orange-red ring of Dutch cheese like a life belt. Without turning his head, he said, as if he were thinking aloud: "Your family's probably been evacuated as well. They wouldn't be able to stay." And he began to nail the lid on the box.

The case with the label neatly written on the top struck straight into Pauline's heart. She had no home of her own now. The place where there used to be a home, an address, was nothing but a black emptiness.

2

On October 16, 1941, the workers at the Karpovsky factory were paid off, handed their work documents and outstanding wages.

The workshops were sealed. Everyone was ordered into the huge engineering shop, which was more like a railway station. The long-serving workers gathered together with the girls in black overalls and leather jackets. They all still had their goggles on their hats, as if someone were about to give them marching orders and they would set off somewhere. But there was no route. They were told they could go wherever they liked. They wandered around aimlessly in their black workclothes.

The trams weren't running. One car lurched past, its platform stacked high with sandbags, a few lucky passengers perched on top. It was a long way from the Dorogomilovsky Gate to the city center, and it was dark by the time Pauline got to the university.

Manège Square was decorated with fantastically shaped frames—rhomboids, triangles. It was Cubism '41 camouflage. House roofs were painted on the surface of the roadway. The university was defaced with brown and gray stripes. Everything was pitch black. Not even the emergency blue lights were burning.

Pauline hurried up the darkened faculty staircase. Assistant Dean Kostin was squatting on his heels burning papers in the stove; the light from the flames flickered over his shadowed face. Pauline began to help him.

They spent the night in the faculty building. The walls were freezing and in the corners patches of hoarfrost had broken through. In the morning they lit the gas and heated some bricks in the flame. The high-ceilinged old laboratory grew a little warmer.

Kostin ordered everyone to leave. The factories were being evacuated, so was the university. He looked at Pauline. "If you have nowhere to go, I'll try and fix you up."

Three days later Pauline traveled to Gorky with the labor force from an evacuated aircraft factory. From the train they moved straight into the engineering shop—assembling chassis. They found space for her in the engineers' hostel. At midnight a bunch of people turned up with a bowl of potato salad, a gramophone, and two bottles of yellowish vodka. Apparently it was someone's birthday. Pauline was the only woman, and everyone asked her to dance.

She sat at the table for half an hour, but as soon as the boys began to sing (could it have been for her?) "There stands a high mountain . . ." she ran out into the street.

The house was set in a dip in the ground, close to the forest's edge. The wind had smoothed the snow into a surface as flat as a skating rink. The snow was deep, far deeper than you'd ever find in the Ukraine. The moon came out, silvery gray, and misty. Pauline couldn't take her eyes off it. The same moon—here over Gorky—as at home.

For a long time she stood there in the bitter wind in her cotton dress. Then she turned slowly back, slipped past the room where the birthday party was still in full swing, and sought refuge in her little cell under the stairs. She couldn't bring herself to dance to the scratchy gramophone.

In the morning she looked into the mail box. Empty. Two days later she got a couple of postcards from Vladislav, a university friend. They hurt: the words he used were so like her mother's.

When she was out of doors, Pauline found herself constantly hurrying after young men. Each of them seemed to be her brother. Sometimes she would run after a small figure—the size he was when she'd last seen him— and sometimes after a tall, thin one; in the last letter she'd had, her mother had said how much he had grown.

Late one night (she worked on the night shift) she noticed a thin, ragged boy going around eating the leavings from the metal food bowls. He kept looking furtively over his shoulder as he scraped out the kasha* with a crust of bread, hunching himself over the bowls.

Pauline went up to him. No, he didn't look like her brother, but her heart went out to the boy and she sat him down at her table, tore off two soup vouchers from her work book, and fed him until he raised guilty but happy eyes to her and said, "I'm full."

On the way home the boy told her about himself. Both his parents were doctors at the front. He lived in Oryol with his grandmother and his brother. When the Germans came his grandmother was too old and ill to move; she told him and his brother to get away. They both cried a lot, but finally left with the retreating troops. His little brother kept whimpering,

* Buckwheat porridge. [Translator]

complaining that his stomach ached. He couldn't bear to hear the child cry from hunger at night, so he gave him what food there was and went around himself surviving on the leftovers in the canteen.

Pauline fed him the next day as well. Then she persuaded the boss to take him on, give him work and a ration card. After some hesitation he agreed. There were still some good people in the world.

With her first wages Pauline bought some textbooks she hadn't been able to find in Moscow; and in the autumn, when she heard that the university was opening again, she bundled up her belongings in her bedding, taking special care with her most valued possessions—Chichibabin's *Organic Chemistry* and Rakovsky's *Physical Chemistry*—and sent them all off to her Moscow uncle. Then she settled down to wait to be recalled to her studies.

Under the clothes in her suitcase she kept the last letter she'd had from home. She used to take it out when no one was watching. There was nothing specific, no pronouncements in the letter, just her father and mother sending photographs—just a feeling . . . All the terror, all the tears lay in one almost accidental phrase—"We hope you'll never forget what you went to Moscow for."

Apart from the university, there was nothing left in life—it was her whole family, her every hope. Finally the letter from Assistant Dean Kostin arrived. All she had to do was get her Moscow residence permit.

The only shoes she had were a light summer pair. The uppers were all right, but practically nothing remained of the soles. She cut her foot putting them on, and it swelled up.

Nobody would issue her a permit. She handed in her notice at the factory anyway, bound her foot up in a rag, and set off to Moscow—permit or no permit. A military train got her as far as a station ominously named Obiralovka ("the place of the robber"). A bitter wind was blowing and she could hardly stand.

An old woman with a bunch of onions in her hand looked at the girl with the threadbare green overcoat and swollen foot, and took her home to get warm before the train came. She washed the wound with her work-coarsened fingers, dressed it with a compress of herbs, and rebandaged it. She put a bowl of steaming cabbage soup on the table and, just before Pauline left, advised her how to get out of the station in Moscow without being spotted—"You just go through this hole . . ."

As she was going through the "hole," Pauline was stopped by a policeman,* his ears red with the cold, who took the limping girl off to the police station. There he went through her documents. No permit.

* *policeman:* Throughout the book the words "policeman" or "militiaman" are used to translate the Russian word "militsioner"—a Soviet policeman. The Russian word "po-

"I won't go back alive!" Pauline threatened.

"Stop squawking. Just like a goddam chicken!" bellowed the policeman as he went through her papers yet again. He even held the letter from the university up to the light. Then he turned Pauline's purse inside out. It held three kopecks.

The policeman looked at her money, took a fifty-kopeck piece out of his own pocket, and said sternly: "Here, that'll pay the metro fare. I never saw you."

She went straight from the police station to the university. Hobbled to Kostin's room. But he wasn't there—back tomorrow. Pauline thought she was going to faint. If she sat down, she'd never be able to get up again.

She stumbled off to her uncle's and rang the door bell. As soon as the door opened, she asked, "Has there been any word from the family?" The Moscow uncle shook his head. He looked her up and down, and took off his huge army felt boots. "Here, put these on."

The next day, wearing the huge soldier's felt boots, size twelve and warm as a stove, she went to see Kostin. Later all the students in her course envied her them.

Kostin was amazingly calm. "Zabezhanskaya," he said, as if they'd seen each other only the previous day, "You're late. Get down to work." Pauline hesitated, then confessed she had no permit for Moscow. Could she still go to lectures without a Moscow registration?

Kostin groaned, scratched the back of his head, and looked nervously out the window as if expecting some sort of inspiration or retribution, then typed out an order on his ancient typewriter, huge and black like a catafalque. To be registered for work, and to be issued with a work and ration card.

"Without the good people like him, I would have died," Pauline said to me many years later.

She was right.

---

litsai," meaning a native Soviet citizen recruited by the Germans during the 1941–1945 war into the Nazi gendarmerie, is rendered as "politsai," or "quisling militiaman." [Translator]

3

Krivoi Rog was captured twice; first in January then again in March of 1944. Pauline wrote to everyone she could think of: to her relatives, the friends she had been at school with, to the Regional Committee. There was no answer to any of her letters.

That winter she reached her twentieth birthday. On the day itself she sat alone by a miserable iron stove writing to a friend. "It's four years since I saw my family. I feel like screaming. And being alone on a day like this . . ."

That evening Vladislav dropped in. Vladya, tall, pleasant, and gawky, a postgraduate physicist, was the only one who had remembered her birthday. In his thin hands he clutched a little bag of buckwheat and a few carrots. He was kind. He made a determined and successful attempt to disperse Pauline's gloom. She felt sorry for him, even more so today, because she hated to see anyone so nice suffer for so many years on her account.

Vladya was absolutely determined to get an answer from her—"Now or never," and even fell back on the old gambit of "My mother said she likes you . . ." but in the end Pauline sent him home with a cleaned carrot still in his hand.

One day there was a call from the dean's office. "Get over here as fast as you can. There are letters from home! Two of them!"

She ran, her coveralls streaming behind her. One was in her brother's handwriting. The letter was very old. Perhaps they hadn't been able to mail it right away? On the envelope were stuck the familiar photographs of Mama and Father. The handwriting was her brother's; her parents seldom wrote themselves because they were ashamed to reveal their semiliteracy. There was a P.S. written on the envelope—"I'm longing to get a telegram from you so I can come to the station to meet you."

She didn't recognize the writing on the second envelope. She ripped it open and took out the folded pages. A sentence caught her eye—"Your mother asked me to show you where they are buried."

Pauline looked back to her brother's letter, which was still in her hands. "I'm longing . . . so I can come . . . to meet you."

She went back to her laboratory, clutching at tables for support as she passed. She could see nothing, everything was swimming before her eyes. A sodium reaction bubbled on in a flask. If it blew up, there would be glass everywhere. No one told her to stop, but the laboratory assistant Varya and Professor Yuriev, the moody old man who conducted the students' practical work, stood close behind her, ready to catch her if she fell.

She could think of only one thing: "Why? Why? Was it because they were Jews?"

That evening there were celebrations in Moscow to mark the liberation of Odessa. The Kremlin fired a salute. The university was lit up by fireworks. The sky overhead seemed to become solid, tangible, a genuine firmament, and rockets embroidered themselves across the medieval heavens, dissolving into green, red, and blue sparks.

She couldn't stay in Moscow. She had to go home, if only for a week. She got hold of a pass which would allow her into the zone near the front. Kostin helped her.

. . . She stepped down from the train at Chervonoye, the station nearest Krivoi Rog, with her belongings in a bag over her shoulder. It was early in the morning. The last carriage clattered past her. As the sound of the train died away she could hear the wind whistling in the ruins where once there had been a neat, whitewashed station building. The red brick water tower riddled with shrapnel holes was the only thing still standing in the naked steppe.

The desolation which surrounded her was suddenly lit up by the beam of a headlight dimmed by its wartime masking.

"Going to Shirokoye?"

She could see yellow grain in the truck. It turned out that the truck was ferrying out of Shirokoye all the wheat the Germans hadn't managed to burn.

"There'll be stacks of it," the driver shouted cheerfully—he was only a lad—"the Fascists set fire to the crops and ran, but a whole crowd of us went to work with spades. You can do anything if there's enough of you! Come on, give us a grin!"

Pauline stood on the load, holding on to the cab. The wind blew into her face, bringing with it traces of the smell of burned grain, a bitter lingering smoke mixed with the sweet scent of almond blossoms. It was blowing from the direction of Shirokoye.

Pauline imagined the village as she had left it—the houses drowning in apple blossoms so dense that you could hardly see them through the branches. Deep purple lilac sweeping down over the fences to touch the passers-by: if you wanted to go around into your neighbor's garden, you had to force a way through the flowers.

The truck rolled into Shirokoye and Pauline looked about her, stunned. All the trees bordering the main street they were now jolting along had been cut down. So had all the telegraph poles. Not shattered by artillery fire, but splintered. The long road, so long that in her childhood it had seemed endless, looked naked, and the old clay houses which had been there as far back as anyone could remember, and the higgledy-piggledy string of garden gates, hanging now crazily on their hinges—everything was stripped naked.

The truck drove up to her own front porch. The house had survived. On the threshold she paused in an agony of horror before she was able to force herself to go in, to step across the familiar, worn door mat. The half of the house they lived in had only just been rewhitewashed—that was why the door had been standing open. The paint was drying.

Empty rooms, newly decorated for new people to live in.

She walked slowly over the squeaking floorboards into the bedroom. Where their beds had once stood, the floor paint hadn't faded, and the freshly scrubbed boards shone yellow . . . in the middle of the room, like two yellow tiles.

Pauline had a momentary vision of the past. The two beds, with the home-made bedside table between them. Her father had made it and it smelled of fresh-cut pine. Home smells! The smell of the dried flowers in the clay vase on the table, near the big mirror. The smell of the yellow chrysanthemums dropping their petals on the windowsill. And the smell of all flowers combined—the heavy dark-green scent of the Chinese rose. And the chessmen sitting there on the bedside table waiting. Her brother Fima, thin, dark, serious beyond his ten years, a solitary, quiet child, sitting on the floor by the chessboard, muttering at himself and at his opponent. "Curse your queen! Your move."

Pauline wept aloud as she tried to gather strength to go back again out into the damp penetrating wind. Outside, she suddenly heard the voice of a neighbor who had come running up.

"It wasn't our fault!"

She didn't have the strength to speak, just stretched out gratefully to touch the woman's hand. The woman's shout had brought her back to reality—into the neatly swept yard, back to the sharp smell of the whitewash, which overpowered everything else.

She just wanted to know if any of the family photographs had been saved—the family groups . . . Not a single one? . . . Why? The woman didn't seem to hear Pauline's trembling voice. "It wasn't our fault!" she blurted out again.

Cautiously, as if she were walking on ice, Pauline went over to the neighbors'.

Her neighbors were the Mukhins. Her parents had rented their half-house from them shortly before the war. They had a kitchen and two rooms. They got on well together. The Mukhins were like part of the family. Lyubka Mukhina had become a teacher. She'd taught Fima's class.

Pauline hadn't the strength to climb the porch steps. But finally she reached the door and knocked. The rooms looked unkempt and stuffy. Sudden horror. The curtains at the window had been made from one of Mama's dresses, her bedspread, and their striped table runner. Lyubka's bed wasn't made; her felt slippers were strewn on the floor. It looked as if she had been late for school.

Indeed, Lyubka wasn't there. Only her sister.

Pauline couldn't understand what she was saying. There wasn't a word about what had happened to the family. She just went on and on, almost violently, self-justifyingly: "Up there in Moscow you think it's been easy for us here. But we almost died. They burned down the trees and the telegraph poles." Then almost casually she added, "They hanged a politsai on the square last night. The one who killed your people." And then carried on again about the trees.

Pauline's mouth had gone dry.

"What about Lyubka? Is she still alive, or did they . . ."

"Lyubka? What about her? Why bring her into this?"

The door flung open. An old school friend of Pauline's, Nina Poluyanova, dashed in with a great clatter of shoes; she was terribly thin, skin and bone, and impetuous as ever. She grabbed Pauline by the arm.

"Come on. Let's get out of here. I'll tell you everything." Nina's eyes looked huge, staring as if she were suffering from goiter, full of pain—eyes that seemed to be screaming, "What are you doing here in this house?"

They ran toward Nina's house at the other end of the main street, jumping over the shell craters and the cracks that had opened in the road surface. Pauline could only gasp out a few words—"The Mukhins—they're our neighbors."

"They used to be your neighbors," Nina broke in harshly. Her eyes blazed. "You can forget about that. Some neighbors."

Pauline stopped and stared around her. She couldn't get used to the sight of the street, almost unrecognizable now. Just a few dirty gray stumps of telegraph poles cut off a few feet above the ground. And the trees gone too.

And the people . . . it looked as if the people had all disappeared. As if they too had been felled. Along the street an occasional face looked out as if turned to stone, as if Pauline was someone from another planet. One old man, the school caretaker, noticed her, crossed himself, and hurried back through his gate.

The others didn't run away—just turned their heads.

At the well, Pauline saw a young woman wearing a full Ukrainian skirt: her head was shaven. Pauline stopped, shaken at the sight. Then she saw that the young woman was wearing Mama's yellow shoes. Could she be sure? Shoes like that, with that metal buckle, weren't sold down here. Their Moscow uncle had brought them. The woman realized she was being looked at, stared back, and hurled her overflowing bucket at Pauline with a shout of anger.

"Pity they didn't finish you all off together! When are they going to shoot you? It's your turn now, Yid! Don't hang around! You might get picked off by a stray bullet!"

As they passed the next house, two small boys in shirts that were a great deal too short for them dashed out, looked at Pauline, and both recognized her at the same moment. She had been their leader in the Young Pioneers.

The children had grown so much over the years that Pauline scarcely recognized them. She embraced them, putting her arms around their thin shoulders, feeling the shoulder blades sticking out.

A teenage girl was standing outside the house, her thin white legs encased in felt boots. She looked ill. She approached uncertainly.

"Are you the Zabezhanskys' daughter?"

Pauline realized that for this girl she was just another teenager, a little taller, perhaps; that was all. Someone who'd lost her mother. What child wouldn't understand?

The children strung along behind Pauline, calling their friends to join them as they went. As they moved toward Nina's house, jumping over the shell holes, the tail of children grew. They were all trying to tell her the whole story at the same time. Loudly, all at once. The children knew it all —where, who had been shot, how. They had seen everything, knew everything. To have seen all that and to be only ten or twelve . . .

That day and the days that followed the children kept flocking in to see Pauline, no matter how hard their parents tried to keep them at home. But every one of them was terrified of going THERE. They told Pauline about THERE, maintaining their bravado with mutual jibes, taunts, and dares. "You afraid?" "I was there, ask anyone you like."

They talked. Talked constantly. They could not be silent for a moment. Pauline was the only person in the whole village who didn't know what had happened. THERE. In the quarry. Their eyes were starting out of their heads, the pupils wide and shining with a black gleam like broken glass as they begged her to hear them: Listen to us! We'll tell you.

At last Nina got Pauline inside the door and closed it against her bare-foot whimpering little brothers, whose noses she wiped casually in passing with an automatic maternal gesture. Then she told the story herself, almost as the children had told it, all in a rush. She told the things she knew and the things she and everyone else had heard from the old driver who had had to round up the Jews in the village Club at the order of the local quisling militia.

But Pauline could still hear the high-pitched voices of the children.

The Germans had poured into the village like bullets from a gun. No one had been expecting them. The villagers were busy digging trenches for their own troops when they heard the motorcycles coming. They looked up out of the foxholes they were working in. Holy God! The uniforms were green, and the helmets were different. It was them. As the motorcycles shuddered to a halt, everyone flung down his spade and ran.

. . . There had been a rumor that Pauline's parents had left two or three days before the Germans came. But Fima was weak after an illness and couldn't walk. While his parents had been trying to find a cart for him to ride in, and then had finally started out along the cratered road, the Germans were bombing the ferry at Nikopol. The motorcyclists caught up with them there and they came home again in the cart, back to their neighbors'. Where else should they go?

A week went by, maybe less, and then the order came that all Jews were to wear the yellow star. They had to register and be issued with one. "What's this for?" asked Fima. "Are they making fun of us?" Mama said, "I'll die before I wear that thing."

Sima, the legless tailor and dressmaker, begged Mama not to leave the house. "Whatever you need, Rosa, we'll bring it for you." They agreed on signals—three taps on the window meant it was a friend.

The next day there were three taps. It was Maria Kurilova, one of the neighbors. "Rosa, we all think it'd be a good idea if Fima came to live with us. Just in case they come."

Pauline knew the Kurilovs. The father was a miner, and there were nine children.

"Ten's much the same as nine," Maria said simply, although if the militia were to find Fima with them, it would mean that the entire Kurilov family would end up in the quarry.

Nina raised her eyes to Pauline's face, and stopped talking. Pauline was whiter than clay; her eyes were closed and she was blue around the lips. As if she too were lying sprawled on her back there in the quarry with her family.

Nina went across to her and took her hand, squeezed it. Then she forced herself to go on. "Every day your mother expected them to come. But she was quite calm. Her son was safe. And that was happiness. She took everything she had of any value over to the Mukhins. There was her winter coat that she'd only just mended, and the green plush tablecloth, the family heirloom. 'If anything happens,' she said, 'I want Fima to have it.'"

The thing they were waiting for came on the Friday. In the evening there were three taps on the window. Friends. Mother opened up. There stood a German officer and a man from the Russian quisling militia. They had a long wagon with them.

"Bring enough food for one day, and get in the wagon," the militiaman ordered, and slung his rifle on his shoulder. Jews never put up much of a fight. They had too much sense for that.

They walked out of the door on their own.

(The quisling said that at his trial. So did the driver.)

The German put his pistol back in its holster as well, and laughed unpleasantly. Get a move on, hurry.

Mama came out of the house and glanced around. A sigh of relief. No sign of Fima. She smiled and went over to the wagon. People who saw her said she was smiling so peacefully, she looked as though she were going to her daughter's wedding rather than her own execution.

Then Lyubka Mukhina came out of her house, arms crossed. Suddenly she dashed across the garden, toward the Kurilovs' house, shouting, "Fima, Fima, Mama's calling you!"

Fima came rushing out as his parents were being jabbed toward the wagon with bayonets. They stopped by the wheel and stood there, motionless, shoulder to shoulder. Suddenly, they didn't seem to feel a thing.

When Fima saw the militiaman with his rifle in his hands, and the German officer with his holster open, he understood it all. He turned to Lyubka Mukhina who had been his schoolteacher and said quietly, "So, you needed some more living space." Then he went quietly over to his parents. And, quietly, helped by his father, he climbed into the wagon.

As the wagon creaked away, Lyubka ran after it, shouting to the militiaman—"And they've got a daughter as well, away studying in Moscow— she's in the Komsomol."

Pauline sprang to her feet, completely transformed from the girl who had been sitting hunched up on the sofa hands resting helplessly on her knees. "Where is she now?"

"Who?"

"Her. Lyubka!"

Nina grabbed Pauline by the shoulders. "What are you going to do, Pauline? Stay here until my father comes."

4

The following day when Pauline heard that Volodya Ganenko was back from the front, she rushed out of Nina's house without waiting for breakfast. She had shared her schooldesk with Volodya Ganenko for ten years. When Volodya had gone off with his father to look for work during the year of the famine, Pauline had kept everyone away from his seat for the whole year. When Volodya came back, his desk was waiting.

Loyalty was a thing to be praised—like naughtiness.

Everyone had lilacs growing in his garden. But the lilacs from your own garden weren't up to much. The neighbors' were always far better. Every morning the teacher would find a whole forest of lilacs on his desk. And once that ceremony was over, the class was free to get on with the business of exchanging work for the lesson ahead. All the slowest pupils had long since been adopted by the bright ones. The stupid ones had their work done for them, but the idle ones never. Each case was treated strictly on its merits. The mathematical geniuses passed a note of their answers along the rows, while the stupid ones checked the mathematical geniuses' dictation exercises.

The teachers were perfectly well aware of all this and gave everyone separately prepared lists of questions. The children competed with one another cracking all the questions like nuts.

About half the tenth class was intelligent. Volodya Ganenko was a mathematical genius. Pauline couldn't be described as a genius—she was just a chemist. But it was something of a stroke of genius to be a chemist in that class at all. The range of subjects was pretty narrow.

Volodya Ganenko came to meet her, as abrupt and as quick as ever, in his cloth battledress with lieutenant's bars. He just put his hand on her shoulder and said, "Hold on, Pauline." There was a banquet in Volodya's

honor—bright red cherries, unripe green tomatoes, pies stuffed with cabbage. Some amber-colored brawn. There was a trickle of yellowish home-
made vodka in the bottom of the decanter, and one withered apple in the
big china bowl. All the guests looked as if they were at a wake rather than
a homecoming.

Vanya Ivanov, still fair-haired but who'd filled out a lot since Pauline
had last see him, was cursing to himself; no one attempted to stop him,
however. His right arm hung useless by his side. He had been invalided out
of the army. He poured Pauline a glass of vodka. She swallowed a mouthful
and put the glass down, coughing.

Lyusya Khomenko was talking. She was a sturdy girl with a sharp nose
like a man's and gestures so emphatic that after each sweep of her arm the
necklace around her white neck produced a tinkling echo. Lyusya Khomenko had been dropped into the village by parachute, and she knew
everything that was going on here. She was talking about Dr. Zholtonog;
he and all his underground group in the mines had been shot by the Germans two days before the Russian troops had moved in. In the same quarry
where Pauline's family had been killed.

Who had betrayed him? There had been no Gestapo in Shirokoye.
The death's head emblem hadn't been seen down there. So the possibility
of the Germans finding out for themselves could be ruled out. But you
couldn't exclude the possibility that one of their own people had betrayed
him. . . .

Everyone knew Zholtonog; he'd saved scores from deportation to German labor camps by certifying heaven knows what diseases. And he had
been betrayed. . . .

"Who could have done it?" Vanya Ivanov exclaimed. "Lilya again?"

Pauline looked at him in amazement. Lilya?

Volodya Ganenko had been the last prewar Komsomol organizer in
the Shirokoye school. When he had left he had handed the job over to
the phlegmatic Lilya. It seemed that as soon as the Germans arrived, she
had put up a notice inviting everyone to join the youth organization Free
Ukraine; everyone, that was, "except for Jews and Communists." They
brought out all the old Ukrainian folk costumes. Nobody had ever banned
people from wearing them, but in the past they had only been worn on
special occasions, and now it was every day. People wore multicolored neck-
laces as some mark, it seemed, of distinction.

The mathematics teacher, Viktor Isaevich, a Jew, had gone to Lilya,
his favorite pupil, and, according to Lyusya Khomenko, had asked her to
obtain a pass for his family, so that the children at least might be saved.
But she sent Viktor Isaevich away, although it would have cost her nothing

to have done what he wanted. Lilya's father, the former chairman of the Regional Agriculture Department, became the German headman of the village, and talked with a whip in his hand.

Lilya watched, her arms folded across her best-decorated blouse, while the helpless little Viktor Isaevich, who had lost his glasses, was herded by rifle butts into the wagon—the same wagon Pauline's family had stood in with their arms around each other. She watched while they threw his three-year-old daughter into the wagon, and the child screamed at the top of her voice, "Mommy, Daddy, don't get in the cart! I don't want them to kill me!"

Volodya Ganenko listened, his head in his hands. Suddenly he got up and hurried out on to the porch; as he lit a cigarette, his hands were trembling so violently that he broke several matches.

"Why don't we strangle her?" said one-armed Vanya Ivanov.

"Stay where you are," Lyusya Khomenko interrupted harshly. "We'll have no amateur executions."

"Could Zoika have had a hand in it?" asked Volodya Ganenko's mother, who was clearing the table. "She had a baby by a German."

Once again they had to restrain Vanya Ivanov. "Goddam Nazi-lover. While we were getting ourselves shot at the front, that's what they were up to back here."

Volodya Ganenko, who had come back into the house, said thoughtfully, "A child's not evidence."

Nearly everyone became members of Free Ukraine. Some of them got involved in real dirty work, others just went to the dances. And some brought up children. Volodya's mother sighed: a child's a child. Others were ready to throw any child of a German to the dogs.

"Filthy Nazi bitch." Vanya leapt to his feet again, and Lyusya had to push him back into his seat, so that he wouldn't dash off then and there to drag the bitches out by their hair.

"And Mukhina. Where's that monster?" asked Pauline in a tight voice. "Where's Lyubka Mukhina?"

"At home, where else?" answered Lyusya Khomenko calmly. "She doesn't have as much to answer for as Lilya or Nina Karpets."

The room swam before Pauline's eyes. The long mirror on the wall was slanting slightly, and Volodya, Lyusya, and Vanya Ivanov, reflected in it, suddenly began to spin and spin. . . .

She ran out of the house into the cold rain. She heard the clatter of boots behind her. Volodya? No. Vanya Ivanov. Volodya hadn't come out. Hadn't even looked up from the table. She managed to get away from the kindly Vanya Ivanov. He shivered in the rain and went back for another drink. She set off for Nina's house.

Evening was drawing in, and the village street seemed to have died. Just the tree stumps gleaming in the rain. She could still hear the jangling of Lyusya Khomenko's necklace. It was wrong to get angry with Lyusya. Parachutist, intelligence operative, she'd seen it all. The rain drizzled on, but it seemed to pale into insignificance compared with what she had just heard. She slumped onto a nearby bench under an awning, her hands around her knees. She began to shiver. So that's where they all came from. . . . Free, liberated Ukraine. They'd lived for three years in their "liberated" Ukraine. And what had they achieved? What had they been trying to achieve?

They had murdered Fima and gone unpunished. And just as freely, just as unpunished, they had murdered her father and mother.

The same for Viktor Isaevich.

The same for Doctor Zholtonog.

Teachers, doctors—all the people she had loved best—all murdered. And how many more besides? She'd heard that there was row upon row of corpses in the quarry.

That was the "Free Ukraine"! No Jews or Communists. She'd heard that Nina Karpets wouldn't be parted from her whip. And Lyubka Mukhina? Pauline gripped the dripping wet bench. So she didn't bear as much responsibility as the others. . . . Pauline had her own personal account to settle with Lyubka Mukhina. Then she'd happily go to jail—or to the grave.

Shaking with cold and with hatred, she ran to Nina's house. Fortunately, Nina wasn't there. She found a rusty bayonet which was still as sharp as a knife, put it in the sleeve of her white blouse, and set off toward the Mukhins' house, her arm swinging stiffly by her side. The bayonet felt cold against her skin and she walked more quickly.

The rain had slackened, and children were looking out of their windows.

Someone called to her and she quickened her pace. Now she was past the well, past the house with the empty, newly whitewashed rooms. . . .

A tousled, disheveled little boy, aged about ten, came out onto the porch as she approached—it looked almost as if he'd been expecting her. He ran up to her, shouting excitedly. "Are you Aunt Pauline?"

She didn't recognize him at first. Mukhin. Yura Mukhin. That was it. The same face. A Mukhin face. Broad cheeks.

She asked coldly, "What's that to you?"

The child's eyes were sunken, nervous. He gave a frightened sideways glance at the windows of the house and began to tell her how he and Fima had played chess together, and how he had been hiding under that bush when Lyubka had given Fima away to the militia.

He didn't finish all he wanted to say, swallowing his words, either out of excitement or sincerity, or some fear that she wouldn't let him finish. Then he asked her with desperation in his voice to take him with her to the quarry the next day. "The Kurilovs over there said that they were taking Aunt Pauline to the quarry to show her where her family's buried. . . . Can I? Please, Aunt Pauline!"

She didn't reply, and the child hunched his body, his hands hanging limp.

A chill swept through her. Suddenly she saw everything from a totally different point of view.

The other children must mock him all the time, torment him. German swine, they would call him, and worse. Torment him to death. And yet when it happened, he could only have been seven years old.

Children can be very cruel.

She was horrified when she realized just why it was that those bony, miserable little shoulders were so hunched under his threadbare shirt, when she realized the pressures he was under.

She squatted down quickly beside him, as she might have done with a three-year-old.

"Yes, Yura. You can come along tomorrow. Of course you can."

And in her heart something gave a great lurch. "Why do they have to do it to the children? Why the children?"

She got up and went quickly away, almost ran from the Mukhins' home, over the rain-soaked soil.

5

She had been right to trust her instincts. Next morning, long before she reached the well where she'd arranged to meet the children, she could hear their cruel, mocking voices.

"Get away from here, little Fritzling!"

"Get out of here!" A boy of about fourteen in a green forage cap took a swing at Yura, who leaped aside like a goat. He stood a little way away from the others, not crying, just cowed, the way he'd been the previous evening, his miserably thin arms dangling at his sides.

Pauline shook hands with all of them. Then she shook hands with Yura, who still stood aside, shifting nervously from foot to foot.

"Hey, don't you know who he is?" said one ten-year-old child in amazement. He was as tattered and barefoot as Yura himself. "He's a Mukhin. Lyubka Mukhina's his aunt."

"I know," said Pauline, firmly.

"His brother's half German. The little bastard's two," explained the lad in the forage cap, and laughed like an adult. "They call him Petro. Some Petro. He's the son of a golden-voiced Nazi truck driver."

"I've heard," said Pauline, as firmly as before, determined to stop this line of conversation. She waved to Yura, beckoning come along, what are you hanging about for? "What's all that got to do with Yura?" she asked the others, and took him by the hand as he came up. The hand was damp, sweaty. The child was scared to death.

The children fell silent, thunderstruck. There were no two opinions in the village about the Mukhins. And Yura was a Mukhin.

The barefoot boy leaped from stone to stone, blurting out words with childish directness, repeating what he had heard other people say—"The Mukhins are all pigs out of the same litter"—and ran off ahead. The only sound to be heard was the boys' bare feet sloshing through the mud. The oldest, the one in the forage cap, tried to catch up with him, but stopped to adjust his cap, which was falling down over his eyes, and said: "Yura nursed his German brother. He wrapped him in your green tablecloth. Mama said, 'Look at those Mukhin swine, wrapping a German baby in that green plush tablecloth. It'll get covered in filth.'"

Slowly, involuntarily, Pauline's fingers released Yura's hand.

Children can be very cruel.

"Well, was there a notice on the cloth to say it was stolen?"

"Even if there was, he can't read," the younger one said scornfully, running back toward them.

Finally they moved on, almost in agreement. There was still some scorn for Yura, but on these terms they were prepared to tolerate him.

At the end of the main street they stopped to knock at Uncle Andrii's door. Andrii had been one of the miners whom the militia had forced to deepen the quarry. He had promised to show what he knew.

Andrii came out at once and shook Pauline's hand so hard in his own red hand, gnarled with ore dust, that her fingers nearly cracked. He saw Yura Mukhin shuffling his bare feet about uneasily, and looked angrily at the other boys as if to say, Why haven't you told her the main thing, about the Mukhins?

The oldest boy adjusted his forage cap and went up to Uncle Andrii to explain.

Pauline moved off, trying to find the drier patches of road. Along the way were tree branches and boards and brushwood sunk in the mud. They jumped from branch to branch, supporting each other as best they could.

They came to the River Ingulets. It had slowed to a trickle between its banks, squeezing between the steppingstones, dirty, storm-flecked, dark brown.

Uncle Andrii stood in the water in his heavy boots and gave Pauline his hand. When she reached the far bank, using the steppingstones the miners had put in, he asked disapprovingly: "So you've forgiven him? They didn't have any pity for your people."

The look on her face told him that it was not a subject for discussion. So he shook his head—well, if that's the way you want it, it's your business.

The quarry wasn't far out of the village; just beyond the nearest fields, where the green was beginning to show through. They were old, abandoned mines, which had once produced ore. The ground was broken by little ravines and craters. Then, higher up, it became criss-crossed by trenches. The rust-red ore-bearing soil showed up like a fiery island among the rich black earth all around it.

Slipping and sliding, hauling themselves up on the few stunted hazel trees, they worked their way up the narrow twisting path. Pauline's legs were scratched and bleeding. She almost fell into a stinking pool of brackish water. She slipped down into a concealed, overgrown crevice. As she pulled herself out again, she broke her nails on the stony soil: below the surface the earth was dry and rock-hard.

But the more they went on, the more rain-soaked and slippery the top-soil became. She slid twenty yards down a steep greasy slope and almost fell into the threatening brown water which had collected at the bottom.

"Are you all right?" called Andrii from the top of the slope. He un-coiled the rope he carried around his waist, threw the end down to Pauline, and hauled her up; he looked at her torn knees and hands.

"That could have been the end of you," he said, taking out his pouch to roll a cigarette. "We'll never make it. We'll have to put it off for a while—until things dry up a little. Hey, you kids, keep away from the edge!"

Pauline herself saw that they could not possibly get there that day.

She looked around, exhausted. From where they stood on top of the old Inguletsk quarries, they could see the river gleaming yellow in the sun, and the nearest houses of Shirokoye. The gardens were just beginning to show the first thrust of spring.

She had already come up this far before, to look along the whole of the route her parents had been forced to take at machine gun point. She could relive every moment of that bloody Jewish Sabbath.

They had been brought out of the Club—she could see it now, with its golden cross and its repaired and gilded onion dome—the only thing the Free Ukraine had renewed.

They had been driven along in a close column, with dogs at their heels keeping them in order. Any local Communist Party members who had been denounced were pushed in with them.

They moved out of the village along the waterlogged greasy track, knowing that these would be the last things they would see. They had to ford the icy autumn Ingulets, and come this way, and on higher up . . .

Then there, behind the bushes, they had been ordered to strip. Men and women separately. Murderous moral propriety.

The German officer stood to one side on a small mound. The people who did the dirty work were their own people, the locally recruited militia. The Free Ukraine.

The first shot had sounded quite quiet—and then the village bells began to ring. The heavy main bell, which they'd spent all night adjusting, went "doom-doom-doom," and the small bells rang out wild and free.

The shots came at random, and the bells rang triumphantly, more and more deafeningly.

At first, Pauline didn't hear Uncle Andrii's hesitant voice.

"Have they told you everything that happened?"

Pauline nodded. Yes, she knew. First the militiaman shot her mother. Then he turned to the men. He shot her brother in the back of the neck. Fima fell forward on his chest, as if he were diving into the river, hands outstretched. But when the man got to Pauline's father, he lowered his rifle and said, "I can't. He was a good man." The German officer had to draw his pistol and shoot her father himself.

Andrii looked at Pauline's gray face, and sighed.

"Why do you want to go, girl? You won't be able to recognize anyone there. They were using explosive bullets, shooting them in the head." And he added quietly, wiping his wiry neck with a rag: "I couldn't eat or drink for two days after."

And Pauline looked over to where the great heaps of bright red soil reared up into the sky. How could she get there?

Keeping her eyes turned away from him, she asked Uncle Andrii why it was that everyone shied away from her, as if she were from some other planet. Only her school friends seemed pleased to see her.

"Well, put it this way," the old miner said confidentially, lighting another hand-rolled cigarette from the butt of the old one. "There you were, coming from Moscow, staying with the Regional Committee secretary . . . Nina Poluyanova's his daughter, you must have known. And down here, everyone was surviving as best they could. They were all afraid of dying. . . . I was forced to go to the quarry to bury the dead, others were made to dig trenches or foxholes, and there were some who were made to drive the wagon . . . and see what happened if you refused."

Uncle Andrii took a drag on his cigarette. It was his friends, the Kurilovs, whom he'd known down the mine for years, who had persuaded him to take Pauline to the quarry. Otherwise he would never have agreed—it did no good to keep thinking over the past. They'd said, "The Zabezhansky daughter's a good girl. She'll do you no harm. Tell her what happened just the way it was."

And then he'd seen her for himself, an unhappy girl, in a shabby blouse, her stockings torn at the knee, her voice trembling. What danger could she possibly be? "Everyone would have been glad to see you . . . but then, you might have had second thoughts. . . ."

Ah, he knows everything. But what was he doing up at the quarry when the shooting was going on? When he was on his own with the militia? He could still be named as a collaborator.

"We're free because of what we did. . . . How can we be collaborators? But we pinch ourselves in the morning to see if we really are alive. . . ."

Suddenly his face brightened.

"Is it true that Sima, the tailor, buried the cloth that your family had asked her to make up, and gave it to you when you came? Sima is really remarkable. . . . Oh, there are far fewer people in Shirokoye, far fewer. Why? Everyone's joining in the war. And the war takes us ready-made, just the way we are. . . ."

Three days earlier, when Pauline had first come up here, she had felt as if she had been shot herself; it was just that they'd missed. For some reason she'd stayed on her feet. Just one more bullet and that would have been the end of her. No more anything. No more pain.

She looked at Andrii, wreathed in smoke. She looked at the faraway white houses of the village, and on the heights of the Inguletsk quarry she suddenly realized . . . until that moment the thought had been suppressed, gnawing at her like an invisible pain. She'd heard that during the Civil War there had been another traitor in Shirokoye. Just one person in the whole village. The priest. The atamans lived in his house, and he'd kept on pointing people out to them.

And now? The militia. Free Ukraine. Three girls out of her class alone at school had joined Free Ukraine.

And now they were like wild beasts. Like primitive people. Anyone not of your own particular stripe—tear his throat out. And yet they all knew that the people around them weren't White or Blue or Green. They had all grown up in the Komsomol. Lyubka Mukhina even taught in the village school.

Pauline sat down on the wet ground. Uncle Andrii looked at her in concern and brought over a piece of wood. "Here, sit on this."

Lilya had been the Komsomol secretary, top of her class in school. She must have changed her personality completely to become a murderess through ideological conviction.

And what about Nina Karpets? A gray, colorless girl. She liked dancing. Did she enjoy having German officers hanging around her? Just for a day or two, then back to her own people? But when she was captured, she was directing the fire of the German batteries, improving their aim against native Soviet troops. What was it that made this empty-headed creature dance to that tune? It seemed as if the dances organized by Free Ukraine had a logic all their own.

And Lyubka Mukhina? When Petlyura's men had come into the village in 1919, it had been Lyubka's mother who had stood at the door of their cottage and said "Typhus!" And saved them all . . .

And yet Lyubka Mukhina . . .

Had she ever had a serious conversation with her? Once perhaps, a long time ago. They couldn't have spent all their time just playing in the forest, or playing ball together. Had they ever talked?

And then she remembered . . .

The only house in the village where there had been a lot of books which you could borrow exactly as if they were in a library belonged to Grinberg, the secretary of the Shirokoye Regional Committee. Once they had lived next door to him, sharing the same garden fence.

The Grinbergs' rooms were rather bleak—no flowers in vases, no rugs on the floor, no carved chests. Just an empty, city kind of flat. Just the bookshelves along the walls.

Across the street lived Stepan Maslyanyi, one of the bosses of the Inguletsk ore quarry. Maslyanyi was a huge, slow-moving, kindly man.

While she was in the lowest classes in the school, Pauline's parents were able to help her with her work, but later there was nothing they could do. She used to run around to see Maslyanyi, who never refused. Whenever he saw Pauline, he would grin behind his bushy Cossack whiskers.

No one in the village had anything but the greatest respect for Grinberg and Maslyanyi.

But one night in 1937 they were arrested. Both of them.

All that day, Pauline's head was in a whirl. A mistake—it must be a mistake.

And once Grigory Petrovsky, the most powerful man in the Ukraine, came to the village. To open the boarding school.

At last the car arrived, dusty and rattling over the ruts. A solid, gray-haired man got out, and ordered the crowd of barefoot children who were peering through the fence to be let back into the yard.

She remembered him as a kindly person, and then suddenly one day it was announced in school that he was an Enemy of the People.

That was the time that she and Lyubka had whispered together in the orchard. Pauline simply couldn't believe that all these people were enemies. But apparently it all made perfect sense to Lyubka. She bit into a crab apple and said: "You mean you really don't know who it is they're picking up? They won't arrest your father or mine. Why not? We haven't got anything worth taking."

But Grinberg had books. Thousands of them. All right, so he must have stolen them from someone, right? Petrovsky had even more . . . and Maslyanyi was rich. He had two bicycles. He rode to the mine himself, and he bought one for his daughter, a special ladies' model.

Whoever's on top grabs everything that's going. "What's mine's mine, and so is what's yours."

Pauline could remember the conversation quite clearly, even down to Lyubka's calculations as to who in the village owned how much and what.

Pauline realized that she was sitting on damp ground, and shivered. But she didn't get up.

"Mother gave the Mukhins everything she had for safekeeping. Surely it wasn't all for the sake of her winter coat, or her dress, or the green tablecloth they used to wrap the German bastard in? For some old clothes?"

On the way back down, Uncle Andrii held Pauline by the arm. She was exhausted, and her legs wouldn't carry her.

Just before she had to leave, the weather turned drier and in the end they managed to visit the ore waste heaps where the family lay buried.

Again it was the boys who led the way. And Uncle Andrii. They brought spades with them. They stumbled along, giving each other a helping hand, clutching at the stumps of burned-out trees. It looked as if no one had been out this way since the liberation. The place was littered with tarnished, rusty cartridge cases and green German flags.

Pauline screamed. There were blackened human legs sticking twisted out of the soil.

Hadn't they even buried them? They began to attack the dry unyielding soil with their spades, and threw up a grave mound. Then they went on to the next. . . .

The new chairman of the Shirokoye Regional Committee, Dotsenko (the Germans had carved the Star of David in the skin of his back), had promised to build a memorial here.

Would he ever do it?

Uncle Andrii couldn't find her mother's grave. It was the boys who discovered it.

"Mama, Mama!" Pauline fell on her knees.

Uncle Andrii laid his hand on her shoulder. Come on, come on, or we won't get back before dark.

Farther along the rust-red earth dug out of the hillside they found the grave where her father and Fima were buried.

The grave was just as it had been left, untouched. Trodden down, no flowers planted on it. It looked as if nothing would grow on this red soil.

And all around the quarry, black earth, newly plowed. Great black clods, with water lying between the furrows. It was a terrible place.

The grave was right on the slope. Pauline climbed up to it over the stony heap of ore, her heart beating in her throat.

"Go away," she told the others. "I'm going to stay here till my train leaves in the morning."

Uncle Andrii argued, pacing about. It began to grow dark; finally, unwilling to stay the night, he left, taking the boys with him.

Pauline lay with her forehead against the stony ground licking her cracked, swollen lips. There was only one sound—her brother's voice. Clearly and quietly he was repeating over and over again: "I can't wait to come and meet you."

He was trying to say something else, to reach out to her—but he couldn't.

His last words on earth: "I can't wait to come and meet you."

Why?

And then, as if in a dream, she saw him—his face with its high forehead, quiet, obedient.

"God got confused," her mother used to say. "Stolen apples, grazed knees—that's my daughter. Quiet around the house, always well-behaved—that's her brother, Fima. Hates candy, that's my daughter, the sweet tooth, that's Fima. God got confused," she whispered. "Confused."

She should be the one lying here, not Fima, a mere child.

It was getting dark quickly now. The bleakness of the steppe gave back a long drawn-out echo: "Confu-u-sed. Confused!"

She felt faint, sick.

Stones rattled and rolled down toward her from above. She jumped to her feet, frightened. Yura Mukhin was scrambling barefoot down the slope, his shirt sticking out of his trousers, his face as white as chalk.

"Aunt Pauline, Aunt Pauline! It's bad here! Let's go away."

"What are you doing here?"

It turned out that he'd gone to the village with the others and had then come back alone.

His teeth were chattering. "Aunt Pauline, let's go, please."

How had he managed to get here on his own?

They crossed the Ingulets in water up to their knees, then stopped for a moment, shivering with cold, listening. Here on the bank, before the war, Pauline and the rest of the school had carved out a little park. They'd dug earth for flower beds, put in some saplings, and had gone away not quite believing that anything would grow. Now there was a whispering noise overhead as in a forest, a spring-like smell of poplars and maple.

The trees had taken root.

PART TWO

6

Near the hostel Pauline saw the tall figure of Vladislav waiting for her . . .
Vladya, her "stickman," as he'd been nicknamed around the university. He
was gazing into the faces of the passers-by, shuffling his long legs in the
cold. He had on his best tie, a broad affair of black crepe, fastened care-
lessly around his long neck.

When he spotted Pauline he dashed up and grabbed her suitcase,
scolding her for not having sent a telegram. She nodded gratefully, having
completely forgotten what they had agreed two weeks earlier. But when he
took her cold hands she buried her head in his chest and wept through
clenched teeth.

Vladya fed her on home-made apple pie and gave her some phenobarbital, which he always carried with him in a match box. Pauline took a
double dose and fell fast asleep with Vladya still holding her hands. In
the morning she awoke at the same time as everyone else, gathered up her
textbooks in their newspaper covers, and set off for the university.

In her first year Pauline had loved to go into the assembly hall of the
university when it was empty and fresh, when it sounded like a church
and you wanted to shout aloud to God.

She sat down by a window. She always used to do that. From there
she could see the whole hall, the ancient hall of the university, with its
eighteenth-century moldings and the triumphant sweep of Corinthian
columns which supported the magnificent ceiling. Usually she felt ex-
hilarated all day, just to know that she was part of something so lofty and
majestic. To work in the assembly hall was like a holiday. From the huge
window she could look out over Manège Square, where for the New Year
they erected the biggest Christmas tree they could find in the woods near
Moscow, and the celebrations went on almost the entire winter.

But this time Pauline went to her desk by the window and felt that she couldn't work here anymore. Everyone stopped to speak to her as they passed. A friend waved a hand—"Haven't seen you for ages." Another came up and told a story, and was annoyed when she didn't even smile—"You've got no sense of humor." The noise of tires and the squeal of brakes from the street outside, the clatter of footsteps, even the whispers of the reading room—everything which before had seemed so soothing, like the far-off sound of the sea—now made her head ache.

Then the windows shook and rang. A salute fired from the Kremlin. Pauline turned to the window. A salute. That meant another city freed. But in the red, blue, and green fireworks, she saw, as she would always see, a reflection of the February salute fired to mark the liberation of Krivoi Rog.

With trembling hands, she gathered up her books and her notes. In the corridor there was a Dutch stove with gleaming tiles. Students sat around warming themselves and swapping gossip. She almost ran past. She had to escape somewhere, hide. Even in a cellar, or in a dark little cell. As long as she could have silence around her. Just silence.

Her friends helped her back to the hostel, put her to bed, where she lay for several days with her eyes wide open. She didn't sleep or eat, nor did she speak, but looked at everyone around her with great staring eyes, like her grandfather, the one who was hanged by Petlyura's men and whose fellow villagers had rescued him from the noose.

A friend telephoned Vladya. He arrived greatly upset and called a doctor. A quiet, gloomy old man turned up and said that what she needed was peace and quiet. "See if you can find somewhere for her to be alone. Even if it's only an attic."

Vladya hurried away, and when he came back insisted that Pauline get up and come with him. They were going to his parents' flat; she would have a room where no one would come in without knocking. Pauline smiled at the determination in his voice and asked, without her usual irony, "Did you go and ask Mama?"

He nodded, slowly. Pauline turned her face to the wall.

It was almost winter by the time they managed to find a room. Finally it was her Moscow uncle who arranged it. Vladya took the felt boots, the coat with the patched elbows, and the pile of books to her new place. It was in a wooden house on the outskirts of the city, at Alexeevsky.

There was no radio and no alarm clock. She had to be up at six every day. The first night she was able to sleep right through until her neighbor woke her. He worked at the tramway depot, and when he left at six in the morning he hammered on her door with his fist.

But the next night she scarcely closed her eyes. She was studying and working as before, and under the wartime laws, it was a criminal offense to be late for work. She spent the night going out into the unlit streets to ask people the time.

If she couldn't hear footsteps anywhere, but just the iron sheets of the roof grinding and scraping together, she ran, slipping over the damp pavement, all the way to the next tramstop in Alexeevsky village, where there was an illuminated electric clock that shone out over the street like a faraway beacon.

It went on like that all winter until Vladya heard about it and produced an alarm clock. The clock would only run when it was lying on its side; and it didn't ring, only shivered and clattered like an old tin can. But it was a joy all the same.

When the standpipe froze up in the bitter frost, she had to go for water to the cemetery, staggering through the snow to where a well reared up like an ice-covered mountain. She was terribly afraid of the cemetery. Rather than make the trip, she preferred to melt snow instead.

One night before falling asleep, she took out a thick exercise book and wrote hurriedly:

From nine in the morning till eleven at night I have been sitting in the university library, in a corner, with my back to the room, studying organic chemistry. Tomorrow will be no easier. I'm exhausted, I can't swallow a thing, although I haven't eaten a scrap of food all day. I just keep working myself into a state of complete fatigue, Mama . . .

She wrote "Mama" automatically, and only realized at that point that she had been writing a letter home.

She fell into bed. If only for the comfort of hugging her pillow till morning. The words of Shevchenko came into her head unbidden, as a prayer comes into the mind of a believer:

> Oh, my dear God,
> Why do you punish the orphan?

No matter what else she tried to think about, the words kept coming back.

> And I shall fly far, far away,
> Beyond the blue skies.
> No more rulers,
> No more sorrow.

By the spring she was very ill. A young first-aid doctor (Pauline had collapsed in the street outside the house) softly whistled a tune as he wrote out an entire page of prescriptions. Furunculosis, malnutrition, influenza, inflamed ligaments—these were only the beginning. He departed with a cheerful shout of "*Au revoir*," leaving the prescriptions in a pile on the table. But she had no money to have them filled. She took the exercise book from under her pillow and wrote in a tiny handwriting no one else could read:

Oh, my darling Mama, why is all this happening to me? I feel as if I've been thrown onto a bonfire. My hands and feet are burning. And there is no salvation. Today I wept from sheer physical pain—that's never happened to me before. I've done nothing to deserve this.

. . . I'm getting breakfast. There don't seem to be any lumps of sugar left. I've been living on them for a week now. I've decided I've been ill long enough. I must put a stop to it. There isn't time.

I tell myself I'm just lazy, that I must get up, tidy the room, make the bed and wash myself. I hate all this filth. So I shall gather my strength and then start work again.

She staggered to the cupboard. There was no food left, no money. Who are you supposed to tell that you've only got potatoes to live on, that you're not strong enough to take your seat in the library, especially when someone next to you is crunching sugar or biting into an apple?

You just have to keep silent. And try not to fall behind the others. And it's no one else's business if traveling to and from Alexeevsky and lighting the stove takes half a day. How marvelous it would be to meet someone who would understand without having to be told, without having to listen to your complaints.

She turned back to the exercise book again.

I would never have thought that holidays would be the worst. I hate them! I never cry as much as I do during the holidays. It's not that people have forgotten me. I have good friends who invite me around to their families. But that only makes things worse. So on holidays I wash the clothes and scrub the floor. I save all that kind of thing specially for then so that I have enough work to keep me busy.

She looked at the alarm clock. Vladya had promised to drop in.

She scraped the ashes from the stove, went to fetch the coal, twisted her weak leg awkwardly, and fell. Finally she managed to bring in the coal, she never knew how. Somehow or other she lit the stove. She beat the Ukrainian rug on the floor, opened the small casement window. It looked clean and fresh. She felt ready to collapse.

She sat for a moment on the edge of the stool, then went for water. She swept out the kitchen, and only then settled down to her books.

She suddenly wondered: If Vladya turned up with a truck, threw all her belongings in the back, picked her up and carried her off, would she be strong enough to refuse the pull of city comfort, of being looked after, of home cooking, of his touching concern?

Vladya burst in scattering raindrops, freshness itself, clutching a bag of potatoes. "Mama sent them!" He shuffled in the doorway a moment and then disappeared, shyly walking backward.

That night and the next, Pauline dreamed about the house in Shirokoye drowning in lilac and gillyflowers, of her father, her mother, and Fima. She and Fima went to draw water from the cemetery well, leaning sideways so that the water wouldn't splash out of the bucket. She heard his kind voice—"What a coward you are, Pauline. Fancy being afraid of the cemetery. That's where we live."

She opened her eyes and saw the bare, clean, whitewashed walls of her room. She reached out for the exercise book, which was now so vital to her very existence.

Darling quiet Fima, wise Fima! Surely we couldn't know what was going to happen to us. How I long for the Ukraine and home. This week, you would have been eighteen. Darling Fima! How I weep for what happened to you, how many nights I spend thinking of you, how I love you, my darling brother!

Fima's birthday coincided with the main examination of the year, and indeed of the whole course. Organic chemistry. It was something like a confirmation day for a student. It always occurred in the spring. And the time had come around again.

The rumor was that Academician Kazansky himself was going to be one of the examiners. Someone once said that Kazansky was as hard as Zelinsky was soft. That he always asked the questions that weren't in the syllabus.

Pauline went through the names of her future examiners. She wasn't at all worried about Professor Platé, although he was the fussiest of all. He was even easier than Professor Shuikin, though you couldn't expect an easy ride from that sly old fox. So long as she didn't get Kazansky!

It seemed as if the night would never end. Her leg hurt her. She could have fought it, but the ache was near the bone. And when you hurt all over, you don't feel up to taking a chemistry exam.

A week ago she had been studying "explosive substances"—a very simple subject, just a matter of rote learning—by no means the hardest subject she faced. But her memory had turned into a sieve. She couldn't hold onto anything. And all after Shirokoye. It had never been like that before. It really felt as if life were trying to cast her aside.

The examination took place in the lecturers' room off the main chemistry lecture theater. The radiators weren't working. Along the walls laboratory tables had been arranged with tall stools beside them like executioners' blocks. It was, indeed, a place of execution. The examiners arrived in single file, wearing their long black robes, untouchable, detached, aloof. Judges.

The Supreme Court of Chemistry, from whose sentence there was no appeal, bowed formally in Pauline's direction. Professor Yuriev, in charge of practical work, actually stopped, disrupting the solemnity of the whole majestic procession.

Pauline waited by the door, her back pressed against the wall. Her own tutor, the tall, lean Alfred Felixovich Platé, came dashing down the staircase. He was twisting his head this way and that, as a result of which his briefcase, fastened only by one lock, swung around in a full circle. His darting, humorous eyes fell on Pauline, and he whispered to her encouragingly, full of French charm as usual: "Concentrate, Pauline! Don't rush. Whatever the subject, whatever the question, always ask for time to think." And he strode off to the door, hurriedly fastening his jacket over his striped red pullover, and setting his shoulders so as to look as daunting as the others.

Dr. Silaev, a quiet, self-effacing lecturer, limped past tapping his stick and whispered: "Come and be examined by me."

Academician Kazansky stalked by, his face showing no sign of recognition, just a satanic smile. He didn't turn his head.

Vladya appeared at the far end of the corridor. He was trying to hide, but how can you hide when you're a head taller than everyone around you? He was whispering something or other to Alik, "Genius-Alik," as he was known in the group. He glanced quickly at Pauline, nodded hastily to her as if to say "You'll be O.K." I must be looking all right, thought Pauline cynically, as she pulled herself away from the wall and walked firmly into the lecture hall.

It was rather dark, and there was a smell like stale fish—probably the result of some experiment with amines and hydrogen sulfide.

The examiners were sitting in their corners on their high stools, smiling. Alfred Felixovich Plate made a sign. "Calm down, Pauline, calm down." Dr. Silaev hissed quite openly, "I'll call you in a moment."

Pauline felt her cheeks burning.

For the moment Professor Platé had no candidate with him, and he waved to Pauline again—come over here! She shook her head, only just then realizing that she wasn't going to be examined either by Platé or by Silaev. Why did they have to make it so obvious? Only one of the examiners had never even heard of her—Academician Kazansky. Do I have to go to him? Heaven help me!

Silaev's candidate had finished. As she left, Silaev stretched and turned his head toward Pauline. "Are you ready?"

Pauline lowered her eyes, refusing to notice the kindly gestures and looks. She stayed sitting where she was, her head sunk on her chest, waiting for Academician Kazansky's chair to be free. Then she rose, but someone was there ahead of her: kind-hearted Genius-Alik already panting out his first answer.

She went on waiting, suppressing her desire to go to Silaev, or even to Professor Shuikin, who sat with a smile flickering over his broad Asiatic face.

When Alfred Felixovich Platé's chair was empty, Pauline didn't want to walk over to him, she wanted to run, so as to make sure that no one got there first. What a coward you are, Pauline. She seemed to hear a childish voice—What a coward! And she stayed where she was.

Alfred Felixovich Platé rose unhurriedly from his seat as if to gather his thoughts and strolled over to her. He looked at the formulas she had written down on her sheet of paper, then looked over at Silaev and shrugged his shoulders uncertainly.

When Pauline got close to Academician Kazansky's place, her head was spinning. Out of the corner of her eye she noticed Platé's striped red pullover, and the soothing gestures being made by its owner.

Academician Kazansky sat in the place of honor, behind a long laboratory bench, a dignified, desiccated, withdrawn figure. His lips were very thin, the kind all villains are supposed to have. He smiled dryly, ironically, a smile that seemed to say, What a fool you are, just up from the country.

Kazansky stretched out a thin white hand, took her list of formulas, glanced at them briefly, and laid them on one side, as if to say, Well, you know about those, so let's leave them: let's talk about something you don't know about.

"Write out Beckmann's equation."

Pauline had a moment of panic. She couldn't remember a thing. Not one unit of the formula. She had a complete blank before her eyes, like a stretch of new-fallen snow.

"May I think for a moment?"

Kazansky looked at her over his spectacles, and said kindly enough: "All right, but not for long."

With an effort that felt like hauling a bucket of water out of a well, Pauline dredged the depths of her weakened memory for the chain of variable formulas, the ones she found the hardest to grasp during the course.

Writing with such intensity that her pen shook, she scribbled down the signs. Out of the corner of her eye she could see Platé looking at her with concern, and breaking off his questioning of the student sitting before him. "What kind people . . ."

As she slowly explained the formula Kazansky examined her piece of paper and laid it aside. Then, as if beginning the oral over again, he asked, "Now please write . . ."

"Let me think about it," Pauline said quietly when she had heard the question.

Kazansky cleared his throat. It was enough to make her pull herself together and answer immediately.

After the next "May I think about it?" Kazansky got to his feet and wandered around the table. All the other examiners were changing candidates, and he had not yet released this girl, who seemed to be deliberately angering him with her plaintive requests for time to think, whether she needed it or not.

Kazansky, the essence of delicacy and tact, looked once again over his glasses at the student, mopped his high forehead with a handkerchief and gave her a bold "four."

"I answered everything!" Pauline exploded, as she sat outside on the staircase, "and the best he can do is a four."

"Hurray." Vladya and Alik were yelling, even waving their arms about. Pauline looked at them and smiled despite herself.

"Shall I tell you who got a four for organic chemistry?" shouted Vladya, leaning over Pauline. "Academician Zelinsky himself. For a chemist to get a four in organic chemistry is as good an omen as Napoleon getting a tremble in his legs before a big battle. Alik, everyone, tell this silly girl it's the truth."

And the whole group immediately transformed themselves into oath-swearing conspirators.

Vladya pulled Pauline to her feet and towed her down the stairs behind him. "Come on! Get a move on!"

"What's the matter with you? Where are we going?"

"We're going to my place! There's a meal laid on!"

They ran out of the university courtyard holding hands. Vladya found a taxi, and a few minutes later they were entering a new apartment block in Gorky Street.

The table was already set, looking as if it would grace a diplomatic reception. Starched napkins lay beside plates decorated with doves which looked real enough to fly away if you came too close. There were pictures on the walls in heavy gilt frames, pictures of biblical scenes, with plump angels in flight. Even Vladya's mother, a philosophy teacher, a portly, pale-faced lady wearing a huge necklace of dark-brown stones, came toward them almost dancing on her toes, ready to take flight herself.

Only the crystal glasses stood firm, although they rang with the footsteps in the room. They looked as tall as Vladya himself—and his father, who came up to the table smiling and greeting them in his deep bass.

"When I was a student we used to say, when you've got your degree you can get married. Well, organic chemistry is about the same as the degree, isn't it?"

Pauline had never eaten such good goose before, never tasted sauce like that, that made her mouth burn. She tried to refuse the Georgian wine, but Vladya's mother lowered her voice and said that this was *his* favorite wine* . . . so how could she possibly refuse it?

Finally, when they had cleared away the café-glacé, Vladya's mother put her arm around Pauline's shoulders and touched her thin, protruding shoulder blades with a sympathetic finger. She took Pauline off into another room where, she said, the girl could feel completely at home.

"My poor love!" she gushed, her eyes moist; "how much you've had to go through! Now it's time to start living and stop denying yourself. Everything's yours for the taking. All Moscow."

As Pauline was leaving and Vladya's father helped with her shabby coat, she overheard Vladya's mother whispering sympathetically to her son: "Vladya, why were Pauline's parents killed? Were they in the army?"

Vladya answered slowly, "They were Jews."

Pauline saw Vladya's mother's face drop.

Vladya only caught up with Pauline at the bus stop. She leaped onto a bus that was just leaving, without even looking at the destination board. The doors slammed shut behind her. Vladya raced after the bus as it accelerated away, hammering on the glass door and shouting in horror: "Pauline, Pauline, Pauline!"

---

* *His*—that is, Stalin's—favorite wine.

7

That evening the door to Pauline's room scraped open and the floorboards creaked. Her Moscow uncle came in, covered in frost, with a bunch of snowdrops in one hand and a newspaper parcel in the other. She buried her face for joy in the damp astrakhan of his collar.

Her uncle took his coat off, carried out the usual inventory of her stocks of food. Had she anything left at all? She would never ask for anything. He knew what the Zabezhanskys were like. He was the same himself.

He peered into the kitchen cupboard and examined the shelves. Just a few grains of corn at the bottom of a tin. And a few handfuls of oats. He poured half a kilo of sugar into a container. That would help out.

Pauline grabbed the teapot, but her uncle stopped her.

"Come on, Pauline, we're expected."

Pauline kissed him and begged him not to go. "It's Fima's eighteenth birthday today. Let's just stay here on our own."

Uncle had been a miner. He'd spent all his young years down in the pits, and his eyes were like coal—calm, and kind. Eyes like her mother's. Full of life, with a sharp anthracite shine to them, just like hers. But the cunning in them wasn't hers—that was his own.

Her uncle covered his eyes with his hand and stood, swaying slightly. Then he said, as firmly as before: "Come on, Pauline, we're going. I've promised." His voice was low-pitched, and something in its intonation reminded her of her mother.

He took her somewhere through Alexeevsky village, leading her through snow drifts past head-high wooden fences. He took her to a house she didn't know, whitewashed on the outside like a Ukrainian cottage. He said, impetuously, "Look, they've got wood carvings on the front, too, like on your house."

Pauline looked at the wood carvings, covered in bright green paint. No, theirs were different.

They were expected. Someone hurried to help Pauline off with her coat, and a woman's voice from inside called, "They've arrived!"

The table was laid in a big room. It was feast day food, Passover food. Stuffed fish, fried fish, steamed fish with red peppers. There was a plate of matzos on the corner of the table.

"Is it Passover already?" Pauline asked timidly, sitting down next to her uncle and looking about her. There was no one she knew. The faces were broad and heavy.

Her uncle didn't answer, but pushed her across to the other end of the table, where there was an empty armchair with velvet arms.

Pauline resisted. She wanted to be with her uncle. But the entire table began to urge Pauline to be kind enough to do them the honor and sit next to a balding broad-cheeked young man in a military jacket with decorations, who was smiling at her shyly. Pauline blushed violently. Surely she wasn't being married off for the second time in the same day?

She nudged her uncle, who was gazing at the jellied fish, and bit back the words, "You wouldn't have dared insult your own daughter like this."

Instead, she said barely audibly, "You arranged this matchmaking for the major."

"Lieutenant-colonel," corrected a guest from the other end of the table, who apparently had a musician's power of hearing.

"What?"

"He's a lieutenant-colonel," repeated the guest, and began to make signs to the prospective bridegroom—go on, help yourself.

The soldier advanced on them in a kind of dive, urged her uncle out of his seat and sat down next to Pauline.

"If Mahomet won't come to the mountain," he said, "then the mountain will have to come to Mahomet."

You've got a lot of nerve, she thought. She could see that there were two stars on his shoulder board.

"Do you have spurs as well, Major?"

"I'm in the construction brigade," the lieutenant-colonel replied with dignity.

"And do you have a dog?"

"Er, no."

"You ought to have a dog, a setter. And huntsmen, and fine horses."

"Oh, I've got a horse. Oppel he's called. Brand new."

Pauline rose to her feet, her anger showing in her voice.

"No hounds, no huntsmen. Do you think that's a proper match for me? You're such fools—and so out of date."

Clutching at the corners of the glass cupboards, the sideboard, the chairs, she stumbled to the door, blinded by her tears.

She ran home in the pitch darkness, falling into snow drifts and having to pull her shoes out when she lost them. She could barely find her snow-covered house. She flung herself face down on the bed.

"Mama! Mama!"

She tried to sleep. But there was no phenobarbital left, and without a sleeping pill there wasn't a chance. Impulsively she pulled out her exercise book and scrawled in huge letters across the page: *Enough. I want to go home to Mama.*

The first person to notice that something was wrong was Alfred Felix-ovich Platé, although nothing in her university work betrayed her. She carried on as usual with the electric motor at her elbow turning the mixer, and Greeniar's reaction bubbling away in her three-necked flasks. All the components dispersed on time, and as her tutor he had no complaints.

But he suddenly realized that she wasn't the same as she had been yesterday—it was her drooping hands that betrayed her. He had never seen her dry narrow hands—the reddish roughened hands of a laboratory chem-ist—lying so weakly and painfully on the bench. He went over and told her that the geologists had brought in a great stack of samples of Guriev oil; she would have to distill and analyze them.

The new oil proved to be hard to analyze. It demanded unswerving attention. There wasn't time to think of anything else. If you took your eyes off it for a second, boiling liquid shot out of the flask, and you had to start again from scratch.

But Pauline had been through the hard school of the Karpov factory. There the analytical laboratory, which checked prepared units of drugs, was under the control of an elderly woman, a Russian-German. She trained her lab workers with a mixture of both countries' pedantry. At all events, she had trained Pauline so rigorously that Pauline was prepared to stay on in the laboratory until midnight to reweigh a sample ten times if need be, until she could stamp her number on the finished unit, her hands heavy with responsibility.

This time it was easier. The oil had been drawn from a variety of depths. One, with a relatively larger water content, behaved like a wild horse, leaping, bubbling in the flask, and bursting upward in a geyser. Another, rich in paraffin, solidified in the refrigerator. "Each oil goes mad in its own way," Platé used to say.

But finally the analysis was complete—much sooner than Platé had thought possible. Glowing with inner pride, Pauline laid her list of tabu-lated constants on his workbench.

When she came into the laboratory the following day, the first thing she saw were his bear-like brows raised in surprise and then his gleaming, almost happy eyes. And how that delighted her—thank God, at least some-one was glad she existed.

He immediately asked her to tackle a new substance, and gradually she found herself, as Platé put it, becoming involved in a diploma. She found the diploma work very exciting. She drove herself unremittingly, in a fever, as though her clothes had caught fire, and she was trying to beat the flames out herself. Everything came out amazingly accurate and the evenings when she could put a flask containing a new preparation on Platé's desk came around more and more often.

But on those same evenings she still needed a family. What a joy it would have been not to have to cope with the coal and the stove, but to come home to a warm room, to be welcomed by her mother, to be given a bowl of soup with dumplings, or even potatoes with home-grown gher-kins, and then to put her feet up on the sofa, to read Shevchenko aloud while her mother listened.

In the evenings she dreaded the thought of going all that way home to her room to stay there on her own. So she worked on until the electricity was switched off or the gas supply was disconnected. As she watched the blue flames of the burners, she often thought of her family, not yet realiz-ing that day by day their faith and the strength of their belief in her in-creased—they had died believing in her. She couldn't let them down. Dared not let them down. For them, that might be worse than death itself.

This unspoken, even subconscious, thought began to heal her, giving her new strength when her hands fell wearily to the laboratory bench. Once, well past midnight, Academician Zelinsky walked up to her unno-ticed, still wearing the black hat he always wore. He looked down at her hands, ruffled his kindly mustache, asked her if it was working out. He looked at her notes, took a pencil and jotted a few words down. He sighed—"Come on night owl, time to go home."

Then from a bulging pocket of his starched white overall he took one of the sandwiches which he habitually shared with the late night workers, gave it to her, and left. Zelinsky lived right in the university itself, but un-fortunately taught less and less in the laboratories.

In the morning the noisy, indefatigable Platé burst in, calling to Pauline as he came through the door, "Old man Derzhavin has actually noticed our work: he's given us his blessing." Apparently Zelinsky had called in Platé and asked him about Pauline's work.

It became a standing joke in the laboratory that Pauline so cherished and cultivated her research that she waited like a child each day just to show Platé what she had done—what would he say? Once she drove away a research student she knew, a member of the Party office, for quite unma-liciously referring to Platé's laboratory as "the French kitchen."

Her friends said that her interest in Platé went beyond her work. Pauline became very angry. She couldn't stand the kind of idiots who fell in love with tenors or famous teachers. Without men like Platé the university would be merely an empty concept. A memorial to times past, nothing more.

Toward spring she fell ill again. Her head ached as if the top of her skull was about to come off, so she said. And her heart—sometimes she felt she wouldn't survive until the morning. She took her temperature—103°.

She was afraid to go to the doctor. He would tell her to go to bed. And where would she find the time to do that? She was just beginning an experiment, so she locked the door, wrapped her head in a wet towel, climbed onto the windowsill and breathed the fresh air at the ventilating window. Sometimes the pain slackened.

Platé burst in like a typhoon. "Have you eaten yet?" He tore off his staff dining-room coupon. "No more work until you've had a meal."

Sometimes he left a bottle of milk on her table. Pauline knew that he had two young children and refused to touch the milk. The next day he shouted at her so that she drank the entire bottle, her teeth chattering against the rim.

"That's a good girl," he said, when she put the bottle down.

Platé was meticulous, like everyone who worked under Kazansky. Before he sent student work off to be printed he repeated the experiments, checking every constant and refraction himself. This time he did it almost in a rage. When Zelinsky had praised Pauline's work, someone had started a rumor that she was receiving special favors, and that if the results of her experiments were recalculated, there would almost certainly be a mass of mistakes. Platé checked every last figure and forced the research student he thought most likely to have started the rumor to read through the whole.

"I'm pleased with you," he repeated. "Every calculation checks out to the fourth decimal point."

Academician Kazansky was named as Pauline's official opponent against whom she would defend her dissertation. She was horrified when she heard. Him again? What sort of a trap was this? Whenever she took her diploma work to Kazansky, she would feel as if she had left her heart outside at the Kaluga gate. Inside she felt empty.

Academician Zelinsky was invited to hear her defend her thesis. Kazansky was sitting at the head of the table, the patriarch of Russian chemistry. With a wave of his hand he dismissed a newspaper photographer. But as he left the man managed to take several photographs of Pauline and Kazansky together. Today these photographs are among Pauline's greatest treasures, along with pictures of her parents.

Kazansky fired off his questions—sharply but with that constant smile.

Platé had made sure that Pauline learned her diploma work virtually by heart. She answered quickly, almost apologetically. The patriarch listened in silence, nodding his head in its black academic cap. He made a few notes and then said, in a businesslike way, that this work was far beyond anything . . .

Pauline left the hall abashed—far beyond what? And where was she going? Apparently on to the competition between diploma works themselves.

Later she was given a scroll with a cup drawn on it—it looked like a scroll for champion footballers. Beneath the cup was printed the information that in the competition of university diploma works, she had won second place.

"There you are," said Platé proudly. "I told you so. Everything came out to four decimal points."

Before that, immediately after she had defended her thesis, Platé's wife, Academician Zelinsky's daughter, had baked her a cake to celebrate her diploma. Platé gave her a copy of his book as a memento. Pauline kicked off her shoes and curled up alongside Fedya, Platé's six-year-old son, with whom she'd always been close friends, and read him Esenin's "To Mother," and when he began to get bored with that, "Kachalov's Dog."

The next day Pauline was summoned to see Academician Kazansky who told her, in his usual dry way, that he would have no objection if she began to work for a higher degree under his supervision.

"Well?"—he raised his eyes to Pauline's thunderstruck face and smiled what she had always thought of as a discouraging smile—"Do you need time to think?"

The summer of 1946 was blazing hot. It was a summer of forest fires and examinations. It even seemed strange to Pauline that she had ever thought about death. It wasn't only failure that lay behind her now, but a great success. She seemed to be flying a glider, borne upward by a rising current. She even telephoned her uncle. He was delighted that she had forgiven him for his idiotic attempt at matchmaking. "Well done, girl. Well done!" he bellowed into the receiver. Once again she heard her native accent, and she was happy.

"Come and see me! D'you need any money?"

"No. I'm wonderfully rich."

And indeed she had acquired some money. The week before, Platé had pulled a wad of ten-ruble notes out of his jacket pocket. Pauline threw up her hands in shock.

"That's your earnings," Platé said calmly. "The work with the oil was commissioned. That's your share."

Pauline stared at him unbelievingly, until the senior lab assistant

Fedosia Ivanovna looked at her in amazement. Surely she must know that they had an agreement with the geologists?

"Rich?" her uncle said in surprise. "How's that?"

"I earned it. Platé arranged it."

She passed all the doctorate examinations with much the same ease and success. And once they were behind her, she found a representative of the Professional Committee waiting at the lecture theater doors for her with a travel permit.

"Sign here, Zabezhanskaya. Travel pass to Gelendzhik. To a sanatorium. Half price."

For the first time in her life there was no one to see her off. Not even her uncle. Two years had passed since her visit to Shirokoye. This time, like the last, she had to change trains in the shadow of the half-ruined, shell-shattered brick walls bearing the name of Kharkov. If only she had been able to exchange her resort permit for a permit home, and if only her people had been waiting to meet her . . .

The doors to the platform at the coach's end were half open. Pauline sat in the doorway, her feet on the step. Along the track was crater after crater. Half-destroyed signal wires, tangled barbed wire.

The coach lurched and shook. Beside her was a soldier who yelled, "Let's have a song," and broke into the inevitable march "Hey, Red-Haired Girl!" And Pauline took up the melody, out of breath from the warm wind and her bitter pride; they were moving into her native country. Yews and poplars passed the windows. The poplars were covered in white fluff, like fledglings about to leave the nest. The wounded fields swung by, green with the tall winter wheat which was just beginning to turn yellow.

"Ukraine, my mother! My beloved Ukraine!"

When Pauline returned to Moscow she discovered that her application to read for her higher degree had not been confirmed.

She went straight to the laboratory, where she found Alik sitting with his head clutched in his hands.

"Alik, is it true?"

Alik raised his head and nodded.

"But . . . Why?"

"Point Five."*

"What?"

"Point Five: nationality."

"Rubbish!"

"Rubbish," Alik agreed. "Total rubbish . . . but let's try and stick to the facts." He took a notebook from his pocket and with his usual thoroughness wrote out a list of twenty names, all candidates for the higher degree course put forward by the chemistry faculty.

The Ministry of Higher Education had confirmed sixteen of them, and these Alik crossed out. They were all Russian or Ukrainian. One Chinese, one German. The list now contained four Jewish names. Among them was the name of the single Stalin scholar of their year, and Stalin scholarships went only to truly outstanding students.

The final name on the list of those refused was that of Alik himself.

"You mean they've turned you down as well?" Pauline was stupefied.

Alik smiled gloomily, distractedly. He suggested they go down to the Ministry. "We'll talk to Figurovsky. He's one of ours—from the chemistry faculty."

---

* POINT 5: The Soviet internal passport lists 1) the holder's surname, 2) his/her given name and patronymic, 3) date of birth, 4) place of birth, 5) nationality—e.g., Russian, Latvian, Ukrainian, or *Jewish*. Plans to alter this regulation in the next few years have been announced. [Translator]

"Their man" was extremely courteous. He explained patiently that judging by the documents Pauline's parents had been in occupied territory, which meant they would have to check out what had happened there.

As Pauline left the Ministry, she was almost reassured. In one sense it could be said they were right. All sorts of things happened during the occupation. People like Lyubka Mukhina or Nina Karpets, from the Free Ukraine, might turn up at the university. So everything had to be investigated down to the last detail.

She went back to her room and wrote to Nina Poluyanova in Shirokoye, asking her to send an official statement of how her parents had died.

She lit the stove. Her head ached—perhaps she had a slight fever. For the first time in her life she considered the fact that her documents contained a Point Five. What did it all mean? For the state, for her personally?

Had there ever been the slightest hint in her childhood that she was somehow different from everyone else? Any hint that she was in any way alien? And what was it, anyway, that could split her off? Religion?

The school in Shirokoye, a pleasant two-story building, had once been the synagogue—and the village Club was in what had been the Orthodox church. The people of Shirokoye hadn't had much time to spare for their gods. She went to school before she was seven. She went barefoot.

"What's your name?" asked the teacher, opening the register.

The whole class shouted back, "Zabizhnya!"

Everyone called her by her nickname: Zabizhnya.

Whenever the head teacher came in and asked "How many in the class?" the reply came "Forty." "How many Ukrainians?" "Forty."

Her real name, Zabezhanskaya, was only written out in full in her certificate at the end of her tenth year. Zabezhanskaya, as in her passport.

At home everyone spoke Ukrainian. When her Moscow uncle arrived, they spoke Russian. Whenever she and Fima heard anyone speaking Yiddish, they fell quiet, very cautious. Her parents only spoke Yiddish to each other when they wanted to keep something secret from the children.

When had she first thought of herself as a Jewess, as something different from her friends? Only here, in the Party Committee room at Moscow University, when they had planned to parachute her into German-held territory, and had then told her they couldn't because the Germans were shooting Jews.

A month later when Pauline called in on her uncle on her way to the university, and he asked her about the higher degree course, she blushed and confessed that they had turned her down. She gave no hint as to the reason. How could you possibly tell sensible people that you had perhaps been turned down because you were Jewish?

At that time her uncle had just been appointed to a very senior job in the Ministry of Coal, almost deputy minister. So what did nationality have to do with it?

But her uncle's wife, a vigorous, aggressive woman, wouldn't leave the subject alone. She didn't approve of Pauline's apparent acceptance of the situation. Why had they turned her down? Maybe she'd got some black mark or other for conduct? She must be hiding something from them.

In the end she had to say it, to use those strange awkward words. "Point Five. Nationality."

Her aunt suddenly flew into a rage. It was as if Pauline's words had put her and her whole family under a threat—a threat that had to be diverted, turned aside as far as possible.

"That's a lie. All that's just idle gossip." She pointed to her husband. "Look, he's just been given this big job. That's nothing like your run-of-the-mill degree course. They were quite right to turn you down if you're capable of thinking that kind of rubbish!"

Pauline was flabbergasted. It was only later that she discovered that on that very same day her aunt's daughter, an able art historian, had been crossed off the list of candidates for the higher degree in the languages faculty—a girl who had already published articles in learned journals, had studied at the conservatoire, and knew the Tretyakovsky Gallery like her own home.

"Just who do you think you are?" her aunt screamed, her pale face contorted with an ugly rage. "Nothing but a country girl who may be able to cook borsch, wash out dishcloths, and scrub floors, but what more can you do than that? That Frenchman of yours, what's his name, Platé, has turned your head. But they soon put you in your place down there at the Ministry. They're no fools. What's Point Five got to do with it?"

Pauline gasped and squeezed her eyes shut as if someone had flung the contents of a slop bucket in her face. Then she turned and ran blindly down the staircase, still hoping somewhere deep inside her that her uncle would call her back.

But he didn't. She went back, shaken, to her room, the room her uncle had rented for her, packed a suitcase, collected her bedding together, tied up her books, left her felt boots in the closet and her blue dress hanging on its hanger. Keep your presents!

She sat by the dying stove fire. It had been a long time since she felt such utter despair.

Finally and painfully she got up. Leaning against the door post she looked around the room for the last time. The walls were white and clean like at home. She'd whitewashed them so often!

It was midday, yet it was dark outside. A fine rain was falling. A cold, autumnal rain. A sharp wind blew the drops into her face. Where could she go now? Moscow was a hard city. You couldn't just find a room overnight.

The tramcar didn't come. The bedding she had wrapped her books and her pillow in was getting soaked, and she hurried under an awning in front of a shop.

There was a squeal of brakes nearby. She jumped to one side, but a cheerful voice stopped her.

"What station d'you want to go to?"

She looked around. It was a taxi.

Pauline stood there distractedly. She had her last twenty-ruble note in her pocket. The driver got out and reached for the bundle and her suitcase.

"You can't just hang around! Who's going to marry you when your bedclothes are all soaking?" He slung the damp bundle onto the back seat and put Pauline in the front with him.

"Right, then. What station?"

Pauline licked her burning lips, and surprised herself by saying: "Zhdanov Street. Ministry of Higher Education."

The driver immediately turned serious and answered with military formality, "Ministry of Higher Education. Very good."

Pauline tried to hand her damp bundle into the Ministry cloakroom, but the woman just shouted at her. So she dropped her things in the entrance hall on the wet floor and walked upstairs. When she got to the door, she looked down at her feet in their tattered sneakers, and nearly turned away.

In the university department they were as pleasant as they had been the last time. She was invited to sit down. She said in an anguished voice that she couldn't wait any longer. She didn't have a roof over her head. She had no money. It was the third month she'd had to make do without a bread ration card. She looked at Figurovsky's full florid face, and he lowered his eyes. She looked at the gray-haired woman standing by his desk holding a file, and she too looked away.

A thought flashed through Pauline's horrified mind: It's just the same as in Shirokoye. Everyone turns his eyes away. It's as if these people here have been digging graves, just like the people back home. They might as well have driven the death cart. As if they were in some way responsible . . . What is it?

Someone came into the room behind her, and Figurovsky got hastily to his feet. Nodding toward Pauline and saying who she was, he announced that she couldn't wait any longer. She had been three months without a ration card.

Pauline turned so sharply to face the newcomer, a dry, smooth-faced man, that he didn't have time to avert his gaze. And Pauline saw the satisfaction in his eyes. Open, eloquent, satisfaction written in fire across his self-satisfied dispassionate face. Everything's going fine. She can't hold out. Pauline suddenly realized that they were out to kill her. Quietly, without firing any shots. An accurate calculation that she would soon be finished. Or would at least give up her work and disappear somewhere or other.

Her head spun. She forced herself to get up and, treading firmly, so as to be sure not to stumble, she left the room.

With her wet bundle and suitcase in her hands, Pauline set off down the Kuznetsky Most, shaking with an awful premonition of trouble to come.

What had happened? Why was it Figurovsky who decided? In the Komsomol office they were saying that there'd never been anyone more stupid than Figurovsky in the university. A real stiff-necked idiot. His students nicknamed him "the butcher." People drew lots to decide who would go to his lectures. So that they wouldn't get their grants withdrawn. And now "the butcher" had found himself a niche in the Ministry!

Now, like a hidden sniper he could fire his shots at anyone, get rid of whomever he liked. Even the most talented ones. Was it just to take revenge on the university?

On her way to the university Pauline went into the Central Post Office and telephoned some of her friends. No one was at home. She wanted to go farther but hadn't the strength. She looked at the next counter—long-distance calls. It was warmer there, and benches to sit on.

She found a corner, and settled down, her things by her side. The operators' voices rang out like bells: "Leningrad, box number eight." "Dniepropetrovsk, number one." "Khabarovsk." "Murmansk."

As she grew warmer she fell asleep, and immediately dreamed about the Inguletsk quarry. She was stumbling about on the red stone, falling, pursued, someone pulling at her shoes, and shouting abuse at her: "You scum. You betrayed them!" Whoever it was went on scrabbling at her tattered shoes.

She looked down. It was Figurovsky, the punctilious butcher in a neat white shirt. What did he want with her shoes? Someone was standing on the mound, a smooth-faced man with white cuffs, watching them shoot Jews. The people with rifles were her friends, people she'd been at school with. There was a scraping sound behind her, and a familiar voice came floating on the wind: ". . . in the back of the neck. Don't you know how to do it?"

A metallic clang, and Pauline jerked awake. A cleaner had woken her. She was wiping the stone floor with a rag on the end of a long handle, and Pauline's things were in the way.

Finally Pauline dragged herself to the faculty with her bundle and suitcase, and after a moment's indecision staggered into the Komsomol office.

Thin gray smoke was drifting through the half-open door, so someone must be there. Thank God.

When the students in the office saw Pauline they immediately gathered around. What had happened? Someone felt her burning forehead, another produced an electric stove to dry her soaking wet shoes. Someone else got out the kettle. She was forced to eat a sandwich and to swallow an aspirin. They left her to spend the night in the office on a ragged leather divan with the springs sticking through the cover: the Komsomol divan, they called it. It was normally used as a seat for people who had been summoned to see Party officials.

By morning she felt slightly better, although her head was still spinning. She had to hold on to the walls as she walked to her laboratory.

It became the practice for whoever left the Komsomol office last to bring her the key, and Pauline would take her tattered blankets and sleep there. She spent almost two months sleeping on the ancient office divan.

Once, in the refectory, she caught herself gazing hungrily at an uneaten potato which someone had left in a bowl on the next table. She dashed out as if someone had put a bayonet at her back.

If she had had a pass to live in Moscow,* things would have been easier. She could have gone to work in the chemical factory until things had been sorted out. But there was no point even in going down to see them. It wouldn't make any difference that she used to work there. Where's your Moscow permit? You might be from the camps.

Her friends wanted to set her up in a student hostel, but it didn't work out. The warden of the hostel was careless enough about broken windows or blockages in the drains, but he came down like a ton of bricks if there was any attempt to have people without permits living within his walls.

She had cast off from one bank of the river, but was nowhere near reaching the other side.

The only firm ground which remained beneath her feet was the oil chemistry laboratory and her bench with its three-necked retorts; she spent one whole month there working on a new compound. Here there was usually a stench of countless hydrocarbons, but there were no smells as

* Before a Soviet citizen can live in a particular Soviet city, he or she must obtain a "registration" from the administrative authorities. Without this registration he can neither rent an apartment nor a hotel room, nor get any work. [Translator]

familiar and encouraging as these, no matter how much they revolted the others.

Pauline used to work beyond midnight, until the night watchman turned off the gas and water. Her greatest pleasure was to come up with some product which had never existed on earth before, as clear as a tear. What secrets did the new substance contain? What gift did it hold for the world?

Finally the long-awaited letter arrived from Shirokoye. Nina Poluyanova wrote that the Regional Party Committee had sent evidence about her parents' death to the Ministry a month ago, as Pauline had asked. "We put the quisling militia on trial. It was said in court that your father told the man who refused to shoot him that he believed in your future and in our victory. Lyubka Mukhina got eight years. She'd betrayed a lot of people."

There was an enclosure in the letter—a copy of part of "A statement by the Commission of Investigation of Nazi-Fascist crimes." It was an ordinary piece of paper, torn from a school exercise book, stamped with the seal of the Shirokoye Regional Party Committee.

The faculty secretary, Mikhail Alexeevich Prokofiev, took the document to the Ministry. He came back looking gloomy, and said to Pauline, "Get on with your work! I'll keep going back until we get it sorted out."

She looked after him as he walked away. He moved firmly, as if he owned the place, broad-shouldered in his blue naval officer's jacket. He still had the kind of strength she had lost.

The entire faculty did everything they could. But it was like banging their heads against a wall. In the end the wall began to crack. After a month, three more of the candidates were accepted, including Alik. She was the only one left.

The November celebrations came around. Pauline was chosen to stay behind to look after things, and they gave her the keys to the laboratory. There wasn't much point in her taking part in the general rejoicing.

She looked down at the red banners flowing below the windows like a huge river, and wept in rage.

Once she was hurrying across the university courtyard when she saw an old man ahead of her. Looking at his thin, bent back, she wondered sympathetically how many years a man must have been under pressure for him to bend so. When she overtook him, she glanced at him from the side, and gasped in horror. It was Academician Kazansky! Boris Alexandrovich Kazansky, who marched into lecture halls like a grenadier, shoulders back, slender, majestic, full of strength. And that's what he was really like when he thought no one was looking.

That day she went to him and told him that it seemed there was no point in waiting any longer. She thanked him profusely, but explained there was nothing else for her to do now, but to try some move on her own account. Kazansky narrowed his lips, and said drily: "This is nothing to do with you at all. You have a research subject. Get on with your work."

If he had looked down at her feet he would have seen that she was standing before him in cracked, rubber-soled shoes, and it was the end of November. But he was gazing out the window. His gray eyes were implacable. "I don't understand anything anymore."

But apparently he *did* understand. The next day he came over to her as she was working on the centrifuge. She heard his voice above the noise of the machine.

"It's not you they're trying to teach a lesson to, Pauline. It's me. But it's only a lesson. Refuse to learn it!"

Another month passed. Pauline was constantly lightheaded from hunger. Her feet began to swell. It was sheer torture to put her shoes on in the morning.

Everyone offered her food, but she just couldn't swallow. Skvortsova, a much-admired chemistry lecturer and widow of Skvortsov-Stepanov,* pressed handfuls of money on her and issued a stern order: "Quick march to the refectory!" Pauline swore to her teachers that she had had enough to eat, and hurried off to the friends she had lived with in the hostel once, and got some food from them. She had no strength left.

Gradually the sympathetic pats on the shoulder and the unthinking, if well-intended shouts from her colleagues died away. No one called out, "Don't worry, Pauline, keep your chin up!" as she passed in the distance. Some asked her quietly, privately, if there was any news. Others averted their eyes, and hurried off somewhere. Everyone had his own worries.

It was only the faculty secretary, Mikhail Prokofiev, who kept the dwindling flame of hope alive for her. She only had to catch a glimpse of his blue naval jacket under his open coat for her to smile to herself and think that there was still a chance left. You could set your watch by the faculty secretary. He always came in at six in the morning precisely, to start work on his doctoral dissertation. There were some mornings when the only people working anywhere in the entire block were he and Pauline, both looking gray and anxious in their black, acid-stained lab coats.

Once he failed to turn up for days on end and Pauline felt despair welling up inside her. After a week of his absence she had let her work go altogether. Was he, too, turning away from her?

---

* Ivan Ivanovich Skvortsov-Stepanov (1870–1928): an Old Bolshevik, who held various high posts after 1925, including that of editor of *Izvestiya*. [Translator]

She hurried out of the university courtyard, only dimly aware of what it was she wanted, and went into a telephone booth to dial a number. She was calling her uncle, who replied, as deep-voiced and slow-spoken as ever, "He-allo! Yes, speaking . . . Whatever's the matter?"

Pauline hung up, and stood as if turned to stone, her eyes closed.

She rang again the next day.

"Hello, Hello. Who's calling?"

She hung up again. Somehow she felt more secure, as if hearing his familiar accent had given her new strength.

Every time her heart rose into her throat, as if she were being hounded with a bayonet in her back into the Inguletsk quarry, she ran to the phone booth. Once when she rang there was no answer. Another time there was a voice she didn't recognize.

December came. One night there was so much snow that it brought the traffic to a halt. Beneath her windows the snowplows roared, rearing their giraffe necks high in the air. The trolley buses swayed alarmingly until their long thin poles broke away from the overhead wires, spraying the streets with sparks.

Everything was falling apart—crumbling.

There was no point in trying to set foot out of doors. It was as if she had been imprisoned within the massive walls of some fortress. What had she left to hope for? It was a mere fifteen-minute walk from the university to the Ministry of Higher Education. And the statement about Nazi atrocities had been sent there two months ago. Wasn't that time enough, proof enough? What more was there to check?

One morning in the laboratory, Pauline had such a sudden sharp heart pain that she had to lie down on the floor. She lay there on her back for a long time, while the pain intensified, moving into her shoulder and down to her waist. This kind of thing had never happened before. It wasn't even daylight, and she realized that her friends might not arrive in time. They would come in and she would have died. She dragged herself to her feet, clutching the laboratory bench, her face contorted from the agonizing pain in her chest. She staggered to the dispensary—but the bottle of heart drops was empty.

She tore a page from her notebook.

Uncle Vitya. Maybe I won't live till tomorrow. No one is responsible for my death; everyone's tried to help me, to keep my spirits up. It's just the way it's turned out. When you go to the Inguletsk quarry to see their graves, write my name alongside theirs. So that we're together.

It hurts to die. But it hurts even more just to be alive.

I love you. Pauline.

She found a stiff gray envelope, stamped with the imprint of the Baku refinery that had sent her their tests for a control analysis. She put the letter into it.

The door squeaked open and Pauline hurriedly thrust the envelope under a chemical journal, mastered the pain in her chest, and stood upright, in her acid-stained, ill-fitting lab coat.

Maria Vasilievna Govardovskaya hurried in. She was a small woman, wearing a shiny yellow amber necklace and patent-leather shoes, as if she had just come straight from the theater. As she came up, her huge frightened gypsy eyes were fixed on the journal and the corner of the gray envelope peeping out from underneath it.

"Pauline! Whatever's wrong? I've got a piece of cheesecake. Let's make some tea. . . ."

Maria Vasilievna poured some water into a flask, and set it on a Bunsen burner, casting frightened glances over at Pauline's bench. She grabbed one of the test tubes which held an iodine solution, shook it, and for some reason smelled the contents. Maria Vasilievna had deep-set eyes which always glowed as if she were on fire inside.

Burnt up with malice, thought Pauline.

Maria Vasilievna was a strange person. Her husband had been declared an enemy of the people—everyone on the faculty knew that. It wasn't just her husband who'd been regarded as an enemy, but her own brother as well. And she was from a landowning family.

Maria Vasilievna's husband, as the Komsomol members had been informed by someone from the Special Department, had helped blow up a chemical factory and had passed on to Berlin the most important discovery that Kazansky and Platé had made in the thirties—the secret of producing oil from coal by distillation. Germany had no oil, but huge amounts of coal. It was because of this that the Fascist tanks, contrary to the calculations of Soviet economists, had suffered no fuel shortages. They just kept on coming.

"How many lives that one traitor cost us!" And the man from the Special Department had looked into the circle of silent faces.

Although Maria Vasilievna was a serious scientist and a faculty lecturer, she wasn't allowed within cannon shot of the students. If only she had had at least the sense of decency to keep quiet. But no! As soon as there was any mention of the war years, she began to try to prove to anyone in earshot that her husband was completely innocent, and that his execution —she called it murder—had been a crime.

Maria Vasilievna steeped the tea in the flask, then poured the aromatic brew into chemical beakers, talking angrily as she did.

"Alik says that Point Five is just drunken rubbish. But it's not drunken at all. It's murderous rubbish. Blood-stained rubbish. How long are they going to keep on murdering innocent people?"

"Maria Vasilievna," said Pauline in a voice of anguish. "What are you talking about? About your own troubles?"

"Mine and yours." Maria Vasilievna broke the piece of stale cheese-cake in half and dropped two lumps of sugar into Pauline's tea. She drank her own unsweetened. "When on the one hand they murder people who built the Revolution and on the other introduce a percentage norm for Jews, only a blind man would fail to see something in common between the two. Haven't you even heard about the daily counts our Acceptance Committee has introduced? In four divisions. Look how many Russians and Ukrainians—the native population—have been taken on, and compare those figures with Jews and the rest. It's a government count."

Pauline and Maria Vasilievna shared one corner of the laboratory, working literally back to back. If it hadn't been for the pain in her heart, Pauline would simply have turned on her heel and walked away. She didn't want to hear that kind of talk. For her an anti-Semite meant only one thing—a Fascist, a murderer. A blood-stained executioner. Yes, there were people like that. But how could you relate them to present reality? Could you make comparisons with 1937?

It looked as if the people who said that Maria Vasilievna was so bitter that she was prepared to slander even the most precious good they shared—Soviet power—were completely right.

It was something that Pauline, a Komsomol member, a faithful campaigner in elections, simply couldn't let pass by. It was Soviet power which had given her the chance to attend university. Her mother had barely been able to write and had learned alongside her daughter. The common people had only achieved equal rights a quarter century ago. Before that, people like her had had to hide in cellars and in stables. Pauline would not hear anything said against the power of the state. It was just as well that Maria Vasilievna wasn't allowed anywhere near the students.

She waited for Maria Vasilievna to go away. But Maria Vasilievna kept on eyeing the chemical journal on Pauline's bench and wouldn't go. She just kept on looking from the journal to the door—Pauline's friends might arrive at any moment—and then at Pauline herself, while her gypsy's eyes filled with suffering. . . .

It was only much later that Pauline understood the full tragedy of the Stalinist wall that had interposed itself between the two of them. The time finally came when Maria Vasilievna was summoned to the Supreme Court and handed a document which declared that her late husband, the leading scientist and comrade-in-arms of Ordzhonikidze,* was guilty of no

---

* Grigory (Sergo) Konstantinovich Ordzhonikidze (1886–1937): one of Stalin's principal henchmen. [Translator]

crime whatever and was therefore fully rehabilitated. Maria Vasilievna, clutching the paper mechanically in her fingers, went back home, and fell to the ground as she opened the door. Her heart had given out under the strain. . . .

Everyone who had known her, distinguished academicians and laboratory technicians alike, came to her funeral, feeling like dogs with their tails between their legs.

But all that was ten years in the future.

Maria Vasilievna finally left only when Professor Platé appeared, and the crowd of research workers and laboratory assistants filled the place with their cheerful racket.

"Your lips are blue," Platé said to Pauline in alarm. "Leave the experiment, and let's get you to a doctor."

Pauline showed him her sheets of notes of the constants she had worked out, all the time seeing before her the huge gypsy eyes of Maria Vasilievna, who had forced her to think about things which had been crystal-clear before, but which were now causing her new agonies—as if she didn't have enough on her mind already.

She was being killed with kindness, that much was becoming more and more obvious. The following night was even more painful. Probably she'd never lived through a harder one. Once she was left on her own, Kurt, a tall student from the German Democratic Republic, strode into the room. He had first appeared a month earlier, his hands held rigidly against his trouser seams, like a soldier, and had asked whether there was any way he could help Pauline.

Pauline's mouth fell open in astonishment. "I don't need anyone's help."

But he didn't leave, and she asked, as she turned back to her test tubes: "Whatever gave you that idea?"

Kurt's face was very serious as he replied, "I am a German. I was in the Hitlerjugend. I learned Paragraph Four, Point One, by heart, like the formula for water: 'A Jew cannot be a citizen of the Empire. He has no right to vote in the resolution of political decisions, and he can hold no public office. . . . Signed Führer and Reichskanzler Adolf Hitler, Imperial Minister of Internal Affairs Frick, Deputy Führer Hess . . .' I believed all that. Can you understand, I *believed* THAT? I believed in everything that led to Auschwitz and Buchenwald. I saw it all with my own eyes. And now I believe that all this is dead, and the right place for what is dead is in the grave. *Verstehen Sie?*"

The sound of the German words made Pauline tremble. That was all she needed—a former Nazi offering her help. What did his "points" have to do with her situation? Moreover, she had been brought up to believe that you don't wash your dirty linen in public. She courteously sent Kurt on his way, grateful for the fact that Maria Vasilievna hadn't heard the conversation. That would be so much grist to her mill.

And yet here Kurt was again, in the velvet jacket he always wore, with its zippers, and his stitched blue handkerchief, and his hands firmly at his trouser seams. In some confusion Pauline indicated the stool. Hesitantly she said, "*Bitte!*"

Kurt clicked his heels, sat on the edge of the stool, and began to ask her about her health.

"What I really came to say, Pauline Ivanovna," he said, finally coming to the point, "is that you must write to Stalin personally. Have you written? No?" He was looking somewhere over Pauline's head and his pale blue eyes were the color of the flame of a spirit lamp—unforgivably sharp. His eyes must have been full of hate like that, Pauline thought, her stomach tightening, when he pressed the trigger.

"You must write. And you mustn't mince your words. Tell him that there's a Nazi on your back, that there are home-grown Nazis in the university. Nazis who carry out orders about Jews."

"What do you mean, Kurt? They're . . . they're nothing but fools. Hooligans! Dogs!"

Kurt jumped up from the stool, sending it flying. Pauline had never seen him in such a rage.

"Don't argue. They're Nazis. I was a Nazi myself. I know what a Nazi is. Everyone knows, Pauline. We had a meeting yesterday, we Germans, and the Bulgarians, and the Czechs—and we all agreed they were Nazis."

Pauline watched him go, swallowing her tears.

She loved the university in the same way that grown people love their mothers. Sometimes they see that their mother is petty or cowardly, or out of date, or that she has other shortcomings. But she is still their mother. And they forgive her everything just because she *is* their mother. But there were people who thought that here—not just anywhere, but here in Moscow, right in the university—hooligans were in charge, hooligans who believed it was in their interest to imitate the Nazis. The thought was incomparably worse than any pain she had suffered before. Her grief and her shame made her want to cry aloud.

What was happening? What was happening?

As soon as it was light, she hurried off to the library through the snow. Her feet were so thinly covered by her rubber-soled pumps that she might as well have been barefoot.

The university library was closed for cleaning. Pauline stamped her feet in the doorway, then ran on along Mokhovaya Street to the Lenin Library.

Yesterday Maria Vasilievna had argued furiously that she should have a look at the newspapers of the Black Hundreds* of Tsarist days, and then she would understand, understand immediately, and wouldn't argue any more.

Pauline filled in the forms for them. But the newspapers didn't come. They were marked "out." They were still marked out a week later—and, again, six months later.

"What does this mean, 'out' all the time?" Pauline asked angrily.

The assistant answered, without the slightest change of expression, "They're being restored, bound. They were all falling apart, crumbling to dust. . . ." "Will it take long to restore them?" "There are millions of copies of ancient books in the Lenin Library. So there's a long queue."

Which sounded convincing enough.

Newspapers were only newspapers, after all. They could wait until the summer. She went off to the bookshelves, where the new red volumes of Lenin stood ready to hand, along with the thick collected works of Stalin, in large format, like books for the blind.

She had read the works only recently, preparing for her examination for admission to her research course. But everyone knows that the same lines sound quite different when you're reading them for an exam, and when they represent your very fate. She opened a volume at random.

> In all European states similar measures and laws against the Jews existed only in the dark days of the Middle Ages, the Inquisition, the burning of heretics and similar delights. . . . In Europe, Jews long ago achieved full equality of rights and have become more and more assimilated into the peoples among whom they live.

See, Maria Vasilievna?

> Apart from the oppression and the persecution of the Jews the most harmful tendency is the attempt to inflame nationalism, to alienate one nationality of the state from another. . . .

Nazis of all kinds might take aim at her, Pauline. They might even kill her, as her parents had been killed. But who allowed them to snipe at Lenin? It was nonsense.

Maybe Kurt's suspicions were forgivable. Who was he, after all? If you burn your fingers in hot milk, you blow on cold water. But how could

---

* The name of a Russian racist and anti-Semitic organization, which was responsible for several pogroms in Russia at the beginning of the twentieth century. [Translator]

Maria Vasilievna fail to understand? It must be a sign of how bitter she'd become.

Because she was hinting . . . God knows what she was hinting. Pauline opened a volume of Stalin. There it was, in black and white:

> Anti-Semitism, as an extreme form of racial chauvinism, is the most dangerous survival of cannibalism. . . . Anti-Semitism is as dangerous for the workers as a false path which leads them from the right road into the jungle. So Communists, as logical internationalists, cannot but be logical and sworn enemies of anti-Semitism.

Stalin's thought still lived!

Pauline hurried back to the university. She was elated, her cheeks glowed. A friend who asked her gloomily, "How are things?" received the shouted response, "They'll confirm me, the bastards! There's nothing they can do about it!"

And confirm her they did.

Pauline spent four months without a ration card, without a grant, without any possibility of getting a job, and then, just before the New Year she was summoned by telephone from the library.

The chemists met her in the courtyard, all yelling in chorus: "They've accepted you!"

"You're accepted!" people called to her from every door as she dashed to her laboratory.

"Have they really accepted you?" Maria Vasilievna asked in a fervent whisper, as she bent over her bench, her back toward Pauline. "Yes, yes, I'm accepted," she replied with passion, as Maria Vasilievna wept and hugged her. "Darling, Maria Vasilievna, they've accepted me. I'm accepted!"

Maria Vasilievna cried, her face buried in Pauline's patched old coveralls, cried silently, and all the more bitterly, more hopelessly. The more Pauline tried to calm her, the more bitterly she wept.

That evening the laboratory benches were pushed to one side, the assistant produced some pure alcohol from her stores, and for the first time in the history of the University of Moscow, the chemistry research students danced on the benches, while the legendary Skvortsova-Stepanova and other senior scientists leaned against the walls beating out the rhythm of the quickening dance.

9

I first met Pauline at a student party given by a physicist who'd been a friend since childhood. He was a creative man who always gave good parties. He lived on Bronnaya Street, near the State Jewish Theater. When he gave a party he sent the aunts he lived with off to the theater, so that, as he joked, the Jews should not embarrass the Russian students.

His guests were never allowed to get bored. That particular day, everyone who came through the door was immediately required to say three lines of verse, without any pause for thought or consideration. Just say the first thing that came into your head!

The door bell rang, and my physicist friend bounded to his feet.

A tall fair-haired girl stepped shyly—almost sideways in her shyness—into the room. She was alarmingly thin, but, despite that, she had considerable presence. She was wearing a light, unseasonable coat, all worn at the elbows. As she came in she was assaulted by shouts of "Three lines of a poem! Come on, hurry up!"

She shivered, biting her lip, and said the first three lines that crossed her mind.

> "Have you seen the rapid river?
> On its banks flowers grow, while
> The bottom is always deep, cold and dark. . . ."*

Then another guest turned up, there was a lot more shouting, and Pauline, kicking off her thin shoes, sat back in the corner of the sofa. She tucked her feet under her and withdrew into herself, sitting there self-effacingly.

So I was able to examine her face, as white as if it had been washed

---

* Authorship unknown. Possibly Shevchenko, the Ukrainian national poet. [Translator]

in snow, with a pink glow on her thin cheekbones, a face that was full of untouched country freshness. Such a good face, but sad. Even her smile had a kind of mournful gaiety, and it was obvious that despite the glow the cold had brought to her sunken cheeks, she had some deep inner sorrow.

I asked if I could see her home, and she thanked me with striking, almost child-like, trust. I think this must have been the result of my naval jacket, nothing more. Mikhail Prokofiev wore a dark-blue naval jacket like mine, though I didn't even know of his existence at that time. For Pauline a naval jacket was a sure sign of a man's trustworthiness.

We walked around the old streets of the Arbat. I told her enthusiastically about the prayer of the monk Daniel, about Kolovrata-Evpatiya, about Evpraksiya, faithful to her knight, who flung herself from the bell tower.* (I was writing a thesis about them, and so considered myself the greatest living expert after Academician Gudzy in ancient Russian literature.) In the middle of Smolensk Square I declaimed Esenin and raised my fairly indifferent voice in an English sailors' song I had learned in Murmansk. An old woman shuffling by with a shopping bag muttered as she passed: "See how he's turning that girl's head! And there she stands with her mouth wide open drinking it all in, the fool!"

I was so embarrassed that Pauline burst out laughing and took my arm.

The following evening I was allowed to sit on a lab stool in the narrow gap between the benches where Pauline and Maria Vasilievna worked, getting in the way of both of them. I courageously concealed the fact that I was suffering agonies from the appalling smell of the chemical laboratory, until Pauline suddenly looked at the clock and exclaimed: "Oh, my God, you've missed the last metro!"

"Then it doesn't matter how long I stay!" I replied in delight, and a long time later I walked home right across the city, from Manège Square to Sharikopodshipnik, swinging my arms as if I were on parade, and singing at the top of my voice, "Even Moscow's got a smile for us!"

The half-frozen watchmen at shop doors huddling in their sheepskin coats looked after me understandingly. "Oh, he's just had a drop too much!"

Once I took Pauline to the philological faculty to hear a lecture by a very talented man who was highly popular in our course—Dr. Pinsky. Pinsky was attacked at every Party meeting, and people said he was bound to be imprisoned soon because of the boldness of his views. Which was exactly what happened.

* These are all references to old Slavonic writings. [Translator]

At that time our faculty was like a cart being jolted over cobblestones. Resolutions about Zoshchenko and Akhmatova.*

About Shostakovich and Muradeli.†

Rasul Gamzatov was to write about it all later in his poem: "Comrade Zhdanov, sitting at the piano, teaches Shostakovich how to play."

But at that time we hadn't come so near to understanding what was going on. We were seekers after wisdom. At first we sought with enthusiasm, later with more circumspection.

We were first put on our guard by a session of the All-Union Biological Assembly,‡ which had just taken place and had burst over us like a thunderstorm on a roof, sending sheets of iron whirling into the wind and clattering to the ground. The differences between the biologists were very obscure. But at the same time the truth had never been more glaring: the press and the radio talked about free discussion, but at the very end of the conference Trofim Lysenko announced with an ironic smile that his report which had sparked off all the row had been *accepted in advance.*

And not by just anyone—by *him himself.*

In other words, what had been happening wasn't a discussion at all, but a trap.

Academician Nikolai Kalinnikovich Gudzy was disgusted. "Trofim chose a good time to dress up all his opponents in cap and bells. Now we all know whom to spit at. What a swine!"

Lysenko's trap was the first trap our generation managed to avoid. Around the university people talked in disgust about the Lysenkization of science. Pauline once asked, "Surely, you people in the humanities faculties couldn't sink to such depths?"

Oh, Pauline, what divine naïveté!

We wandered through winter Moscow, and our courtship was more like a scientific debate from which we would emerge momentarily to gulp fresh air before plunging back in again.

I once asked Pauline about her parents. She abruptly and painfully changed the conversation, and I didn't return to the subject. But we weren't able to keep silent for long about the things that came to mind of their own

* Decree of the Central Committee of the Communist Party of the Soviet Union August, 1946, condemning these two writers and expelling them from the Writers' Union. [Translator]

† Decree of the Central Committee of the Communist Party of the Soviet Union February, 1948, which condemned the latest works of the composers Shostakovich and Muradeli. This decree, like the previous one, was drawn up by Zhdanov. [Translator]

‡ This was a famous session that took place in 1948 declaring the absolute truth of Lysenko's theories of the transmission of acquired characteristics and denouncing his opponents as heretics. Many of them were deported. [Translator]

accord, thrusting themselves right into our nostrils, as if we were drowning in deep water.

. . . We ran up an iron staircase into the faculty building, and stopped in a corridor full of excited and angry students. A red-haired, tousle-headed Czech girl, Miroslava, from the department of Slavonic studies, was explaining that they were going to carry out a "social experiment" as she called it. So that all doubts could be either contradicted or confirmed. From what she'd seen, she had reason to believe that lecturer B. was giving Jewish students especially low marks.

"Oh, that can't be true!" protested Gena Faibusovich from classical studies. "That's absolute nonsense!"

"Well, why don't you try being examined by him," someone said gloomily.

Several other voices joined in. "Yes, you try it yourself."

I began to try to push my way through the crowd. We were late for Pinsky's lecture, but Pauline stopped me. Her voice was low and tense. "Wait a minute." "We'll be late." "It doesn't matter."

Unwittingly I stopped. I didn't want to inflame an old wound, a wound of which, in my opinion, Pauline still understood nothing.

From somewhere on the fringes of the group, a voice spoke up uncertainly.

"Look, why don't you take the exam in my place?"

A war veteran student was sitting by the wall. He had only one leg. His crutches were propped up alongside him.

"I can't remember a thing. My memory's like a sieve."

There was silence.

"Go on, Faibusovich, take the exam for him!" suggested a boy I didn't know, someone wearing horn-rimmed glasses. "You're a genius. It's nothing to you. Let's get going with this experiment. Is B. an anti-Semite or isn't he?"

Faibusovich shuffled his feet uneasily, adjusted his glasses, which were always sliding down to the end of his long nose; thin, with narrow shoulders —one higher than the other—long-nosed, he looked like a caricature of a Jew out of some anti-Semitic paper from the time of Shulgin and Purishkevich, and would, of course, be the best candidate to carry out this public experiment.

Faibusovich began to walk slowly back to the staircase and pulled away his hand when Miroslava tried to grab hold of it. His voice shook with despair. "Taking an exam for someone else! That's cheating!"

Faibusovich was open and honest—so honest he couldn't even conceive that within the walls of this ancient university there could be liars, or flagrant anti-Semites.

"He's too good," said a dark-haired girl from classical studies. "He simply couldn't do it!"

"He's no saint, he's a holy fool!" came a sharp response from the crowd.

Faibusovich shuffled in the doorway in total confusion.

"Look," he said at last, forcing the words out. "He probably knows me. Who is this B.?"

"Have a look!" several voices invited.

Faibusovich eased open the squeaky door of the lecture hall and sighed deeply as he was obliged to acknowledge that "he doesn't know me."

"Gena!" Miroslava shouted excitedly, "we won't get another chance like this. Let's find out the truth!"

Gena paused.

"Are you afraid?" Several voices together.

"Oh, the hell with him!" cursed the boy in horn-rims. "What are we groveling to him for?"

Then we heard a quiet, husky voice, almost a whisper.

"Genochka!"

It's voices like that, girls like that, who can compel young men to walk through fire or dive off cliffs into frozen rivers.

"Genochka, please . . ."

"But what about my card?" Gena said, his voice shaking. "The photograph'll be different."

A broad-shouldered boy with a pock-marked face pushed to the front of the crowd and said, "That's no problem." Within seconds Gena's photograph had been transferred from one card to another.

In normal circumstances only three or at most four people put their ear to a crack in a door, but there must have been ten with their ears against that one. They were society's representatives: the ones lower down squatted on their heels, and the ones at the top scrambled onto chairs. But even that wasn't good enough. So they opened the door a fraction. So that society could listen directly, without intermediaries.

What they heard wasn't merely a student replying to examination questions—it was a beautiful song.

"Do you know Belinsky's letter to Gogol?" the examiner asked in a surly voice.

Gena Faibusovich started off by heart, from the beginning without any hesitation: " 'You are mistaken if you think that my letter to you is the words of an angered man . . .' "

He declaimed the text like a prose poem, until the examiner said sharply, "That's enough."

Then Gena explained the letter, as requested, in his own words.

I had never heard such brilliant answers—Gena was well aware of the ear of society listening behind him, waiting for him outside the door. The boy in the horn-rimmed glasses gave a whispered running commentary. "Now he's taking the card. He's looking at it. Now he's marking it. Hurray!"

Everyone leaped away from the door. No one even asked what mark the examiner had given. There couldn't be the slightest doubt.

Faibusovich, as red as a tomato, came out, opened the card—and his mouth sagged open in horror. "He's only given me a three!"*

There was a silence. It grew deeper, then was suddenly shattered by a joyful yell from the war veteran, who grabbed his crutches and leaped about on his one leg. "That's marvelous! It's all I needed to pass." His face shone with genuine triumph. He went out gleefully, waving his crutch. The rest of us stayed silently where we were; then dispersed just as quietly, our heads hanging, as if at a funeral.

A short time later Gena Faibusovich found himself under attack. One of the people in his group, a girl, said in a report that he was a "bourgeois internationalist."

I met Gena Faibusovich twenty years later, in a corridor in the Lenin Library. I asked the name of the girl whose libel had landed him in prison. His face crumpled, reddened, and he said, "There's no need to talk about it. She went into a psychiatric hospital after that—after they told her everything."

Gena was on his way to the hospital where he worked. It turned out that when he'd been released he hadn't been allowed to go back to the university, as everyone else had, and he'd had to start again from scratch. He had a glance, as he put it, at some books on philology and then joined the Medical Institute. What he didn't tell me was that he had become one of the best doctors in Moscow.

We joked about the "social experiment" outside the lecture room doors so many years ago. Then suddenly he said that strictly speaking it wasn't a good experiment. "You see," he said, "it may have been that the examiner wasn't so upset that I was a Jew, but that I was a Jew with a Russian name. You know—trying to hide the fact. After all, the card belonged to that fellow with one leg!"

He grew more serious and talked about the camps. "What they taught me," he said, "was that the most hated people are always the ones who try to conceal the fact that they're Jewish. I was only beaten up once for being a Jew. And that was by criminal prisoners. They chased me into a

---

* In the Soviet Union examination marks run from one to five, so the mark of three means just average. [Translator]

corner. 'Jew, dance.' It was far worse for the Jews who tried to pass themselves off as Byelorussians or something. No one liked them. Neither the good people nor the bad. You know, that's not anti-Semitism. People are instinctively against liars; they're repelled by them."

And Gena set off down the stairs—desperately shy, wise Gena Faibusovich, who had remained so pure even after being dragged by the hair through all the mud of the earth.

. . . The "social experiment" was barely over and the students scarcely dispersed when Pauline turned back.

I caught up with her. "Where are you going? What about the lecture?"

"Let's get out into the air, shall we?"

We left the university building, ran across Manège Square, and turned into the Alexandrovsky Gardens, a wonderfully clean haven in the hell of motorcars. Pauline sat down on a bench but got up again immediately.

"It's cold," she said. "Life is cold." She was looking at me without blinking and her eyes were full of pain.

"What's going on? I must know. I have a right to know. All of it. So do you, for that matter. Because these people will soon be going all over the world, that Czech girl, our German friend, the Bulgarians, and the Hungarians; what are they going to tell their people back home? It's a stain on our country's reputation."

There, on a damp bench in the Alexandrovsky Gardens, beneath the walls of the Kremlin, I first learned to my astonishment that Pauline was a Jew, and heard the fate of her family. Later my memory was jogged by a line by the poet Anna Akhmatova:

He who is transfixed forever by your terrible fate . . .

I sat motionless, living the truth of that quotation.

She sighed, then began again. "What *is* going on? When did it all begin? Was it really during the war when the Germans were shooting Jews? I just can't get it into my head. You've got to tell me how it first broke out. What made it spread? Why did it happen? Here, at home, along the front line. Do you know from personal experience, or is it just rumors you've heard? Tell me. Have you really seen it for yourself? I've got to find my way out of this maze, for myself. It's vitally important. During the war did you ever feel you were being hurt or insulted because you were a Jew? Or not you but your friends, people you knew? Did any one of you ever feel, just because you were Jewish, that you were the kind of miserable creature who could be mistreated with impunity? Try to remember! Please!"

10

On June 4, 1942, the Germans sank convoy PQ17—made up of both English and American ships—in the Barents Sea. The convoy was making passage to Murmansk, and a staff order had dispatched us to Vaenga. At base airfields on the Baltic and Black seas the alarm went out at four in the morning, and by midday our brothers were landing on the very edge of the world, at blazing Vaenga.

Anyone who served at that polar airfield in the summer and autumn of '42–'43 knows what hell must be like. Any front has reserve airfields, decoy airfields, airfields which can be shifted into service when necessary. Aircraft can be switched about, hidden. In Byelorussia we held out for a month and a half simply by dodging from one airfield to another like grasshoppers.

But up near the pole there is nowhere to hide. The one airfield had been hewn by convicts out of solid granite. They had dynamited the rock, dragged it away in trucks, and an airfield had appeared, surrounded by little hills.

I went out into these hills in the polar night, cold but bright as day. I looked around, and for a moment forgot a war was on.

The engines were quiet, and I could hear the sound of the little streams that criss-crossed the slopes. A man in a naval uniform with an engineer's silver stripes was picking berries. He held out his uniform cap to me, full of fruit, and invited me to help myself. They were juicy. Blueberries: the hill was knee-deep with them. Here and there were white-capped mushrooms, and farther off the dark color of veronica. Rosebay willowherb swayed in the wind. Pale pink, tender, and standing as high as polar flowers could, the willowherb grew thick and strong by discarded ammunition boxes.

Down below fighters were revving up for take-off, raising little whirl-winds of dust. As soon as they were off the ground they retracted their undercarriages. Only after they were airborne did we hear the sound of the alarm bell, as the orderlies leaped out of their dugouts and grabbed metal rods to hammer the rails which hung on a wire.

"Here they come again!" the engineer shouted. "Run for it!"

As if to confirm his words, close by, in the Kola inlet, the ships' guns opened fire. We flung ourselves to one side, landing up to our ankles in clinging brown mud.

All the ships seemed to have taken up the firing. Salvos from the heavy anti-aircraft batteries on the hilltops shook the earth beneath our feet. There was a sharp screaming sound overhead. I was about to follow the engineer, then someone else shouted hoarsely, "This way!"

I turned to follow the voice, and leaped into the shelter of a huge granite boulder, curling myself up away from the satanic noise of the falling bombs.

The first explosions were in the middle of the airfield. The hills shuddered. It seemed that the earth was vibrating like an overstretched bass string.

"That was a whole series. They're heading this way!" someone beside me shouted in a hoarse bass voice.

I used what strength I had to burrow deeper into the mud, squeezing myself as close as I could get to the boulder. The explosions drew nearer and nearer, turning the air into smoke, shaking the earth and sending thousands of shrapnel splinters hurtling in every direction.

The earth split open. The huge granite boulder, which had lain motionless for centuries, swayed, and something hard hit me on the side.

The explosions began to recede. The bomb series was moving over me with giant strides and then was gone. I slowly raised my hand, reluctant to discover what had happened to my body. There was no pain. . . . Finally, I managed to touch the spot. My fingers found a lump of damp earth which had been thrown up by the blast. I immediately leaped to my feet and shouted for my unknown companions.

There was no reply. The man who'd been lying near me had already set off down the hill. I could just make out his military greatcoat some way below me. But where was the engineer?

I ran around the granite boulder. On the other side a small crater was smoking.

"He-e-y!" I shouted again to the engineer.

Silence.

I dashed back and forth, jumping over chunks of rock. And then on the very top of the mound, lying among the blueberries, I saw the sleeve of a naval jacket with an engineer's silver stripes. That was all there was.

I stared down at the airfield, where the tractors were already at work, dragging trailer loads of stones and gravel to fill in the new craters. Soldiers with spades were running along behind to do the necessary work.

"Welcome to the North Pole!" I said to myself, spitting out soft muddy soil. "Nice quiet place you've got here!"

When I had called the ambulance people and got back to my aircraft, someone was in the cockpit. A pair of legs in green soldiers' overalls were dangling out of the lower hatch.

While we were serving on the Volkhov front we had been issued bell-bottom trousers, as we were now called something with an alarmingly long name: Special Naval Air Strike Group. No one was particularly pleased about that, as we already knew we were liable to be thrown into any breach that appeared anywhere. But we wore our bell-bottoms proudly, and so wide that our commandant once set up a post near the airfield equipped with sheep shears to cut out the gussets that the dressier ones among us had sewn in. It seemed there must be some immemorial rule: the farther a sailor from the sea, the wider the flare of his bell-bottoms. And yet there I saw a pair of green overalled legs sticking out of my airplane. One of the soldiers must have decided to climb in and have a look around. Likely as not he'd hit some switch with his elbow, and then there'd be an accident. Idiot!

I ran up to the legs in the green overalls and heaved on them with all my strength. The metal spring-loaded steps on which the soldier was standing slid aside and he fell to the ground. As he stood up, he brushed down his dirty army greatcoat, which was charred at the hem, and said in a slightly nervous tone: "What's the matter with you?"

"I'll give you 'What's the matter'!" Then I broke off. The soldier looked well over forty, although I suppose he could have been less. At all events, he looked like a grandfather. "Aren't you ashamed of yourself, old man?"

The "old man" had a broad, brick-red face, with high cheekbones, and a chin as wide as a barn door. It was the coarse, simple, open, kindly face of a foot-soldier from a guards regiment, the face of a man who'd spent all his life in the open. There was something about his eyes—motionless, self-deprecatory. As if he were in some way persecuted. The eyes of a man expecting a blow.

But he said calmly and with dignity: "I'm the new navigator."

I felt myself go hot all over, and froze as if I were on parade. I realized the kind of person I was dealing with. We'd had men from penal battalions before. And then—could this be the man who had just saved my life?

"Sknaryov, Alexander Ilyich," he introduced himself. "Private."

Alexander Ilyich became our navigator. Within a week he was the squadron navigator. Why not? He was the only real sea-wolf among us.

The rest of us just wore bell-bottoms. And when you're over the sea there aren't any landmarks. No chance of following a railway or a river as we'd been used to doing.

Only yesterday one bell-bottomed boy, nineteen years old, had boxed his compass. He flew his plane, not to his target, but back to his own airfield and bombed it. Fortunately he didn't score a hit, and equally fortunately our station commander, General Kidalinsky, wasn't a vindictive man. He was always yelling "I'll have you shot for this!" but throughout all his years in the service he never actually did it.

Sknaryov flew with everybody. He never turned anyone down, not a single pilot in the squadron. He worked so hard, flew so many sorties that there were times when he was too tired even to get back to his dugout, and he would fall asleep by the plane, lying on a padded engine cover.

The planes never stopped their dogfights overhead. The Messerschmitts came diving over the inlet leaving long white trails behind them. And Vaenga catapulted her MiGs, Hurricanes, and Kittihawks back at them, with crocodiles' teeth painted on their engine cowlings. They came home on their last drop of fuel and others took over for them.

The ack-ack guns sounded spasmodically. Had the Junkers broken through? I looked up at the sky with the clouds of white gunsmoke drifting in the wind, and wondered whether I should wake Alexander Ilyich. As usual, I decided to let him lie. Why disturb him?

After that meeting up on the hill with the engineer who gave me the berries he'd picked as a farewell, I became a fatalist. You can't escape the bomb with your name on it, and no other one will get you. That bomb had frightened me—but at the same time, oddly enough, it had calmed me down.

Actually, somehow or other, everyone at Vaenga calmed down if they didn't want to end up in the madhouse. People passed through the barrier between life and death very quickly, as men later passed through the sound barrier. And no wonder. The airfield was being bombed six or seven times a day. Often by thousand-pounders. Sometimes they even used four-ton bombs, the ones originally intended for the English battleship *George* V, which they didn't seem able to find.

That was the time I kept remembering the words of the Bible. "And the earth shall gape open . . ." That was how our day began. Forty or fifty Junkers broke through to Vaenga with a mission to crater the airstrip as badly as they could so that our fighters would be unable to take off. When they succeeded, a second wave of Junkers overflew us and passed on to the port of Murmansk to bomb the allied freighters waiting to unload, their smoke drifting over the Kola inlet.

On the hilltops around the base the moss blazed all summer. The peat bogs smoldered constantly; it seemed that the earth and the inlet itself were permanently aflame. There was no chance of putting them out. The smoke and the smell of fire were always drifting over the airfield.

"What's going on?" Sknaryov asked sleepily, when the ack-ack began to stutter, and he turned over on his other side.

When the crescendo howl of the German dive bombers convinced me that time had run out, I would kick the navigator into wakefulness and we would plunge into the slit trench we had dug out of the stony ground right by the aircraft park. It was here, crouched on engine covers at the bottom of a narrow, crumbling trench, that Alexander Ilyich Sknaryov told me his story.

He had been a major, a squadron navigator in the Far East. That winter his aircraft, the slow-moving corrugated monster known as the TB3, had had a forced landing in the taiga. The engine had quit. They ran out of supplies after a month, and Sknaryov and his flight engineer/gunner, a boy my own age, had set out to see what they could find. In one of the scattered villages of the region they had come across a bunch of half-drunken recruits, coats open to the winds, one of them playing an accordion. When they discovered what Sknaryov needed they just roared, "Give him what he wants. We've got flour to spare—loads of it. No one feels like fighting anymore. It's all there for the taking." And then, unexpectedly soberly, "Give us your jacket in exchange!"

Alexander Ilyich took off his leather flying jacket, and brought a sack of flour and a box of meat back to the plane.

After another week they managed to get the TB3 off the ground somehow or other and limped back to their airfield near Khabarovsk. Alexander Ilyich gathered together all the widows and orphans of the squadron and divided what remained of the food between them. "He divided up the meat to a hair's breadth and the flour to the last grain" was the way I heard the story in Severomorsk, where I met an old pilot, Colonel Gorkov, who had served with Sknaryov in the Far East.

. . . They had barely finished when the station received a message that a military dump in a taiga village had been raided, and that the guilty parties were to be found immediately.

And where were they, these guilty parties? Where were the half-drunken "comrades" from the infantry regiment? Fighting near Moscow? Near Stalingrad? Maybe they had already been killed.

The search for the guilty men was relentless. They wanted every single one of them. A law had been passed about the theft of state property just before the war started, it was said, and at the personal initiative of Stalin himself. However small the amount a man had stolen—a handful of wheat, a hundred grams of meat, a loaf of bread—the penalty remained ten years in a camp. A new decree is like a new broom. Sknaryov was arrested. He was taken away, dishonored and disbelieving. He was tried by a field court-martial. . . .

"The blood of a guilty man is mere water," Alexander Ilyich said quietly, looking up at the clear sky, where despite the apparent emptiness we could still hear the crack of machine gun bullets. "I was sentenced to be shot. And they put me in the death cell."

It was a long way to Moscow. It was fifty or sixty days before the recommendation for mercy could get there and back. When they took him out of the moldering, windowless death cell, his hair had turned gray. They read the new sentence to him. Ten years. The same as for stealing a loaf.

And then, thanks to the efforts of the local senior officers, the ten years was replaced with a sentence to serve in a punishment battalion. Which was how Sknaryov came to be in Vaenga, sleeping on tarpaulins.

It was to these tarpaulins that a letter was delivered. It came from the Far East. About his wife, and how she had a new husband, a captain someone or other. And about how she didn't want even to think about her old husband.

It wasn't until much later that we discovered the letter wasn't genuine. Someone had been desperately eager to get at Sknaryov. Eager that he shouldn't return from the war. But both Alexander Ilyich and I took it at face value. I flew into a rage, and cursed every member of the female sex with childish thoroughness, starting with Eve. And then the marauding captain who had displaced Sknaryov. Worse even than a marauder.

Alexander Ilyich calmed me down, smiling sadly, wisely, determinedly. "Come on, Grisha! After all, look what the fellow's taken on himself—two children—belonging to a man who's been shot!"

I glanced up at this quiet man with his coarse, red face, colored by the eternal polar sun. And I fell silent. From that moment I grew very close to Sknaryov. Whatever I was doing—as shells whined overhead, as tracers slashed through the sky, as fires raged—I thought of Sknaryov. How could I help him?

I felt guilty when I looked at his face, such a strong face, lined beyond his years, and then, almost a surprise, his eyes, gazing, hurt, silently accusing.

What could be done?

What could I do, there on the blazing airfield, a simple fitter, on first-stage stand-by, a man who didn't have the right to leave his aircraft even during air raids? What if it should suddenly catch fire?

No one tried to hide the fact that the bomber was worth a great deal more than my life. A great deal more. Who was going to listen to me? Never before had I felt so useless.

But I couldn't go on living like this. I thought and thought and finally came up with an idea. I borrowed Sknaryov's navigator's pencil, and hiding behind a newspaper I wrote out his story on the back of an old flight map and sent it off to the newspaper *Fighting for the Fatherland*, so that everyone should know what kind of a man Alexander Ilyich Sknaryov was.

That was the first article I ever wrote in my life. I sent it on an off chance to the headquarters building where the editorial offices were. Then I sent a second letter, then a third. There were six in all. . . .

No response. It was like sending letters to a grave. No answer, no acknowledgment. Luckily, Sknaryov didn't know what I was doing.

A month later I was summoned to see some senior lieutenant or other—on the double.

I washed the oil off my hands, straightened the belt of my stained leather jerkin, and set off to H.Q.

It turned out that the senior lieutenant was a journalist. He was a short man, wearing an army jacket with several buttons missing. It looked as if he was a reservist. He bawled me out for writing about a man from a punishment battalion. "Don't you know that you mustn't say a word about the punishment men? Not a word, my friend, not so much as a sigh." He obviously *was* from the reserve.

I made the lieutenant sit down on an ammunition box, and told him about Sknaryov. I told him all the things I hadn't written about in the articles, which had, of course, only dealt with his heroism in action.

The lieutenant's shoulders, one higher than the other, like Faibusovich's, twitched nervously. He adjusted his thick-lensed glasses, slumping as he sat and looking like a bookkeeper who couldn't make his balance sheet come out right.

He wasn't a born soldier, this pathetic little man. That much was plain. And I didn't yet know he was the only mobilized naval journalist who had been transferred to the army. The fleet commander, Admiral Golovko, had happened on him one day on the quayside and had barked: "We can't have sailors looking like that!"

And so there he was, the only man on the airfield wearing an army uniform. They promoted him but refused him his bell-bottom trousers.

But it was our good fortune that this was the man we got.

As we said good-bye, he stroked his badly shaven cheek with his hand, looked at me very seriously, and said, "What's your name? . . . Right then, Grisha, go on writing, and I'll keep your stuff. Whenever my bosses see me, they seem to grin or snigger a little. Maybe we can turn that to our advantage. Let's take the risk."

When Sknaryov's name finally made it into print, I tore across the whole aircraft apron, waving the paper like a flag. I must have looked utterly crazed, because heads in Balaklava helmets came popping out of every hut. At the very least, the war had to have ended!

Of course, it wasn't actually my article in the paper. But there on the front page under the headline, instead of a leading article was an announcement in bold type that a bomber flight under fleet navigator A. Sknaryov had carried out such and such a mission. The main thing was that his name was there. Set out in real type. Legally. A. Sknaryov!

Soon after that, a group of naval officers turned up at the airfield, and people whispered apprehensively among themselves that a board of inquiry was being held.

In a staff dugout, on a circuit sitting of the Tribunal of the Northern Fleet, Sknaryov had the finding of guilty against him formally removed. He came out of the dugout wearing a modest grin and new pale blue shoulder boards. "His epaulettes are as clean as his conscience," was the pilots' joke. They embraced him, hugged him. I handed him a bunch of rosebay willowherb, which I had picked down in the valley, and was holding behind my back just in case.

Sknaryov may have had his finding of guilt expunged, but there's truth in the saying that bad rumors spread while good ones don't. Granted, he was no longer numbered among the punishment battalion, the outcasts. But he remained someone who was always pointed out as a man who *had* been in the punishment battalion, one of "those." He had probably earned three decorations by the time he was awarded his first.

After each of his triumphs, I wrote about Sknaryov. I celebrated every time he acquired a new star on his epaulettes. He soon became a lieutenant, and a senior lieutenant the month after.

The military store was in lower Vaenga, in the port. I used to go down there to buy the new stars for his epaulettes. I had a stock by now—first his captain's stars, and then the bigger ones for the rank of major. I would probably have bought his marshal's badges, except that they didn't sell them in Vaenga. There wasn't much demand.

When Sknaryov was promoted to captain, I waited by the dugout (by now he lived alone, at the regimental command H.Q.) to congratulate him. I said he'd once been a major, and it wouldn't be long before he got back to that rank. Everything was reverting to where it should be. And by now he'd even been given two decorations, although that was a mere shadow of what he ought to have had.

Sknaryov's arms flopped to his sides. He was holding a tattered map case.

"Come off it, Grisha," he said, "I'm going home. Don't you think that somehow or other my major's stars'll pass me by? People'll say, 'Who's this Sknaryov?' 'Oh, he's the one who was sentenced to be shot. Remember?' That's ruined my name right through the fleet. I'll never get away from that, no matter how long I live. And my children'll suffer too, I'm afraid." And then, suddenly, with a heavy sigh, "If only they'd make me a Hero of the Soviet Union."

He spoke in the same voice I once heard a peasant use after the war, when he said to me, "If only the bread lasts till spring."

My head was full of that secret wish. Like the air gunners who put on their flak jackets before taking off, Sknaryov was looking for stronger and stronger armor, something that was impenetrable. That was his dream, and I knew about it. If he got what he wanted, and anyone asked, "Who's this Sknaryov?" there would only be one answer—"He's a Hero of the Soviet Union. One of the best."

I wrote about Sknaryov like a man possessed. I persuaded the air observers to give me copies of photographs of the German freighters he'd sunk. The military editor of the paper would pace the floor of his office as he was putting the edition together, and say, "That crazy Grisha'll be tearing in any minute. Leave him a column breaker—say twenty lines."

They gave Sknaryov another decoration and promoted him to major. With his promotion he was transferred to the other regiment on the far side of the airfield.

But they didn't make him a Hero.

When the weather was unflyable, and there was nothing to print about Sknaryov, I was furious. But finally I had an idea. When the all-clear sounded, Sknaryov and I would sit together, and he would tell me (he didn't like writing) about his wide-ranging theoretical ideas. I made up plans to go with his ideas and gave them unpronounceable but convincingly scientific titles—"The torpedo bombing of a single freighter on the traverse of the Cape of Kiborgnes." I was also very fond of headlines like "In the narrow neck of the fjord . . ." They were so poetic.

They still didn't make him a Hero.

Once Admiral Golovko, commander-in-chief Northern Fleet, came to the dugout. Several men were standing nearby. The most senior of them was Captain Shkaruba, a Hero of the Soviet Union. Shkaruba was a legend and his decorations countless. His picture was always appearing on the front page of the paper.

Shkaruba rapped out the usual order to those around him: to the men, to the sea, to the very heavens, he bellowed, "Atten-*tion!*" And he marched up to the admiral to report.

While he reported, for some reason the admiral was gazing at his jacket. Suddenly everyone realized why. All his decorations were there, except that where the golden star of the Hero of the Soviet Union should have been, there was only a hole.

"Why are you improperly dressed?" snapped Admiral Golovko.

Captain Shkaruba shifted uneasily from foot to foot in his fur-lined flying boots, perhaps preparing to explain that his star was on his other uniform jacket, that he had wanted his family to have it, if . . . But then he said loudly that the reason was something quite different.

"Comrade Admiral! I have sunk six enemy freighters. And I am a Hero of the Soviet Union. Major Sknaryov has sunk twelve enemy freighters and naval vessels; twice as many. And he is not a Hero of the Soviet Union. So what right have I to wear this star? How can I look my comrade in the eye?"

The other pilots stood as if turned to stone. What would happen now? It was only a few days since the polar ace pilot Gromov, four times holder of the Order of the Red Banner, had been threatened with a punishment battalion.

Fortunately, Admiral Golovko was both young and wise. In a voice that everyone could hear, he ordered Captain Shkaruba to be put under house arrest for five days for being improperly dressed. And then he said something, in a much quieter voice, to the staff officer standing beside him, which set the aide off into frantic activity.

The very next day, by never-failing bush telegraph, it became known that the papers recommending Sknaryov for the award of Hero of the Soviet Union were on their way to Moscow.

We waited and waited for the announcement, but it never came.

At about this time I was transferred to the staff of the newspaper *North Sea Pilot*. The regimental commander, Colonel Syromyatnikov, gave me his fountain pen (a rarity in those days) as a parting gift, and said, "There you are then, Sknaryovite. Go and see what you can do."

The next morning the General Staff reported that some torpedo bombers had destroyed a German transport carrying five thousand mountain troops. I leaped into the editorial jeep and drove off to the airfield. I got there just in time.

The ground crew were just opening the lower hatch—Sknaryov's—and setting up the stairs. One boot and then another appeared, groping for the ladder rungs. The leather sole of one boot was ripped through by a piece of shrapnel; it flapped, and felt wadding stuck out of a rip in the flying suit's leg.

Sknaryov jumped to the ground, yelling cheerfully to Syromyatnikov, who looked as if he didn't have the strength to climb out of his cockpit: "Come on, Boris Pavlovich, let's get out of here. We might get hurt!"

That night there was a banquet in the dugout. In honor of the victory. This time, finally, he must be awarded his Hero for sure.

It was the tradition of the Northern Fleet that every time a military transport was sunk, we'd feast on a suckling pig. Sometimes a rabbit or two would find their way into the pot. When there were so many victories, you couldn't always provide the real thing. But this time there was a genuine suckling pig. Milk-fed. No substitutes.

Everyone who was around was invited, even red-eyed fat Selyavka, the "son of the fugitive" as he was known, a widely disliked senior sergeant. (He once explained his nickname—"My mother fled from the kolkhoz."*) He was known around the airfield as a hoarder, a sneak thief, and a squealer.

Once in the winter we were trying to find some felt boots for a wounded man who was being sent to Murmansk. No one had an extra pair, so they had to take the man away in ordinary shoes. Then the next day it was discovered that Selyavka had a spare pair tucked away in his huge wooden chest. He was beaten up for that, and from then on anyone at the airfield who showed the same kind of inclination was warned not to "do a Selyavka."

But even so, that night Sergeant Selyavka was invited too. He was given a tin mug of liquor, and he began to talk.

Selyavka had recently returned from Mogilev, where he'd been visiting his mother. As he talked about the dreadful prices in Mogilev, about the sufferings his mother had undergone during the occupation, he added his own descant: that everything would somehow be bearable if it weren't for one thing—the Jews. They'd come back when the Germans were driven out, descended on the place like a swarm of locusts. His mother had fixed up an empty apartment and they'd demanded it back from her. Swaying drunkenly at one end of the table, he suddenly bellowed passionately, his red eyes gleaming: "All Jews should be sent to Novaya Zemlya."

Sknaryov hurled a can of bully beef at him with all his strength. Selyavka dashed for the door, and Sknaryov set off after him.

I had been late for the party, and was coming in just at that moment. I was groping my way along past the boulders, and barely had time to leap out of the way. First Selyavka tore past, waving his arms and screaming something in his high-pitched voice—you could tell it was he by that voice of his in the inkiest darkness. Then came Sknaryov, swearing and running heavily in his flying boots. Then, behind them, was someone else I recognized as Iosif Iokhvedson, Sknaryov's pupil, shouting at the top of his voice, "Alexander Ilyich! Alexander Ilyich! There's no need to beat him up! There's no need!"

* Collective farm.

Sknaryov stopped, gasping for breath. Captain Shkaruba looked out of the dugout, jacketless in his shirtsleeves, and came across, his flying boots crackling through the snow. "Well, you certainly blew up, Alexander Ilyich! What bit you?"

And in the heavy silence of the still polar night we all heard the answer.

"I'm a Jew myself."

Shkaruba burst into muffled laughter, shaking so much that he had to sit down on his heels. "You? With that Ryazan face of yours?" Everyone began to laugh, even Lieutenant Iokhvedson, who was still trying to locate Selyavka through the darkness. It was wild, hysterical laughter. Then they all fell quiet, and through the silence came the husky voice of Sknaryov. A firm angry voice.

"I'm a Jew. There it is. Somebody up there did something wrong, and they shoved the whole lot onto me. I'm the loser." Into the hush, broken only by the sound of boots in the snow, he added, "Well, am I a Jew or not?"

No one said a word.

So there we all stood at a distance from Shkaruba—I, Sknaryov and Iosif Iokhvedson—and the clouds over the polar airfield seemed to grow lower and blacker and heavier. Finally the cold all-pervading silence was broken by Shkaruba's bass voice.

"Right then, Jews. Let's move. Let's drink all this out of our minds with Russian vodka!"

On October 14, 1944, fleet navigator Sknaryov died when his plane, flown by our regimental commander Syromyatnikov, was shot down over a German convoy. The next day, caps in our hands and tears pouring down our faces, we heard over Moscow Radio:

> The honor of Hero of the Soviet Union has been accorded posthumously to Guards Colonel Syromyatnikov, Boris Pavlovich, and to Guards Major Sknaryov, Alexander Ilyich . . .

11

"Do you want to hear any more, or is that enough for today," I asked Pauline, who was sitting silently. We got up from the seat and walked along the pathways of the Alexandrovsky Gardens. Pauline said good-bye quietly and asked me to come around the following evening. After midnight, when we were the only people left in the chemistry laboratory, she said, as if in passing, without taking her eyes for a second from her flasks and test tubes, "I always want to know what *you* think. You, personally. You know—'Tell us about yourself,' the way people are always shouting at Party meetings. By the end of the war you were a journalist. So you've traveled a lot, seen a lot, talked to a lot of people. You must have thought about this trouble-maker, this Selyavka. What did you think about his behavior? You must have thought something! It's no joke when someone sets fire to your house.

"Now I know about Sknaryov. Or more than just about Sknaryov. But there are other things I want to know as well. About what you saw and felt and thought all that year when Selyavka first appeared on the scene. All right?"

The year had ended with Sknaryov. But it had begun with Katunin. Katunin, too, had been shot down over a German convoy. The Barents Sea doesn't leave a crippled pilot a great deal of choice, not even a painless one. Katunin dived his plane, streaming black smoke, into the deck of the German guard ship, and the sea erupted up to the sky in a great explosion. And he, like Sknaryov, became a Hero of the Soviet Union—posthumously.

Immediately, my friend Kostya Zarodov, the king of polar journalism, turned up at the airfield. Overnight, Kostya wrote a splendid piece about Ilya Borisovich Katunin. It was a whole page, with photographs of the exploding ship, and his friends' recollections of him.

Usually Kostya's articles were printed just as they stood, with no corrections. But this time the editorial blue pencil took out one and a half lines: "Katunin was born to a poor Jewish family . . ." and rewrote them: "Katunin was born in Byelorussia . . ."

Quite soon afterward we did another piece about a famous pilot—Turkov the reconnaissance specialist, also a Hero of the Soviet Union. Turkov was a Mordvinian, and we mentioned that in the article—again, just in a line. But on this occasion the editorial pencil took the phrase and turned it into a banner headline right across the page—"SON OF THE MORDVINIAN PEOPLE!"

"Kostya, what's it all about?" I asked anxiously one evening when we were on our own in the tiny room that housed our double bunks.

Kostya mopped his jutting forehead, and talked about a time in the middle of the previous century. An epidemic of plague had wiped out a city, and even the doctors had become infected. "In this war," he said, "we are the doctors."

"But they isolate plague victims," I argued. "They build plague huts for them. They don't make them into newspaper editors."

"Well, what's the editor got to do with it?" Wise old Kostya wrinkled his forehead. "He's no more guilty than you or I."

We argued till midnight, until he gave up and waved his hand wearily. "Stop quarreling. This isn't a Russian disease, Grisha. And anyway, you and I aren't involved."

We left it at that. But it was quite incomprehensible that the first one to be infected had been the colonel who edited a newspaper, and whose censor's pencil moved over the pages more and more heavily every day. Ordinary pilots showed no signs of the infection. Nor did it reach the ground staffs (Selyavka excepted). No doubt that was because on a polar air base every infectious disease is swept away by the whistling wind.

But were the men in the staff offices likely to catch it?

Once, when I was night duty editor, I was sitting drowsing by the stove in the printing room. The printers poked me awake and thrust the proofs at me, still damp and smelling of printing ink. Were there any deletions? One line had been removed from a column; the line referred to the Jewish birth of the navigator Iosif Iokhvedson, who had sunk a warship.

Formerly I had been totally convinced that on our paper we paid no attention to Selyavka and his kind, any more than we had paid attention to the squeaking of the rats in the cellar when we had been down in Volokogamsk, sheltering in the few peasant huts left standing. Let the beasts squeak, and to hell with them. Not worth the trouble of killing them. But now, it seemed, people *were* taking notice of the rats in the cellar. Everyone. Did that mean we had to cede the victory to Selyavka?

That was something else again. Unwillingly my ear began to pick up the rats' noises. "All the Jews are in Tashkent."* "All Jews are cowards."

What about Major Shnei, I thought, as I worked on the proof removing all the misprints. I signed the damp sheet. Vladimir Markovich Shnei, our omnipresent staff officer, whom we'd met on June 22, 1941.

At that time my regiment had been retreating toward Gomel. One by one our pilots returned to their unit, breaking through the frontline in boots stuffed with straw, in peasant clothes, their faces covered in stubble, exhausted. The first thing they all asked when they came in was "Has Shnei got back yet?"

Shnei had flown off to Staryi Bykhov, where the wives and children of the officer pilots had been stranded. There were rumors that General Guderian's tanks had already reached the place. For nights on end the pilots hardly slept. They turned away their faces so they wouldn't see the tears in each other's eyes. Day after day they went out to bomb German airfields, and all the time they were thinking about Staryi Bykhov.

Before taking off, Major Shnei had tried every possible means of contact with Staryi Bykhov—but there was no way of getting through. It looked as if the only way of finding out was for someone to take a light plane and risk flying there. Shnei had volunteered for the job, even though his family didn't live there.

Shnei was the pride of the regiment. Small and agile, always dressed in yellow gaiters, with foreign decorations covering his chest, Shnei sometimes brought a smile to the lips of our well-built pilots, who'd been selected for air force service by prewar standards of height and fitness. It was said that he'd flown every old crate there was from the time of the Civil War. He was indescribably pedantic, and working for so long in the roar of aircraft engines had made him deaf in one ear.

But none of that would have mattered if the chief of staff hadn't been a fanatic for military training. And his idea of training was something out of the ordinary for an air force regiment. Before the war, the station had had a brass band. All the commanders of neighboring garrisons had tried to steal it from us, on the grounds that there was nothing in regulations to say that an air base should have a band. But Major Shnei defended his band with all the bravado of a legendary warlord. When circumstances changed, and it was finally no longer possible to justify a band at all, the best technicians on the base took it on themselves to train the musicians—all conscripted students from the School of Military Music— as weapons armorers. They worked alongside me, loading bombs—I remember them well, two double bassists and a cornetist.

* That is, far removed from the battlelines. [Translator]

To the strains of this magnificent band we marched around Mogilev air base, none too keen, let it be said, on Major Shnei's enthusiasm for parades, and never suspecting that Major Shnei in those days kept a scientific drill diary. It seems that after parades like these (the diary was published later) there were far fewer breaches of discipline when people were on short leave in the neighboring town. The ceremonial marches had their uses.

Shnei dealt with me individually, as well. The chief of staff was attracted to educated people. One day he stopped me at the main gate and ordered me to march up and down in front of him, changing step, saluting on the march, and so on. Then he said in his usual terse style: "You—are a student. You have knowledge. But what has happened to your drill? You should have it down pat." And he sent me to the garrison commander, to the parade ground, so that I *should* have it down pat.

In the end, the news from Staryi Bykhov came through.

When the rattling little plane landed on the deserted, abandoned Bykhov strip, a car roared up with a group of armed men who obviously weren't Red Army. The young pilot stood up in his seat and pulled back the earflap of his helmet in time to hear Shnei say, "I'll go over and find out." Shnei heaved himself up on his thin arms, leaped over the plywood side of the plane, and dashed off toward the armored car shouting, "If they're Fascists, I'll shoot myself and you take off!"

I sat listening to the hum of the printing machines and thought about things which I could no longer bear to think about. All right, then. Shnei was a long time ago. But what about now?

I tried to look at the world through the eyes of a Selyavka: on the one hand, sailors who were Jews, on the other, sailors who weren't. But I couldn't manage it. For a start, who was a Jew, and who wasn't? They didn't stick questionnaires on the conning towers of submarines and the tails of airplanes. In Vaenga no one was interested in the nationality of a pilot, except possibly the personnel officers, who spent their time deep in their dugouts never appearing above ground. One flight over the Barents Sea was enough to tell you all you needed to know about a man—without questionnaires.

Should we suspect all dark-haired men? The darkest of them all was Hero of the Soviet Union Osyk, a dark-haired, handsome, mustachioed fighter pilot. But I was sure he was either Russian or Ukrainian. How about their names? Was the famous submarine skipper Kautsky a Jew or not? Or the fighter pilot Roldin—Jew or non-Jew? There was no point in this guessing game.

"Why don't you ask Selyavka?" suggested the typesetters, cheerful men from Vologda, who had seen the line about Katunin dropped from the article—the line that described him as coming from a poor Jewish family—and who had themselves said that this was a dirty business. "Selyavka's sure to have a list of who's a Jew."

I decided to get by without Selyavka's help.

I found a clerk in the Political Department, a happy drunk, who launched straight into a string of names without even glancing at his documents. Hey, there's an entire list, I thought, just like in the Gestapo. The clerk went on and on. My eyes got wider and wider. How come there were so many Jews in the polar regions? On the table before him lay the latest telegraphed dispatch. A dive bomber had crashed into a hillside. The squadron leader, Senior Lieutenant Zilberg, had been killed.

An hour previously there had been a phone call to the newspaper office. There'd been a gun salute in the Kola inlet. One of our submarines, the black boat skippered by Fisanovich, Hero of the Soviet Union, had returned to port after a mission.

I had articles lying in my desk drawer waiting to be corrected. They irritated me, as I'm always irritated by work that isn't completed on time. One had been written by the famous air gunner Misha Wasser, who the day before had shot down a Fokker-Wulf 190. The other was by fleet navigator Peisakhovich, the daredevil Peisakhovich, who served in the same advance regiment as Sknaryov.

Katunin, Peisakhovich, Wasser—in the end, I simply didn't have enough fingers to complete the count. "It's an entire flying synagogue," joked the clerk from the Political Department.

When I got back to the office, there was a note from the editor waiting for me. *Iokhvedson has destroyed a ten-thousand-ton transport. Urgent. Get it in the paper!*

Ah, Iokhvedson and Zavelband! The two inseparables—and over them both, the shadow of death . . .

Zavelband was slender and moved like a ballet dancer. He was totally carefree and so young that he still played childish games in his head.

"We—that is, the low-level torpedo bombers—" he said, "we're the torero, and a torpedo attack is like a *corrida*. Everyone's a bit afraid of the battle, and only the torero can master his fear. Only he can face an angry bull with razor-sharp horns."

The slow-moving, ponderous, thoughtful, and modest Iokhvedson was always worried about Zavel. He once told me jokingly that after the war they were going to set up as a double act, with Zavel as the torero and him, Iokhvedson, as the bull.

A week later, the Norwegian town of Kirkenes fell, and in the ruins of a pillbox we discovered the transcripts of the interrogation of Soviet pilots who'd been shot down over Norway and captured. I saw some of them at headquarters. Almost every captured pilot had been asked, "Are those two Jewish torpedo bombers, Iokhvedson and Zavelband, still flying? We'll get them yet."

But Iokhvedson and Zavelband had forgotten they were Jews. So, for that matter, had I. While no one is shooting at you, no one is spitting at you, you don't stop to think about whether you're a Jew or a Turk. You're a Soviet citizen, and that's good enough. But when you've heard "All Jews are cowards" or "All the Jews are in Tashkent" once or twice, then you start to think.

Over the last few days the only topic of conversation had been Iokhvedson. Iosif had brought a torpedo back from a raid. He hadn't been able to drop it during the attack, and his plane had been riddled like a sieve. The launching gear had been shot away, and no matter how Iosif wrestled with the red release knob, nothing happened.

Some people admired Iokhvedson for bringing the torpedo back. After all, a torpedo was worth a million rubles at least, and he was a brave man to lay his reputation on the line and land with the torpedo still in place rather than fire it manually on the way home and sink all that money in the sea. Others cursed him under their breaths. Selyavka, who'd been turned down for the guards torpedo regiment and who lived at the other end of the airfield, came running across simply to make a fuss. He was terrified, almost crazed with anger. "That kind of idiocy is more than I can understand," he yelled in his high-pitched voice. "It's like a man taking his trousers down and saying kick me! If the damn torpedo seized up over the convoy, the Barents Sea is big enough, he could have got rid of the thing somewhere and kept his mouth shut." And then with complete contempt—"Trust a Jew!"

It was curious how Selyavka's red eyes functioned. Certainly not like other people's.

Pravda printed an interesting article on Heroes of the Soviet Union. It appeared that Jews, who made up only two percent of the population (about eleventh in order of all nationalities) stood in fifth place for the number of Heroes of the Soviet Union they'd produced. "They certainly know how to get themselves medals," Selyavka explained.

No one could suppress him. Jewish pilots could die before his very eyes, one after another. You could show him statistics. "Jews can prove whatever they like!"

Once a week I had to do my night shift as duty editor. The night, the sharp smell of printing ink, and the rhythmic beat of the presses churning out the news all made for an atmosphere that was conducive to thought. My mind kept returning to the increasing tribe of Selyavkas and I would curse myself. I used to spend my time looking for minor misprints, but

Selyavka was no minor misprint—he was a huge typographical error. Everyone could see him but no one seemed to notice.

So what was going on? Was it evil intent, a huge diversionary tactic, or official stupidity?

It was difficult to find an answer. The time for answers hadn't yet come, and didn't even seem to be near. But one thing was clear. There were no more editorial quarrels with Konstantin Zarodov.* "At least we're standing on the sidelines," he used to console himself. "No, we aren't on the sidelines, Konstantin. You can't be on the sidelines on a battlefield. You're either in one trench or the other."

Despite all the facts it published, our daily paper consistently, resourcefully, and—why not admit it?—fraudulently, avoided spelling out a repudiation of the lies the North Sea slanderer Selyavka spread so shamelessly. Selyavka remained victor of the field.

And, wriggle as I might, I, a frontline journalist, was just another link in the chain Selyavka had forged. I marched shoulder to shoulder with him. If I stayed silent, I was working alongside him, even if I was a mute protester. It made no difference to the Selyavkas of this world if I were protesting inside my head. The main thing was that they were still on their feet.

That was probably the longest, hardest night of my life. "Even if I bang my head on a brick wall, I'm still guilty."

When I first came to Vaenga, within a couple of weeks of my arrival, I went to visit the torpedo bombers, who were all unknown to me. Some of them had downy hairs on their upper lips—they looked as if they'd never shaved. There wasn't a single older pilot in the hut. Where had they all gone?

I stood in the doorway of the hut. Some of the pilots were lying down, some fooling around, others writing letters. They were wearing clean, new-looking flying suits, with new badges of rank. Some of them were even wearing flying helmets, with the white silk of the helmet liners showing around their faces. The field telephone stood on a table in the corner and everyone kept looking at it uneasily. Around the stove a group of boys were sitting drying their flying boots and quarreling. A childish voice, almost falsetto, broke in: "Stop it! We're torpedo bombers. That makes us condemned men!"

(They don't like that kind of conversation at headquarters: "Unhealthy preoccupations. It frightens the young ones. They exaggerate the

* Konstantin Ivanovich Zarodov, at the time of writing editor-in-chief of the magazine *Problems of Peace and Socialism*; later editor-in-chief of *Sovietskaya Rossiya*, deputy editor of *Pravda*. [Translator]

dangers." Twenty years later, when I went back to Vaenga with Mosfilm to make the movie *It's All Quiet Here,* I learned the official statistics, which had been declassified some time previously. In two and a half years of the war, the guards torpedo regiment lost three hundred percent of its flying complement. It was completely renewed three times. . . .)

When they saw me, the torpedo pilots stopped quarreling. A fresh-faced, red-haired lad in a flying suit open to the waist looked warily in my direction, stretched, and greeted me with a mild insult: "Ah, one of the scribblers!"

Then he turned on me and began to blame me for every mistake in every paper. It seemed the papers were read very closely, especially by these young and as yet unknown pilots. "Look, even in *Pravda,* in a leading article no less, they got Shkaruba's name wrong—they printed *Skorubo.* They know nothing about us or our job."

"Well, how could you expect them to know?" asked someone I couldn't make out in the half darkness. "After all, they get paid for writing, not fighting."

Six months earlier I might just have laughed. Supermen! I, as a sergeant mechanic, had more battle experience than these precocious youngsters. They should have tried what I'd done, stuck in the tail of a heavy transport, the kind of aircraft called the "flying coffin." They hadn't even smelled powder yet, and they were already handing out white feathers.

But during those six months a lot of water had flowed into the Barents Sea.

I walked into the dark, dimly lit hut.

"What's all the fuss about? That I don't understand what a torpedo attack's like? Of course I don't. Take me with you, and then maybe I will!"

The hut fell quiet. A few curious heads popped in from the corridor. Someone wanting to join a torpedo attack of his own free will?

The boy in the gaping flying suit said uncertainly: "Well, that's nothing to do with me. If the squadron commander says O.K., then by all means fly. He's out at the dispersal point right now."

I cranked the handle of the field telephone. "Hello, dispersal? Give me the squadron commander." I knew his name. He was one of the bravest pilots of the Polar Division.

The commander was brought to the phone. When he heard what I wanted, he screamed down the line that he couldn't have me flying in one of his aircraft. "You wouldn't be a member of the crew, right? So if you don't come back, how am I going to account for you?" He coughed and spluttered. "If the regimental commander clears it, I'll fly you any-where you like—to hell and back if it suits you."

I couldn't get through to Syromyatnikov (he was still alive at that time). His deputy mumbled something noncommittal, from which I gathered I could certainly fly if the divisional commander gave his permission.

The pilots laughed when they heard what the replies had been, and someone from deep in the hut said soothingly, "O.K., drop it, you're getting nowhere." I cranked the telephone again nervously. It was no easy thing to get a call through to the divisional commander, General Kidalinsky. But I was lucky. He chuckled hoarsely into the receiver with a sly humor that made prickles run up and down my spine. "What's up with you? Who's chasing you? No, of course you can't. You just get on with your newspaper. There's nothing you can do that'll get you on a trip."

I swallowed cautiously and explained that the air crew refused to take the newspaper seriously at all, and that wasn't the way it ought to be.

A further burst of laughter was the answer. "Have you been drinking? Svirsky, I like my flying Jews—I have a weakness for them. But I'm afraid I can't let you go."

I felt myself getting angry.

"So do I take it, Comrade General, that your plan for flying . . ." I bit back the word *Jews* (after all the airmen couldn't hear what the general was saying) ". . . your flight plan is complete?"

Kidalinsky stopped laughing, as if he'd caught my change of tone, and said kindly, in a tired voice, "Svirsky, you can fly straight into Neptune's teeth for all I care. There's no percentage quota for dying. If the C-in-C of the air force allows it, then good luck!"

When the air crew heard what Kidalinsky had said, they leaped out of their bunks and waddled toward me, stumping along like bears in their heavy flying boots, all trying to persuade me to abandon the idea— "You've made your point. We can see you wanted to come. The bosses have hides like drumheads—everything bounces off." "Don't worry—when we get back, we'll tell you everything exactly the way it happened."

I sat there silent, clenching my fists.

I couldn't go straight to the air force commander: I didn't have the necessary rank. They'd never put me through. Then suddenly I had an idea. How about the commander of the Political Department?

The previous evening I had gone to see him with a proof of the paper, for his signature. He had half smiled at me. A gentle, kindly, intellectual man.

Well, no harm in trying!

It was difficult to get through to Garznoi. Time and time again I had to start working my way through the labyrinth of switchboards. First one line was engaged, then another. Finally, through a whistling and scraping in the receiver that sounded like a string orchestra tuning up, I suddenly heard his voice, low-pitched and unhurried.

"Well?"

I started to explain, and kept having to go back and start again.

He broke in sternly. "Very well. You may go."

I put the phone down on a wooden case, looked around to shout—"I did it! I've got permission!"—and then my heart sank. There wasn't a soul in the hut.

I had been so wrapped up in my conversation with high command that I hadn't even noticed an orderly dash in, shouting "Scramble." The air crew, shuffling their boots over the muddy floor, had rushed out of the hut.

I dashed out after them, all but flattening the orderly in my hurry.

It looked as if Syromyatnikov was in the command post structure, improvised out of a wood-and-cloth-patched section of a Hurricane fuselage. It was right at the other end of the airfield, and smoke—very white and almost invisible, as if they were burning old papers—was coming from its stovepipe.

On the stands, the aircraft engines were already turning over. Their props were spinning faster and faster, filling the narrow gap in the hills where the airfield lay with a deafening roar. They revved up still further. The pilots in their yellow flying helmets, looking like ducklings sitting in broken egg shells, were waiting for the start flares.

I'm going to be late! I thought in horror, and dashed at top speed to the command post.

Its ramshackle door was half open. I stopped to get my breath, and suddenly heard the voice of the chief of staff from the depths inside. It was quiet and sad—more of a sigh than a voice. "We'll be lucky if half of them get back."

I froze to the spot. It was as if my boots had suddenly turned into divers' boots, metal ones, and had magnetized themselves to the earth. My soles were glued to the ground.

Colonel Syromyatnikov looked out of the door.

"Svirsky? What are you doing here? The operator phoned me. Get going—number three!"

It was as if someone had driven spurs into me. I set off at a gallop toward the aircraft.

I tried to gesture to the young pilot, sitting there in his cockpit goggles that made him look like a Martian, that I had been told to fly with him. He eased off the revs so that I didn't have so much dust blown into my eyes.

The air gunner came out of his hatch without any argument. He hurriedly handed over his faded helmet and his life jacket. The parachute seemed to have been made for a giant, and it bounced around on my chest like a sack. I tried to shorten the straps, looking apprehensively at the torpedo, with its circular stabilizers, that was hanging from the belly of the aircraft. It glowed in the rays of the setting sun, as long as a python basking in the warmth and yet somehow innocuous-looking . . . in no way associated with that terrifying, monstrous death which could overtake ocean-going ships like a plague.

"Leave it!" said a mechanic who'd come running up, seeing me fiddling with the parachute straps. "There's nowhere to jump to anyway. The Barents Seas's no place for parachuting." With that encouraging farewell he bundled me in through the lower hatch.

On take-off the bomber lurched like a farm cart, clattering over the craters and ruts which had been roughly filled up with earth. There was a strong smell of hot plexiglass, something like enamel. The gunner/wireless operator, a freckle-faced youth of eighteen, nudged me and went through the motions of asking if I suffered from airsickness—if I did, to take my boot off, and use that.

I grimaced to show my extreme indignation at the very suggestion. While we were getting to know each other, the heavy aircraft, after another couple of bounces, heaved itself off the ground.

A hilltop flashed past my yellow porthole, and soon I could see the gray-green jumble of rock, grass, and water that was the coastline. Then there was the sea, endless and black as oil, so close below that it looked as if you could reach out and touch it.

Surely not even a bird could fly any lower, let alone a Messerschmitt? I tapped the gunner/wireless operator on his white boot, and asked whether it would be any help if I kept a lookout above us. He gave a slight nod, and I shoved my head up into the upper turret, and asked who the pilot was. Behind us, wavering slightly in our slip stream, flew four more torpedo bombers, their cockpit windows shining over the dark sea. The clouds were thick, soiled, hanging like sunlit airships in the huge transparent blinding sky: there was no end to it, no limit, neither this leaden black water below us nor the blue above.

The planes dropped right down to sea level. The air from the propellers sent tracks of foam scurrying over the surface. Somewhere on our flank, terrified sea birds rose from the water. A whole flock of them. They fluttered to and fro in panic, and were left far behind.

I breathed more easily. Only the week before a bird had crashed through the window of a navigator's cabin and wounded him. As if there wasn't enough to worry about!

Now we were on our own. There was no one between us and the

North Pole. A fresh wind was driving the foam-topped waves in toward the shore. Over them two flecks of white turned into two sea gulls. They flew slowly ahead, battling with the wind. When they tired of the unequal struggle they turned and let the air carry them rapidly back to land.

In the eyes of the gunner/wireless operator I could see a hidden pain, a longing. They're flying, he seemed to be thinking. And once we've been shot down, they'll still be in the air! When he spotted me looking at him, he pulled himself together, and his face became impenetrable.

The engines droned on for an hour, two hours . . .

The weather was closing in. A mixture of damp snow and rain which had come across our course dribbled down the windows in long streams. Then we had sun in our faces again.

I was just getting to the point of feeling that I was an indispensable member of the crew, when the wireless operator, without taking his eyes off the sky, pulled a magazine folded in four out of his boot and thrust it into my hand. "Here, have a read."

I took it, feeling discouraged. It turned out to be the latest number of *Krokodil*. I looked below me to where the sea was still churning in white foamed crests, and went back to the magazine.

I have never flown in such comfort as on that incredible attack. Except, possibly, after the war, in TU104 airliners. I was chuckling over the cartoons when I suddenly heard in my headphones the navigator yell "Ships!"

I thrust the magazine aside. Pressing my face to the yellow plexiglass of the cockpit window, I could just make out dark-gray smoke rising from the sea. It was a huge creeping cloud.

"Twenty-three of them," counted the navigator. "Petro, twenty-three," he repeated in excitement to the pilot. "And there are more coming."

The only reply was silence. Just the roar of the engines. Their insistent throb was now our form of silence—solid and defensive. I felt the usual kind of alarm, the kind you feel before an air raid, a slight tightening around the heart. As if someone were squeezing it with strong rough hands.

"Petro!" The navigator's voice was getting hoarse with the strain. "Forty-three ships. Their escort is in three rings. They'll eat us alive. . . ."

The engines droned on. Just so long as they kept on doing it. That would mean we were still alive.

Then suddenly the desperately longed-for silence was broken, torn apart by a panic-stricken yell from the navigator.

"Petro, what the hell are you playing at? You asleep or something, dammit? Where the hell are you going? I told you, forty-three of them. Petro!"

It sounded as if someone had lassoed the man and dragged him into a bonfire, and we were all screaming hysterically.

I learned later that the crew had the right not to go into attack against a convoy as large as that, a convoy that was a more appropriate match for a combined attack using all kinds of weapons—submarines, MTB's, planes . . .

I had seen the calculations before we left the ground. Within five minutes of the time the aircraft opened up against a convoy of twenty-five ships, the Germans would have fired off something like fifty thousand shells and half a million bullets. And the navigator had already counted forty-three ships.

"Petro!" he broke into our headphones again.

I stayed silent, feeling as I imagine someone must feel who's tied onto a galloping horse, facing its tail, while the horse rushes toward a bottomless canyon.

After a terrifyingly long drawn-out almost eternal silence, we heard the young high-pitched voice of the pilot.

"Navigator, give me a course."

That was his answer.

The navigator replied in a voice only just under control, but businesslike, as if he hadn't been shouting his head off a moment before: "Steer two hundred seventy-eight degrees."

The gossip died down. The real work had begun.

Seconds passed, and suddenly everything seemed to explode, both sky and sea. Dark-green columns of water rose up before the side windows, huge and massive, then subsided slowly back to the surface.

It was still too early for the German machine gunners to open fire. It was the convoy's destroyer screen that had opened up . . . with their big guns, along the surface of the water. The splash from a high-caliber shell can rise to eighty meters, and we were flying at thirty. If there's a shell-burst in the water under your wing, that's it.

The sea was boiling to the right and left of us. The water spouts followed us like an escort. Suddenly the plane lurched and staggered, as water cascaded on top it, leaking through the plexiglass, drenching the cockpit. The motors roared, and we pulled away.

"Number eight's gone!" yelled the wireless operator, and danced about in his white flying boots as if the water had got to his feet. I moved to the opposite lookout port; where number eight had been waddling along in our wake with its torpedo slung below its belly, there was nothing but a column of water. No plane, no sky. Just water. A boiling, heaving, foaming whirlpool.

The ships kept crawling over the sea, getting bigger and bigger.

"Right flank!" the familiar high-pitched voice came in the headphone. The planes began to disperse for the attack. "Don't go in over the destroyers. They're at the head of the column!"

I had the comforting thought that this boy really knew his job.

The leading destroyer suddenly put out a cloud of dense smoke, and fired a red flare. At the signal the entire convoy opened fire.

From horizon to horizon the sky was full of red, green, and white tracers moving slowly toward us in a stream of fire. They were getting nearer. "Well, they're nicely bunched together," came over my headphones. And then, right in front of my face, the red bursts of shells. At that second I closed my eyes.

The plane lurched, and I opened them again. The multicolored tracers were passing to the side and above us. There were so many of them that it seemed as if the plane had been caught in a net woven out of the chaotically intertwining flares. Like some wild beast. Sometimes the shellbursts were so close that they seemed like direct hits. The plane staggered to one side, but leveled off immediately.

The headphones crackled again. "Let's go! It looks pretty frightening, but you can still use your hands."

The plane lurched upward, shuddering, swerved sideways, just like an animal in a trap.

It turned out later that a shell had knocked out the navigator's instrument panel and pierced the fuselage with hundreds of shrapnel holes.

We could feel a wet wind now; it tore into our eyes, and whistled with a terrible, threatening keening.

The firing intensified. Now the tracer tracks were like scissor blades of fire, intersecting along the plane's path, and threatening to cut it off as soon as it got within torpedo range.

The destroyers kept up rapid fire, their Oerlikons pumping out stabs of flame. The frigates maintained their fire as well, and so did the launches—the subhunters and the armed trawlers. The fire corridor was as tight as it could possibly be, often threatening to engulf the aircraft, before widening out at the last moment. One of the subhunters hurried to the side of a huge freighter to intercept the torpedo that had been meant for her . . . Too late!

The aircraft swooped up, the torpedo bounced once on the surface of the water, then plunged beneath, and set off behind our tail, through the foaming waves, trailing a wake of bubbles.

"Well, God give it legs!"

Our impressions became momentary reflexes. Out on our right, one of our aircraft turned and began to go for home, apparently unaware that immediately below there was one of the subhunters following the turn with its Oerlikons pounding away at the red stars on the wings.

Both engines immediately blew out and began to stream black smoke. Our plane didn't even try to turn back. It dived straight on to the ships steaming away beneath. What could have gone wrong? Had the pilot lost control?

But no, he kept the plane right down above the surface of the sea, so that its engines set up a stream of foam on the surface. We flew hopping along the water at below-deck level, below the level of the guns, between two freighters, so close that I could see the gun crews in their yellow life jackets crouching behind their shield. Their Oerlikons kept on pumping until we were within a few dozen yards of them. Then they stopped, apparently afraid of hitting their own ships steaming alongside. Only a momentary pause, but long enough for us to get through the gap.

As soon as we had overflown the ship, and it came into my field of fire, I squeezed the trigger of my machine gun and a blaze of pale fire came out of the muzzle, as if the barrel were white hot. Making just enough height to clear the jagged rocks of the shore, wreathed in pink smoke, the plane turned again, and I was able to see the freighter we'd attacked explode into a million pieces.

That evening, before we got to grips with our roast suckling pig, I walked over to the airfield with the pilots. Two machines hadn't made it back.

An aircraft stand looks like an orphan when its plane hasn't returned. Where the engines waited for the signal only a short time ago, there's nothing but dark oil stains on the concrete. The steps stand there, leading nowhere, stretching out their wooden arms to the dark blue sky. . . .

A trampled piece of earth, surrounded by rocks and green water—what is it? Wave after wave of young men come here in their leather flying jackets, and stand shivering in the icy wind. You can call to them but they won't hear you anymore. . . .

As usual, we went out for a drink to celebrate. But it wasn't very gay: a victory and a wake at the same time. Two crews is eight men. The squadron sergeant packed their belongings in their cases and made a list. The round-faced, pink-cheeked pilot, a senior lieutenant, drained a jug of vodka. I, as an intellectual, half a pint. He told me what a splendid airplane the Ilyushin-4 was (a Russian plane—they keep on pumping bullets into her, but dammit, she keeps on flying). And he told me how today his mechanic had hauled him out of his flying suit. "There was steam pouring out of it—like a samovar."

I'd seen that for myself. I listened to him affectionately, with great tenderness, although we had only met for the first time that afternoon, as the airplane stood on the runway. Would this ever happen again—just one flight, and you were ready to give your life for a man?

When the men around us burst out into nonsense choruses of the squadron songs, I admitted to the pilot in a whisper that I had been very frightened. That I'd closed my eyes. He shook his head in surprise. "And when the tracers were coming in," I whispered confidentially, "and didn't reach the plane . . . and then the red shell-bursts . . ."

The lieutenant laughed, and said calmly, reassuringly, "You idiot— that's when I *always* close my eyes."*

A friend of his came over from the next squadron to join the party. He was just as beardless and pink-cheeked. He asked quietly, with a nod in my direction, "Who's that?" The freckled gunner/wireless operator whom I'd flown with, who was sitting nearest to the new arrival, rose to his feet and, pointing me out with his oil-stained forefinger, began to praise me in his own way. "Oh, he's all right, that one. He's made his mark!" Then, more quietly, "Even though he is a Jew."

For a month or so, I suppose it was, I flew as often as I could. I flew with every squadron in the Polar Air Force. I flew with the pathfinder Kolenikov, who managed en route to shoot down a sea plane marked with swastikas. We flew as far as the table-flat rocks of the North Cape looking for Fascist convoys.

I flew with modest Misha Tikhomirov, who came to Vaenga after a mere four-month training period. The older pilots joked that if they were getting people like that, they'd soon be more frightened of their own planes than the enemy. They joked—but they lived to learn.

Then I was back with the guards regiment, the torpedo bombers. With cheerful, brave Kazakov and Muratov. Muratov dropped flares over a convoy that was then sunk by the motor launches of Shabalin, awarded Hero twice over.

It was a fairy-like spectacle, incredible. The night sea was lit up with a blinding white light, like molten metal. I left the airfield happy, although with a kind of gnawing feeling of irritation, which I couldn't for the moment quite place.

I didn't immediately understand that in the chances I was taking, in the pleasure I derived from the fight, there was something deeply hu-

---

* He was killed on his next sortie, the now legendary Petro Gentov. It's a quarter of a century since his former comrades in the North Sea battles have been trying to get him a posthumous award of Hero of the Soviet Union. But the documents always seem to keep going astray.

miliating. I was having to prove again and again that "even though I was a Jew," I was no worse than anyone else.

When Sknaryov died, someone took me up without waiting for permission. "Come on," said the pilot, a friend of Sknaryov's, "they can't demote me any lower than kolkhoz worker,* or send me farther than the frontlines."

And I thought I had won.

---

* A kolkhoz is a collective farm. Living conditions on such farms were notoriously hard and wretched. [Translator]

12

When I came back from the war, I was not accepted at the university. They returned my slightly yellowing certificate with its gold border that gave me the right to enroll without examination. Looking past me, the secretary explained politely that they were indeed obliged to accept me but that unfortunately I had brought the documents in too late. It was only then that she jotted the order number on the file. I had been among the first to hand in my papers.

The assistant dean walked firmly into the office; he was a sharp-eyed man dressed in khaki, and there was a naval air to him.

"Is your name Selyavka?" I asked quietly, when he invited me to sit.

"No. You must be mixing me up with someone else." He was whispering too.

"How do you mean?" I lowered my voice even more. "You won't admit Jews to the university. To the Department of Russian Literature. You must be Selyavka!"

"*Sh-sh!*" hissed the assistant dean, springing to his feet.

It was only 1946, and already people were crying "Hush!"

"You know the rest, Pauline." I broke off my story. "It's what happened to you over your second degree. Only I had to do my fighting on my own."

We were standing in the Lenin Library metro station, which was utterly deserted. The cleaner was pushing her mechanical brushes back and forth over the damp floor. They made a squeaking noise, which grew louder until you'd have thought they were splitting the stones, not washing them. She finally stopped the machine so she could make herself heard, and yelled at us to board the train, since it was the last one that night.

But Pauline didn't seem to hear anything. I grabbed her arm and dragged her into the carriage, otherwise it would have left without us.

It was obvious that she hadn't even noticed. Her gray eyes were blank and staring. "What's happening?" she said at last. "What can we do . . . what *can* we do?"

I kissed her pale lips. It was the only thing I could give her.

Pauline usually arrived at her laboratory at eight in the morning. At night, at twenty to one, we would dash out of the university so as not to miss the last metro. The philologists waved good-bye to me; I transferred to the chemistry faculty.

For me, the laboratory replaced library, home, theater, sports stadium. I was already used to its stuffiness, to its multicolored bottles and flasks, to its bubbling baths of chemicals. Even the stench didn't seem as awful as at first.

Pauline looked after her flasks, and I usually read aloud to her. For some days we had been going through Klyuchevsky's *History of Russia*, trying to find an answer to all our "Whys?"

We were thus occupied one day when the door of the laboratory was flung open by an elderly, thick-set man who walked in as if he owned the place. Something about him repelled me. He came in and stood gazing silently around him. His bald head looked as if it had been polished—it positively glowed. His face was puffy, formless, with the eye sockets sunk deep in the flesh. If you looked closely you could see that he did in fact have eyes but they were pale, watery, and empty.

He came over to us and stared at Klyuchevsky. Or maybe not—it was hard to tell, when one eye was staring at you and the other trying to read your mind. He stretched out his hand for the book. Authoritatively. It was the same gesture that Squadron Sergeant Major Tsybulka had used to take books from me.

Hands off, I thought, and pushed the book under my arm.

"This is Kostin," Pauline said in her gentle voice. "The assistant dean. Don't shy away from people so."

Uncertainly, I handed over the book. Kostin looked at it, flipping through the pages disapprovingly, almost as if he were sniffing at it, as if Russian history would subvert the whole university.

(Incidentally, it could indeed be said to be subversive—not for the university, naturally, but . . .)

Pauline and I realized this when we reached the volume in which Klyuchevsky was dealing with the collapse of the university, brought about at the beginning of the nineteenth century by Speransky's successor, a certain Magnitsky, who later recanted.*

History shows that nothing is as damaging to progress as a progressive

* Mikhail Mikhailovich Speransky (1772–1839), minister under Alexander I. He supported a number of social and political reforms. He codified Russian law under Nicholas I. [Translator]

who recants. Magnitsky sought royal permission to make a public example of the university, riddled, as he put it, by the spirit of Robespierre. And by "example" he meant physical destruction—that the very buildings should be razed to the ground. When that was refused, he decided to root out learning from the other end. He fought the Voltairean spirit of the university singlehanded. The new spirit he inspired was very straightforward: "The Russian state pre-empted all others."

"The seat of higher learning has always paid for the sins of society." Thus Klyuchevsky begins his epic account of the destruction of the university. That account ends with the sentence: "The man who symbolized this line of thought was the famous Arakcheev."*

Joseph Stalin read Klyuchevsky. Of that there can be no doubt. Otherwise, he could never have described this last period in one of his books as the Arakcheev regime. Stalin was accurate in his description of the way Arakcheev brought certain social processes into being, but Pauline and I were still as far from understanding this as we were from traveling to the stars.

This second convulsion was permitted to take place. "The Russians always came first." It was allowed to become the cornerstone of every teaching course, of every lecture given in the university. The inclusion of names of foreign scientists in essays and theses was a sure sign that the candidate would fail. French breakfast rolls were renamed "city rolls."

The time found its own heroes. In the university, hard men—stone-hard, devious-tongued, and unsmiling men—took the upper hand with their mission to "uplift" and "purify" the institution. In their worn jackets with the military badges removed, in their old, cracked officers' boots, wrinkled and battered, or in gray military felt ones, they honed every question to the sharpness of a Cossack pike. But there was one thing they didn't take into account. It was more than a hundred years since the time of Arakcheev. And it was from this that confusion was born—especially in the natural science faculties.

One day I came into the laboratory to find Pauline rushing to wash out her equipment. She struggled out of her lab coat and said, "Come on, quickly. We'll be late."

We hurried to a lecture hall that was already crammed full. Below, gleaming like a piece of naval brasswork, was that bald head.

"There's that terrible man." I pointed out the shining dome to Pauline. "Next to Platé."

* Aleksey Andreevich Arakcheev (1769–1834), minister of war under Alexander I. Stalin, in his book *Marxism and Problems of Linguistics,* denounced the "Arakcheev regime in linguistics." [Translator]

"He's a splendid man," retorted Pauline, looking around, searching for her friends.

"A terrible man," I insisted, and got to my feet.

"A splendid man," she repeated, just as firmly.

It was getting to be like a family quarrel. We looked at each other and burst out laughing.

When Pauline stopped laughing, she said, "Kostin! Don't you know that but for him I'd be dead by now?"

There he sat on the dais, at the presidium's table. Taking the chair at the meeting was a quiet, tough man, Academician Nesmeyanov, who opened the proceedings with all the precision of a main-line train guard.

But what was going on on the platform? A coarse-faced boy in a faded battledress top, the back of his neck rigorously shaven, was pounding the lectern and denouncing the two most outstanding scientists in the country, Academician Frumkin and Academician Semyonov, the future Nobel Prize winner. They were, he said, of no value to the Russian people.

At the presidium table, next to Nesmeyanov, who had blushed deep crimson, sat Frumkin and Semyonov themselves, their faces buried in their hands, listening as though bewitched to the crude ranting of this boor. Then Frumkin, sounding like a scolded schoolboy, promised to mend his ways, to come closer to the desired standards.

"Who's that?" said Pauline, meaning the loud-mouthed youth. "People like him shouldn't be allowed."

She tore off a piece of newspaper and scribbled a note to the presidium, asking to be allowed to speak. She wasn't called. There wasn't time enough. She was told she could speak on another occasion.

A week or two later the open meeting continued. This time it began with a beaming and regal Nesmeyanov congratulating academicians Frumkin and Semyonov on the award to them of the Stalin Prize. The awards had been made a few days earlier—in confidence*—for outstanding discoveries of vital practical value.

The laughter that broke out in the university, in every lecture hall, in the courtyards, in the students' dining room, grew so loud that the pigeons, who usually perched on the windowsills, spent the whole day wheeling in bewilderment over the rooftops. It looked as if the revival of Arakcheevism was over, once and for all.

But it was nothing of the kind. Pauline showed me an article in which this time the chosen scapegoat was the world-famous Academician Linus Pauling. Once they'd made their mistake over Frumkin and Semyonov, the ringleaders had selected a new victim—they needed someone, or they

---

* The Stalin Prizes in some sciences were not publicly announced. [Translator]

would have looked as stupid as inquisitors without bonfires for burning their heretics.

Pauling fitted their bill perfectly. For a start, he was American. Secondly, he was the author of a theory of resonance which was self-declaredly idealistic. And moreover he was a cosmopolitan. No one would ever award *him* the Stalin Prize. And he wouldn't be able to go up on that stage to defend himself. They couldn't have found a better candidate.

And so Pauling was dragged, figuratively speaking, to the place of execution. One wit suggested that an effigy of him be burned in public, but then word came down the Komsomol line that the wit should curb his tongue.

So Pauling began to be painted as a beast of a very different stripe. He became a reactionary, a cosmopolitan. And while this was going on, the papers began to report that at about the same time, Pauling had been summoned to Washington by the Committee on Un-American Activities under Senator McCarthy. For investigation. The points against him were that he was an active fighter for peace and a friend of Moscow.

The ringleaders in the university agitatedly announced that this was quite a different man: the reactionary was Polling, and the friend of Moscow was called Pauling. Just a matter of spelling.

Again the students laughed, and in their various ways, in their various faculties, began to remark more and more frequently that the designated puppet leaders of the "cosmopolitan campaign" were dredging the stinking canal of anti-Semitism (which one had hoped had dried up in Russia) only to keep on dragging up garbage.

Then suddenly there was a new explosion. The philosopher Professor Beletsky was accused of being a Jew and concealing his nationality. Why should he? What good would it do him? But Beletsky was a Byelorussian, and so he couldn't recant even if he'd wanted to. The party office sent a special investigator to his homeland to search for the missing documents, registers, and birth certificates. They went through them looking for the word "Jewish" as one might look for a criminal past, for hidden murders. Finally, Beletsky proved that he was the son of a priest. So he received complete rehabilitation.

Our professor of history, Yudovsky, a sickly man and always short of breath, during a lecture I attended named the hue-and-cry over Beletsky's alleged "Jewishness" for what it was. He was immediately condemned as a bourgeois internationalist, a militant Zionist, and more besides. He died soon after of a heart attack. His death angered some and frightened others. People waited for an inquiry.

A young teacher of Marxism, a woman partisan who'd been wounded in the war, looking as pale as if she'd just lit a fuse that was too short, in a seminar read to us from Lenin's attack on Great Russian chauvinism. Like all our generation she didn't so much lean toward Lenin as grab for him the way one grabs for a life belt, or a stone to throw at the hooligans who surround one.

The students stopped going to lectures given by anti-Semites. One of them was chased from the platform. The most often told university joke of 1949 was one that related to Russia's claim to be first in everything: "Russia is the birthplace of the elephant."

The wife of the rector of the university, the straightforward and dominating Galkina Fedoruk, who was giving me an examination in modern Russian language, suddenly and kindly asked me: "Excuse me, but are you a Jew?" After which she explained that, Heaven help her, she wasn't an anti-Semite. Some of her best friends were Jews.

Even the most careful people, the most highly paid people were waking from their lethargy.

"They really knew how to curse in the Middle Ages," Academician Gudzy said quite casually to me one evening, as we were strolling along deserted Vorovsky Street to the Writers' Union. "Yesterday I was reading an old manuscript. Such splendid use of words: 'Spawn of the serpent'— 'the brood of Antichrist'—'Satan's hound'—'thrice-evil monster'." And he looked at me with those wise, sharp eyes.

I looked back at him—and it was enough to make me realize that I wasn't alone in the wide, wide world anymore.

We went into the Writers' Union, and stopped for a moment to bring some life into our frozen hands and to absorb the dry heat of the old building. From the restaurant upstairs, punctuated by peals of laughter, we could hear the quiet voice of the secretary of the union, Anatoly Sofronov, declaiming something in his excited stammer.

A man I didn't know came stumbling and rushing down the wooden stairs right into us. He was thin. His cheeks were cavernous, his nose unnaturally pointed. He bumped into me. His eyes, misted with vodka, couldn't focus. But he realized he had landed on something soft—he hadn't run into the wall but into a human being. Looking somewhere above my head, he spoke with a sadness that was all the more affecting for being unmalicious.

"What do they want of us? Eh? We already sing their song."

Gudzy stood as if turned to stone, looking after the departing figure. He took me by the arm like a child.

"Let's get out of here, Grisha."

"Who was that?" I asked, for some reason in a whisper.

"Mikhail Svetlov."

Nikolai Kalinnikovich Gudzy and I walked through the side streets of the Arbat. They were deserted, and the doorkeepers watched us suspiciously. There was a cold fine drizzle mixed with snow. The dirty frozen slush of the streets squelched beneath our feet. We stopped in a doorway, and then set out again to brave the icy rain. My student shoes were cracked and leaking, and my soaking feet grew numb. I felt as if I were walking barefoot in the snow.

"The Danes hid their Jews. They say that the king put on a yellow star himself, and so did all the people. How many of our people sheltered their countrymen?" Gudzy shouted in a voice in which even a deaf man would have heard the suffering. "Six million Jews were shot. A whole nation. Did anyone hide them? Did anyone *try* to hide them? I know of two or three cases—that's all."

"And then Mikhail Svetlov. A brilliant, brilliant* man. Of course, his name is a pseudonym."

The despair in his voice! And the fatalism! Gudzy stood clutching his heart, panting. "But he's a Russian poet. Genuinely Russian. A Russian Levitan!"†

Where was the way out?

"The Jews are as ancient as the dinosaurs. Dinosaurs had a defective nervous system. A dinosaur's tail was its main point of balance—if it was bitten off, the beast didn't feel it; the huge creature would simply turn around, fall over, and die.

"They're taking away our point of balance. Taking it away!" he suddenly shouted in a voice that cracked with emotion. "They're taking people's balance away. What will be left for people to believe in after this? As long as I've lived there's always been someone beating at us—Petlyura's men, the Hitlers, the Banderas, the Sofronovs—there's no end to it. It's like being a squirrel in a wheel. First they beat you till you're blue. Then they cast doubts on the quality of your blood because you're blue. A Jew bruised blue—that's dangerous. He might get the idea of striking a blow in retaliation. Then they peel off the scar tissue, so that you turn red with your own blood. And so on—endlessly. It's appalling."

Then Nikolai Kalinnikovich repeated Mikhail Svetlov's words, and his voice, hoarse and yet still mellifluous, transformed by his powerless rage into an old man's falsetto, still rings in my ears to this day: "What do they want of us? We already sing their song." No memorial to Svetlov can be greater than that. . . .

---

* The Russian word used is *svetly* meaning *luminous* or *brilliant*. Svetlov, a pseudonym, was a play on *svetly*. Svetlov's most famous work was his poem "Grenade." [Translator]
† Levitan: One of the most famous Russian painters of the nineteenth century—he was a Jew. [Translator]

"Just what is it they want of us?" I asked Pauline, when I finally reached the laboratory, exhausted. I felt ill with tiredness.

She made me take off my shoes, heated some bricks over a Bunsen burner and put them under my feet. Then she made tea. "What do the Sofronovs want?"

She looked at me, glancing away momentarily from the solution that was simmering in the retort. She said, "They want the green-plush table-cloth. The pogrom-makers have no other ideas in their heads."

My heart ached. She had a perfect right to use words like that, though I still thought she was oversimplifying.

But I listened to what she had to say with a good deal more attention after the funeral of Mikhoels.* We stood for three hours in the funeral procession which moved along the Bronnaya to the Jewish Theater where Mikhoels lay in state. At such long-drawn-out, crowded events, people usually whisper among themselves about their own affairs, or sometimes even smile.

There were no smiles this time.

There was a terrible, desolate silence, emphasized by the coughing of a single old man. It made a deep impression on me—and Pauline's anger made an even deeper one.

"Why did they have to kill Mikhoels?"

I was dumbfounded.

"What do you mean, kill him? What are you talking about?"

It was all so much clearer to her, seen from the vantage point of the Inguletsk quarry.

Among the pall-bearers stood People's Artist Zuskin, his eyes closed, his neck arched, and his tie as tight as a noose around it. Perhaps he was as perceptive as Pauline. Not months but only measured hours remained before that second night of St. Bartholomew, when the Jewish Anti-Fascist Committee,† of which that great artist Zuskin was a member, when that committee was shot just like Pauline's parents. Only a few escaped.

---

* Salomon Mikhailovich Mikhoels (1890–1948) was a distinguished actor and director. From 1921 he worked at the Moscow Jewish Theater staging the greatest works of Russian Yiddish playwrights—Sholom Aleichem, Mendele Mocher Sforim—and the classics, including an unforgettable King Lear. He was a member of Stalin's wartime Jewish Anti-Fascist Committee, which was dissolved in 1948. [Translator]

† Jewish Anti-Fascist Committee: During the war Stalin summoned prominent Soviet Jews to serve on this committee. After the war the committee was disbanded, and some of its members were shot as traitors. [Translator]

13

The Anti-Fascist Committee was shot on Stalin's orders.

I only came to understand this on April 4, 1953, when I elbowed my way through to the long fence-like hoardings with the day's copy of *Pravda* stuck on them. I read as I walked along the hoardings. But suddenly I stopped, dumbstruck.

Pravda had printed a report saying that the Doctors' Plot* was nothing but a vile provocation.

Behind my back I could hear the indrawn breath of the others who were reading. People were mute with amazement. Someone swore softly. A girl with her hair in plaits protested, "That can't be!" An old woman in glasses standing next to me said nervously, "Well, with our government you never get bored." An elderly kolkhoz worker with a bag stuffed full with long loaves of black bread spoke in his plain, deep voice. "I never could make out what was supposed to be going on."

I shivered; I felt as if someone had pushed a handful of snow down the back of my neck. I still believed in HIM.

Then suddenly I recalled the acid remark of an old language teacher I'd once had: "You belong to a generation with retarded powers of thought!" That had happened at a mutual friend's house. Pauline attacked the teacher with all her usual Komsomol energy. In reply he yelled angrily that Pauline and I were deaf and blind, that we were both in an intellectual stupor. We left the house silently, stony-faced, like ambassadors of a state which has just been insulted.

And there, by that newspaper hoarding, I suddenly became aware

* Early in 1952, fifteen doctors, some of them Jews, were arrested. They confessed, it was alleged, to murdering Shcherbakov and Zhdanov, and to collaborating with the American Joint Distribution Committee—a Jewish aid organization (referred to elsewhere in the book as "Joint"). Shortly after Stalin's death they were formally declared innocent, and released. [Translator]

of something I had heard of many times, but which had always flowed past me, as water flows past the reinforced concrete of a bridge pillar: during all those years Stalin was involved in everything. He trusted no one. Without his signature no one could go ahead with anything—not the building of a country village for academicians, not even the replacement of a lift in the *Izvestiya* editorial building.

Could so much as a hair fall from the head of anyone without his being aware of it? Could one single shot be fired at the Old Bolsheviks who had taken the Winter Palace? Was it possible without his signature? Or at least without his tacit approval?

What was supposed to be going on? The voice of the people is the voice of God!

Now, after so many years, so much has come out, so much has become known, and facts keep pouring in like floodwater, so that even one-tenth of what is known would be enough for the most modest revolutionary tribunal—if, of course, it were truly revolutionary.

In which case it would be enough for the tribunal to consider just one of the questions posed by the Russian Revolution: the national question, and within that question just one facet—the injection into it of anti-Semitism.

In his family life Joseph Stalin was an anti-Semitic hooligan, fiercely so, to the point of violence—not even his own daughter, Svetlana Allilueva, now tries to conceal it; she has told of Stalin's Jew-phobia as it came out in his family rows with the Jews who were her boyfriends and husbands. But let us leave the question of Svetlana's husbands and lovers aside—it's a tragic enough subject in its own right. And even though Old Bolsheviks have talked about Stalin's anti-Semitism as far back as his exile in Turukhan, we won't deal with that either. What we are concerned with is the anti-Semitism of the general secretary of the Bolshevik Party.

Was he an anti-Semite in that high office? Or indeed was he a victim of deception, of provocations by the satanic chorus of Berias, Yezhovs, Abakumovs, and Ryumins,* who moved around him in their eternal bloodstained dance?

Unfortunately the Institute of Marxism that was attached to the Central Committee of the CPSU, the Institute of Philosophy and History of the Academy of Science of the USSR, and other official bodies were all unable to help me in this line of research.

---

* *Lavrenti Beria:* sometime head of the NKVD under Stalin. Executed after his death. *Yezhov:* head of the NKVD from 1936. *Abakumov:* security chief, one of Stalin's henchmen, also executed under Malenkov. *Ryumin:* head of security, also Beria's colleague, executed for his part in the Doctors' Plot affair. All four were instruments of Stalin's terror. [Translator]

Officialdom remains silent. It remains silent just like our frontline newspaper, which didn't intervene to prevent the Selyavkas of this world from getting on with their dirty work.

So let the documents take the witness stand. And let us call first those enthusiastic scholars who for years have studied Stalin and his times. We call the archives of the old revolutionaries. Just the facts. Just the work of serious historians. Just the documents.

Was Stalin a progressive politician? Was he in any sense a progressive figure—if we ignore the mistakes and the crimes which the human conscience cannot forget, however much some of us seem to want to try?

And where is Stalin's ghost leading us—those of us who are his successors, overt and covert?

To answer this question, according to G. Pomerants,* who has made a lengthy study of Stalin, we must first pose it correctly. We must distinguish between the mandate which a statesman must necessarily fulfill, and his own personal share of what is done over and above that.

Stalin took power on clear conditions, and until the time when he transformed that power into absolute power he could not afford to ignore those conditions. He had to carry out a program of industrialization, he had to bring about the establishment of the cooperative system of agriculture, he had to lead the international working-class movement, he had to give thought to the defense of the state. Any other person elected general secretary would have been mandated to tackle exactly the same problems. So what is important is not *what* Stalin did, but *how* he did it. Apart from the written mandate—the Party program—Stalin obeyed other, unwritten mandates, which were in the air around him.

First of all there was the mandate that Lenin called "asiatchina." You probably remember the article "In Memory of Graf Geiden": the slave is not guilty because he is a slave, but a slave who cannot live without his master is guilty of whining and groveling. The ages of the Tartar hordes and of serfdom left behind them a well-entrenched tradition of whining and groveling. The Revolution shook that tradition, but on the other hand the Revolution suddenly turned masses of peasants from their long-established way of life, and they lost their old foundations before they could master a new ideology. These masses wanted nothing to do with the deepening and strengthening of their freedom, and didn't even understand what use freedom of personality was to them. They wanted a master, and they wanted order. That was Stalin's second mandate.

* *Pomerants:* Grigory Solomonovich Pomerants, born 1917. Served a term in Stalin's camps, later rehabilitated; became a prominent dissident. The article referred to was published clandestinely in the Soviet Union under the title "The Moral Make-up of Historical Personality." [Translator]

Mandate number three was the mandate of the headless religion. The peasant believed in God, and for him the images of Christ or of the Virgin of Kazan were objects of love and selfless devotion. The peasants had it explained to them that God did not exist, but that did not eradicate their religious feelings. And Stalin gave the workers a God of whom it was impossible to say that he did not exist. The unconscious religious feeling which gave Stalin mandate number three was pure. (I am inclined to include the self-interested elements of religious feeling in mandate number two.)

The word *Stalin* here could be easily replaced by any other word meaning an all-blessed, all-powerful, all-controlling being, the source of all perfections, or, as people said in those days, the inspiration for our triumphs.

Now, how could Stalin accomplish three such diverse mandates simultaneously? For that of course he had to have a special talent. In Stalin's jargon this talent was described as twohandedness.

As I have already said, we shall deal with only one aspect of this special talent. But we shall try to examine it in as much detail as possible. We will go deep, not wide. . . .

1924. Stalin's oration over Lenin's coffin included an oath that he would be a true internationalist; but he betrayed internationalism right then and there over the coffin.

This is widely known to historians of the CPSU and to veterans of the Revolution. Here in particular is the testimony of M. P. Yakubovich, an old revolutionary who spent half his life in prisons and camps.

Vladimir Ilyich had two deputies to help him in his capacity of Chairman of the Council of People's Commissars—A. I. Rykov and A. D. Tsyurupa. When Lenin fell ill, and needed not so much a deputy as someone who would to all intents and purposes take over during his illness, the Central Committee, following Lenin's advice, chose L. B. Kamenev.

Lenin handed over the reins of power to him for the duration of his illness.

After Lenin's death, Stalin, as is well known, immediately removed Kamenev from the post of head of the Soviet government. Here we are concerned not with the fact of Kamenev's dismissal, but rather with the arguments which Joseph Dzhugashvili (Stalin) employed.

Here's Yakubovich again.

Stalin persuaded the Central Committee to divide the duties of the Chairman of the Sovnarkom into two, and to apportion them between a Sovnarkom chairman and a chairman for labor and defense, on the grounds that it was unfitting that the Chairman of the Sovnarkom in our peasant country should be a Jew by descent. [Kamenev's father was a Jew, and in his Tsarist passport his name was given as Rosenfeld.] This argument would not have convinced the Central Committee had it not immediately been supported by Kamenev himself.

(Let us note, incidentally, that Stalin applied no such racialist considerations in regard to himself, Dzhugashvili, as leader of the Russian Social Democratic Party.)

Stalin was not the first national-revolutionary in Russian history. "The Russian list" revealed social revolutionaries who in their time, and for the very same reasons, withdrew the candidature of the Chairman of the Constituent Assembly.

"We have always distinguished, and will continue to distinguish peasant considerations from peasant prejudice," said Lenin.

The Solovetskiye Islands received wave after wave of arrested social revolutionaries, but their guiding vision, as the future was to show, remained on the mainland. . . .

"Now, thank God, there are only two masters in Russia, you and me," said Stalin to Rykov, as Maria Ilynichna Ulyanova testified, when Rykov had been chosen as chairman of the Sovnarkom.

"I remember feeling a chill on my skin," Ulyanova told the writer Stepan Zlobin.

That happened in the same year as Stalin swore over Lenin's coffin to be faithful to the principles of Leninism.

On the Solovetskiye Islands and in Pechora, people were already being shot without trial. The wastes of Archangelsk were gradually being turned into a vast concentration camp.

So, who in fact learned from whom? Stalin from Hitler, or Corporal Schickelgruber from Stalin?

Völkischer Beobachter* and other Fascist papers expressed their displeasure at the fact that Soviet newspapers printed Jewish surnames. Stalin immediately moved to meet the wishes of his ungrateful pupil. One after another, world-famous names of journalists disappeared from the pages of Pravda and other central papers.

I will give just one example—an example of great courage, for the journalist concerned did not give way to threats and blackmail, and despite everything, preserved his good name as an investigative reporter. In 1936 the deputy editor of the paper For Industrialization, A. Khavin, was summoned by the editor-in-chief, Vasilovsky, a Polish Communist, himself

---

* Nazi daily newspaper. [Translator]

soon to be exterminated by Stalin. Vasilovsky asked Khavin to change his name.

"Take any other name you like, Comrade Khavin. As long as it's got a Russian ending to it. Something in '-ov.' How about Khavkov, for example? You refuse?" He got angry. "Are you blind? Look, there was Ierukhimovich, *Pravda*'s London correspondent. He was known all over the world as Ierukhimovich. What name did he take? Ermashov." And the editor produced a whole string of further examples.

The names of national newspaper correspondents which displeased Hitler disappeared from the papers in those days, like falling leaves in autumn. All you need do to prove it is to go back through the old files.

Many people saw nothing prejudicial in being asked to change their names. After all, if it's necessary to lower your visor before the jousting starts . . .

But it was not long before Jewish journalists often came under fatal fire for "hiding" behind pseudonyms. Mikhail Sholokhov was to write an all-revealing article called "Behind a Closed Visor."

But that was still in the future. For the time being, correspondents were not actually driven from their jobs and killed for being Jews. Stalin always loved to say that he was a gradualist. Everything in its proper time.

The next year was 1937.

I am writing these lines in a hospital ward where I've come to visit a friend. They have taken him away to have a dressing changed, and I'm waiting for him. In the bed next to him there's a desperately sick Old Bolshevik. His friends have all come to see him, and he won't let them leave because he knows that he's got only a short time to live. I try not to overhear, not to eavesdrop, but one phrase keeps coming through like a refrain, always pronounced with great emotion. First one, then another voice says—"And then they sent him to a camp." And so it goes on for hours together.

"And then they put him in a camp!"

I've nothing else to do, nowhere to go, so I begin to listen. The dying man, his face yellow and sagging, says, "In Loyola's spiritual exercises, there's a thirteenth point which says that if the church declares black something which our eyes tell us is white, we should accept it as being black."

Stalin had similar traditions.

My God, what a bitter cup it must be, to have to talk about that in one's last hours of life! Only of that . . .

The year 1937 set the anti-Semitic wheel turning faster. In a TASS document Stalin personally "corrected" the names of Zinoviev and

Kamenev, telling the population the pre-Revolutionary names of these victims of the process of the terror—Radomyslsky and Rosenfeld. That encouraged the timid Selyavkas and the careerists, who could finally be sure which direction the wind was blowing.

The year 1938 brought the official destruction of Jewish schools and Jewish departments in institutes in the Ukraine, thus making a ghetto of all Soviet literature in Yiddish, which lost its readership with catastrophic speed. And that wasn't the actual act—the culminating act—of assimilation, thanks to which Jewish schools in the Ukraine had been losing their pupils year after year. Those were merely the first salvoes.

In 1939 Stalin announced that Hitlerites must not be labeled Fascists—an ideology is an ideology. The word *Fascism* disappeared from the papers. Soon after that, the papers printed the speech of Adolf Hitler, in which the Führer explained that his aim was the struggle with godlessness and the Jewish plutocracy. Today there is no one left in the world who doesn't understand what Hitler meant by those words.

The screams of Auschwitz, the Inguletsk quarries, the Babi Yars— millions of graves of murdered Jews, workers, craftsmen, scientists could have become a firebreak against the smoldering anti-Semitism that was rampant on earth.

Stalin didn't try to extinguish the fire—he put another match to it, the better to make it blaze—from both ends. In 1942, on Stalin's instructions, two booklets were written about generals Suvorov and Kutuzov. When the first copies were brought to him, still damp from the press, Stalin gave vent to his extreme displeasure at the fact that the authors had non-Russian names. At about the same time he refused to approve the list of editors-in-chief of army newspapers because Jewish names were among their bylines. He expressed his dislike of the composition of an orchestra that went on a concert tour in England. "All these Flier-Miers— where are the Russian names?"

It was at this time that the scandalous behavior I saw on my newspaper on the Polar Sea began to occur.

Anti-Semitism arose directly out of his instructions, just as the snake-charmer's pipe awakens a slumbering cobra. Stalin couldn't stand Jewish names in the days of the pact with Hitler. "It's high politics," lecturers for regional committees used to explain, when people asked them why Ierukhimovich had suddenly become Ermashov.

And Stalin was still hunting out Jewish names in the days of the holy war against Fascism, when the pro-German militia were shooting Jewish children with explosive bullets in the back of the neck. On this topic the lecturers muttered about the Germans reviving peasant prejudices.

"Throughout the four years of the war, the High Political Command of the Soviet Army, which every month sent the various political departments subjects for political discussion and matters of political information, never once devoted a single exercise, a single lecture, a single information bulletin to the subject of anti-Semitism, to the role of anti-Semitism in the politics of Nazism, to the murder by the Nazis of virtually the whole Jewish population of Europe," writes the historian R. Medvedev in his definitive work on Stalin.*

In the postwar period, Stalin, masking his actions beneath references to the counterrevolutionary activity of international Zionist organizations, began the gradual removal of Jews from the Party and Soviet apparatus. The majority of establishments of higher education, scientific institutes, and even many businesses, introduced an unwritten quota for Jews.

A long time ago, Stalin once said that "the path of anti-Semitism could lead only into the jungle." But he himself left direct evidence of the "path" he had chosen to follow.

In his report to the Twelfth Congress of the CPSU, he gave this exhaustive definition of great-power chauvinism: "Great-power chauvinism is expressed in the attempt to bring together all the threads of government into one Russian source, and to suppress everything non-Russian."

In 1945 Stalin proposed a toast to the Russian people as the "ruling nation."

Is that simply an evolution of his views? Hardly. It is simply a case of the "rule of Arakcheev," to quote Stalin himself, having grown stronger as any possibility of criticism waned. Why, in that case, be ashamed of one's fatherland?

Stalin's practice of genocide yields nothing to that of Hitler, not even in scope. Historians calculate that Stalin forced the migration of unwanted national minorities to the tune of more than five million people.† And the majority of those who were driven from their homes perished.

Not trusting his descendants any more than his contemporaries, Stalin wrote his own history, or at least a short course in it, and cunningly titled it a *Short Course of the History of the Party*; he erected gigantic statues to himself along canals, in parks—and great visionary that he was—wrote this verdict on himself to be pronounced by the revolutionary tribunal of

---

* Roy Medvedev, *Let History Judge*. It includes documents on Stalin's anti-Semitism taken from the archive of NKVD Colonel E. P. Frolov which have been in my possession for some time. I am not therefore including them in this book but I would refer readers to Medvedev's book.

† Among the minorities and ethnic groups so treated were the Chechens and Ingush, and, most notably, the Crimean Tartars. [Translator]

the future: "In the USSR active anti-Semitism is punishable by shooting."

In order that the sentence should be final and that history should not be able to appeal against it, Stalin, this time perhaps subconsciously, immortalized his pogrom-making, chauvinistic incursion into the country in stone.

In the Stalin years there were no statues in Moscow to Marx or Engels, or even Lenin. But one statue was erected to Yuri Dolgoruky, an independent prince of the twelfth century, and to make a space for it to stand in Sovietskaya Square, opposite the Moscow City Council building, the Obelisk of Freedom set up by Lenin was destroyed. How many people have been crushed by the bronze hooves of the Prince's horse, now the symbol of Stalin's rule? How many millions of Soviet people?

The bloodiest wrongdoers of history, the Duke of Alba and Philip II, in all their orthodox religious ferocity, killed less than fifty thousand heretics. The Holy Inquisition in France in a period of a hundred years killed about two hundred thousand. In Tsarist Russia from 1825 to 1904, only forty-two people were sentenced to death. Even Alexander III in thirteen years of his reign only sent five thousand trouble-makers to prison.

And Stalin? The records are accurate only with regard to actual members of the Communist Party. One million two hundred thousand party members were exterminated. Four out of every five Old Bolsheviks died in prison or in exile—these were the men who stormed the Winter Palace, who fought in Spain.

And how many wholly innocent people never returned to their homes? Historians consider that the number who died can never be accurately calculated. Or perhaps it's that they don't want to try.

By 1949 there was no question of Pauline and I not being able to see what was going on—the guns had begun to aim at us.

We were enthusiasts of the age, we used to carry placards on demonstrations, or the big balloons they used to hand out, and we used to shout with all the strength of our young lungs, "Mao and Stalin, listen to us!" Moscow had agreed that at the end of the year Mao would come on a visit. We secretly hoped that Mao might tell Stalin how much the ridiculous Black Hundreds were compromising Soviet ideas. Would he say it or wouldn't he?

The sniping in the newspapers became stronger and stronger. Then the shooting began to come in salvos—just like the Tsarist army, where the platoon commanders, not trusting the privates an inch, would yell, "Platoo-oon! Load! Aim! You, you fool, where d'you think you're pointing that gun? Get it lower! Fire!"

Who was in command of that fire of provocation? Who was the

provocateur crawling toward the great high chair? Who? For us, and if I may say so, for our generation (there may have been exceptions, but if so I didn't know about them), that was a great secret, sealed by seven seals. Lies fell on youth like an avalanche. And for many years people remained buried under them. We were sure of only one thing: the main enemy of those who were conducting the pogrom was human memory, and most of all Russian history, and we were instinctively drawn to the libraries and reading rooms.

Once Pauline complained that for more than a year she hadn't been able to get the newspaper *Russian Banner* from the Lenin Library, and yet we were continually told how instructive the paper was. Naturally, the next time I was in the Lenin Library I ordered the bound copies for the last five years. It's true that to do this I had to produce an official document stating that for my particular line of studies access to *Russian Banner* was as vital as axle grease to a wheel. The conveyor belt eventually produced virginally dusty folios with cardboard bindings protecting the yellowing pages of newsprint. I began to leaf through them, sneezing violently from the clouds that rose from them. It turned out that *Russian Banner* was the official organ of the Black Hundred Union of the Russian People. The paper of the Russian pogromists. Well, well, as they say, it's good to meet you at last.

I found a clean sheet of paper and prepared to take notes from this prime source, according to all the rules of good scientific research, for Pauline. The basic questions repeated themselves again and again. "Can a true Christian be a Socialist?" Answer: "To be a Christian and a Socialist at the same time is impossible: one cannot at one and the same time serve God and Satan."

The completeness of the argument overwhelmed me. *Russian Banner* was a paper of abuse and cursing. But granted even that, it was remarkable what lengths the paper could go to when faced by the opposition.

"Yiddish Samovars! Don't drink tea from samovars made by dirty Yids. They'll give you stones in your stomach."

"What have we come to now?—Jews are being admitted to the sugar refining business."

"Get the Yids out of the army!" Perish the thought; Jews had been allowed to become military bandmasters.

"Look out, look out, there's a Jew about!"

"Save us from the Jews!"

No voice raised in the defense of the Jew. Headlines poured out: "I AM AFRAID." "BEWARE!"

"An undermining of the very foundations of our civilization." Somewhere, of course, under the evil influence of the Jews, there had been moves to shorten the working day to eight hours. And so there should be no more doubt—"The whole world knows the evil that Jews can do."

The whole world knows! What proof is needed? Why batter at an open door? For the evidence of sense, of logic, even the investigations of what the Tsarists did, can't shake that belief.

"BEILIS ACQUITTED. THE JEWS ACCUSED."*

And then there were other, unhappily familiar slogans in the newspaper headlines: "ON PSEUDONYMS." "ON THE INTELLIGENTSIA."

Of course, the intelligentsia is enemy number one. After the Jews, of course, who are even worse than the intelligentsia. "The intelligentsia has never expressed the desperation of the people."

"The brittle Moscow intelligentsia."

It speaks of students, of course, only in certain terms: "From the murky depths of student life . . ." A regular column.

"The politicking gangs of the intelligentsia"—that was about strikers.

What a paper! When did its last number appear? It turned out to be the very day before the February Revolution of 1917. And what's more it was Kerensky who closed it down. In every edition, there were black anti-Semitic headlines—appeals unshakeable in their stubborn fanaticism, and as fierce as an order to shoot.

"Jews are impermissible as teachers!"

"The employment of Jews in the service of education is impermissible."

"In Russia we cannot tolerate Jews as doctors, chemists, or pharmacists!"

"The Jews are poisoners!"

"We cannot tolerate the presence of Jews in Russian schools at any level, lower, secondary or higher, either as teachers or students!"

"Jews are not to be tolerated as newspaper proprietors or editors, or indeed anywhere in the Russian press."

In the end my hands became black from their contact with the pages of *Russian Banner*. I spent a whole evening washing them.

I gathered together the heavy, dust-laden files, and went back to the desk to return them. As I stood in the queue, I spotted an old comrade of mine from the front, who'd been invalided out and who had finished his university course before me. He came up to me. He was sweating and distraught. His eyes flickered from side to side. He whispered to me that he'd just been dismissed from Moscow Radio. And not only he. Every editor

---

* Beilis: Ukrainian Jew who in 1913 was accused of having committed the crime of ritual murder of a child—a crime which anti-Semitic propaganda frequently accused the Jews of committing, particularly in Russia. He was acquitted after a worldwide campaign was conducted in his defense. [Translator]

who was a Jew. Even a pregnant woman, even people who'd worked there all their lives.

"I know they're all off the same list. No explanations. Just out to the street, and that's it."

The files slipped from my hands to the ground, and pages fell out. Until then I had thought these loose leaves were packing, and had paid no attention to them, but as I picked them up I looked at them absent-mindedly. They were official Lenin Library forms torn in half. On the back of each of them I found the instruction: "Not to be given out. Readers are to be told that they are under restoration."

I don't remember returning the newspapers or how I reached the street. I only noticed that I was still holding my naval cap in my hands when my head began to grow numb with cold.

For some reason I was in the Alexandrovsky Gardens, near the brick walls of the Kremlin. My head was splitting. Did that mean that all of them—Molotov, Kaganovich, Malenkov, Shcherbakov—knew what they were doing? They knew the road they were following? That must be why there was the instruction that the files weren't to be handed out. That's why the files were always being restored—so that no one could follow their tracks.

What were these swine doing with Russia? What were they doing? And how did they manage to deceive the whole world?

I slowed down by the tightly closed and mysteriously dark gates of the Kremlin, in the state of mind that drives men to attack tanks with their bare hands, to shoot themselves or to try to force a way in to see Stalin as a petitioner.

Suddenly two figures detached themselves from a lamppost and moved in my direction. They stopped a short distance away, wearing identical hats. Their long shadows combined and engulfed me.

I stood as if frozen to the spot, clenching my fists, waiting to die. I shuddered as a hand touched mine. There was a frightened, anxious voice: "Lord, where have you been so late? I went to the library and you'd gone. I've waited so long. Just waited."

It was Pauline. Her headscarf had slipped to her shoulders.

"I've waited so long, waited and waited."

14

We were married on St. Tatiana's day—a traditional student festival. About that time Pauline rented a tiny room in Engels Street, on the ground floor, with a heavily barred window. It was a cosy single room; everyone liked it. And we moved in with all our possessions in one suitcase and a bundle.

For Pauline's friends it was the only place they had to go to where there were no parents in the way, almost a bachelor apartment, and almost all the postgraduate students from Selinsky's department had gathered there several times already. Even in frosty weather we had to open the windows, or it would have been impossible to breathe. And we launched into the traditional "graduates' jig," to the delight of the children in the street outside, who pressed their white noses against the glass.

Sometimes, someone would bring around some chemically pure alcohol; and once someone proposed the half-joking, half-serious toast: "Down with the Jews and the postmen!"

I took the bait and asked in surprise, "What have postmen got to do with it?"

There was a shout of laughter. It appeared that for years no one had ever asked, "What have Jews got to do with it?"

We lived cheerfully enough. But we decided to celebrate our marriage just with the family—not with the graduates' jig. My old mother came with a stuffed fish, and there was also Gulya, Pauline's closest friend, an oceanologist, a bright girl, a devil in skirts. My mother had left her husband, my father, twenty-five years before—Gulya had only just left hers, and with some violence. She had proudly slammed the door in his face. For both of them marriage had ended in bitter tears.

Mama looked cautiously at Pauline, busying herself about the table, and Gulya looked at me with just as much doubt in her eyes. How would it all work out? Mama had already asked me twice in a whisper. "Is it true that Pauline is Jewish? Perhaps she's pretending? You could have looked at her passport?"

I laughed, and then got angry. "And what if she'd been an Eskimo, or Lithuanian, or Ukrainian? Would that be worse?"

"No, no, I didn't mean anything," Mother agreed, thrusting a fork through the fish. She waited until Pauline and Gulya had disappeared into the communal kitchen at the end of the corridor, and then explained, blushing slightly, that she wasn't really a total fool but she didn't want to live to see the day when, if times got hard, Pauline could yell at me— "Get out of here, you Jewish scum!"

"No, no. I didn't mean anything. Sorry. Marry who you like, Eskimo, a cannibal, if you want. The law isn't made for fools. I never thought my only son was an idiot!"

The evening passed in true family spirit.

The next day our friends descended on us without any invitation, and everyone promised to kill me if I detached Pauline from the collective.

"Goddam philologist!" That's what I was always known as. Finally, I was dragged off to the kitchen to cook the horseradish. As I scraped the roots and tears flooded my eyes, I could hear the sounds of the graduates' jig filtering through the walls in a growing howl.

There's a saying that the tongue is a razor. In Gulya's mouth her tongue was a company of machine gunners. But that day she excelled herself. She rapped nervously on the window, and yelled through the open pane as she ran by: "Switch on the radio! A wedding present from the government!"

I switched it on, and the room was filled from wall to wall with the ominous voice of the announcer. "Bunch of jackals . . . Mad scribblers . . . trying to degrade . . . to poison . . . noxious spirit . . . cowardly sneering laughter . . ."

"Has a new trial started?" I asked Gulya quietly when she came in.

"Come off it," said Gulya. She was very pale. Her father, one of the country's leading experts on Arabic and Semitic languages, had had a heart attack after a discussion about "language." "A trial? It's just a high-toned literary debate. About the theater." She handed me a newspaper with an article about "an anti-patriotic group of theater critics."

And the doom-laden voice of the announcer droned on, warning of the danger from Jews. ". . . the bankrupt Yuzovskys, Gurviches, . . . Borshchagovskys . . . they have entrenched themselves . . . they have constantly run down . . ."

"A wedding present," said Pauline in a tense whisper, padding around the room in her bare feet. She pulled out the radio plug and cried hopelessly: "Surely Stalin must be reading this stuff. He can't fail to read it!"

The circles widened. There were reports from Leningrad, Kiev, Odessa; in Kharkov alone, "G. Gelfand, V. Morskoi, L. Yukhvid, A. Grin, M. Grinshpun, I. Pustynsky, M. Stein, and others have been unmasked." Almost every time the list of newly revealed vipers in the bosom of the state ended with those well-worn words, "and others," which were immediately explained as "they were uncovered with their accomplices . . . their stench has also poisoned . . ."

"They really knew how to curse in the Middle Ages," I remembered Academician Gudzy saying. "Their stench has poisoned" was almost on a level with "brood of antichrist." And again, on almost every newspaper page—"and others . . ."

"Find them, then indict them." In our faculty there were frequent "Chinese ceremonies"—tedious conversations in the office, when, politely and warmly they asked, "Where do you spend your time? With whom? What do you talk about?" That's what the students called them— "Chinese ceremonies"—although at that time, of course, there wasn't the tragic depth of meaning in the phrase that has been revealed since.

In our communal flat in that crumbling house there was no standing on ceremony. Our neighbor, an unhappy, hungry woman who had lost both her husband and her son in the war, used to listen at our door. Once when I caught her at it and attacked her, she began to cry and said that she had been forced to do it by the house manager.

We calmed her down as best we could, and fed her some thin student soup. She told us in a whisper, stammering and darting her eyes toward the door, that the house manager found us suspicious. We had guests, he said, a whole synagogue. And we locked our doors and whispered behind them. Who were we locking ourselves away from? What were we whispering about? He had said to her, "You're a responsible tenant. Look after them both. And if there's any hint, you know where to come."

As he left her he went further. "The Jews are tricky customers. If they seem to be up to anything, you'd better get on to me right away. People aren't made of steel, you know!"

Pauline and I genuinely tried to cut ourselves off from the world. We had indeed locked our doors, and had even whispered behind them. We turned our backs on the watching eyes. We ignored the literary hysteria going on about us. We turned our backs on the anti-Semitic venom in which, it seemed, the pages of the newspapers had been steeped.

We wanted a son. I didn't have anything against the idea of a daughter. But Pauline wanted a son, nothing but a son. There's a saying that life goes on even when the executioner's axe is poised to strike. A man goes on living in hope until the moment the blow cuts through his neck.

And although, as time was later to show, we had only seen the first act of the bloodstained tragedy dreamed up in every last detail by that great stage director, there were still two or three years to go to the planned St. Bartholomew's night, when a policeman, admittedly from another street, was to place us on his secret list of proscribed "Huguenots" and when all the drunks and criminals of our old, downtrodden street would feel themselves part of a fighting vanguard against the Jewish threat.

But all the same, from time to time snowballs and clods of earth were flung through our windows, and once a drunken voice bawled, "Hey, Mozart, pack your bags. Kolyma's waiting for you!" (I never did understand how Mozart suddenly turned out to be a Jew.)

And in the apartment exchange, and in the "free housing market" of Moscow, where we went to try to get a bigger room, we were sometimes met with an undisguised sneer: "Oh, you're trying to expand, are you?"

But nevertheless Pauline and I were happy in our place of execution, although I sometimes came home to it with a split lip or a black eye, the result of one of a series of cultural discussions with anti-Semites I'd come across in the street or on the tram. For newlyweds traveling in a private compartment on a train are no less happy up to the moment of the crash about which they've never thought, even though they knew in advance that the track was dangerous. There were the two of us, and I looked into Pauline's icon eyes, and was happy because they were shining.

The metallic clang of the alarm clock marked the end of the fairy tale each day—but the fairy tale went on. It went on in Pauline's deep, rich voice when I telephoned her at the end of every lecture, it went on in the movement of her work-roughened hands, placing as many as ten flasks at a time on her Bunsen burners and achieving success after success.

And I was delighted that her eyes did not lose their happiness even when one day we saw, peering through our barred window, the coarse, red, worried face of a policeman, who simply couldn't resist the temptation of trying to find out what we were up to in there—printing pamphlets maybe. You can so easily get confused with these Jews! Can't afford to take your eyes off them for a minute!

But, alas, a place of execution is always a place of execution. When the blow came it was stunning, violent. And it came from the opposite direction—from where we weren't expecting it at all.

Everything suddenly became clear. The constant persecution, the years of hunger had taken their toll. Pauline lay there growing weaker day by day. Her cheeks were so pale, no one would have believed they had ever been otherwise. Her blood analysis was so grave that the doctor came hurrying around with it himself in the middle of the night. It showed a hemoglobin count of 38. And then the hemorrhages began. All through each night I had to keep dashing off to storage chests for ice, and rushing back with it melting in my hands, never knowing whether I'd find Pauline still alive when I got back.

Blood came in sealed glass ampoules from the Blood Transfusion Institute. I held them above my head in the crowded trams, while a friend would keep the press of the crowd off me so that I wouldn't bang the containers against the side of the car. Each ampoule bore the name of the donor—the names were Russian, Tartar, Ukrainian . . .

"The party hacks'll be falling in behind you," joked Alik, when he came to visit Pauline on her sickbed. "After all, you've got the blood of all the brotherly republics flowing in your veins."

Pauline laughed, but then grew quiet and sad again.

For almost a year I took her to see every doctor I could think of, unknown and famous, allopathic, homeopathic, to people you had to wait six months to get an appointment to see. The allopathic men dismissed the homeopaths as rogues and vagabonds, the homeopaths regarded the allopaths as medical ignoramuses.

Pauline could only walk by propping herself up against walls. The blood transfusions went on hopelessly, out of sheer desperation. If anyone had told me there was a holy man who could perform faith cures, I would have taken Pauline to him.

The bitter path of illness eventually led us to Zinaida Zakharovna Pevsner, a rank-and-file physician at a clinic on Pirogovka. She looked more like the kindly plump grandmother from Gorky's *Childhood* than one of the finest diagnosticians in Moscow, who had brought back hundreds of women from the edge of the grave. Pevsner's diagnosis was rejected outright by the chief doctor at the clinic, and by a whole string of distinguished consultants. However, she turned out to be right.

But all this happened only after seven blood transfusions. We came across Pevsner quite by chance. Pauline was refused admission to the clinic, and I demanded a note from the duty doctor guaranteeing that she would survive till the following day. Of course, he wouldn't give any such thing but allowed the hemorrhaging patient to be placed in a corridor. It was here that Zinaida Zakharovna Pevsner almost literally stumbled across her.

"Can we manage without an operation?" Pauline asked her later. Because of the transparency of Pauline's skin and her great burning eyes Zinaida Zakharovna had dubbed her "Pauline the martyr."

"You can live," Zinaida Zakharovna replied sadly. "But you won't be able to have a baby."

I expected the phone call about the outcome of the operation about midday. It came at three in the morning. "Come as quick as you can!"

At the clinic I was met by a surgeon looking more like a butcher in his overalls with the sleeves rolled up to his elbows. He waved his strong hairy arms and yelled at me that I should take my wife and get her out of there—take her to the devil's grandmother if you like. "To the devil's grandmother!" he yelled again, and disappeared back into the theater.

I found Pauline at the dimly lit end of the corridor. She was sitting there in her hospital nightdress, bent double and clutching at her stomach, as if she had been winded by a blow in the solar plexus. She was weeping silently. It turned out that when she had been placed on the operating table, all the preparations completed, and the anesthetic injections all finished, she asked the surgeon standing there, scalpel poised, whether she would be able to have a child after the operation.

"That'd be a surgical sensation," he laughed. "Whoever gave you that idea? That's pure charlatanism. There's one fraud like that in the Sklifosovsky Institute. I'm a surgeon, not a charlatan. And anyway, it's not so bad to be childless these days."

With one jump Pauline was off the operating table dashing away in her bare feet, fleeing from the operating theater pursued by furious looks and the shouts of nurses.

I put my arm around her shoulders, feeling her painfully sharp shoulder blades sticking out under the pitifully thin and ugly hospital nightdress. I took her home.

During this period everyone in the chemistry faculty used to drop in on us. There was no lack of advice. Finally it became clear that the rumors were true. In the Sklifosovsky First Aid Institute, there was a miracle-working Professor Alexandrov, who performed the most artistic plastic surgery operations. When he removed tumors he would stretch the cut-away skin over the scar, stitch it into position, and then, people said, you were almost as good as new. Even that rather vague "people said" was good enough for us.

I went to see this short, lean, nervous man, who couldn't stay in the same place for more than a moment. His white coat was spattered with blood. He kept his arms very close to his body, and on his hands for some reason he wore two pairs of transparent surgical gloves, which made his fingers look clumsy. I discovered later that he suffered from eczema, brought on by the iodine which rinsed a surgeon's hands so often. He never complained about this, but he always had to operate wearing the two pairs of gloves.

He inclined his close-cropped head, running with sweat, toward me and rapped out, "Well, what do you want? Make it quick!"

"Your wife said that she wants to come to me?" he interrupted my nervous babbling. "I have so many enemies. You're just innocent children. . . ."

"You mean that plastic surgery would be possible, Professor?" I asked anxiously. I could hardly believe it.

"Possible?" Alexandrov sounded surprised. "I have done four hundred plastic operations. It's just that I'm not recognized by . . ." and here he mentioned the names of Moscow's most famous surgeons. "I'm a charlatan and a crook." He laughed nervously and his hollow cheeks twitched. "If I wasn't Orthodox, they'd probably be putting it around that I crucified Christ. Or rather poisoned him. That's more up to date." He spread out his hands, which still looked clumsy to me. "Oh, twentieth century! We're on the way to Communism, single file ahead." He moved quickly over to the door, and stopped on the threshold. "I can't guarantee success. We'll only know for sure after the operation. Bring her along, if you're not frightened. But bring her yourself, through the reception room. Otherwise they'll say that I've fixed it all for a bribe."

The greater part of Professor Alexandrov's department was under reconstruction. Iron beds were everywhere, in the corridors and even in the Red Corner, the Communist reading room. There were at least thirty of them. I could barely find those familiar thin shoulders.

The noise of people talking was so loud that it gave even healthy people headaches. And they were all talking about the same thing—the Doctors' Plot.

"They pay them huge fees, and yet they still go on with their poisoning," declaimed a thin middle-aged woman, clutching the head of a bed like an orator behind a lectern. "If you ask me, all Jews should be shot—no trial, no investigation . . ."

A plump lady, with an almost intellectual face, spat the medicine the nurse gave her on the floor. She said, in an aggressive and hostile tone: "I get mine sent from the Kremlin."

"Theirs is even worse," her neighbor urged. "The Kremlin Hospital is where the real nest of traitors is."

In the next bed to Pauline's there was a woman with a face as pale and bloodless as a corpse. She was an engineer. She knew that her operation had done no good, and that she would be dead before the spring. She was the only one to protest; she was probably trying to shout, but her voice was so feeble it hardly rose above a whisper. Everyone fell silent to listen.

"If you've let people stuff all this garbage into your heads, making out you're being poisoned, why are you here at all? Get out of here, you silly people! And this is taking place in the year I'm going to die. Just when have I been living? In what century?"*

* The idea of doctor poisoners, began, it seems, long before the gutter-press paper *Russian Banner*. I have before me a book published in Poland whose preface states that the

In every hospital, people were on the lookout for poisoners—and invariably they found them. No, that's not true. I do know of one exception, so remarkable that it's worth recounting. In one medico-chemical laboratory, the victim chosen was an old man called Aaron Mikhailovich, a chemist and engineer, who had created a new drug. Pauline asked that it should be tried on her. That was how I came to meet its inventor, a quiet, skinny man with a modest smile.

A chemist who invented new drugs! How could he not be a poisoner? So a trade-union meeting was called with the specific purpose of naming him as a poisoner. With very few exceptions the scientists didn't turn up. But the conference room was full, although for some reason no one was sitting in the front rows. They sat there, chatting among themselves, knitting, eating the packed lunches they'd brought from home. There were the lab assistants, the cleaning women, the dispensers, the housekeeper, the plumber, the carpenters, the night watchman.

"Never mind. There are enough people here," observed the personnel director with some satisfaction as he surveyed the hall. His wife angrily accused the poisoner. She claimed that he had deliberately produced an incorrect result in calculating the composition of the air in a mine near Moscow. He had put the oxygen content too low, and as a result some of the miners had been poisoned.

Then it was if a dam had burst. "Get out!" the old night watchman screamed at the woman on the platform. "It's not Aaron Mikhailovich we should be getting rid of, but you. You just stand there yelping away while he keeps the world going!"

A young girl, a pharmacist's assistant, came to the platform and told how Aaron Mikhailovich helped the lab assistants prepare for their examinations, and refused to accept money for it. "Nastka was always bursting into tears because she said she couldn't understand anything. But Aaron Mikhailovich would come and help us every evening as if it was part of his job."

Another girl recalled how whenever there was a forced loan collection, he would always give more than anyone else to make sure the laboratory gave what was expected, so that the cleaners and lab girls wouldn't be squeezed out of their last kopeck.

Then the plumber rose from his seat in the back row, shouted down everyone who was trying to stop him speaking, totally ignored the personnel director's desperate gestures, and bellowed: "Before the war I used

___

book contains clear proof that anyone who employs doctors who are Jews, Tartars, or other infidels, contrary to the dictates of the Holy Church, shall in both body and soul be condemned to death everlasting. Published by Priest Sebastian Selszkowski, in the Year of Our Lord 1623.

to work in a Jewish collective farm near Kharkov. They were fine people!"

It was a dreadful scandal. The representative of the Regional Party Committee turned quite green with fright and crept out of the room, followed by the personnel man.

How right old Gena Faibusovich was when he said that the people were strangers to lies. They hated lies. It might be that the people often didn't realize they were being lied to—they were trusting, easily deceived by the press. But if once the truth leaked out! . . . People have burned the truth on bonfires since the creation of the world.

One day in the hospital ward, a young nurse rushed in, shouting, "Switch on the radio. Stalin is dying!"

She couldn't reach the switch: the ward was filled with the sounds of a Chopin sonata. Pauline's dying neighbor gave a convulsive shudder, sat up in bed, and like lightning stretched out her hand to the knob.

And suddenly there was a shriek, full of pain, as if someone had been struck in the face. Pauline's eyes filled with tears. Her gray, pain-wracked face revealed her suffering. "What will happen now? What will happen to us all now?"

She began to weep, the tears pouring down her cheeks like a child. Horror had frozen in her round eyes. What would happen now? He was no longer there. Who would there be now to check the flood of newspaper lies, the drunkards, the officials who were spare-time executioners? Now they would have their way, they would spread. . . .

Toward evening, Zhenya Kozlova, the short, fat "minidoctor" who'd become a friend of ours, bounced into the ward. Zhenya was so small that when she operated they had to put a bench next to the operating table for her to stand on.

"Telephone Grisha and tell him to stay indoors!" she called to Pauline, not noticing me standing there.

Pauline shuddered. "Has it begun already? Has the pogrom started?"

"Everyone's on the streets," shouted Zhenya, out of breath with emotion. "Everyone's dashed off to the House of the Unions. The place I first met you when you came in here is piled high with corpses. They just keep on bringing them in."

A day or two went by, and Pauline, running down the stairs in her nightdress, told me with astonishment about Alexandrov. "He's an iron man! The day of Stalin's funeral he didn't even cancel his operations. How could he go on operating? On a day like that. You'd have thought all his instruments would fall from his hands."

But Alexandrov's instruments didn't fall from his hands. He went on operating. From morning till night. Eventually it was Pauline's turn. "Tomorrow it's execution," she wrote to me, "—or salvation."

In the morning they brought the newspapers into the ward, as usual. That day they had printed an excerpt from a speech by Dwight Eisenhower—"The Stalinist dictatorship is over."

"They're obviously out of their minds," said the nurse who was selling the papers. "That's where blind hatred leads you."

Alexandrov, who had come in unnoticed behind the nurse, seized the newspaper from Pauline's hand and shouted, "It's time to think about other things. Other things! Get her on the table!"

I wasn't allowed to see her until the following day. Then they let me stand at the half-open door to the ward where she lay after her operation. From behind the door I could hear Zhenya Kozlova sounding unusually severe. Her voice rang out authoritatively: "Her temperature's only 99°, yet she has the nerve to say she doesn't feel well. Rubbish!"

The old orderly, to whom I had given the bottle of fruit juice I'd brought with me, grumbled good-humoredly: "I've been working in the postoperative ward for twenty-five years now, and they always moan. I can't think what'll happen when people stop moaning."

Zhenya bounced out of the ward, and observed, in her professor's voice: "She woke late from the anesthetic. Gave us some peace anyway. Mikhail Sergeevich phoned every two hours through the night. Tomorrow she can have some chicken broth. Good-bye!"

I dashed around three or four markets in Moscow. The chickens must have been somewhere else. Finally, in the Central Market, I heard an angry voice complaining, "Even if she laid golden eggs, I wouldn't touch her at that price. . . ."

I pushed through the crowd of women, angering them still more. They were clustering around a young girl in a skirt covered in feathers, and they were telling her in no uncertain terms what she did and didn't deserve. On the ground in front of her lay a big yellow chicken—just one. And a ticket showing the price—90 rubles.

I snatched my one neatly folded hundred-ruble note from my wallet and dashed to the exit, clutching the hen to my chest, while the women cursed and swore, firmly convinced by now that I was some kind of crook and that my money was stolen. It was only when the soup, clear as crystal, was finally made and poured into a chemical flask with a ground glass stopper that I realized that Pauline's university friend, the thin, pedantic Irinka, whom I'd asked to make the broth for me, shouldn't have been there. It was almost midday.

"I didn't feel very well," Irinka answered imperturbably, turning her eyes away. She didn't tell me that she had just been fired from the Oncological Institute, where she, a research chemist, had just synthesized a new drug for one form of cancer.

Almost every morning I heard the agitated voice of Zinaida Za-kharovna Pevsner on the telephone, but she never told me either that she had been thrown out of the Pirogovka Institute with the mob baying at her back, on the very day she was due to give her doctoral dissertation.

Pauline kept the flask with the ground glass stopper for a long time as a kind of family heirloom. She swore that it was that mouthful of home-made chicken broth that had saved her life—and I, weak man, didn't try to persuade her to the contrary.

When Zhenya Kozlova finally gave me back the fruit juice bottle I had brought for Pauline, she stuffed it into my briefcase distractedly, took me by the arm, and led me off to the dispensary. "Sit down." she said firmly.

I sat down nervously on the edge of a chair and asked, "What's happened?"

She calmed me with a wave of her hand, coughed and cleared her throat as if she were about to declaim poetry, and said in an elevated tone that she wanted to congratulate me on having such a wife. I stared at her and made some light remark to bring her down off her podium. But she angrily told me to be quiet and listen.

She spoke softly and her voice was full of a surprise she found hard to express in words. The tone was even more striking than what she had to tell me, for Zhenya was a staff doctor in the Sklifosovsky First Aid Institute, where the doctors worked in shifts on a bloodstained conveyor belt. They had long since stopped being surprised at anything they saw—they had seen everything.

"Grisha, remember every word I say to you. You'll have to tell all this to your childen and your grandchildren. Whenever they're born, they should know that they were born here, in this institute on March 18, 1953. On the anniversary of the Paris Commune. All your family from now on is under the star of the Paris Communards."

"Thank you," I said in amazement. "But what have the Paris Communards got to do with this?"

She didn't think that worthy of a reply. She nervously lit up a cigarette, just as her boss might have done. I realized I had better keep quiet. Obviously, something incredible had happened.

"Now then. Pauline asked us not to put her to sleep. I told her that a spinal anesthetic could be a great deal more dangerous, and she'd be better off with a general anesthetic. She wouldn't listen."

So they gave her a spinal.

"After forty minutes we took a biopsy. That means we cut off a piece of the tumor for histology tests. Mikhail Sergeevich gave it to me to take to the path lab. Suddenly I heard Pauline's voice: 'There's no need to take it to histology. I haven't got cancer. I've had a biopsy before.' I stopped in my tracks. Mikhail Sergeevich almost bellowed at me: 'What are you doing listening to the patient—particularly when she's got her stomach wide open?'

"After twenty minutes or so I got back from the lab. The tumor wasn't malignant. We could go ahead with the repair work without cutting out everything in sight.

"I told Mikhail Sergeevich, and then I suddenly noticed that Pauline was desperately pale, and she was clenching her teeth the way people do when they're in the worst kind of pain. Then she said—and I could feel her forcing the words out—'Professor, I can't stand any more.' Mikhail Sergeevich shook so much he nearly dropped his scalpel. It turned out that her nervous system was all shot to pieces, and the anesthetic wasn't working properly. But she had kept quiet. She was afraid of the same thing happening that had happened at the Pirogovka. She thought we were going ahead to do what was easiest—just take her womb out— and then there couldn't be any children. And so she had just rolled herself up mentally, kept quiet, so that she would know everything we were going to do, so that she could resist, poor girl, if we began to go ahead with the hysterectomy.

"Do you understand what this all means?" It was an attack. Apparently my face wasn't showing enough emotion. "If you cut your face when you're shaving, I bet you yell! And she was an hour and a half under the knife. It made no difference how many layers down we went, she never groaned, never flinched. I remember she was tense, clutching the theater gown to her chest. I thought she was just nervous. But she was suffering. . . ."

Zhenya lit another cigarette from the butt of the old one, and went on in the same quiet but amazed tone.

"And when it finally became clear that everything was all right, that we weren't going to do the full hysterectomy, then of course she lost the power to resist, and that's when she whispered, 'I can't stand any more.'

"When Mikhail Sergeevich got over the shock, he yelled like a madman for the mask. He'd never seen anything like it either. We gave Pauline a massive dose of ether and began to stitch her up."

A year and a half later, I took Pauline to the Grauerman Maternity Hospital on the Arbat. "I'm going to have a son!" she said happily to the duty doctor, when he registered her in his book.

He looked at her rather dubiously, and said, "It could be a daughter, you know."

"No," said Pauline. "It's a son!"

The doctor looked at her again, and then at me, wondering whether both of us were idiots, or only the mother.

In the operating theater, where Pauline was being prepared for a Caesarean, the two nurses handed over syringes of novocain, and the woman doctor injected the incision line she was going to have to make. Ten injections, one after the other.

"You'd better make a good job of sewing it up, doctor," said Pauline. The doctor looked at her in alarm. She was talking as if it were someone else being injected.

"Can you feel anything?" she asked.

"Oh, yes," Pauline confirmed.

Around her there were about twenty student midwives and doctors, and all twenty voices came out simultaneously with a triumphant, "It's a boy!"

The doctor took the baby by the foot, and as she was going out said again, "It's a boy. Black-haired."

"Good God!" exclaimed Pauline. "Who does he look like then?"

The operating theater rocked with laughter. The chief doctor, standing at the head of the operating table, said, "You should know better than we do."

When I turned up at the maternity home, I was called in to see the chief doctor, who looked curiously at me and then called in someone else, who also had a good look. In the end they explained why they were staring.

"We were certain you must be fair, or a redhead—or possibly even Chinese. Why in the world was your wife surprised when the baby turned out to have black hair? What else did she expect with a father like you?"

Pauline wasn't discharged as soon as we expected. She developed mastitis, and she had to have another series of operations. The doctor said sympathetically, "It's like in the old song—one damn thing after another. She's very patient." That son cost Pauline six surgical operations.

We had to think of a name for him, so I turned up one day with some suggestions.

"Fimochka's been feeding well today," said Pauline. "He really grabbed hold of the nipple."

"Fimochka?" I shouted. And suddenly I felt a chill down my spine.

Of course it *had* to be Fimochka. That's why Pauline wanted a son so desperately—and only a son. She had even imagined that he would be fair-haired—like her brother who had been shot. Fima.

Of course all my suggestions went out the window. Fima would go on living. Despite racism. Despite wars. Despite the bullets in the back of the neck.

15

But there was still a long time to go before Fima was born. For the moment the year of 1949* was cracking and smoldering along like a torch in a Fascist procession. It was a year of bloody *autos-da-fé*, a year of jubilees which fused together with the *autos-da-fé* into one indissoluble unity.

They drew nearer like a heavy train. Everything around began to shake and tremble—even the earth. And Pauline and I as it were stood by the throbbing railway line, longing to lie down on the ground so as not to be dragged beneath the wheels by the whirlwind.

By now it was not only *Pravda* but all the papers that were being gutted of Jewish names. One highly placed anti-Semitic writer remarked wittily that the papers had all taken on a Sholom Aleichem tint. *Krokodil†* went mad with jokes about Jewish names—and it has to be admitted that they were funny.

People prepared for the festivals as they did in Tsarist times for the raising of the Banner. People tuned up their voices. The windows in Jewish houses rang from the sound.

At first it was only a small banner that was raised. The chorus of newspapers sang out in one voice: "A true son of the Soviet people. Throughout your whole life and in all your work you have been an inspiring example." That referred to Lavrenti Beria. The fiftieth birthday of a true son. That festival passed, the stench increased.

For some reason, Japanese names were beginning to crackle in the jubilee bonfires. It appeared that they were generals poisoning us by the use of bacteria. They set aside a special festival for the poisoners. Like poisonous smoke bombs, they gave the jubilee stench a sharp and repulsive savor.

* The year of Stalin's seventieth birthday. [Translator]
† Illustrated satirical magazine published three times a month. [Translator]

"Why stand on ceremony with these Japanese and with our own criminals?" I heard at one of the meetings. "String them up on the same tree."

The preparations were almost over. We were waiting for the raising of the Great Banner itself. The organs of law and order, of course, were brought up to a state of full military preparedness: our local policeman excelled himself. He rushed into our room without knocking. Or rather, he knocked and flung open the door simultaneously without waiting for an answer. He wanted to take us by surprise.

Which he did. Pauline was sitting at the table with a pencil in her hand leafing through a reference journal—*Chemical Abstracts*. I was at the windowsill correcting four copies of the manuscript of a novel. The whole room was white with paper—it looked exactly as if we were preparing leaflets.

The burly young man, his cheeks afire with the true Komsomol glow, asked to see my residence permit. What else could he do? He had known for a long time that I was a native of Moscow, registered according to all the regulations (if we hadn't been, he certainly would have had something to talk to me about!), and so he didn't bother to listen to my reply, but stared anxiously at the papers on the windowsill, the table, the floor.

"Did you type all this yourself?" he asked, when the silence had stretched on unendurably. "No? You must be spending a lot to have it typed, then?"

Another silence.

"What language is that book in?" he asked, stepping over to Pauline.

"English," she replied.

"English? I see. And you can read it? Just like our own books?" he asked, almost amicably.

"Yes," Pauline answered, "I can read it." Then suddenly her eyes widened and flashed with mischief. "Would you like to hear a page? It's good."

"Very well," the policeman answered, perplexed, and took a seat by the door, staring around the walls and the corners of the room as before, then suddenly standing up again, as if he were searching for a secret hiding place.

Under Pauline's big hand-embroidered cushion there were several red volumes. Pauline had bought them, even though we didn't have enough money to buy bread at the time. They were marked with colored bookmarks to show the places Pauline turned to when the tide of anti-Semitism was splashing at our feet. It was from these quotations that she drew strength whenever she felt herself weakening.

She leaned over the chair and took one of the volumes, stuffed with its markers, from behind the cushion, and began to read in a high, clear voice, exceptionally distinctly, so that each word, as they say in the theater, bounced off her teeth.

" 'There has been a great deal of witty comment regarding the fact that *Russian Banner* has more often behaved like *Prussian Banner*. Chauvinism remains chauvinism, no matter of what national brand it is.' You understand?" asked Pauline, raising her eyes.

"N-no," he admitted honestly. Then he looked at the binding—"Vladimir Ilyich? What volume is that?"

Pauline slowly took out another volume with a marker. Even he couldn't fail to understand this quotation.

" 'The hatred of the Tsarist regime was directed principally against the Jews. Tsarism knew very well how to employ the vilest prejudices of the most benighted sections of the population against the Jews, to organize pogroms, if not to run them directly.' " Pauline didn't look up, but went on to the next quotation.

" 'The organization of Black Hundred pogroms, and the beating of Jewish students, Jewish revolutionaries, and Jewish workers goes on progressing and spreading. . . . The school, the press, and the parliamentary tribune are all being used to disseminate this dark, wild, evil hatred for Jews. It is not only offshoots of the Black Hundreds who are involved in this black and evil work, but reactionary professors, scientists, journalists, and members of parliament. Millions and millions of rubles are being spent in order to poison the understanding of the workers. Not one nationality in Russia is as persecuted and humiliated as the Jews. Persecution of the Jews has taken on completely incredible proportions in the last few years.' "

Pauline read more and more slowly, pausing at each punctuation mark as if she were about to ask the policeman to summarize the arguments. I began to feel a certain sympathy for him. He shuffled his shiny boots with their crumpled tops and wiped his crimson face with a handkerchief he kept grasped in his fist. He had been ready for anything except this—quotations from Lenin were for him, as for us, almost a national anthem which should be listened to standing up.

Pauline raised her eyes to his, and, good soul that she was, decided to offer him some reward for his suffering. She asked him as she might a guest whether he would like some tea. "A glass of tea? With cherry preserve. We've got stoneless cherries?"

No, no. He shook his fuddled head.

So Pauline carried on. She warmed to her theme. Now the most basic truths had to be demonstrated.

" 'Greater Russian chauvinism, like any other form of nationalism [she stressed the word *any other*, so that the young lieutenant shouldn't feel himself too isolated], goes through various phases. Until 1905 we were familiar with national-reactionaries. Then after the Revolution we had national-liberals. And inevitably, later, there will appear national-democrats. . . .' "

The policeman vanished as swiftly as he had come. Pauline heard the sound of the door closing and looked up to find him gone.

We didn't fall asleep until morning. The red-cheeked policeman with the child-like wondering eyes of a simple country boy had aroused disturbing thoughts; the injection in the vial marked "Chauvinism" had a great deal in common with Hitler's injections that brought such horror to the people in his concentration camps. Would many survive? We remembered Lyubka Mukhina and the Free Ukraine and realized that many things of which we had once been proud were rolling downhill now, rolling toward the jubilee.

Soon the Great Banner was raised higher than ever. It floated in the blue sky as from a balloon, shot with the colors from the searchlights, crimson and blue. And the printing presses and the rustling pages of the jubilee newspaper outpourings resounded like a mellow church bell. Who could have even entertained the thought that Vladimir Ilyich's righteous anger against Russian obscurantists would not be enough to prevent him from becoming one of the precursors of Stalin's obscurantism, and that he would bear a definite share of responsibility for today's pogroms? Thoughts like that could have occurred to our deceived generation only in a nightmare.

I shall be obliged to return to this agonizing twentieth-century paradox later.

But everything in its own time.

"They're beating the Jews." "No way out for them." "They're the lowest of the low." "Victims of Point Five." The students of the Russian literature department sometimes wisecracked. They weren't malicious jokes—more often sympathetic.

"They're just poking fun at you," repeated one of the professors, the wife of the rector, Galkina Fedoruk, meaning well. Then she moved on to subjects which excited her much more. Indeed, what was there for her to worry about? She wasn't the butt of the jokes.

But for Pauline and me matters were worse than they had ever been, although on the surface things seemed to be going very well indeed; Pauline had defended her candidate's dissertation, and it had been a festival day in the faculty. I received a congratulatory letter from Konstantin Simonov, the editor-in-chief of *Novy Mir*, telling me that my novel about the university would soon be published in the magazine. Simonov was going off somewhere for six months and asked me to go and see his deputy, Krivitsky.

In the *Novy Mir* waiting room was a man of about forty whom I didn't recognize. He was sitting on a sofa, a thick-set man with a high forehead and the shoulders of a boxer. He told me with a calm smile that he was gathering material for a novel. "I've decided to try another genre," he said jokingly.

From the way that the people around me listened to him, trying to catch every single word, I realized that he must be highly respected, a very important writer, clearly someone who was widely known. He had an air of confidence, self-collectedness, a force for good, and I remember that I lost my nervousness and went into the newspaper office somewhat encouraged.

When he left I asked who he was. "Borshchagovsky, Alexander Mikhailovich," I was told.

Borshchagovsky! I leaped to my feet and dashed to the window. I watched him go. He walked along the pavement in much the same way as he talked, not hurrying, confidently, as if he owned the paving stones. And yet all around him, from every newspaper kiosk, the headlines had been shouting for days that he was a literary saboteur, a Judas, an agent of imperialism.

What reserves of inner strength he must have had to remain calm when every newspaper hound in the land was baying at his heels, when any knock on the door might mean that they had come for him, and to go on working as if nothing had happened.

"Your p-piece will be in the n-next n-number," said Alexander Krivitsky, a cheerful stammerer who was nevertheless a business-like man with brisk impetuous movements. "The back-door Simonov," as people called him, was talking to me in the editor-in-chief's office, a big room, two or three times larger than the waiting room. "It's been d-decided."

Of course I dashed to buy the next number of *Novy Mir* and went through it at the newsstand. The first thing was a poem by Nikolai Gribachov. Then there was Vadim Kozhevnikov's play *The Fiery River*.

"Well, n-next time. I p-promise you. On my word as a gentleman!"

In the next number there was Anatoly Sofronov, the chief orator from the Writers' Union for the banner-raising ceremony. He contributed a stillborn play called *Becket's Career*.

"Well, it'll be in next month's. Here's my hand on it."

Next month's had another play—*The Green Street* by Anatoly Surov, who wouldn't have let go of the staff of the banner even if it had been white hot.

Even today it's hard to believe that *Novy Mir* was the spiritual home of the banner-bearers.

I realized that there was no point in my expecting anything when Alexander Yulievich Krivitsky, rolling those cheerful, slightly protuberant, round Jewish eyes, which seemed so well-suited for taking a broad view of things, returned a play by someone unknown to me about the heroic uprising in the Warsaw Ghetto, without so much as reading it. "Even if it's a work of genius," he said, "the Russian people aren't ready for it yet—Seryozhka!" he yelled.

And he dashed off, his jacket flying open, to greet his next guest. Seryozhka—Sergei Vasiliev—was a gloomy, square-faced newspaper poet with arms that dangled down to his knees. He had come straight from the Writers' Union, where that morning he had been reciting his new poem, "People Russia Would Be Better Rid Of."

A pause to consider the poem: It's worth it! Give the rostrum to the "poetic encyclopedia of 1949," whose heroes:

> . . . met and argued how they could
> The closer get together,
> To smear and slander everything,
> And smear and slander better.
>
> They tried to choose a number one,
> A leader, a commander,
> Someone who could show them
> the finest way to slander.
>
> One said, "I'm for Yusovsky."
> "Borshchagovsky," said another.
> "Plotke-Danin's the man for me,"
> Said Holtzman and Bleiman.
> Brenstein backed Finkelstein,
> Cherniak came out for Goffeshefer,
> B. Kedrov wanted Selektor,
> M. Gelfond favored B. Runin.
> Munblit, he wanted Holtzman.
> They raised such bedlam,
> And let themselves go,
> Until they decided to live in anarchy.

At points like this the paper *Russian Banner* would scream *"Gewalt!"* in parody of the persecuted Yids.

What was left that could possibly deceive anyone? Even the most stupid first-year student could deal with a learned, well-thought-out article as he would with a cabbage head, quickly finding his way through to the stump, the core, the real center, whose meaning was always the same—"Beat the Jews!"

And what a smell there was in the kitchen itself. When the editor-in-chief of *Literaturnaya Gazeta*, Professor Ermilov, signed a column in 1949 containing the latest anti-Semitic material, he defended himself with a cynical grin: "Senile decay setting in." It hadn't, of course, set in of its own accord. It had been brought on in a most efficient way. And in the evenings that same paper provided space for the outpourings of the amateur "form and truth" ensemble which mocked everything that had been done during the day, even, sometimes, by themselves.

I remember one well-nourished lady journalist playing the role of a fighter against cosmopolitanism, using histrionic pathos to describe a certain female critic with a Jewish nose.

> She does not belong to us.
> *I* belong to us.
> There is no room for her.
> There is room for me.

Laughing, they beat the Jews. Jeering, they turned them out into the street. But they buried them quietly. In the traditional way.

Grossman, Yuzovsky, Altman, Zavich—the older, better-known writers were trampled to death. If you go through the yellowing pages of contemporary papers, you'll find the headline "RENEGADES!" and confusion below. The younger ones were dealt with more calmly, just so that they should learn their place. I was the greenest of the prose writers. I wasn't even a member of the Writers' Union. I was simply kicked aside, like a small animal.

People say of 1949, "Oh, it was like the Middle Ages." That maligns the Middle Ages. For example, in 1388, the Jews of Trotsk and Brest were granted a Royal Letters Patent, which declared that "If a Jew is found to be not guilty of the offense of which he is charged then his accuser shall suffer the punishment which threatened the Jew." What would have happened if Sergei Vasiliev had been made to answer under the law of 1388?

Ours was a medieval nightmare. The jubilee year of 1949 moved on into the summer, devouring the bones of our Jews to an extent matched only by the way the Tartar Khans gorged themselves on the bones of captured Russians. Then came 1950, and Stalin's personal re-creation of the regime of Arakcheev. Then 1951.

I received more congratulations for my work, this time by telegram from Fyodor Panferov, the editor-in-chief of *October*. "We'll print it soon, very soon."

Pauline was presented with her diploma for Candidate of Chemical Sciences, in a thick binding with gold tooling on the cover. But for some reason she wasn't appointed to a job. Nothing in an institute, or in a factory, even though the desk of the chairman of the employment commission was piled high with requests for organic chemists.

Then Academician Kazansky told Pauline that she should go to the Kaluga Institute of Mineral Fuels, where they were in great need of a scientific assistant. Everything was agreed.

In the institute, Pauline was received by a taciturn middle-aged woman in an old lab coat. She was the lab director. Her hands were yellow from handling chemicals. She shook Pauline's hand firmly, like a man. It was clear that she was a hard worker, one of those academic women who are always to be found in the shadows of the Russian academy, which is so proud of its men. Her round, tired face—tired like almost all women's faces after the war—showed genuine happiness. She so much needed an assistant. So much! She could not believe she had been lucky enough to find a graduate from Kazansky's school.

She went to the personnel department herself to fetch the form. Pauline filled it in immediately; as the laboratory director laid it on one side ("That's just a formality, we'll look at that later") and showed Pauline her desk, her extractor hood, her fan, and introduced her to the two lab assistants who were to work under her. "Come back in three days," she said as Pauline left. "No, don't bother to telephone. Just come ready to work!"

Three days later she said to Pauline in genuine surprise: "You know, for some reason the personnel people won't accept you."

Seeing the dismay on Pauline's face, she said, to give her time to recover herself, "I'll see what I can do. . . ."

A year and a half later, there was an excited postcard, "I've done it!" But by that time Pauline was in the Sklifosovsky Institute Hospital.

In the next academic institute, Pauline was received by a polished, elegantly dressed assistant director, like an English lord, one of the breed of administrators for whom a scientific laboratory is something like a kitchen—if you do condescend to look in, it's only for a moment—and who have now appeared in vast numbers throughout the scientific world. He was kindness itself. He didn't so much speak as sing: "A recommendation from the chair of Academician Zelinsky and the letter from Academician Kazansky provide the best guarantee we could ask for. It's beautiful. No problem at all. Zelinsky's school is the pride of Soviet chemistry. You need have no doubt . . ."

He was just as kind and mellifluous a week later: "Unfortunately, you were too late. They've already taken a man on. So annoying." And his shameless, slightly protuberant eyes betrayed almost genuine sympathy.

In the next institute the assistant director couldn't maintain the tone required of him, and for an instant—no more—his eyes showed something of the expression of an unfortunate footman who's been ordered into the hall to lie, to say that her ladyship is not at home. . . .

How kind, how attentive, how beautifully dressed all the respectable murderers were, and how self-righteously angry they would all be if anyone were to call them that. But they were all able to produce the attentive smile and the barely noticeable shrug of the shoulders that pushed Pauline one step nearer the precipice.

Kazansky was deeply embarrassed. Whenever he saw Pauline, his confusion showed all over his face. She even began to feel that he was deliberately avoiding her. But that couldn't have been the case. It was simply that he had so much else to do. He went into battle with his visor open and his face in full view, alongside other old university teachers. Sometimes they fought singlehandedly, but more often shoulder to shoulder.

When Kazansky finally realized that he wasn't going to be able to defend Pauline alone, he gave her diploma work to Academician Nesmeyanov to read. Nesmeyanov swiftly telephoned the Ministry of Higher Education to tell them not to be fools.

When Nesmeyanov hadn't been able to defend the talented chemist Lev Bergelson, the son of the Jewish writer Bergelson who had been shot, and who had himself been condemned to death by starvation, he brought Academician Nazarov in to help.

Ivan Nikolaevich Nazarov, who at about that time received the Stalin Prize first-class for the Nazarov Adhesive and who was at the height of his fame, took on translation work in his own name. Lev Bergelson did the translating, and Academician Nazarov received the fees through the mail and passed them on to Bergelson. Everyone was aware of what was going on, and there was a flood of work in Nazarov's name.

It wasn't that they were protecting Jews per se. They never divided people into blonds and brunets. They defended their talented students with their own bodies—the way a mother will protect her own child, and if need be take the bullet meant for him.

It was this instinctive protest that allowed them, when they were accused of conniving with the Jews, to respond with an angry challenge, as did Academician Vladimir Mikhailovich Rodionev, a man of remarkable directness and courage: "The Russian intelligentsia has always shielded the Jews from pogroms. And I count myself a member of the Russian intelligentsia."

But "the black raven" carried off Academician Balandin, one of the country's most outstanding chemists. And our university friends fell one by one, including Gena Faibusovich. Inside the university, people whispered the names of those "scientists" who were really stool pigeons, who had only to lift the telephone for a man to fall. Their reports were never checked.

And the reports gathered strength. For those who wrote them, reports were like indulgences. So why did our old professors remain so inexplicably frank with many of us, so defenselessly open, when at meetings of the academic councils they would sit in motionless gloom? But the main thing was that they protected us and put their hope in us, for what else was there for them to put their hope in?

"Work. Don't let yourself be distracted," Kazansky kept telling Pauline. "They won't have an effect on me. . . ."

"Separate the wheat from the chaff, Grisha," Academician Gudzy advised me constantly. "Be sure your eyes don't stop distinguishing the light from the dark."

"Saadi once said no one throws stones at a tree that doesn't bear fruit," said the professor of languages Pyotr Stepanovich Kuznetsov consolingly, looking at Pauline and me with his kindly blue eyes. Kuznetsov was a stooping, jerky man, with a nervous habit of wiping his palm down his threadbare jacket. (Drying his hands, his students called it, and to avoid having to deal with his nervousness, we would rush over and shake hands with him.)

Our old professors weren't guilty of anything, but they felt it all the same, because of their burning shame for what was going on in the university that was their home. . . .

Kazansky telephoned everyone, and finally found a job for Pauline. He told her to go at once to the Veterinary Academy, where they'd been searching day and night for a good organic chemist.

The whole thing turned out to be a tragi-comedy. Two such different academies of science—hundreds of people laughed as they told each other the story. What a step down! Everyone found it very funny. But Pauline was at the end of her tether. When she set off to see the veterinarians, she put on her only decent dress, a light blue one, so that she wouldn't look like a starving beggar.

She was shown into the institute where they were making a serum from horses' urine, which was believed to be useful in many illnesses, including cancer. The main difficulty was that while they had obtained the serum, they didn't know its chemical structure, and so could not discover why it worked. They wanted a chemist; they longed for a chemist. This latest panacea for all ills attracted such a flood of suffering people that the institute lived under a state of siege. No one was allowed to visit the laboratories. "A chemist is coming" sounded through the corridors like a watchword. No one even asked Pauline for her passport.

The short, thickset, balding professor rose in delight when she came in to his office and showed her the rooms he'd set aside for the chemistry laboratory; he then took her off to meet the colleagues she'd be working with. He asked her to write out a list of the chemicals she would want. "We'll get everything you need," he said. "Come tomorrow, Pauline Ionovna. See you in the morning."

While Pauline was sitting at the professor's desk writing out her list of requirements, a young woman in a black velvet dress stormed into the room. Pauline had noticed her previously while she was being introduced to the other workers. They were all wearing white lab coats but she'd seen this one woman in evening dress. Pauline had thought she was probably going straight to the theater after work. The woman paid no attention to Pauline, nor to the colonel who had just arrived to see the professor, but screamed angrily at the professor himself: "Why have you chosen this girl? What can she do for you?" The professor cut her off in midsentence and took her out of the office.

When Pauline left, she met someone she knew in the corridor, and told him in a state of complete bewilderment that she probably wasn't going to get the job after all. Some woman had come charging in and . . .

"In a black dress?" her friend asked and began to shake with laughter. "You should have told her that you already had a husband and weren't thinking of changing him." He was laughing so hard that he almost fell over.

But that was actually what happened. In the morning when she went to get her pass for the institute, a head was thrust through the window to tell her that there was no pass ready for her, and that it looked as if there wasn't going to be one at all. Two academies, and half the university went on laughing. In the academicians' sanatorium they lived on the story for a week. Laughter's a great healer.

The only people who didn't find it funny were Pauline and myself. Our money was running out. I had a student grant which in today's money would be about 24 rubles a month (10 pounds or 25 dollars) and the doctors who came to see Pauline seemed to know only one phrase—"Feed her up, feed her up." I tried to earn a little extra where I could. I taught in a literary group. I edited, or rather totally rewrote, the memoirs of a colonel. I took wartime sketches to the Soviet Information Office, until one intelligent elderly woman who was an editor there told me that a new boss had taken over the information office and my name had been crossed off the list of writers.

We lived in debt. Once a week we went to buy bones. They were sold from a booth near the meat market. We used to have to stand in line for long periods, never less than two hours. It was a windy corner. That winter it blew so hard that the people in line would look at each other and wonder who would get frostbite first. We used to stuff the bones into a big bag and hang it out of the window. That was our refrigerator. The bones lasted a whole week—at least our soup wasn't totally devoid of nourishment.

Once Pauline had to wait for half a day. In front of her was a worker in a quilted jacket, ragged with acid burns. He was stamping his feet to try to keep warm. A woman wearing horn-rimmed glasses came up and asked what sort of bones there were today, was it pork or beef? Someone answered that it'd probably be pork. She went away, and the worker in the quilted jacket turned to Pauline and said angrily, "Jews, they expect a choice. But we take whatever they give us." As he stepped closer and saw how white Pauline's face was, he grew concerned. "You're absolutely frozen. Look, take my jacket. It'll warm you."

Every morning Pauline set out to look for work. She looked at advertisements in the papers, on street boards, at factory entrances. From time to time her university friends telephoned to tell her of openings. She went around to all the big chemical plants—Dragomilovsky, Derbenevsky, Karpovsky, where she'd worked during the war. No one would take her on. She didn't even bother to ask anymore what kind of work it was or how much the pay was—she'd have taken anything just to keep alive.

One day there was a phone call from the University Komsomol Committee, to say that she was on the roster for holiday office duty at Regional Committee headquarters. Pauline turned up at the committee with the paper the university had sent. The instructor looked at the document and cursed.

"What's this rubbish you've brought with you?" he bellowed. "Filth like this to do a responsible job at the Regional Committee!"

"Filth?"

The document from the University Komsomol showed the names of the two girls who'd come. There was Pauline, and a second girl called Freedman. The instructor jabbed his finger at the name Freedman.

"Can't you see for yourself what I mean by rubbish?"

Pauline's turn of duty lasted half a day, and she sat there in headquarters forcing down her tears, and freezing in the north wind. She was determined not to tell her friend, who was even bluer from the cold than she was herself, what their reception had been like.

Young people these days may find all this hard to understand. Why didn't Pauline just walk out? Why not take her friend with her? Was it that she was afraid? No, she had been brought up in the war years. People might behave like swine, but discipline is discipline. That morning we didn't even have any bread in the house.

I have remembered all the events of that day because in the evening after Pauline's duty was over we met at her uncle's house where to mark the festival they'd prepared the traditional bowl of vegetable salad—as they'd managed to do all through the war. Everyone came, all the relatives, and I almost wept as I watched Pauline waiting as the salad was piled onto her plate, sitting there like a little orphan, her hands folded on her lap.

To her uncle she was an orphan. To the Regional Committee of the Party—an orphan. To the personnel departments—an orphan.

It was almost an inborn trait. Her own uncle, her own Party, her own personnel officers . . .

I counted the days to the date of publication of the magazine with my novel about student life, although even when it came out we wouldn't be so well off that we could afford to forget what it was to be hungry. But when the magazine did come out, the money was only just enough to pay our debts. And to buy some felt boots for my mother so that her feet wouldn't freeze when she was lining up for bones.

No matter how much it makes me blush now, I feel obliged to write something about that half-forgotten student novel. I have no right to pass it by in silence.

"Grisha, during the war were you by any chance in the demolition squads?" Fyodor Panferov, the gloomy editor-in-chief of *October* asked me reproachfully. "You nearly blew up the whole magazine! Just imagine what a row there'd have been if *October* had brought out that novel of yours about students in the philology department without making any reference to Stalin's recent discoveries in the field of linguistics? It's all right, don't worry. I know it wasn't deliberate malice," he said to calm me down. "You've got an alibi; you wrote it before Stalin's discussion on linguistics took place. But there's no alibi for the magazine . . . understand? Would you like some tea?"

Aromatic tea was brought in. I was discouraged, and yet proud that Fyodor Panferov was talking with me so forthrightly. And even giving me tea . . . I respected him for the fact that every year, at the risk maybe even of his life, he bombarded Stalin with letters about the tragic state of ruin of the Volga kolkhozes and others, of peasant children who hadn't seen sugar since the day they were born. Fyodor Panferov was a true son of his native soil, and he was ready to lay down his body to defend it. He did not have to go as far as that, but despair had driven him to drink.

I looked at his pallid yet strong face, and I remember that I didn't feel in the least frightened. I was ashamed. Moreover, I felt that I had been brought to my knees—I had stopped believing in myself.

If HE, amid all the hubbub of affairs of state, from among all the branches of learning, had chosen linguistics to write about, then that must mean linguistics was the most important subject of all, the spearhead of the ideological life of the country. Yet about that time I was listening to lectures by Galkina Fedoruk, and it had never even crossed my mind that her linguistic course could have any social significance at all. A friend of mine spent his time jotting down "Galkinisms," linguistic pearls perpetrated by the good-hearted lady, which made the whole class roar with laughter.

What kind of writer must I be if I couldn't even penetrate the real essence of those lectures? I couldn't see the woods for the trees. There I was, enthusiastically scribbling things about youthful egoism, about the small-minded Komsomol noisemakers who were so active among the young, and had no more influence on them than the moon and the tides.

It was just like being at the epicenter of an earthquake and not noticing the ground tremble beneath your feet. If I was so blind and deaf, then there wasn't much future for me in literature!

It wasn't till a year and a half later, constantly encouraged by Fyodor Panferov, who seemed to feel real goodwill toward me, that I finally made myself sit down at the windowsill that served me as a writing desk and selflessly stuff the book with all the newspaper-linguistic "Marrist"* problems that I was convinced were vitally important for the life of the country . . . no matter how remote they seemed to me.

Yet, alas, after all that, I still managed to turn my long-suffering novel into rubbish! And now, looking back over the past, I ask myself the bitter question: I, as a then-young writer, an "intellectual" as Fyodor Panferov persisted in regarding me, was I so very different in depth and independence of mind from the simplest country boy, from the policeman who looked so anxiously at Pauline and me as if he were afraid we were up to something bad? Simply because *Pravda* had issued a warning about what the Jews might be up to? Following the truth to the end of the road can be terrifying. But once you've started, there's no going back. Was I so very different from, say, those private soldiers of the internal security forces with machine guns in their hands, who drove the Crimean Tartars from their homes—old men, women, children? Those boys in uniforms were told that it was Stalin's orders. That all the Crimean Tartars were traitors—including babies still at the breast. And the soldiers, just like me, had taken Stalin's word unques-

* Marr, who had been for many years the undisputed arbiter of Russian linguistics, was a particular target of Stalin's essay on linguistics and Marxism. [Translator]

tioningly, blindly, with unswerving confidence in him and—consequently—
in his infallibility.

When HE said something . . .

So how was I in any way different from them—I, a writer, and an
intellectual, God forgive me? The only thing, perhaps, is that if I had
been in their place I might not have actually massacred children. . . .

As I stood in the muttering, angry bone line, cursing at the miserable
life we all had to lead, I learned that I had been invited to present myself
at the Union of Soviet Writers of the USSR. From today's standpoint, it's
obvious that I almost deserved the honor, although, of course, that day I
had no suspicion of the real reasons for the summons and proudly invented
all sorts of significance for the invitation.

It was my first official invitation to the Writers' Union, but the names
of the secretaries were widely known and respected, and Pauline came running up with the news, quite out of breath. Maybe the phone call meant
that our fate had finally taken a turn for the better.

Who it was exactly that was so anxious to see me, I don't know to this
day. Almost all the leaders of the Writers' Union—Alexander Fadeev, Fyodor Panferov, Boris Gorbatov, Leonid Sobolev—and some generals were
gathered in the smoke-filled office.

The generals left. Boris Gorbatov went and sat by the window. Then
he rose and began to pace the room, up and down, up and down. Alexander
Fadeev was leaning back in a chair at the desk, which had a pile of folders
on it. One of them turned out to be my personal file. Fadeev rose ponder-
ously to greet me and shook hands as if we were old friends. He gave my
name to someone who was standing by humbly with his hands full of
papers, and as the secretary went out he looked at me, his eyes sparkling
with excitement, as if I were some rising film star, or the student Gavrilo
Prinzip, whom no one had ever heard of that day but who tomorrow would
fire the shots that killed the Archduke.

Fadeev immediately began to address me with the intimate form "ty."

"I'm delighted to welcome you, my friend. This week we're bringing
you into the Writers' Union. Pleased? Good. We need young men like you,
just back from the war. People of character. Your election is all settled.
We've been waiting a long time for someone like you. People who are
coming into literature from the battlefield. As we all did in our time. Men
who've been face to face with death don't give in easily. Have you got a
flat? . . . No? . . . Well, we'll find you one. Has your novel been published
in book form yet? . . . Only in *October*? We'll get things moving."

He stopped talking and smoothed back his gray hair, stroking his
silvery scalp, as if he were a trifle embarrassed, and finally began to speak
again, hurriedly, using those same excited tones Pauline had heard so often

from people who were lying to her when they told her there was no work to be had.

"The thing is, my friend, we want you to declare your support for the Party—loudly, so everyone can hear what you're saying, all over the country. You know, bang your fist on the table. So people can see that here is a man! A soldier!"

He smiled, and took a sheet of paper from the table.

"This week there's been all that discussion about Vasily Grossman's* novel *For a Just Cause*. Have you seen the reviews?" He took out a file of cuttings, and leafed through them, reading out the headlines: " 'On a false course . . .' " Then, with great emphasis, "And this is a leading article. Here's another one—'On Grossman's novel *For a Just Cause'*—the same sort of thing."

He kept on flicking nervously through the cuttings, throwing several of them to one side. Then he closed the file and put it back in his drawer. He held a slip of paper out to me. It had several topics set out on it—the framework for an article. *Distortion of the subject. One-sided presentation . . .* "Just think about them. It's important that these ideas should come from a boy like you. Someone young, someone who isn't tainted by all the old squabbles. Someone who's seen service, got a few medals."

"And who also has curly black hair and a hooked nose," I said, pursing my thick Jewish lips.

For some reason he glanced at Boris Gorbatov, then stroked his gray hair and looked me in the face, talking haltingly, tensely, but as though he and I were in full agreement.

"I'm glad you're so quick on the uptake. Judge for yourself. Why are we getting all these accusations of anti-Semitism? We don't want them. It's not a question of that. Let the truth about Vasily Grossman be told not only by Arkady Perventsev or Mikhail Bubennov—they'll say it anyway—but by Grigory Svirsky as well. Like an equal."

I jumped to my feet and thanked the world-famous writer for putting me on equal terms with Arkady Perventsev even before he'd met me. And even with Mikhail Bubennov, who had once managed to get himself convicted for anti-Semitism. Admittedly that was after his famous drunken brawl in Moscow with the playwright Surov, in the course of which Bubennov had jabbed Surov in the backside with a fork.

Not surprisingly, that was the last invitation I had to the Writers' Union for many years. Of course, that didn't stop the literary pogrom. Pedestals don't stay empty for long. Another candidate was found, one whose particulars were similar to mine on paper. A Jew who'd fought in

---

* A Jewish writer. [Translator]

the war, and who was a young writer. All the essentials. I noticed him that very day, in the waiting room. A puny individual with shifty eyes. He was clutching a folder and talking respectfully with Anatoly Sofronov himself, then he dashed to the door of the first secretary's office as if he were running for a bus. But no, he wasn't too late, this totally unknown—at that time, anyway—energetic boy in brightly colored foreign-made socks. Two days later everyone knew his name. Not only the members of the preparatory plenum of the Writers' Union, warmly applauding the man who had so passionately revealed the truth about Vasily Grossman, but the whole of reading Russia. . . .

Alexander Chakovsky's star was in the ascendant.* A yellow star with a red border, which indicated a useful Jew.

Pauline knew from my face that the official reception with the secretary was not going to bring about any changes in our life. At least, not good ones. And what about bad ones? Well, things couldn't get any worse.

Except for the Inguletsk quarry. That was worse. And the gas ovens. But we didn't believe that they could come. We didn't want to believe.

Pauline dressed in silence to go out to look for work. For a year and a half now she had been getting up each morning as if she had a job and going off to nowhere in particular. All she met were sneering rejections. She went out for today's insult—that's what we used to call her daily excursions: "Looking for insults."

Everywhere people needed chemists. Yet everywhere they spat in her face. She had been around not only to all the institutes and factories, but even small workshops where people looked at her candidate's diploma in its gold-tooled leather binding as if it were a crown. But what would a small workshop do with a crown?

Finally she hid her diploma in a closet and tried to get a job as an ordinary engineer, even working on the production of mercury, one of the most dangerous of all processes. Perhaps they'd need her there. In the factory personnel department they didn't so much as look at her passport. Three men came into the room. They looked her up and down and went out again furtively—to phone somewhere. They needed her desperately, yet they didn't take her on. What were they afraid of? That she might throw a bomb into the mercury workshops? That evening she was so downcast that the following day I refused to let her go out alone. I went with her. . . .

In the metro we met an acquaintance, a lieutenant-colonel, a journalist who was also a candidate of sciences. He was wearing a short, tight civilian

---

* At the time of writing, Chakovsky was the editor-in-chief of *Literaturnaya Gazeta*, the official weekly newspaper of the Soviet Writers' Union. [Translator]

overcoat, with the hem coming down. It turned out that he'd been dismissed from the army on some fabricated pretext and he'd just been offered a job in the City Committee of the Party—as a newspaper-seller.

"What's wrong with that?" the boss of the press department had screamed at him. "Your people have always been traders."

I refused to believe the colonel. I simply couldn't accept that on the City Committee people were coming out into the open with such anti-Semitic babble.

I still had a lot to learn.

Pauline and I traveled out to the edge of the city, to an institute which Academician Shemyakin had told Pauline was not so much an institute as a pig-in-the-poke.

"It might not even be an institute at all, but a rubbish dump," he warned. "There isn't a single serious scientist on the staff."

"Doesn't matter, I'll take it," Pauline answered swiftly.

"It may be very dangerous to work there. You'll get sick."

"I'll take it!"

And so there we were, Pauline and I, walking the streets of a rundown part of town. I asked her to give me her word that if the work was really dangerous to her health she wouldn't take the job. It wasn't right for anyone as sickly as she was . . . But she clenched her teeth and wouldn't reply.

It was getting dark already. Ahead of us we could see the windows of what looked like a palace, burning brightly in the dusk. There were rows of grenadiers on parade. And on the other side, dozens of cars were drawn up in more rows, black and green. Even the trees opposite the palace were pruned back hard to an equal size, like new recruits. And a brass plate polished like gold caught the last rays of the setting sun.

Pauline slowed down.

"We're wasting our time. They'll never take me in a place like this. Not a chance . . ."

My heart sank. She hadn't even been turned down, yet her steps were faltering. That old orphan feeling again.

We got near enough to read the brass plate: THE STALIN TANK AND ARMORED VEHICLES ACADEMY. We stopped, defeated. If even small workshops wouldn't take her . . .

But then Pauline suddenly shouted that we'd come to the wrong place. Look at the number. What a relief. And she dragged me farther along, away from the palatial columns.

We wandered about for a long time. Around little side turnings. Behind sheds. It took a long time to find the place we were looking for. From a distance it looked more like a garage or a stable. Its walls were peeling, like an army barracks. It looked as if it had been stuck into the earth and left there. It had no brass plates.

"This is quite a different matter," said Pauline cheerfully.

At the entrance we were stopped by a soldier with a machine gun, who phoned for an officer to come. Pauline was given a pass, and I was sent out to wait in the street.

Pauline reappeared after a couple of hours, and set off across the road toward me, not looking at the traffic. She was almost run down by a tram. Her eyes were shining the way they had done on our wedding day. From the other side of the road she shouted, "They may take me."

The tram roared past, and another one rang its warning bell at us. We were still standing on opposite sides of the road.

"What about the danger?" I shouted.

"I didn't ask!"

Another tram groaned past.

"Did they look at your passport?"

The tram moved away, and she flung herself at me.

"They said we've got a business to run. We don't worry about points like that."

And indeed they did take her on. True, not immediately, but six months later when she had filled in a sheaf of forms and had gone through a very severe security check.

Right up to the last minute we couldn't believe that she had done it. How could she? She'd been spurned by every institute of higher education in Moscow, even by the worst, by places where in normal circumstances she would never have shown her face. She'd been turned down by every factory, every workshop. She'd even been refused work by a kind of mobile thing on iron wheels that melted wax in the marketplace.

And yet now she'd been given access to the greatest military secrets—secrets on which the whole future of the Soviet Union depended. The secrets were so secret that Pauline never told even me what she was doing, and I, despite my burning curiosity, never questioned her about them.

O, Russia, Russia! You're completely mad.

When Pauline left the institute that day she didn't know what it was called, nor the names of its senior management, with whom she'd just been talking. The whole thing was like a dream.

A week later she suddenly asked me if it were really true that we had been in . . . that institute. And finally she set off again in search of a job. While the security check was taking place we couldn't just live on the thought of it. Not far from our room there was a chemical factory which was always poisoning the air with chlorine. In the summer we couldn't even open our window. Sometimes the smog was so dense that passing cars had to switch on their headlights and trams kept their warning bells ringing constantly.

"Let's go in," said Pauline with a deep sigh. As usual, her candidate diploma was at home. They might just hire her on the shop floor. The head of the personnel department was an elderly, determined-looking woman in a green denim battledress top and a gun belt. You'd have taken her for a heroine of the Civil War.

She was on the phone for a long time, talking about someone's funeral. Finally she turned to Pauline and said, overjoyed: "Oh, we're desperately short of chemists! There's such a turnover. Take these forms and sit down here to fill them in; it'll be easier for you."

Then she looked at me and barked in the tone of voice used by military patrols when they stop a suspicious character—"Passport!"

I remember being shouted at like that once in Byelorussia: "Halt!"

She glanced at my passport, and didn't hand Pauline the application forms. She just said in a tired voice that perhaps we'd like to ring again in a week or two.

I saw that Pauline had clenched her fists. She went over to the woman, and said in a tense, passionate voice, the like of which I'd never heard her use before: "Then you should write your advertisements differently, like they did in *Russian Banner*. Without lies! 'Chemist wanted. No Jews!' So we could have passed by your stinking factory. That's why you poison us all with chlorine, why we can't open our windows—because you haven't got enough specialists. You haven't even got to the stage of the Kremlin Hospital yet, have you—polished floors and doctors who are there just because they've filled the forms in right? But somehow or other you've still got to make ends meet. Is this the way you're going to do it?"

She stopped. And then she spoke with a pain and despair that frightened me and rang in my ears for a very long time: "All my misery began when the Soviet Army left Krivoi Rog. I always thought they'd recaptured it." She turned to me, her lips trembling. "Recaptured it? If they did, why did the German militia stay there? Why were they never tried? Wherever I turn, there's always Lyubka Mukhina!"

PART THREE

16

You can always feel the omens near the bulletin board of a maternity hospital, which is always surrounded by tired, anxious grandmothers. The board has circles of paper fastened to it. A green circle means that a boy has been born, blue for a girl.

"There are more boys—that means a war's coming," says one anxiously. "Don't ever hem a diaper—that brings bad luck," is the business-like advice from another.

Omens and superstitions surround the newly born.

"Well, your husband's no Russian," said the friendly nurse who brought Pauline her snugly wrapped, bawling son for his feeding. "He must be Armenian, or a Jew."

"A Jew," Pauline replied in the same lighthearted tone, smiling happily and stretching out her arms for the child. "What about it?"

"Well, you're so fair, and the baby's as black as a beetle. There was a woman here once who had a Chinese baby. He was yellow all over, liked boiled milk. And then her husband came along—a boy with a little snub nose, and as fair as can be. She was fair, too. And there they were with a Chinese baby. What a business . . . And you've got a little Jew." She sighed heavily, sympathetically, as if to say, well, it's your bad luck my dear for getting mixed up with these people. But she didn't utter another word.

By the autumn of 1954 the adults had become more restrained; even those people who a year and a half earlier had been spitting medicine in the faces of Jewish doctors held their tongues. But the children . . .

At that time we were living with my mother, in a single cramped room of ten square meters. When Fima appeared we'd been thrown out of our room in the flat. Our son's wooden cot, made in Czechoslovakia, had to be pushed right under the window—there was nowhere else for it. We couldn't let in the fresh air, and at night the stuffiness would keep us awake.

The children played beneath that window. The house was in a workers' district. Just opposite was the "Sharikopodshipnik" ball-bearing factory, where my father had been a fitter before the war. It was *our* factory, almost in the family, the pride of the five-year plans. It had risen out of the swampland. Then a little farther on there was "Dynamo," and the Stalin car factory.

The children who played around under our windows were not of the merchant class. I knew their parents. I'd been at school with some of them. One day the children, smeared from head to foot in clay and sand, were building the "Tsimlanian Sea" in a corner of the courtyard. They towed along their toy dump trucks loaded with soil for the embankments. And two of the lads staggered up with water for the sea in leaky buckets.

"Here comes the Volga!" yelled a thin little Tartar girl, oblivious to everything else, wiping her hands on her ragged dress, with its sleeves rolled up above her elbows. Her narrow eyes were gleaming. "Where are you pouring it? Over here, look! Hurray!" The children gave the dam a name of their own—"Tsimla"—and discussed details of dam building most of us had forgotten.

It was hardly surprising. I remember how they learned to read. The biggest letters around them were the letters in the newspaper headlines of the day, that formed words like "Volga-Don," "Tsimla," "Canal," "Excavator." Fortunately they were still too young to understand the headlines of the anti-cosmopolitan and other similar campaigns. As the children grew into conscious life, year by year, so did the great building programs.

My thoughts were disturbed by loud cries. The boys were fighting over the bucket and calling each other names.

"Yid! Look at him running at the end of a rope!"

"Ugly bastard! Bloody Jew!"

The girl with her sleeves rolled up tried to separate them, but they both yelled at her to keep her nose out of it.

A few windows opened, and worried faces looked out. But by this time the children had dashed off to mend a leak in the dam.

Their parents' heads went back in. The curtains were closed again; why worry, if they weren't killing each other? No one was getting hurt. . . .

I looked angrily at the children, crawling on their hands and knees around their crumbling structure. Once I hadn't been able to restrain myself and I had gone out to them, sat them all on a bench, and told them about the Nazi racists, and how shameful it was for a Soviet person to descend to this sort of name-calling.

The following morning I was awakened by a voice as high-pitched and pure as a bell: "Jew, Jew, makes me spew!" and a bellow of "Dirty Yid!" My lesson hadn't done much good.

The children took what they heard in the communal flats out into the street, the way a foaming stream sweeps up rubbish. Dirty, like winter snow in the city streets, hate spread out into the courtyards, into the school corridors, and one could judge the quality of the father, no matter how he held his tongue, by what his son was shouting out of doors.

Once, in a jampacked hairdressing salon Fima saw two huge portraits hanging on the wall. "That's Grandpa Lenin," he said confidently about one of them. "But who's that?" pointing at the picture of a man wearing the star of a generalissimo.

The shop rocked with laughter. The older men looked at each other in amazement. It seemed that there was now a generation on earth who didn't know who Stalin was. Didn't know at all, didn't even recognize his picture.

Time passes. . . .

When Fima was three he came running home one day in tears. "Papa, I'm not a Tartar, am I?"

It turned out that the boy next to him had taken his sand shovel and pushed him away from the sandbox, telling everyone to have nothing to do with him. "You're not Russian, you're a Tartar."

When he learned that he wasn't a Tartar, he calmed down. But not for long. A year later, when we'd moved and the children in the new neighborhood were mainly the children of well-educated majors and colonels of Pauline's secret institute, my son finally learned who he was. He was told very specifically, in great detail, and the lesson was driven home by a huge black eye.

Fima didn't cry. It seemed he wasn't even worried by the bruise, although his cheek swelled up and must have been painful.

"Papa, is it true that you're a Jew?" he asked, staring at me. It sounded as if he were asking, "Papa, is it true that you're a thief?"

I was busy and muttered some joke in reply.

"And mummy's a Jew too?" he asked, his voice a little more hopeful.

I confirmed that she was, still trying to turn everything into a joke.

"And Granny?" Fima's eyes grew round with horror.

By this time I was seriously worried. My son looked at me with his unwavering child's eyes, the look of someone who's received a terrible blow.

I caught my breath. Was it his turn now? I took him on my knee, hugged him, and, calling for the help of every great man of Jewish birth from Marx to Levitan, whose paintings we'd just been to see in the Tretyakovsky Gallery, managed to restore him to some state of mental balance. But the main thing was that I taught him how to reply if he was chased, insulted, attacked.

"Put your fists up!" I said and began to attack him.

From that day on, whenever my son struck a blow, he did it not with his fist alone, but with his whole body behind it, so that his fist should carry with it the whole weight of his tension and anger.

I had learned that in my time from Sergeant Tsybulka, who admired education and didn't like it when he saw me lurching about on the gym bar like an old sack, while the rest of the air force school roared with laughter.

"Put your fists up, student!" he yelled, and came at me, swinging his iron-hard peasant fists. "It'll come in handy later!"

And it did. My son broke a few "Aryan" noses, and racial equality was established in our courtyard. It was established to such a degree that when we moved to another part of town, the boys from the old house often came over to see Fima, even though we lived at the other end of Moscow. But unfortunately it only held true for the inhabitants of our courtyard.

Once I was taking a bunch of children to the Museum of Fine Arts. We piled onto the back platform of a trolley car, very excited, our shoes well-polished.

As the tram started, a boy jumped onto the platform, holding the door open while he threw his cigarette butt onto the road. He bumped into Fima, who in turn was pushed into a fat woman, who was standing there with a dirty white overall in her hand.

She looked at the boy, and her face turned a sudden bright red, as if she'd been burned. "Hah! There's no getting away from your kind!"

Then Fima became the object of a ceaseless stream of anti-Semitic abuse. It was really high-class stuff, straight out of the Black Hundreds and Fascist papers.

If I hadn't had all the children with me on their way to the museum, I would have hauled her off to the police, as I did when the incident was repeated about a year later. But on this occasion I simply separated her from the children without saying a word. I was tempted to toss some remark at her over my shoulder, but one of the boys grabbed my hand, and whispered that I shouldn't pay any attention.

"It's only Glikeria. She works at the beer-shop by the metro station. My mother calls her the Screamer."

I turned away from the Screamer. She was still carrying on. She seemed unable to stop herself, like a heavy train that can't brake immediately when it's heading down a slope.

The other passengers included a wide cross section of people. There was a soldier with the rank of a colonel in a tank regiment and a cheerful group of students. There was an elderly woman in spectacles, carrying a roll of plans, perhaps an architect with designs for a new town. And several workers in quilted jackets. Some of them buried their noses in books and newspapers, and others looked out of the windows at the building of the Regional Committee headquarters where there was a huge poster calling on us to increase the friendship between peoples.

The Screamer wasn't worrying about the language she used. A girl with a blue bow in her hair, who was sitting next to the conductor, shut her mouth firmly, trying to stop herself uttering a word. The whole car, full to bursting, kept silent. But when the woman began to use really foul language, there were angry protests from all parts of the car. "Stop that! There are children here!"

Then the Screamer would stop swearing and return to her original theme—and the car would fall silent again. It was as if people had blocked their ears.

What had happened to people? There must have been complete confusion in their minds, like the two colonels arguing about why Beria was arrested. One said because he'd been sending the Jews to jail, and the other because he'd let them out.

Or was it just indifference? A stupid, bovine refusal to be involved; maybe even silent approval? They didn't want to tangle with a market scandalmonger. Yet she was attacking a child. . . . What was going on in people's minds?

The Dragon in the play by Schwartz,* Pauline's favorite play, brags that you won't find souls anywhere else like the ones he's got in his town. "Armless souls, lame souls, legless souls, deaf-mute souls, souls in chains, accursed souls . . . souls with holes, souls for sale, dead souls . . ." Surely we hadn't gone as far as that.

In no European capital would anyone utter such anti-Semitic abuse in a public place; or, maybe some drunken priest might—someone who refused to accept the ruling of the Ecumenical Council and kept on saying, "They crucified Christ!" I heard about one such man recently from a friend of mine who'd just got back from Vienna.

The Screamers bit back their words even in Berlin, although there too one can find storm troopers who've taken off their Hitler uniforms for the time being. Once on a trolley car in Berlin three years ago, I realized that I was being stared at with open hostility by a one-legged man

* Evgeny Schwartz (1896–1958), allegorical playwright whose best-known piece *The Dragon* is officially described as "unmasking Fascism." [Translator]

carrying a crutch. He pointed me out to a little flaxen-haired girl, his granddaughter probably, who apparently had never seen a Jew before, since they'd all been exterminated before she was born.

"*Jude!*" he whispered quietly to her, so that I wouldn't be able to hear.

In Moscow the Screamers don't care who hears.

I couldn't live with myself until I'd found some way to voice my anger and dismay in protest against the Screamer's silent collaborators. So I wrote an article called "The Trolley Stayed Silent."

I took it first to *Komsomolskaya Pravda*, then to *Literaturnaya Gazeta*, to editors whom I'd been at school with and who I knew for certain weren't anti-Semitic. For two or three years that article went around every Moscow editorial office. It was seen by every one of the bosses. They all read it, but only one of them, on the magazine *Friendship of the Peoples*, scribbled on the corner: "I'm in favor of printing! Boris Lavryonov."

Lavryonov merely asked me to supplement the article with some facts about our propaganda for friendship between peoples. Why didn't it work?

I got hold of all the pamphlets on friendship between peoples that had been published over the last few years. They were strange productions. They appeared to have been put together on an assembly line from standard parts. Once you'd seen five of them, there would be no difficulty in using the same ingredients to do a sixth, or a tenth, or a twentieth. And you could guarantee in advance that the twentieth would be up to standard in every way. But what a standard!

> The immense effect of the friendship between peoples in our country shows itself in the Socialist competition between the miners of the Donetsk, Kuznetsk, and Moscow coalfields.
>
> —Verkhovtsev, State Political Press, 1954

> The competitions between the miners of the Donbass and of the Kuznetsk coalfields have become a tradition. And the friendship between the miners of the Donbass and of Karaganda has shown a new strength.
>
> —Rachkov, 1954, Alma-Ata

> The friendship between the Karaganda miners and the Donbass grows and strengthens. Many of the miners of Kazakhstan have visited the Donbass.
>
> —Kupyrin, Knowledge (Znanie) Press, Moscow 1954

> The miners of the competing coalfields of the Donbass and the Kuzbass systematically exchange production and technical information and experience.
>
> —Malyshev, Znanie, 1955

Exactly the same lines appeared in pamphlets published in 1957, 1959, and so on.

Stanislavsky once said that a cliché is an attempt to speak about something you do not feel. This unfeeling, dead propaganda, DEAD for so many years is a truly LIVING witness to what has been going on.

Anti-Semitism was fanned with considerable invention and verve, with reports "From the Courtroom" and biting articles like "Pinya from Zhmerinka"* and theoretical articles about the native and non-native sons of Russia. But how can those sparks be extinguished? Why is there no water in the fire hydrants? Why are the hoses unusable?

"We absolutely must print 'The Trolley Stayed Silent,' " the editor-in-chief kept assuring me. "It's so important at the moment."

But as became clear, editors-in-chief only have a final say over insignificant matters. The trolley went on staying silent, and when the Screamers began to scream that Hitler should have got rid of Pauline, me, and our son, in the whole of the Moscow newspaper world I found no one brave enough to do anything about it.

* An anti-Semitic article published in *Krokodil* in 1952.

17

Pauline and I stood at a bus stop, by the kolkhoz market, clutching bags of potatoes and a frostbitten cabbage. The market was closing, and the country people flowed out of it at the end of their day's trading, each of them heaving bulging canvas bags. The bags were strange shapes—they were stuffed full of loaves of black bread.

Pauline's gray eyes filled with tears. "In the hungry years, Mama used to have to bring things back from the market like that to feed us," she said. She wiped her eyes and went on, "How long will this awful poverty last?"

We rode as far as the Byelorussky station where there was a butcher's shop and stood in line again. An old woman with some rattling empty tin cans and a shoulder bag took ten chunks of meat for soup. She threw the bony, frozen blue lumps into a can, and they clanked in it like stones.

The line began to protest. "Why so much? Don't give her so much!"

"You don't need it! She does!" Pauline followed the peasant woman out of the shop, paying no attention to the dirty look the shop assistant gave her.

In the corner of the shop was a group of workingmen in quilted jackets and boiler suits. One of them whipped out a half-liter of vodka, unseated the cork with a blow of his hand to the base of the bottle, and with a furtive glance around him poured it out into paper cups. A young boy, almost a schoolboy, was staggering about in the doorway. He slurred guiltily, "Ex-excuse me," and tried to let us pass.

Pauline sat silently in the trolley bus. I asked her about her work, but she replied in monosyllables, thinking about something else. It was a Saturday, and of all the men sitting around us the only one who was sober appeared to be the driver. Two were already sleeping peacefully, sprawled along the seat. They would go on like that until the trolley bus pulled into its depot.

At last Pauline spoke—but her eyes were still far away. "The war's over.

Millions of people are dead. And millions of the survivors seem to want nothing better than to be dead drunk."

She turned to me, and her eyes were full of incomprehension and pain. "All they want is their half-liter? Why?"

I knew that every time she saw them, she had a sharp feeling of guilt— over these peasant women who hauled the huge weights on their backs, the impossibly heavy sacks of bread, and for these young boys who only a short time ago had been polite and courteous, but who had lost all human dignity in vodka. When would the drinking stop? Pauline had made a better life for herself, but what about them? . . .

One of the drunks, wearing a cap pulled down over his prominent ears, opened his eyes. He looked at my gray fur hat and said, not apparently speaking to anyone in particular, "That kind, they've all got fur hats like colonels."

Pauline trod on my foot. "Don't bother with him."

The man in the cap muttered something, and I pretended to be stone deaf. A Jew in Moscow or Kiev, particularly one with a broad Armenian nose like mine, can't avoid being stone deaf, at least sometimes. Otherwise he'll turn into a fighting cock or a hysteric. The man in the cap took my silence for cowardice, and began to expand on his theme. Pauline stepped on my foot again, harder. Finally, I couldn't stand this pressure from two sides any more, and got out at the next stop. Pauline only just managed to leap off behind me.

"What's the matter with you? We aren't there yet!"

At first I didn't reply, but then I said angrily: "It's not easy being a Jew in Russia at the moment. And when you've got a wife who behaves like a Christian saint!"

Of course, basically she was right. But I know that often—in most cases even—the racism of the workingman is very shallow, and that a mere word or gesture is frequently enough to give a man back his humanity.

I couldn't forget the meeting where the chemist Aaron Mikhailovich was to be marked out as a prisoner, and how his slanderers fled from the hall.

I was convinced of this in another way on May 9, Victory Day. As usual there was to be a reunion of war veterans in the Writers' Club. I put on my naval jacket and my decorations, pulled on a raincoat over the top, and set off.

In the metro a young man of about twenty-five fell into conversation with me. He was in his best suit with a Komsomol badge in the lapel of his jacket. We stood jammed together by the door, and he told me with all the freedom of a man who's had a few drinks that he had just been to see his father-in-law, who'd been in the war—he'd even got a decoration before the Revolution. Then the man leaned toward me, giving me a taste of his vodka-laden breath, and, without any further ado, remarked in a confidential and ironic way: "Not like your kind—spent the whole war in Tashkent!"

I didn't reply, so he began to elaborate. When I got bored with this, I unfastened the top button of my raincoat and opened it. When he saw the medal ribbons he flushed bright red, right down to his neck. Then he said, all right, Jews in general should be shot, but ones like me should be saved.

"What proportion should be allowed to live?" I asked, in a business-like tone.

"Ten percent, no more."

"You're as merciful as Hitler," I said. "Hitler had useful Jews as well. That's what the Germans put in your passport—'useful.' He made an exception for them, just like you."

"You mean I'm a Fascist?" the young man said astonished.

"Oh, no. A profound internationalist."

I got out at my stop. When I reached the Writers' Club I glanced around and saw him hurrying after me as if he wanted to say something.

I stopped. "What d'you want?"

He shuffled his feet, apparently sincerely distressed. "It's awful . . . I'm a Fascist."

I looked at his simple open face, at his big red workingman's hands, and I realized just how guilty the people were who'd stuck his Komsomol badge on his chest and then left him to sort things out for himself.

. . . February. Snowdrifts. Soon the Twentieth Party Congress would be starting. Pauline and I were waiting for it hopefully. Maybe it would change some of our day-to-day troubles. Maybe the time was coming when we wouldn't have to pretend to be deaf. We'd had enough. During the Congress our room was covered in newspapers. Stalin's crimes laid bare. Only his anti-Semitic persecutions were allowed to be passed over in silence. As if they had never happened. Strange. Not one word to the effect that Pauline and I were just as much people as they were. And that we couldn't be insulted, discriminated against, spied on with impunity.

Had Khrushchev forgotten? Was that what it was? After all, he'd never had to sit on a trolley car with people shouting "Dirty Yid" at him. Over and over again I looked through Khrushchev's speech, until it was worn into holes. Surely there must be a word somewhere? Even if it was only where he talked with such passionate and righteous anger about the Doctors' Plot.

But no, not a word . . .

I even began to doubt whether the trial of the doctors had actually been the torch that lit the blaze of anti-Semitism, the criminal short circuit that sparked the fire. Maybe it was just in the air then and not in official texts. That kind of thing did happen. So I looked up the *Pravda*s of the time. . . .

"Devious spies and murderers under the guise of professors and doctors . . ." "Criminally undermined the health . . ." "The victims of this band of beasts in human form were A. A. Zhdanov and A. S. Shcherbakov . . ." "The first target of the criminals was to destroy the health of military commanders like Marshal Koniev and Army General Shtemenko. . . ."

So who were these monsters, these murderers?

"Most of the members of the terrorist group—Vovsi, B. Kogan, Feldman, Greenstein, Etinger, and others—were members of a branch of American intelligence—the international Jewish bourgeois nationalist organization called Joint."

"It was shown in evidence given by the accused Vovsi that he had received a directive that the leaders of the USSR were to be destroyed. This directive was passed on to him in the name of the espionage and terrorist organization Joint by Dr. Shimeliovich and the famous Jewish bourgeois nationalist Mikhoels."

That's how far the lie had been built and twisted. And not a word about all this from Khrushchev? Why?

When the doctors were declared not guilty, the papers printed the names of those who had been set free. Among them were the men I have already mentioned, except for one who had died in prison. And to everyone's surprise there were other names which had never been reported at all. The names that had been suppressed were for the most part Russian and Ukrainian (Vasilenko, Selenin, Preobrazhensky, Zakurov, and so on), which might have made it harder to establish the impressive picture of a Jewish plot, and so they had been removed to preserve the purity of official thought.

And not a word about that? A fine lover of the truth, you are, Nikita Khrushchev! Aren't you just as great an anti-Semite as Stalin ever was, you great fighter for internationalism?

"You're right! But thank him for what he has done," said Pauline calmingly. "If it weren't for him, millions of innocent people would still be rotting in the camps."

The warm winds of change were blowing. The goddess of justice was gradually lowering her protective wing. But she couldn't reach down far enough to touch us.

Pauline and I had to renew our passports. We waited our turn in the stuffy passport room of the 72nd Militia division in our factory region of Sharikopodshipnik. A young worker pounded on the closed window and demanded that they stop messing around. He'd lost a half day already. The door opened and a tired-looking militia officer came out. He looked at the youngster, who was slightly drunk, and grinned kindly.

"What's all the fuss about? Take care, or I'll put you down as a Jew, and see how you like that!"

Everyone in the room laughed.

Pauline's family was a deep-rooted Ukrainian Jewish family, and it's not difficult to understand what she felt when she fully understood the new attitudes toward the Jews. It isn't necessary to have shared her fate to understand that, either. All that happened was that Khrushchev shook the evil Beria apparatus as one might shake a tree covered in ravens. The ravens merely rose in a frightened crowd and settled on the next tree. And more often than not, that tree was the personnel departments of institutes and firms.

It is true that it was becoming more difficult to force the Russian people to follow the official line just by shouting at them. But the way ahead was clear, as far as the unfortunates marked by Point Five were concerned. Especially if you were a scientist competing for certain posts. The courts refused to become involved in any way, and simply sent anyone who complained back to the administration. The administration referred them back to the courts, knowing full well that because of Point Five their decision was final. The administration had already telephoned the Regional Committee to tell them they had an overweighting of the Jewish element—that it was time to have a purge.

I could help almost no one except for one or two unfortunates. In many cases the affair ended with the man they were after having a heart attack.

Everywhere you could find the former *politsai*, ex-members of the Russo-German quisling militia, their arms bloodstained up to their elbows. The authorities were still supposed to be looking for them.

In the Writers' Union, a mysterious, semiliterate, yet not untalented poet called Fyodor Belkin came to the fore. He launched attacks on Ehrenburg and on Margarita Aliger. Especially after Khrushchev had announced in public that "Leonid Sobolev,* even though he's not a Party member, is closer to us than Margarita Aliger, who is." How could he fail to be galvanized into action given an opportunity like that?

The little chorus of supporters helped the truly Russian Belkin to get

---

* *Leonid Sobolev, Margarita Aliger:* Sobolev, born 1898. Orthodox Soviet writer, but not a member of the Party. Aliger, born 1917. Poet who didn't entirely follow the Party line, but was nevertheless a Party member. [Translator]

his poems published, book after book of them, without having to take his turn in the line of waiting writers. He believed so determinedly that his time had come that when he was asked to appear on television he did so without a second thought.

One of the viewers recognized him, and the KGB called on him at once. It turned out that during the war Fyodor Belkin had been the head of the regional gendarmerie, the boss of the *politsai*, and had personally shot hundreds of Jews and Communists.

The newspapers printed reports of hooligans who had been shot,* hooligans with Jewish names. Of course, no one had any sympathy for the hooligans, although everyone understood the deliberate point of the "Sholom Aleichem" coloring of the reports. People had learned to understand.

It was about this time that Pauline's uncle—her Moscow uncle, the one she would telephone when she was in despair, even if it was only to hear his voice, so like her mother's—invited us both around for a visit. We very rarely saw him. But that evening was his sixtieth birthday. He worked at the Ministry of Coal under Zasyadko and Onik. He never stopped. He was known as a workhorse who hadn't kicked the traces over even in 1949; he just kept on pulling away.

His sixtieth birthday was the zenith of his working life. The jubilee table was laid from noon onward—everyone was invited. There would be all kinds of guests, friends, and acquaintances. And they did turn up. Totally unknown people, young men all wearing identical hats. We waited to hear who they were. Where had they come from? Had they brought a special birthday greeting?

"Sit them at the table," Pauline's uncle shouted cheerfully in his white starched shirt, looking into the corridor. "We'll sort it all out later."

"Does Granovsky live here?" the new guests asked politely, still standing at the door.

"That's right!" Pauline said happily. "Come in, come in!"

Then, a little shamefacedly, they produced a search warrant for the flat. And the work started.

They didn't finish until almost dawn. It was a thorough, professional job. They rapped the walls for secret hiding places and so on. To the astonishment of the searchers, Granovsky's savings bank books showed that he only had 800 rubles.

"Is that all?" the leader of the group asked incredulously. "Fancy going on a pension with only that."

They resumed. But they found nothing. No gold ingots, no jewelry.

---

* In 1961 a law was passed establishing the death penalty for "economic crimes" (i.e., fraud, stealing state property, etc.). [Translator]

The only gold was his wife's wedding ring. Later they explained the reason for the warrant: "We had an anonymous letter about you." And then it was the birthday. They thought that might be the best time. For if he'd been working for the government for so many years, and he'd stolen millions, he wouldn't be able to resist temptation. . . .

The leader of the search squad mumbled, "Excuse us," just as if he'd accidentally trodden on someone's foot on a bus. And that was it. They filed silently to the door, settling their identical hats on their sweating foreheads. There was no sign of penitence on their faces. Why should there be? The national papers still sounded the refrain: Jews are crooks. They're an economic hazard. Nikita Sergeevich had made the law that it was right to shoot currency speculators. So in that case, why not turn over another one of *them*. Just in case. He might be a crook too.

But this time it was a decent, selfless, hardworking man who didn't survive the insult which had crowned his life. He fell seriously ill and then died.

Of course no one was punished. The only thing that happened when the case was closed was that the man who'd been in charge shook his head and sighed, "What a bastard the guy who wrote that anonymous letter must be. Ai-ai-ai!"

All this had happened before, when the floorboards of Pauline's parents' hut were torn up by Hetman Skoropadsky's men and again by Ataman Zelyony's men. "We were looking for gold. We smelled Jews." Then it happened again under Stalin, in the famine year of 1934. Once again they "smelled Jews," and Pauline's grandmother fell dead because she couldn't take the arrest of her sons. Of all that big, friendly, country family, the only ones who remained alive were Uncle Vitya and Pauline, who by chance had avoided the bullets of the *politsai*. And under Khrushchev they got her uncle too.

Surely I, a writer, would be able to tell people about this one little local crime? Shouldn't I be able to raise a voice in protest? Against murder? . . . Editors threw their hands in the air and said, "How terrible!" and then asked me instead to do a piece about the Socialist competition between the Communist brigades. Everywhere I went—*Pravda, Literaturnaya Gazeta, Komsomolskaya Pravda, Izvestiya*—the polite sentence of rejection masked the real message: "DON'T WRITE ABOUT THE VICTIMS, IT UPSETS THE EXECUTIONERS."

There was one course left open to me. I could send a letter to the Central Committee. I had been in touch with them for ten years consecutively, after almost every visit I made to the Caucasus, to the Baltic States, or to Central Asia. The metal safe in the office of the head of the cultural department of the Central Committee, Comrade Polikarpov, had become the repository, the sarcophagus, of my anger, my disillusionment, my pleas. That was where my article "The Trolley Stayed Silent" had found its last resting place, along with my letter about the talented graduates of the University of Central Asia, Russian girls, Tashkent born and bred, who had not been allowed to go on for higher degrees because they were non-native, although there were plenty of places free.

That same safe also held the galley proofs of an article the censors had rejected about an incredible idiocy, but an idiocy preserved forever in stone. The city fathers of Odessa had fought against concessions to the West to such an extent that they had renamed streets once named after leading revolutionaries—Jeanne Labourbe, Vaclav Vorovsky, and Sholom Aleichem and Mendele Mocher Sforim—so that they shouldn't have non-Russian names and spirit.*

Not one of my pieces of investigation, not one of my general articles, no matter how sharp, lay around the shelves for long. They even published an article on the way the University Chair of Marxism was misteaching its students. But if I twitched the curtain however slightly to reveal deep-rooted nationalistic barbarity, breathed a single word in defense of the persecuted, that word, like the worst disturber of the peace, was immediately clapped into Polikarpov's iron burial vault.

But this time I got a call from Polikarpov's office. We fixed a day for a meeting. When I appeared they apologized. Polikarpov was busy. He had asked them to pass on the message that he had the material about Granovsky's murder. It was a most unfortunate and regrettable incident . . . but it wasn't the Department of Culture's business. It wasn't a literary matter.

What about helping me to get the article published? But clearly he couldn't dictate to editors what to print and what not to print. . . . All right, could I have a pass to leave the building? Certainly.

There was a fine cold rain. Among the people sheltering in a foyer I noticed a man who seemed very familiar. He was a dried-up little figure in a worn greatcoat with blue buttons; he looked flabby, depressed, and wet. I looked at him first from one side, then the other. There was no doubt about it. It was Major Vladimir Markovich Shnei, our former adjutant, whom I had thought was dead. The legendary hero.

---

* Jeanne Labourbe was a French teacher shot in 1919 in Odessa by the French occupation forces. Vaclav Vorovsky (1871–1923): militant Bolshevik, an ambassador after the Revolution who was killed in Lausanne. Sholom Aleichem (1859–1916)): the most famous Russian writer in Yiddish, who described in his largely humorous and satirical works all strata of the Jewish population in the Tsarist empire. Mendele Mocher Sforim (1836–1917): Russian writer in Yiddish, novelist and playwright; his *Voyage of Benjamin III* was one of the plays staged by Mikhoels at the Moscow Jewish Theater. [Translator]

Shnei recognized me, and said bitterly that he was going through hard times. He had been thrown out of the Party, out of the army, out of everywhere. Why? He raised his eyes and looked at me. They were the eyes of a Sknaryov, of a man from a punishment battalion.

"They took a sentence from a lecture I gave and turned it upside down. That was in 1949. . . . Grisha, you wouldn't believe that such things are possible."

Oh, yes I would, Vladimir Markovich, I would indeed.

His eyes filled with tears. Lucky that it was pouring outside and that he'd ducked in out of the rain; that way no one would notice that he, an old pilot who had flown aircraft as far back as the wood and string Farmans, was not as tough now as he'd been in 1941, when he flew every day with death.

We walked through the torrential rain to the metro hunched and clinging to each other. The puddles sparkled and splashed but we didn't bother to walk around them. The bitter wind and the water swirling down the gutters assailed us from all sides. We just clung closer and closer. People standing in doorways out of the rain stared after us. We looked like two men on their way back from a funeral.

18

It was Shnei who encouraged me to create Yasha Gilberg, a pilot who was to appear in a small role in my novel *The State Examination*. But it wasn't only Shnei, who was physically sound; the idea also came from a student-philosopher who had lost his arm during the war and who later became the best volleyball player in the university and captain of a champion team. And from a young and taciturn research student.

Z. had fought as an engineer in the war. His sight had been destroyed in a bomb explosion, but he received a degree and became a physicist. When I heard him lecture for the first time I didn't realize he was blind. His mouth was so mobile, his words bright and deep, and his face lit by such a brilliant smile that he gave the impression of being a kind, perhaps slightly mischievous person, someone with no sight problem at all. It was only when he stopped talking that his face wore a strange, sadly guilty smile, as if he were apologizing for his blindness. Z. worked somewhere beyond the Urals, and I had long ago lost contact with him. But I shall remember him all my life.

There were more severely wounded war veterans in the university, people of amazing strength of character, who both astonished you and made you feel very proud. I don't know who—except the administration—would have cared what nationality they were. And among them was this friend of mine, a former bomber navigator, whom I called Yasha Gilberg in my novel.

Yasha was forced to jump out of a burning aircraft. It was in Norway, over the icy waters of the Tanafjord. The pilot jumped after Yasha, and his flying boots came off in the slip stream and fell into the water. When they came down, Yasha cut the sleeve off his fur flying suit and wrapped the pilot's feet in it. That saved him. But Yasha himself lost his arm. It took the rescue party three days to get through, and he got frostbite. Then he studied at Moscow University and was ultimately sent to a remote village to teach, although his professor tried to keep him in the university.

I was asked to pay an urgent visit to the editor-in-chief of the Soviet Writers publishing house, Valentina Mikhailovna Karpova, a youngish woman with tightly drawn cheeks, an educated girl who used to talk to authors almost like a mother.

"Why did you write this, Grigory Tsezarevich?"

She had the manuscript of my novel there opened to the chapter about Yasha. She waited patiently while I explained the importance of the passages her blue pencil was hovering over. At last she said cautiously, "I see. But what precisely did you have in mind? Was it the heroism of a man of Jewish nationality?"

"He lost his arm in the war. And then he was packed off to a remote village."

"But we don't have any anti-Semitism here."

"I haven't said a word about anti-Semitism."

"Well, I'd leave the chapter out if I were you."

"You mean that to mention Jews like the Landers doesn't disturb the international feelings of our publishing houses, but to mention Jews like Gilberg does?"

Karpova sighed heavily and put her pencil down. In her eyes I could read the familiar message, "DON'T WRITE ABOUT THE VICTIMS, IT UPSETS THE EXECUTIONERS." Disobey and you'll be left hanging on the barbed wire of a publisher's caprice. You'll hang there till you compromise with fate or . . . die of starvation.

"I'd take it out, Grigory Tsezarevich. Why reopen old wounds?"

That's when I finally decided to see the head of the culture department of the Central Committee, Comrade Polikarpov, although the old writers warned me against it. "Karpova, Polikarpov, they're all the same—all part of the Khrushchev defense platoon."

The plump, well-educated, and seemingly benevolent head of culture, as the writers called him, encouraged me to speak with nods of his big high-domed head. I told him about that Hero of the Soviet Union, the North Sea pilot Ilya Borisovich Katunin, who wasn't allowed to be identified in our newspaper as a Jew, not even posthumously. I told him that the same sort of thing was going on now in books, magazines, and newspapers, and that all he had to do to convince himself of the truth of what I was saying was to have a look in his "sarcophagus" safe.

"There isn't a single literary organ where I'm allowed to defend a national minority from abuse and discrimination," I said angrily. "I can't defend the Soviet Constitution against discrimination, our Constitution which proclaims equality of races and nations. Not even here—in my novel about scientists who were fired or imprisoned in 1949. The novel was held back by censorship, even though I didn't write specifically about that."

Here Polikarpov became more alert. "Excuse me, but surely no one was interned in 1949?"

I reminded him, and he gave a drawl in his bass voice, as if he were trying to suppress a yawn: "Oh, the Jews." He immediately sounded uninterested, saying to himself, "Oh, the Jews, not us."

He looked at me kindly, paternally, not at all loftily, and said good-bye in the quiet friendly voice of a man who was prepared to change nothing but his position in his chair when his feet got numb. He shook my hand in a way that indicated no acquiescence, and in his handshake I could feel those unmistakable words, "DON'T WRITE ABOUT THE VICTIMS, IT UPSETS . . ."

Well, whom does it upset? It upsets everyone.

It was a day of discoveries. That same evening I received a phone call from the office of the magazine *Friendship of the Peoples* to tell me that Vasily Smirnov had been appointed editor-in-chief. The phone nearly fell from my hand. The elderly, irritable, jaundiced Smirnov was the only member of the Writers' Union who remained unshaken in his invincible pogrom mentality. He was the best-known, the most rabid and malicious chauvinist and anti-Semite. Anti-Semite Number One. The Writers' Union had nicknamed him the Iron Chancellor—like Bismarck.

Smirnov's appointment was the most flagrant insult to writers to date. The first thing he did when he took over the magazine was of course to insist, "Get rid of the smell of the Jews."

I got a phone call from the prose department to ask me to come around quickly and retrieve the manuscript of my novel *Leninsky Prospekt* and then get the hell out of there.

"You know the reason," the sub-editor told me. But the novel had been approved by the magazine, and I'd been paid my fee.

"The money isn't his, it belongs to the state," said the sub-editor soothingly. And when he became irritated by my bewildered questions he yelled down the phone, "Since when have anti-Semites brought the state any profit? They just spit at government money!"

I sent several letters of protest about Smirnov's promotion to the secretaries of the Central Committee of the CPSU, P. Ilyikhov and A. Suslov, and to Nikita Sergeevich Khrushchev himself. It was a meaningless exercise and I stopped when I heard something that made me realize the letters would just pile up in Polikarpov's sarcophagus.

When the recorded speeches of Lenin were reissued Khrushchev ordered that his speech against anti-Semitism, which was entitled "The Pogrom Persecution of the Jews," should be excluded. A speech of the leader and teacher dropped—just like that. Why be ashamed of your parentage?

On January 20, 1965, G. Mekhanik, a member of the Party since July 1917, asked at a meeting of propagandists why this speech had been removed. The secretary of the Bauman Regional Committee of the Party, Comrade Voronin replied: "It was dropped for technical reasons." And added hastily, "There's no time to pursue this question further."

Once I heard Nikita Khrushchev, his hand raised in a Lenin gesture, telling a group of guests from abroad, including Wladyslaw Gomulka, all about internationalism. He spoke passionately, with conviction. The microphone shook, and in its shaking I could distinguish the martial call of Khrushchev's internationalism, a call that was echoing before our era and is known in many languages: "Juden! Yids! The non-native population!"

So that it should be made unmistakably clear to all that he, Nikita Khrushchev, was leading the country along Lenin's path, so that everyone should know it—from the old peasant woman bent double under the weight of the sacks of bread she had to carry out of town to the country, to Pauline, in tears at her uncle's funeral—at every crossroads in our cities they put up gigantic billboards with a portrait of Vladimir Ilyich and the slogan: "You're going the right way, comrades."

Only people who owned the original gramophone record, now very rare, were able to hear Lenin's voice speaking through the hiss, like listening to a radio station through a jamming device: "NOT EVERY VILLAIN IS AN ANTI-SEMITE, BUT EVERY ANTI-SEMITE IS A VILLAIN!"

Everyone held his tongue. They'd even silenced Lenin. I wonder if he foresaw it all, as he lay struck down by paralysis? When the horror froze in his eyes at the moment captured forever by the Kremlin photographer?

19

These are the methods of a Hitler. When there isn't enough bread, burn down a few synagogues, and the people will be convinced that their bread is being eaten by the Jews. Anti-Semites, even if they live on different continents in different epochs, are as like one another as rusty knuckle-dusters thrown on the roadside.

I thrust the newspaper at Pauline, indicating that there was something in it that had really impressed me. She sat quietly leafing through *Pravda*, which in those days was like a theatrical spotlight directed on the Premier. Wherever the hero happened to be the light was there too. It followed him from the cornfields to the United Nations, where he hammered with his shoe on the desk, and from there to Cairo, where on his own authority, without any preliminary formalities such as a decree by the Presidium of the Supreme Soviet, he awarded Gamal Abdel Nasser the decoration of Hero of the Soviet Union. Pauline lowered the paper to her lap and said thoughtfully: "How quickly absolute power corrupts."

Then she said—sadly, for she had a weakness for Khrushchev—"He began so promisingly, so humanly, but all that'll be left of him is a blood-sucker—like all other statesmen."

So what was there to be done?

Just turn your back on everything? Pull out the plug of the radio when the announcer with his educated accent reads out the daily ration of the Premier's doings, on account of which even the corn stops growing and shrinks in the northern fields to a miserable weed?

Perhaps go to my own Party organization with a protest. But Khrushchev had dissolved it. Even the quietest, most biddable of the Communist writers voted against the dispersal of their organization. Unanimously . . . And the result? For a week already the secretary of the defunct Party Committee, Elizar Maltsev, had been handing out vouchers showing that members were now unattached. That we could go and join whatever branch we wished.

Margarita Aliger, I remember, looked like a hurt child. She kept saying despairingly, "What's going on? How can they?"

When Konstantin Paustovsky heard of the break-up of the Party organization, he smiled sadly and said something which many at that time failed to understand: "Seek and ye shall find." There are times when people are united by happiness and hope. On this occasion the writers of Moscow were united by outrage.

"What is to be done?"

. . . If we were to resort to the law? To Soviet law. Our militia, our courts, our public prosecutors were there for our protection—no, not against Khrushchev, of course; to him I'd been sold body and soul. Maybe against unrestrained drunken hooligans?

I had almost no doubt that such protection still existed. I should have brought the matter to the courts earlier. A matter of sneers and jibes in the street is not the pogrom in science, not the massacre of the scientists. But in the street—that should be clear to any militiaman. Usually they don't stand on ceremony with ordinary lawbreakers. Even if the spirit had largely gone from the law, the letter remained in force. Next time, no matter how much Pauline tried to pull me away, I would take the first bawling Jew-hater to the militia.

I didn't have to wait long. It began, as usual, on a trolley car. A group of fifteen Bashkirs got on, new to Moscow. Some of them had overcoats, others furs. Judging by their faces they were workers, probably oil workers. They stood on the platform, talking away in their Bashkir language. Their eyes were lively, and the conversation was animated and friendly. It was good to see them.

Behind me someone was breathing noisily. A woman's voice said sourly: "They must know Russian. But there they are babbling away in their own language."

The Bashkirs got off, and at the next stop three Caucasians, Azerbaijanis, got on. They were having a row about something or another—in Azerbaijani. The woman behind had stopped talking, but was hissing like a goose working herself up to the attack, while a hoarse male voice grunted an approving refrain.

When I got out at the metro station, I forgot about her. But when I got onto the train I heard the same voice again. Quarrelsome, brazen. The familiar woman in her lint-covered headscarf was abusing a frightened old gypsy woman, wearing huge earrings and carrying a child. The baby woke up and began to cry. The old woman said something in a guttural voice, and then suddenly the drunken man in the dirty jacket who'd been in the tram began to bellow. And it's what he said that was decisive: "Hitler should have finished you off as well! Go on off to your Israel!" Hatred is always the same. But why consign a gypsy to Israel?

Should I write yet another article? And hang about the doorways of editorial offices?

No! There was Article 74 of the Criminal Code of the Russian Federation.* The inflaming of racial hatred. It was a law, dammit. It must be enforceable.

Unfortunately the drunk managed to punch me in the face as I was hauling him off the train to hand him over to the police. I was relieved that the policeman didn't notice it, as my bruise would have put all racial considerations out of court.

The scandalmonger in the headscarf had dropped her drunken boy friend or husband and disappeared. It seemed she had a deep-seated dislike of militiamen. And the gypsy woman with the child had disappeared as well, just as the automatic doors were closing. So both offender and offended avoided the law.

Gently, supporting him under his arms, we deposited the cursing racist in the militia office of the Kursky Vokzal metro station, and I told the duty officer, a senior lieutenant, what it was all about.

"This citizen has got it all wrong!" I heard from behind my back. It was a strong, confident voice, the voice of a university lecturer or a radio announcer. I turned. Another passenger from the train had followed us into the militia office. He was a gray-haired man in a gabardine raincoat. From beneath the brim of his velour hat little sharp eyes looked at me with hostility. "He's got it all wrong," he repeated relentlessly. "He probably has a mania about it, and so he gets it all wrong. Slandering an honest working man!"

But the unshaven drunk couldn't get away with it as easily as that. Nor, apparently, did he want to. He banged his fist on the wooden counter, and went through his whole routine again. "Hitler should have got rid of them!" he concluded, tripping over his tongue, and looked at me with swollen red eyes as if to say, "There you are, make what you like of it!"

The false witness turned smartly on his heel, and went out without saying another word, accompanied by the rhythmic blows of the fist on

* Article 74: "Violation of national and social equality: propaganda or agitation designed to provoke national or social hatred or antagonism or to lead to direct or indirect limitation of the rights of citizens, or to furnish them with direct or indirect privileges arising from their national or social classification are punishable by deprivation of liberty for a period of from six months to three years or by exile for a period of from two to five years." [Translator]

the counter. He didn't hurry. He preferred his dignity even under such humiliating conditions.*

"Well, he's done it now," said the senior lieutenant in amazement, staring at the pounding fist. The young officer was quick to get the point. "Documents!"

When he had taken the particulars, he asked me to come outside with him for a moment. In the foyer, people were streaming past like a river in flood.

"What charge shall we put?"

"What do you mean, what charge?" I didn't understand. "Charge him with what he did."

"No." He shook his head. "Let's put down 'breach of the peace,' or 'creating a disturbance.' Whichever you like?"

"Put down what he was actually doing."

The senior lieutenant looked at me as if I were out of my mind. His eyes grew round. He had obviously grasped the situation. "We haven't got that charge. . . . You can't . . ." He waved his arms indignantly. "Do you want a hooligan like that to get off scot-free? Just walk out of court? No? Then why are you making it impossible for me to get him convicted?"

"Me?"

"Of course! You're just being stubborn! Listen, I know about these things. He'll get off scot-free. So what do we put?"

I didn't believe that if we put down what actually happened the man would get off without punishment. Something was wrong. So the next day I went to the People's Court and picked out a judge who looked as if he knew his business—a research student in an institute of jurisprudence. When he'd heard what I had to say and examined my red, almost crimson membership card of the Writers' Union, he looked at me curiously. His face was honest enough, but his eyes looked uneasy, as if I had caught him out in something. He adjusted his tie mechanically and laughed. He asked me to go through it all again to give himself time to think.

"How do we deal with cases like that? Well, it's hard to explain. Come tomorrow. There's a similar case on then. You watch the court stenographer's fountain pen. She's our mainstay. She knows everything."

The mainstay turned out to be a middle-aged woman. The judge asked the Tartar night watchman what words the woman tenant had used toward him and he replied, "Swine." The mainstay wrote it down.

"Filthy pig." The mainstay again scribbled on her pad.

---

* Later I met him on the main stairway of an academic institute. I have no doubt it was he: little eyes and the face of a lackey. I inquired who he was. He was a major specialist in modern history.

"Wog bastard."

The fountain pen didn't move.

"All Tartars are speculators!"

The pen as before stayed motionless in the secretary's poised hand, like a dart aimed but not thrown.

"Slavering jackal." This time the pen went to work.

The mechanics of lies seemed as plain as day. There was a sieve that let pass what you might call clean dirt but which excluded anything with a smell of national insult about it.

Stalin's internationalism! I had followed the whole course. I had seen it with my own eyes, felt it with my own hands. There was no one left to protest to, no one to write to, no one to go and see.

And yet I set off over the whole course again, with mulish stubbornness. I hung about the offices of what seemed like every literary appointee, everyone in the prosecutor's office; they all listened to me and looked somewhere out the window. I tried to protest, to appeal to their consciences, to their hearts, to their beliefs, to what remained of their ideology . . .

Internationalism! It's almost like a game. First of all you come up behind a Jew and hit him over the head as hard as you can, then you stretch out your hands as if to help him, with your thumbs turned up. Guess who just hit you? Everyone's faces are as impenetrable as stone. He can't guess, so he turns away. Then you hit him again.

In the end I got bored with it all. I played deaf for two years. I acted color-blind. We weren't living too badly. It was almost peaceful. I was only called "Yid" two or three times, and then only by faceless citizens, in passing. If it had gone on a little longer I might have got used to it. I might have gone along.

But I had a son. What could I say to him? How could I explain what was going on? Had I the right to destroy his world, his impressions of justice, for which he was already paying with his body, sometimes covered with bruises?

In my son's new class there was a huge, clumsy boy. He was strong, with big hands. He came from a Don Cossack family, but he got beaten up by everyone in the class who tried, at every break in the day. The children used to ride him around the room, which earned him the nickname of Horse. My son was struck by the fact that this powerful boy submitted to all the insults and the jeers. Then he found out that he'd grown up in Magadan, in a family which had been victimized under the repression. Fear had been born with him in the womb. And he was afraid of complaining. He was afraid of everything.

My son said to anyone who cared to listen that he wouldn't allow anyone to beat up the Horse. Anyone who hit him was hitting Fima as well. Of course my son was treated three times worse as a result.

A little later the fuss was to start, when the Regional Committee began to examine the question of whether I was right or wrong. When I came home, my son would look at me sideways, as if an incautious direct glance might hurt me, and then ask—or rather whisper—"Well, how are things?" And then he would dash over to me, and fling his thin arms around my neck.

My son was growing. "Fima's begun to clean his shoes without being told," Pauline said one evening. "I suspect he must have a girl friend."

"But he hasn't started washing his neck yet," I replied, hoping she was wrong. "From that we can deduce that things haven't got very far."

We took Fima to Leningrad, to show him the holy places. We walked on Senate Square, where the Decembrists had threatened the throne, and I told him who had stood there and where the cannons had fired from. We looked with excitement around all the sites connected with Pushkin.

I realized that I had brought my son to *my* holy places. To the holy places of Russia. But about the rise of the Jewish hero Bar Kokhba, or about the Hungarian Kossuth, he would learn much later, and this was natural—for these were the holy places of other people.

Apart from that, he could see that for some reason I was finding life difficult, that sometimes it was unbearably difficult for me to work. Before our trip to Leningrad, when he was looking at a map he saw on the Volkhov River the legend "Literary bridges," and asked in an everyday tone of voice, "Did they throw writers off them?" But he still didn't understand what the Progressivists proclaimed, and what had been thrown in his face more than once—that the holy places of Russia were not his places, that he should get out of them.

How could we save our children? How could we shelter them from grief, from repression, from discrimination? How could we do it?

My grandfather, a saddler, and my father, a metalworker, had been given the status of full citizens in 1917. They were able to leave the ghetto and go to the Baltic States, where even though they swelled up with hunger they still won equality and human dignity. But I, the son and grandson of workers, tireless fighters for internationalism, had been turned into a second-class citizen. "Non-native population"—a Jew. And my son, the son of a writer, and at the same time a Jew, was already being turned into a third-class citizen. If it were to go on like this, where would my grandson end up? And my grandson's grandsons?

Until then I had never been able to bring myself to tell Fima that it wasn't only the five-year-old son of a watchman who could turn on him and say scornfully, "You're not a Russian, you're a Tartar." It wasn't only a drunk in the street who could shout "Yid" after him. These were the kinds of actions that were being proposed now by a totally sober government. And if we were to complain, he would find no laws to protect him: they were blocked by inflamed "internationalism": they were dead letters.

I didn't know when I would tell him all this.

Fortunately he was a healthy boy, and he rapidly forgot about his spiritual wounds and settled down to look after his bird and guinea pigs, went out on biological expeditions, slept out in the forest, kept a herbarium of river grasses, won prizes in the city biological olympiads, dreamed of his studies, of science, and I watched with a lump in my throat.

What was ahead for him? What was ahead for his friends, who still didn't know that they'd already been divided into "native" and "non-native"? As time passed, perhaps they would poison him, as they poison dogs, as they've already tried to poison us.

Would he begin to get "greeting" cards on big festival days? Cards like those received by David Markish, the son of the savagely exterminated Jewish poet? They called David Markish "Yid's litter" and threatened that he hadn't long to live, that he'd go the same way as his father.

Khrushchev's boat had developed a list, sometimes it was difficult to keep a foothold on the deck, there was a danger of going over the side. And I wondered what would happen if some time my son lost his footing, went off balance, or if the racists tried to throw him overboard, as they've thrown many—who would support him, help him? Hate, alas, is stronger than benevolence.

As I wrote these lines, in the next room my son and his school friends were listening to their tape recorder. Vysotsky* had won the boys' devotion. I knew that their faces were serious as they listened to the husky, strong voice of the singer: "You're cutting down the forest to make coffins; through the gap come the punishment battalions."

O happy generation, who can't even imagine what it was like face to face! Not in a thousand years!

What are these coffins? The winter woods around Moscow in 1942, for example, were full of "snowdrops." That's what they called the corpses of soldiers sticking through the drifts. They showed black under the thawing snow, twisted and terrible beneath the surface. The demolition corps blew great holes in the frozen ground, and the burial parties—old men with frozen beards, young boys, convalescents from the hospitals—dragged the corpses to the craters and flung them in, one man holding the hands,

* Vysotsky: A popular singer and songwriter. Most of his material is not published officially, but circulates on privately made tape recordings. The songs are satirical and often anti-regime. [Translator]

the other the feet. About a hundred cropped-haired lads to one crater grave, which stayed open till the spring.

Robbed by the Germans of their last clothes, the country people, who were freezing to death, came out at night to steal clothes from these craters, and in the morning you would see the dead soldiers propped up against the earth walls, stripped of their quilted trousers and their underpants. Over the lip of the crater hung naked blue legs.

And the children used the frozen corpses of Germans as sledges to slide down hills on.

The cruel fields of 1942.

I too carried those frozen "snowdrops" to the edge of the airfield, just like the burial parties, one at the head, one at the feet, hundreds of them, so that our planes could land without nose-diving on the runway.

And I dived into that same snow myself, under the whine of tracers and heavy shells, when there was a sudden attack on those strips deep in the forest, or "back-up airfields" as headquarters used to call them.

And then I jumped out of the snow and dashed over to the airplane—all so that my son would never have to come face to face with Fascism . . .

To go through all that and then to see that racism, like a many-headed hydra, has grown new heads?

My son's name was Fima, in honor of another boy called Fima, betrayed by his teacher; in honor of Fima, killed by a dum-dum bullet fired by a quisling militiaman. Surely my Fima wasn't going to live with a feeling of persecution, feeling like a man with a target pinned over his heart, as in a German death camp, with the target labeled "Point Five"—there for anyone who cared to take aim at it?

20

Once at a writers' meeting our home-grown pogromists were condemned by the writer Blyakhin, the maker of the famous film *Red Devils*. He was followed by Professor Shukin of the Literary Institute, who dared to quote Marx on anti-Semitism: "No nation can be free that persecutes other nations." Finally, Konstantin Paustovsky, in discussing Dudintsev's novel* in 1956, accused some of his highest-placed comrades of being anti-Semites.

But these words went unheeded, the more so after Khrushchev's rise to power, and they were not repeated. There was no attempt to repeat them. . . .

I hoped that the old writers would receive the support of the leaders of the Union. That the first to join them might be the secretary of the Union, Alexei Surkov, who hated the Black Hundred.† Surkov kept silent. I waited for Alexander Tvardovsky to raise his voice against anti-Semitism. But Tvardovsky had his own worries, his own sorrows.

I tried to persuade many writers, famous throughout Europe, to speak out. Some of them seemed not to hear me; they were paralyzed by fear, the nerve gas of the twentieth century. They would quickly change the subject. Others slapped me on the shoulder and said cheerfully, "Ask me to do something easier." To know the truth and to live it are two very different things.

The wrinkled, flabby faces of the third category at times reminded me of Polikarpov when he and I were talking and he was barely able to keep from yawning—"Oh, the Jews." One of the old writers actually did yawn, a great big yawn, which he covered with his sclerotically veined hand.

Once, at a New Year's Eve party where we didn't know all the guests,

---

* *Man Shall Not Live by Bread Alone.* [Translator]
† In 1949 Surkov was the only secretary of the Writers' Union who was brave enough to dissociate himself openly from the cosmopolitan campaign.

my son was sitting slumped at the table. I automatically said to him, "Sit up straight, or you'll get a hunched back!" Then I saw the look in the eyes of a boy sitting opposite. He stood up and left the table and I saw that he was a hunchback. A chill ran up my spine.

I couldn't forget this incident and I couldn't forgive myself, although of course I hadn't meant to hurt anyone.

But as for my old friends among the writers—they knew perfectly well that I too had been numbered among the hunchbacks and as a hunchback wasn't allowed even to cross the threshold of the Moscow Worker publishing house and a number of other publishers. The old men told me about that, so that I shouldn't waste my time.

They could see and hear that people were shouting hunchback at me, in the firm conviction that if someone is called hunchback often enough, sooner or later he'll grow a hump. They saw all this and yet they did nothing. What happened to people?

With very few exceptions the trolley car is silent, it seems. And there sat the direct successors of the great Russian writers, staring mutely out the windows while publicly proclaiming to the world their proud motto "I cannot stay silent!"

It was only several years later, in 1962, that I met and became very close to a remarkable man, a descendant of an old noble family, who had taken part in the Revolution and then served time in Russian prisons, a man who stood by my side shoulder to shoulder, and who in my eyes at least saved the honor of the Russian creative intelligentsia of the Khrushchev period.

Stepan Zlobin.

Stepan Zlobin was a writer and a famous scholar. Everyone knew that. But how many knew what he stood for to those around him? Zlobin was a bright-eyed man, with a fine, intelligent face, high-browed and angular, like Don Quixote. But who was Stepan Zlobin for us?

Stepan was the author of *Salavata Yulaeva* and other historical novels. He enlisted in 1941 and was taken prisoner. Behind the barbed wire of a German prisoner of war camp, he, although not a Party member, became the leader of the Party underground—in the camps, a man was what he was, not what his documents said he was.

When the Nazis were retreating and preparing to destroy the camp, the prisoners, led by Stepan, seized the guards and all the quislings; they held out for three days until the American tanks arrived. It was here in the camp that one of the writers, Boris Gorbatov I think, found Stepan thin as a skeleton, clothed in rags with wooden clogs on his feet.

When Stepan got home, one of the English soldiers who'd been in the camp and who had heard that Russian prisoners of war were being sent to

Siberia, wrote to the Party Central Committee in Moscow to say what Stepan had meant to them, the anti-Fascist prisoners. This letter was to become document No. 1 in the thick file against Stepan Zlobin, English spy.

Beria's men arrested a number of former inmates of Stepan's camp so as to obtain incriminating evidence against him. But not one of the former prisoners, however much they were tortured, would produce any damaging evidence. The investigation only stopped after Stalin came across Zlobin's novel *Stepan Razin* and Zlobin—to everyone's surprise— was awarded the Stalin Prize, first class.

What happened was this: Alexander Fadeev and other members of the Stalin Prize Committee, selecting the candidates for the 1949 prize, were received by Stalin in the Kremlin. Stalin looked through the prepared documents and asked calmly why no one was being put forward for the first class order. "I see you managed to find a second-class prize-winner," he said, "and a third class. But no first. Why?"

Alexander Fadeev turned white as a sheet and answered hurriedly, "It wasn't a fertile year, Joseph Vissarionovich. That sometimes happens in literature. There just weren't any really outstanding works."

Stalin puffed on his pipe and said, with barely detectable sarcasm, "Really? But I've just read a historical novel called *Stepan Razin*. In two volumes. It struck me as a first-class book."

. . . How the literary rabble feared Zlobin! Fifteen years running he spoke out at writers' meetings when no one else would take the risk—he and his words were all that we had to take pride in. But he was never allowed to speak unheckled at congresses or meetings. Whenever he began his walk toward the platform alarmed shouts of "To hell with him" arose. He always managed to let his enemies know what he thought of them and made a practice of striking out unworthy names from the lists of candidates for election. On one occasion he stepped to the microphone, said what he had to say, then turned to the presidium, where Konstantin Fedin, Leonid Sobolev, and other writers were sitting, having just returned from a meeting with Khrushchev. They had been praising Nikita Sergeevich. Stepan didn't mince his words. "Look at you, nothing but a greedy rabble, crowding around the steps of the throne—you don't even care whose throne it is!"

Naturally enough, Stepan was so viciously attacked by the critics that people thought he would finally be silenced. After all, he wasn't a healthy man, and he should have been taking more care of himself. But six months or a year went by, and at the next writers' meeting Stepan once again turned the fire against himself, when he protested against the hard core of self-promoted literary generals, against their lies, against the deep-seated, malevolent hysteria they represented as fidelity to ideas. "Russian Man remains a revolutionary only to the age of thirty," wrote Chekhov. Stepan Zlobin was the living refutation of this pessimistic view of the Russian intelligentsia.

One day I heard the duty secretary at the Writers' Union calling an ambulance. I asked what had happened. He said, "Stepan Zlobin's ill. It looks like a heart attack."

I dashed to the room where the secretariat of the Moscow division of the Writers' Union was having a meeting. Stepan Zlobin was lying on the floor of the smoked-filled room, waiting for the doctor to come. Around him clustered the "leading writers," but they were behaving in a way that seemed incomprehensible in the presence of a sick man. They were clearly excited about something, waving their hands and talking at the top of their voices. Stepan Pavlovich, lying there on his back, was shaking his head bitterly as he talked back at them. They were finishing their quarrel.

When Stepan Zlobin became really ill, he asked for one of his old friends to come and sit by his bed.

"Why an acquaintance, why not one of your family?" the doctor asked in surprise.

"These boys have been in prison with me, they're my sons," answered Stepan.

He called us his sons as well. We were proud of this, but we knew that so far we'd done nothing to deserve his view of us. His "sons" were in and out of his house all the time. He insisted that we should stop calling ourselves young writers.

"Here writers are described as young until they are fifty years old. It's nothing but a tactic for the suppression of youth—and a very dubious one at that. Because they use 'young' to mean 'immature'."

There were about forty of us writer-sons, and the youngest of us was over thirty. We had all written several books. We knew that we were considered young writers, but that seemed to us to be quite natural, the literary norm.

"It looks as if you've all let yourselves be convinced that you're inferior," said Stepan Pavlovich in distaste. "I disapprove of thirty-year-olds behaving like infants! Can't you see that this is just another form of Philistinism? Let others think us inferior! Let other people rack their brains! We're still being educated. There's nothing easier than to let yourself be thought immature. It's such a comfortable, irresponsible position!"

Stepan Zlobin's "sons" read a great deal. An ill-informed person was no match for Stepan. We read Plekhanov and Kropotkin. He'd thrust your nose into the right book once, twice even, but after the third time, if you weren't prepared to read it then you could go your own way.

He often took Maxim Gorky's articles on the petty-mindedness of the bourgeoisie from his shelves. " 'The ambition above all other things to achieve peace and quiet and plenty,' " he read to us, " 'is the hallmark of the narrow-minded bourgeoisie. A deep desire for inner and outer peace is the same as a deep-seated dark fear of everyone who might in some way or another disturb that peace.' "

Both in the Nazi prisoner of war camp where he produced leaflets* and after the war when he defended Jews who by some miracle had survived the Nazi camps, Stepan fought anti-Semites all his life, although he didn't always succeed. "The fact that a Jew has survived," their accusers insisted, "must mean that he was a traitor."

As he lay on the stretcher carrying him out of the Writers' Union, Stepan waved his thin arm and said to me, "There is no room for me, a comrade of Heinrich Heine, in a place where when they say 'Jew' they mean 'Yid'."

When the stretcher had been placed in the ambulance, he beckoned to me and asked that I go to his home to reassure his family. "And bring any documents you've got with you to the hospital. Anything on the history of anti-Semitism. From Genesis onward . . . I can't keep quiet any longer! As soon as I'm on my feet again . . ."

The ambulance drove away.

I went to see his family, then went home and sat down to work on my play about the pilots of the north sea squadrons. But all the time my thoughts kept turning to Stepan's request. As far as anti-Semitism and racism were concerned, they had never engaged my whole mind, they were never my whole concern. Anti-Semitism was a nagging pain, a wound which sometimes just throbbed, and sometimes spouted blood.

"Documents, Genesis . . ." This was something serious.

I went to the Lenin Library and began to do research precisely at the point I'd left off fifteen years earlier. I began with the last numbers of the pogrom journal *Russian Banner*. The Bible of the Russian Black Hundreds—hadn't it become out of date now, in the sixties? At first I thought it had. There was too much old material—nothing you could use. I doubted whether it would pass muster now. Indeed, the old Black Hundred tree

* The Minsk Museum of the Patriotic War holds a manuscript copy of "Camp Pravda" written by Stepan in the German concentration camp. It's his work from the first line to the last. Here, among other selections like "Our Truth" and "Chronicle" is an article "What Is Anti-Semitism?" It begins with these words: "A bestial survival of the Middle Ages, practiced by the most reactionary sections of society . . ."

was showing its age. Almost all its leaves had been blown off by the winds of history, and turned to dust.

Its best slogans were on the rubbish heap. "They crucified Christ." (Even the Catholic Ecumenical Council had decided that that was nonsense.) "They spill the blood of innocent children." "The Yids are usurers, bleeding the Christians." "The Jews are poisoners." All so much garbage.

So what remained? As Konstantin Paustovsky said, "Seek and ye shall find." Here was one leaf that certainly hadn't blown off the tree. It had lasted for centuries, renewed in particular by the Imperial Decree of 1914: "All persons of the Jewish faith are to be removed from the area of the front, as disloyal citizens who *might* come into contact with the enemy."

MIGHT!

My great-grandfather, Girsh, for whom I was named, was a soldier in the Tsarist army. He served his Tsar and his country for twenty-five years. He was wounded during the first defense of Sebastopol. And he was evicted from his family home near Vilna, together with his sons and grandsons, "on the basis of the decree." None of his services to the Tsar or the country could prevent it. They sent the people away on carts, miserable, weeping, under a guard of Cossacks.

"MIGHT come into contact . . ."

Centuries, governments, banners came and went . . . my comrades and I, returning as if by a miracle after a cruel war, had to realize, just as my great-grandfather Girsh had had to realize, that we were coming home as second-class citizens.

"MIGHT . . ."

But still, a hundred years had passed. The Wright brothers had flown. Medical science had overcome typhus. The nations, for the most part, had got rid of their kings. Communication satellites were circling the earth. Plans were going ahead for a moon landing. . . .

From morning to night the radio spoke constantly of the victory of Communism. So what? Are there any new theories, new ideas? No. All there are, flashing like neon signs, are street curses: *Anti-patriots! Rootless cosmopolitans! A mob of scientists! Agents of Joint! Mercenaries of the Imperialists! Wanderers without passports! Enemies of the people! Fifth column! Zionists! Ideological foreigners! Disloyal!*

In a word—"who MIGHT."

They! They! They!!

If you look for more "scientific" evidence, then the signs flash *native population, non-native population.*

And most recently new words have been coined—for the connoisseurs:

"A people having a state beyond our frontiers must not be given advancement. . . ." I.e., the English, the Germans, and . . . the Jews. Before Israel came into being—beat them! After Israel was formed—beat them!

A few drunks dared to yell "Israel" as a new term of abuse. Before, they shouted normal, unoriginal things. But now they've learned a new tune. *Israel*—and that's it in a nutshell. You can understand what upsets them and there's no point in complaining.

Quite recently an important writer—one of the "true Russians" as the pogromists like to call themselves—condescended to conduct a theoretical argument on this point. We met unexpectedly at a conference, and in an interval he asked me to share his table at the bar. "If you aren't too fastidious," he said, making a cautious joke. He poured himself a glass of vodka and whispered confidentially that personally he liked me, that I really did strike him as quite specifically Russian. That was meant to be the ground shot from under my feet: "I really like you."

Then he began to pour out his obsession about the alienness of the translators' section in the Writers' Union ("They've got a lot of your people there"). He wiped his lips, then suddenly, very loudly, as if he were about to launch into a lively version of his favorite song, he said, "Whatever you say, they sympathize with Israel! And we've beaten Israel, we're beating them at the moment, and we'll go on doing it. That's historical reality!"

I've known about reality for a long time: Before Israel existed—beat them! Now that Israel's there . . .

I said with a grin that the Communist Party had adopted a special resolution on the Jewish question, which answered all the questions raised by our home-grown racists.

My companion suddenly turned gray. His forehead broke out in a sweat. Tugging his tightly starched collar away from his neck, he asked in a tense whisper, "A Party document? Saying something new about the Jews?" His Adam's apple jerked as he spoke.

From my jacket pocket I took a pamphlet, with the English title "Political Affairs, August, 1966."

"Oh, it's something from abroad," he said as the truth dawned on him.

He brightened up enormously, relaxing in his chair, when I told him that this was a resolution on the Jewish question passed by the Eighteenth Congress of the American Communist Party.

There are dense clouds in the Atlantic Ocean. It's not easy to see far through a thick fog, especially to see what those on the other side are doing. Our groans don't carry over that distance. It's a long way. So for some years now the American Communists have been claiming that the biggest problem the Russian Jews have is the shortage of prayerbooks. All the other information about Russian racism is of course just so much yellow press propaganda.

My "true Russian" companion tolerated my reading the document up to the point where it said that Russian anti-Semitism had helped the instigators of the Cold War achieve their ends. Then he stood up, drummed his fingers nervously on the table, and said in a tone which brooked no contradiction that what the American Communist Party said was not binding on us. "They ought to stick to their blacks. We've got our own problems and our own ways of coping with them."

That's true. Our own ways . . . And the most widely used way is the essentially Russian formula of the "native population." This is now a term of government and Party practice. The small change of officialdom. It insulted me worst of all, I suppose, when I first got back from the war. Where did this expression, now so deeply rooted, come from in the first place? Who worked it out? Who wrote it down? Maybe it really was one of the greats of Marxism? Marx himself? Engels? Lenin? I tracked it down in the end—it was in a decree promulgated by Alexander III:

"Jewish craftsmen, by their very existence, interfere with the development of craft trades among the *native population*."

Jews as such were singled out from the native population by this decree of His Imperial Majesty, even if they had lived in Russia for a thousand years. And by the same token they were marked for a loss of rights in every sphere.

But surely the Soviet government, I thought, couldn't hide behind this Tsarist doctrine of separation. Surely they must have worked out some more scientific rationale? In fifty years they must have been able to come up with something? How many years must a nation live in the world to put down roots, to receive its certificate as a "native people"? Are there any criteria? You be the judges.

The decree of the Presidium of the Supreme Soviet of August 20, 1964, cleared the Volga Germans of all charges against them. But they were not allowed to return to their homelands. Why? Because they "had taken root in new places."

In September 1967 a decree of the Presidium of the Supreme Soviet withdrew all the accusations against the Crimean Tartars.* There was no question of restoring the Crimean Tartar Autonomous Republic, as the decree affirmed—"Tartars formerly living in the Crimea have taken root in the territory of Uzbekistan and other republics of the Union."

* The Volga Germans were deported by Stalin to Siberia in 1941. They were described as "a German spy nest." In 1944 the Crimean Tartars were deported to Siberia for "collaboration with the occupying enemy." [Translator]

Superb dialectic! The Tartars took root in new places—(in twenty-two years). The Volga Germans took root in new lands—(in twenty-three years). According to archaeological findings, the first Jewish settlements on the territory of the present Soviet Union were made in the first century A.D. In Kiev, at the time of Vladimir Monomakh, there was even a Jewish street. For two thousand years Jews have lived on Russian soil—and they are still not native.

When I went to see Stepan Zlobin in the Botkinskaya Hospital, he dug around in the pile of books which wobbled dangerously on the chair next to his bed and handed me a tattered book with yellowing pages. It had been written in 1905 by Amfiteatrov* after one of the bloodiest pogroms. Stepan pointed to a paragraph with his long finger. I read it, and reached out mechanically for the stool so that I could sit down.

"At the moment, Russian anti-Semites allege that the Jews are behind the Russian Revolution. Let twenty years go by, and Russian anti-Semites will be alleging that the Jews had nothing to do with the Russian Revolution."

* Aleksandr Amfiteatrov, 1862–1923. Anti-Bolshevik who before the Revolution wrote for the Black Hundred Press. [Translator]

21

"The beetle has fallen into the cellar," the guard of the express train proclaimed joyfully, and the whole coach seemed to erupt, staggered by the news.* In the narrow corridor people drank toasts to each other until wine was splashing literally everywhere. Friends drank together and so did total strangers. A corpulent, crimson-faced MGB† colonel, probably in retirement, embraced an emaciated old Bolshevik lady with shaking hands who had spent half a century first in Tsarist and then in Stalinist prisons. Khrushchev had managed to set both the one and the other against him.

But was she right, the old lady Bolshevik, to go so far as to embrace her former jailer? After all, she had been freed by Khrushchev's order. Or were my friends and acquaintances nearer to the truth, when, like Pauline, they received the news of Khrushchev's fall with no rejoicing?

At the Twentieth Congress Khrushchev of course spoke about the tragedy of Stalin. But Stalin's shootings and pogroms were the tragedy of the people, and theirs alone. Not the tragedy of the murderer himself . . . it is unconscionable to speak of the "tragedy" of a man who has killed millions of people.

But are historians right to stay silent about the tragedy of Khrushchev himself? He was the first, with peasant stubbornness, to tear apart the strands of Stalin's net of lies which had enmeshed the country. It is possible that even though he himself didn't see right through to the logical conclusion of his thoughts, he awakened an entire generation from lethargy. "He pushed a hedgehog under our scalps," as Pauline used to say.

Thousands and thousands of totally innocent people streamed out of the prisons and the camps, among them Alexander Solzhenitsyn and

* The Russian word for "beetle" is "khrushch." The word was the popular way of referring to Khrushchev. [Translator]
† Ministry of State Security; the previous name of the present KGB (Committee for State Security). [Translator]

Evgeniya Ginzburg, and since then it has become much more difficult to choke the historical paths that Russia has taken with filth and garbage. The country has begun to recognize itself, no matter how much the healing process has been slowed by such mortally terrified pupils of Stalin as Khrushchev himself—a passionate enemy of Stalin who was still condemned to wear Stalinist blinkers.

Have you ever seen a pit pony who's spent all of its life in the blackness of a mine, walking round and round in a circle, and who then comes to the surface for the first time? It comes up into the sun and to the straight roads, but at first it cannot lose the ingrained habit of the treadmill, and keeps moving in its dark circles. It was a true tragedy—to begin so bravely and energetically, to throw open Stalin's prisons, to start building houses—and then to end one's career as a capricious, self-important loudmouth, the muddle-headed "Khrushch" as he was always called.

The news of his fall was soon followed by that of the death of Stepan Zlobin. I flew back to Moscow overnight, and managed to be there for his funeral so that I could stand beneath the mournful walls of the Novo-Devichi Monastery and say what Stepan had meant to me and my comrades.

He was a leader: a man like squadron navigator Sknaryov and the pilot Syromyatnikov, who died in flames over the Barents Sea. . . .

The whole sea was black from the smoke that streamed from the doomed airplane: although Syromyatnikov and Sknaryov had only minutes left, the commander led his young pilots into the attack on the German convoy the way a father leads his children across a dangerous road. "Don't hang back, Valya. Come on. Quick! Come on!"

When they'd launched their torpedo, Sknaryov, who had apparently been set on fire by the blazing smoke as the aircraft banked, screamed out in agony, and Syromyatnikov spoke to him hoarsely and firmly: "Take it easy, Sasha. Easy . . ."

And that was all. The explosion blew the plane into fragments. But the young pilots got back without a scratch.

The only other man I ever met like my wartime commanding officers was Stepan Zlobin.

Everyone has his own holy place—his Mecca. When everything gets too much for me to bear, I go to Stepan's grave. It's at the very edge of the Novo-Devichi cemetery, where the wind is stronger, and where the wheels of the freight trains clatter past overhead—there is no peace even here. Beside the jutting chunk of raw rock—elemental almost—which marks Stepan's grave is the grave of his friend Vsevolod Ivanov, under a huge boulder, rubbed to a sheen by the action of the ice age. The great Vsevolod, who wrote *Armored Train 14-69* and then defended himself as a writer from behind that train. Nearby there's a granite colossus with the inscription "Nasim,"* and an invisible message to all those of us who remain behind on earth—to disperse the fog. Beyond that, lit up with an inner smile, is the great round head of Gudzy. It's made of a hard gray stone, the kind they use for making harbor walls.

That unconquerable individualist Ilya Ehrenburg isn't far away either. The lies told about him are piled so high that you'd need a shovel to clear them away. How much of Syromyatnikov's boldness, his heroism, did Ehrenburg need to get up alone, all alone, and stalk so eloquently out of the Pravda conference hall in 1953, from the meeting which had been called at Stalin's order to bring together the "government Jews," to approve the expulsion of the Jewish people from their homes? . . .

When I buried fearless Stepan, I also buried my hopes that any of the old and well-loved writers would raise a sword in public against our native Russian Black Hundreds. If I had found one such man, I could have given him a truckload of documents. If need be I would have carried them to him barefoot over broken glass. Even at the cost of my own life. It's bitter to have to write that I found no one.

The open, all-Moscow conference of Soviet writers was approaching after an eternity of silence. As the time drew close, it became clear that the conference was going to ignore the single most important subject for discussion, the one that disturbed anyone who still had any sense of shame.

Of course a turbulent pre-election conference was no place for the calm development of an argument. The old Khrushchev "automatons" would try to interrupt, shout us down in their hoarse voices. They would be looking for someone new to hire themselves out to—to prop themselves up against, as they say. If only we could thrust the truth down the throats of this confident Black Hundred Mafia. If only—and who cared by what means—if only we could get hold of one of these swine by the ears and drag him out into the sun, just to throw a little light on the subject, to remind them all that out there beyond the windows, we weren't all living in the Hitler Reich.

That morning I shaved carefully, put on my best starched shirt—and told Pauline of my decision. Her eyes grew wide and her lips tightened the way they always did when she was afraid for her son. She laid her rough, chemical-stained hand on my shoulder and we stood still, cheek to cheek, as I listened to her make the longest speech she had ever made in her life.

"You haven't forgotten Lyubka Mukhina. She turned into a murderer, yet we grew up together. We played games around the trees, played *lapta*. She was like my own sister.

* Nasim Khikmet, Turkish-born writer who settled in the USSR in 1951. [Translator]

"But those official dogs from the Ministry? Those chosen few? They pulled the trigger silently and smiled—a murder committed in silence isn't really murder at all. Who heard the shot? Where are the witnesses? The people who'll be listening to you also bear the marks of time. Will you be able to get through to them?

"Do you remember when Professor Elsberg, the specialist on Saltykov-Shchedrin and Dostoevsky, was accused of treason? He was an executioner who had sent innocent people to the torture chambers. 'You are condemning me by present moral standards. That is immoral,' he said. And what about that publisher Nikolai Lesyuchevsky who was an expert witness at the trial of Boris Kornilov? They shot Kornilov and afterward Lesyuchevsky defended himself point by point just the way Henrich does in Schwartz's play *The Dragon*: 'Let me say this: if you really consider the matter, you'll see that I'm not personally guilty of anything. That's just the way I've been taught.' And there was no one to give him the answer Lancelot gives Henrich in the play: 'Everyone was taught like that, but did you have to come out on top of the class, you filthy animal?'

"When you and I first met at university, the word 'humanism' was usually used in conjunction with 'false.' And it always sounded like a curse, an accusation. 'Morality,' 'goodness,' 'conscience' were all put in quotation marks. In the end, even 'social honesty' was put in quotes, as if a man could be honest to 'the people' even though he lied to his wife, his children, and his neighbors. Now the quotation marks have been removed. But they haven't removed Professor Elsberg; he's an inveterate traitor, but he's still teaching literary morality just like before. And they haven't removed Lesyuchevsky, who still controls the fate of so many Soviet writers. And Vasily Smirnov has been promoted. He's so prominent you can't get away from him.

"So whom are you going to reach, hothead? What about your great 'progressives'? The ones with a firm reputation for having clean hands? Those are the very people who disowned you, pushed you away as if you were the very devil himself. And covered their eyes so that they wouldn't have to acknowledge our troubles. You know they've long since convinced themselves that they're not keeping quiet out of cowardice, or any desire to save their own skins, but because they think a voice crying in the wilderness is laughable. That it's stupid to beat your head against a brick wall. And so on.

"They're very comfortable, these literary Napoleons, perched on their pedestals—very proud of themselves. But some of them are a little worried that the pedestals may be rather full of cracks. And if you come along and shake them up . . . The very fact that you're going to speak is going to shake them—it'll shatter them! They're going to hate you.

"Who do you think is going to support you? The ones like yourself? The ones who are never allowed onto the speakers' platform? Or the poor honest devils who grind their teeth under the pillow at night so their neighbors won't hear?"

Her eyes were looking more and more alarmed, and her pale cheeks were flushed.

I understood exactly what it was she wanted to say to me, she who was so cautious, who saw the world from the heights of the Inguletsk quarry. But—she didn't say it. . . . Her lips trembled, and she remarked thoughtfully, with a little smile, that always when she had been on the brink of disaster, some remarkable, good, or brave man had appeared to help her. Weren't they breeding good people anymore?

"Of course they are," I said cheerfully. I was so eager to get away from her gloomy predictions. "The logical conclusion to your chain of good men is me." But she responded with such a nervous and sarcastic laugh that I didn't go on.

She tugged at my elbow and we both sat down, as if we were about to set out on a journey.

That night she didn't sleep at all. Before she set off for work the next day she said, "Go and see Gudzy. He's ill."

Gudzy was, indeed, very ill. He lay in bed, his feeble hands resting on the sheets. He looked dried up, and his skin was a deathly gray-white. When I told him what I intended to do, he looked at me as if I, not he, were under sentence of death. He tried to say something but found it hard to speak—so he gestured toward his bookshelf, usually stacked high with ancient Russian manuscripts.

Today there were no manuscripts to be seen. Instead, the shelves were lined with pictures of historical subjects. He was too weak to read, and so the indefatigable old man spent his time looking at paintings. Behind a picture of a naval battle I found a dust-covered folio. Gudzy leafed through the yellowing pages; he pointed out a sentence and whispered, "Remember this: 'The boyar was right, and he punished his accusers. . . . But the boyar was killed later for another wrong.' "

I felt shaken. The world's greatest specialist in Kiev-Rus was dying. A good man, beloved by his students. And this was the message he was leaving to the world?

That evening by chance an old acquaintance looked in—an elderly lady who worked as a translator. She had known me since the war; she had been noted for her courage. She clenched her thin hands and urged Pauline to lock me up at home. "He'll be arrested as soon as he leaves the platform." She took some validol to calm herself and quoted Saltykov-Shchedrin from memory: " 'The truly unrepentant criminal is neither a robber

nor a murderer, but a freethinker.' You'd be better off robbing a bank,"
she said, her voice quavering. "Organize a brothel or something. Don't pay
your Party dues. They'd forgive you anything like that. But rake up the fact
that building Communism is incompatible with anti-Semitism and stick it
under their noses—and they'll hound you to death! After all, they know that
already without your telling them. So to hell with you! You're just acting
out of pride. Forget it. You can do what you like to yourself, but think of
Pauline and your son. They've got to go on living."

O Lord, what has time done to the beautiful, good people?

Pauline came to the metro station with me. She pressed her warm
mouth to my cheek. But her lips were tense. Then, as a joke, she whispered
cheerfully—"Don't back down."

At the Writers' Union the guest of honor was expected any minute.
He was the most eminent guest imaginable—the secretary of the Central
Committee of the Commuist Party of the Soviet Union, Comrade Demichev. Several paunchy, round-shouldered writers in evening dress stood in
a semicircle near the main doors, like a column of amazed penguins eyeing
the discoverers of the Antarctic. They were all at attention. And if they had
to shake hands with a friend, they rapidly disengaged again so that their
arms could return swiftly to their sides, trembling like black vestigial wings.

Heaven knows why the reception party should have been so nervous.
The order of business of this pre-election meeting had been laid down with
all the rigidity of a May Day parade. The list of speakers had been drawn
up a week ahead, thoroughly checked and approved. And anyway, they'd
known for a long time which writers could be allowed to speak. There
wasn't even any need to listen to what they were saying—you could be sure
that they wouldn't deviate from the norm. And they knew who couldn't
under any circumstances be allowed on the platform. Yet they were still
nervous.

The Party organizer of the City Committee attached to the Writers'
Union, Viktor Telpugov, a narrow-shouldered, quiet-mannered nature
writer, the "singer of spring," as his friends called him, had written my
name on the list of speakers on his pad. I was number four. He even showed
me the slip of paper—"There you are—that proves it. Fourth . . ."

The first three speakers came and went. A fourth was called, then a
fifth and a sixth. I realized that they were using the well-worn tactics of
the "fixed race," the "don't hurry, my dear fellow," where the chairman,
like a crooked jockey, uses his reins to determine which horse will win the
race, and which one comes in last. I'd seen this happen time and time
again over the years, putting men like Stepan Zlobin and Konstantin Paustovsky into last place. Of course, it was flattering to be in such good company, but still . . . Any moment now a new speaker would be called, and

then it would be—"And our next and final speaker is the secretary of the Central Committee of the CPSU, Comrade Demichev." And that would be it. A well-organized plan. Down into last place . . .

So I had to make a move. If one writer on his own meant nothing here, perhaps they would pay some attention to the wishes of twelve hundred. For about ten minutes there was a tremendous uproar in the hall. Some of them were shouting, "Let him speak!"; others the very opposite. And over and above the clamor I could hear the penetrating high-pitched voice of Karpova, chief editor of the Writers publishing house, who rushed to the highest part of the stage where Demichev was sitting and shouted that it was disgraceful to demand the right to speak when the writers had gathered to hear the speech of the secretary of the Central Committee. She sounded really frightened.

In all the din a vote was taken. The fight continued even when I began to speak. My first words were lost. But then everyone calmed down and the hall was quiet. This time at least the goodwill of the writers had overpowered the literary officials hovering nervously on the sidelines.

I had written the first half of my speech in advance. If anyone tried to interrupt, began to shout or to create a disturbance, I could go back to the exact point where I'd broken off. But the second part—well, there was no point in writing that out. By then no one would be able to stop me.

Allow me to quote the official transcript of my speech at the open Party meeting of the Moscow writers, held on October 27, 1965. We will call it Document No. 1. For this, alas, is not the end of the story. Only the beginning of the end.

Document No. 1

"At all the meetings I have attended in this hall, the leaders have usually begun and ended their speeches with the words, 'Writers don't know about life.' That has been their leitmotiv. And in this connection I have often been reminded of the words of a wise writer, now dead, who when he left one of these meetings, muttered to himself, 'Study life! Study life! Good God, if only we could manage to forget even half of what we've lived through.'

"I think that this formula, 'We don't know life,' springs from the fact, first of all, that writers ask, and have always asked, those acute questions which most disturb an inert leadership. They go straight for the so-called forbidden subjects, the undesirable themes, and, from the point of view of officialdom, that clearly displays a lack of awareness of the facts of life.

"These forbidden themes are something like back rooms. They are full of the abomination of desolation, and no guests are allowed in. But writers are not guests.

"So let me speak on two forbidden subjects.

"The first is one that has been 'closed' for many years. It is the subject of the education of public thinking in the State of the Common Man. It is a direct and honest question to ask—how to involve the masses in the direction of production, how to attract the 'silent ones' who sit in the electoral colleges like so many pieces of furniture. How to attract those who always avoid public duties. How do we move from a political formula to direct action?

"In my journeys around the country I constantly come across widespread evidence of the apathy of the workingman. Time and again I hear, 'It doesn't make any difference what you say—nothing ever changes.' 'The bosses just read the papers, listen to the radio—let them worry about things.' And this indifference to public and social matters drives ordinary people to drink. In one pulp collective I went to, 92 percent of the wages are spent on vodka. And dominoes! People are literally frittering away their free time, just killing time with games. And football. The English have a saying that it takes your mind off politics.

"But the most important thing is that the older workers are teaching the mass of youngsters how to drink. The young aren't involved in social life (with very few exceptions), are not attracted by badly run, overformal *Komsomol organizations*. When I was at the *Bratsk Hydroelectric Station*, I saw drunken youths careening on their motorcycles along cord roads and leaping over precipices like circus acrobats. I asked them why they didn't want to do more useful social work. The answer was that the club had room for three hundred people, and there were thirty thousand workers on the site.

"The most important task we have is to find a practical way of involving the workers, of getting away from verbose abstractions and finding practical things to do. That essentially is what my work is all about—all my books and articles. But precisely because my books are about ideological problems, I worry about them, I fight on their behalf for any amount of time—from two to twelve years.

"My article on the unwitting reinforcement of thoughtlessness was described in some editorial offices as anti-Party. Later, after two years of worry, it was published in the magazine Party Life. The novel Leninsky Prospekt, which the reviews described as dealing with present-day problems from the Party point of view, began its journey round the publishers to the accompaniment of accusations that I had written a slanderous anti-Party work.

"And it's the same with every book, every article. Until the Central Committee makes a ruling on a particular problem, in the view of editors that problem doesn't exist.

"Because I deal in ideological problems, I find myself in the position of Nekrasov's peasant, waiting at the main door until someone inside decides to hear his petition.

"What is the matter? There is a great deal wrong—in the ranks of the editors who are determined to overinsure themselves, who still suffer from the trauma of the Stalinist era, who still believe that heads must fall for every error made; it is only natural that they prefer not to publish than to risk it, particularly since there's more than enough material at hand, and we have very few publishers.

"Many editors fail to notice the more painful manifestations of our lives until they become an actual danger to the state and are condemned by a Central Committee resolution. Such editors condemn articles and short stories and novels for being mere illustration, for chewing over old themes, for being repetitions of what has already been said.

"I think that this kind of editor is objectively—and not just subjectively—the main anti-Party force in our institutions . . .

(Applause; shouts of "It's true!")

". . . since they reject anything that's daring, anything that's up to the minute. And this material must wait for years. Some of my colleagues have written books which have waited eight, ten, twelve years for publication.

(Shouts: "And you'll find most editors like that at Voenizdat [the military publishing house]!" Laughter in the hall.)

"We need brave men who are not afraid of asking painful questions, who will prevent our sicknesses from being driven deeper within ourselves, who will bring them to the surface. We need editors who are committed to ideas, otherwise we will get no good results.

"Recently I took a pile of books which had just been published and well received by the critics—they were written by friends of mine—and I checked back. . . . What had been dropped just before publication, what had been removed by the censors? I was horrified; all the blue pencilings, all the cuts had an anti-Party, anti-Congress bias. Everything that supported the ideas put forward in the Twentieth and Twenty-second Party Congresses, everything which was written straightforwardly and directly about those ideas had gone.

"The problem of finding brave and ideologically sound editors for literary organizations, it seems to me, is our problem No. 1.

"I want to ask Comrade Demichev why this mass of Communist writers who are sitting here in this hall have been excluded from any part of the decision-making process? Why do they have no say in the selection of editors? At this very moment, the editor of Literaturnaya Gazeta is being appointed! Why not ask all those who are sitting here how most writers feel about one candidate or another!

(Applause. Shouts from the hall—"Quite right!")

"Why have Communists been excluded from this question, which is vitally important to them? Why aren't they asked whether this or that candidate would have the right kind of authority or not? What actually happens is that some people clamber onto the escalator to advancement and it simply carries them from height to height.

"If we were to strengthen the structure of Party democracy, at the same time we would be strengthening the fighting efficiency of the organization. If we have simply been gathered here to listen to speeches and then go home, there has been no increase in our strength.

"The great majority of editors I know are honest men. They fight for those books they like, but they are rendered nonentities, humiliated now as never before by censorship, which has taken unprecedented, anti-constitutional powers on itself.

"Nowadays the censorship is referred to as 'Special Literary Consultation.' The job of Glavlit* is to preserve state and military secrets, not to run literary trials, and not to interfere in the creative process.

(Applause. Shouts from the hall: "That's true, that's right!")

"This interference has now reached the farthest limits of stupidity.

"It is interesting to note exactly when the censorship acquired the right to act as it thought fit. It was at the time the great Khrushchev decennial celebrations were being prepared. A big lie was thought necessary and so the Moscow Party Writers' organization was disbanded—we were told to join Party groups in our apartment blocks and in other institutions, so that we could study life there.

(Applause.)

"Having dealt with (a) I must now go on to the (b). The time of our great flood has passed. Let censorship return to its rightful banks. Let editors return to being editors.

"We have already overcome the cult of personality. Now it is time to end the cult of incompetence."

(Applause.)

While people were clapping and shouting their approval, I looked

* The official censorship, which operates in every newspaper office and publishing house. [Translator]

around. Behind me I had been hearing something like a gramophone record stuck in a groove. It was bothering me: time and again, quietly, insinuatingly, it kept on repeating, "I wouldn't have said that."

Sitting just behind me, it turned out, was one of the most active and nervous secretaries of the Writers' Union, Alexander Chakovsky. There he was with his shoulders hunched, constantly muttering, "I wouldn't have said that. I wouldn't have said that." What was he trying to do? Was he trying to shoot me down in full flight like a crow, the way he usually did? Trying to put me in my place—"Come to your senses"? Or was he just mechanically repeating the phrase without even knowing he was talking out loud?

I turned back to the presidium, where the sweating Viktor Telpugov was pointing out the time to me and the assembled company, to indicate I had passed my limit, while he faced the leaders of the Writers' Union, Fedin and Simonov, sitting side by side, and also nodded toward Demichev.

I looked at Konstantin Simonov and at Konstantin Fedin. Was I getting through to them or not? Was there any human spark left in them? Simonov's yellowish, flame-colored eyes held all the unquenchable interest of a scientist looking into a microscope at some creature which was behaving in a totally uncharacteristic way. But Fedin's eyes had gone dead. They were frozen with horror.

"Please"—Viktor Telpugov finally managed to blurt out to calm the meeting down as he nervously twitched his shoulders.

"Now to the second subject. Even if articles and books have been published on the first subject, despite everything the second remains firmly closed.

"Once I was in the Ossetian Republic with a group of mountaineers and tourists. In one village an old man came up to us and said, 'We invite you all to the wedding. The whole village will be there. Except you'—and here he indicated me—'you are not invited.' So I stayed behind to take care of the bags. I sat there reading a book, and suddenly a cloud of dust appeared in the village street, moving toward me, as if Budyonny's cavalry was on the charge. I was seized and dragged away by the bride and bridegroom, yelling, 'Forgive us, dear friend,' and hauled off to the wedding feast. They poured the local vodka—arak—into a drinking horn and tipped it down my throat. I asked my friends what had happened, why they hadn't invited me in the first place, and why I was now being treated as the guest of honor. It turned out that my friends had asked the old man why I hadn't been invited, and he said, 'We don't invite Georgians!' My friends had explained that I wasn't a Georgian. Then the old man had yelled that he had mor-

tally insulted me, and that I must have my revenge. In order to forestall
any such act of revenge, the entire wedding party had set out to fetch me.
The next day the old man came around to ask whether I had forgiven him.

"When the tour was over, we came back to Tbilisi. That evening we
went out for a stroll. Two drunks came up and said something in Georgian.
I didn't understand. Then one of them took a swing and hit me in the ear.
I fell down. Someone in the hotel foyer shouted, 'They're beating up our
people.' The mountaineers came piling out of the hotel and a brawl started.

"We ended up in the militia post. All the proceedings were conducted
in Georgian. Then suddenly the man who had hit me picked up my passport which was lying on the table, leafed through it, and came over to me
saying, 'Forgive me, we thought you were an Armenian from Erivan. Come
on, let's go and have a drink.' It took me a long time to get away from them.

"Half of the climbers in our group were from the Baltic States. First-
class sportsmen. After all that, we became close friends. But whenever they
talked among themselves and we came up, they stopped. I would say,
'What's up?' and they'd say, 'Well, you're a Russian.'

"When I got back to Moscow, I learned that I had been turned down
as a member of the editorial board of a literary journal because I was a Jew.

"That's the way the subject of the battle with chauvinism came into
my life. I tried to fight it, but I came to the conclusion that there is no
real battle being waged in our country against great-power chauvinism.
What's more, there appears to be some kind of incomprehensible collaboration with it. For example, Vasily Smirnov. Just as water is wet and snow is
white, so Vasily Smirnov is a great-power chauvinist. In fact, he's the only
chauvinist who doesn't even bother to hide his views. He has compromised
himself to such an extent that it even became necessary to remove him from
the secretariat of the Writers' Union. But within six months he was appointed editor-in-chief of the magazine Friendship of the Peoples.

(Laughter.)

"Comrades, we know that he is not the only one to share and preach
these views. We here in the Writers' Union have our own Black—no, not
a Hundred, but a dozen—and the way they are allowed to get away with
things is truly remarkable. Those who allowed Ivan Shevtsov's pogrom
work The Louse to be published go unpunished. Then there are several
Ukrainians who have not been reprimanded. When I was in Kiev I was
amazed to see how far they had been allowed to go. Let me get home as
fast as I can, I thought, to my own native pogromists!

"I must repeat—there has been a total lack of condemnation of the
man who published a work like The Louse, and also of those who refused
to publish I. Konstantinovsky's great book The Term of Ages. This anti-
Fascist book was described in the prose department of the Soviet Writers

publishing house as nationalistic. And in the publishing house's internal newspaper there was even an article saying that more attention should be paid to the war against Zionism. Now Konstantinovsky had been published in many countries and has been wonderfully well received.

"We should punish not only those who release bad and harmful works, but also those who keep fine Party works off the market.

"In 1953 I wrote a short article called 'The Trolley Stayed Silent.' A drunken fool started abusing the Jews in public, and the rest of the passengers in the car didn't have a word to say. I'm not so much interested in one stupid racist as in the rest of the passengers. Why did they remain silent? I have tried to analyze that. But for twelve years I have been unable to find a publisher for the article.

"I think that fact alone is sufficient evidence of trouble in this area.

"When people criticize the leadership from the platform of writers' meetings or turn against irresponsible people—and the Writers' Union has its share of irresponsible people who are prepared to climb to paradise on other people's backs, on other people's blunders—these same irresponsible people reply that writers don't want the Party leadership. So, for I don't know how many years, we all have to feed off rumors, since they seem to be the only directives from our leadership. We hear, 'Egorychev said such and such, Demichev said such and such, Pavlov had these views.' What is this? Party leadership? We are tired of being harassed and having to run for cover."

(Applause.) . . .

I came down from the rostrum into the roaring body of the hall, which applauded far longer than I deserved. But strictly speaking, it wasn't me they were applauding. It was the relief from dumbness, from unspoken, cowardly fear. "Fear is dying in Russia," Evtushenko prophesied.

Maybe, but slowly. Very slowly.

I sat down where I could—by the wall. Nikolai Chukovsky came to sit next to me—a good man, a talented translator and prose writer, the son of Kornei Chukovsky, who even in the worst years had, like Schwartz, been able to speak the truth. He sat forward in his seat, protecting me from being seen from the presidium table. He stroked my arm in a fatherly way, and murmured quietly, "What will Demichev say now? What will Demichev say now?" Yet all the time, his face remained turned toward the presidium table, stonily unmoved. He was dissociating himself from me, his neighbor.

At last the Central Committee secretary Demichev rose from his seat, smooth-faced, slow-moving, holding himself stiffly erect like an officer. He was middle-aged, about the age that people get to be the secretary of a university Party Committee. Pauline had told me he was a chemical engineer, which for some reason cheered me up a little.

He said that we Communists had indeed broken off the struggle with anti-Semitism too early. Anti-Semitism was still with us. . . .

"Anti-Semitism should be a reason for expulsion from the Party!" shouted the Old Bolshevik Landres, pounding the floor with his crutch. Landres was a publisher, a colleague of Ordzhonikidze and had probably served time in every Russian prison.

"That is correct," confirmed the Central Committee secretary, who was responsible for the ideology of the Soviet Union. "The penalty for anti-Semitism should be exclusion from the Party!"

Although I write these words from memory, they are accurate. At the same time that I heard them they were heard by twelve hundred Moscow writers—tragedians and historians, humorists and rhymesters, in addition to several prose writers from Leningrad and other cities who had flown in for the conference. The Central Committee secretary talked long and passionately about the need for the fight against anti-Semitism to be continued.

A week later Demichev repeated all this in a speech to teachers and students of Moscow University, then again in a factory—and that finally ended the remarks about our home-grown Black Hundreds; he'd only said it because he'd been forced to.

There was a telephone behind the stage. As soon as Demichev finished, I rang Pauline, who had been waiting for the call more dead than alive. "Everything's all right!" I whispered, covering the receiver with my hand as I was being complimented by those who were waiting to use the phone to let Party instructors and *Pravda* correspondents know what had happened. "Everything's all right!"

A week went by, full of embraces and congratulations. The old lady translator wept in our house, saying that Demichev had saved me. If it hadn't been for him . . .

It was late autumn. But the sun shone as if what lay ahead wasn't winter with its Russian snowstorms but an Indian summer, time for holidays.

"Lord," said Pauline, "Is our son really going to be free of the Yellow Star and Point Five?"

Yes! I believed a new era was dawning.

22

A week later I was summoned to the Moscow City Committee.

The head of the cultural department, Solovyova, rose to meet me. She was a stocky lady with a round face and curls, a comfortable domestic person. She beamed as if welcoming a favorite guest and adjusted her white lace collar. Then she said with a smile, as if she were offering me a slice of cake, "Admit that you got too excited."

"What?"

"Well, that your speech . . . on anti-Semitism. And Vasily Smirnov. All that. You were just overexcited. And now you've thought it all over. Why don't you write that you were overexcited?"

In some way her face reminded me of Karpova's, and I realized later that the resemblance lay in the soft exterior and the false smile of the official who has to talk every day with writers, playwrights, and painters— people whom it's safer not to anger, whatever you may think of them. Her face shone with benevolence and a willingness to forgive all. After all, who among us has never made a mistake?

A man with impenetrable coal-black eyes, who until now had sat silently in the corner, said firmly that I had no reason to accuse anyone of anti-Semitism, which of course didn't exist in our country. I had even less reason to name the Russian writer Vasily Smirnov, who for five years had been in charge of the international all-union magazine *Friendship of the Peoples*. "So what do you think is happening? Who is the leader here?"

Solovyova's kindly face grew kinder yet. "Look," she said. "See what you've done. All we want you to do is to put everything right and say 'Forgive me, friends. I got carried away. . . .' And her kind, soft expression suddenly turned into the hardest, stoniest face I had ever seen.

The man with the impenetrable eyes said sharply that I had spoken incorrectly. No one needed my speech. More than that, it was harmful.

It just poured more water on the millwheel—whose millwheel he didn't say—but when people talk of millwheels it always means that things are getting really serious. Any minute now the shouting would start. (After they've given you the bit about the millwheel they always start shouting.) I turned to look at the only person I knew in the room. Viktor Telpugov.

Telpugov had always shown me goodwill and had even once admitted (ah, these after-dinner confessions!) that he liked me. Indeed, we had become friends after a tourist trip to Scandinavia, where he maintained I had saved the honor of the Russian writers.

The first time was in Oslo, where our official speakers had reduced their audience to a complete state of bewilderment by their vacuous speechmaking. I had had to stand up and depart from the program by pointing out on a map exactly where and how my friends had died freeing Norway from Fascism.

The second occasion was in Helsinki, where we were meeting in a small wood near our hotel. The intention was to talk about our affairs with trade-union directness. Like a May Day meeting. And suddenly a desperately drunken Finn advanced on us from out of the trees. He was enormous, with his arms dangling around his knees, and several fingers missing from one hand. It was clear that he was full of memories of the Russo-Finnish war. . . .

From that time on Telpugov had called me his friend, and once when the City Committee had been agonizing endlessly over whether Svirsky should be allowed to meet the old Canon Kir* he said warmly that there was absolutely no reason why I shouldn't. And we had met. I even embraced Kir. I was able to prove to my own satisfaction that the heroic mayor of Dijon, despite his ninety-four years, was absolutely in full command of his faculties. Apart from embracing me, he gave the young Intourist interpreter a hearty kiss.

In short, I believed that Telpugov, even if he wasn't my friend, was at least a true comrade, and so, in Solovyova's stuffy room, which for some reason was full of people who wanted to see me, I looked at him expectantly.

But Telpugov stayed silent. He looked away, and when he finally did open his mouth he too uttered something about millwheels.

I began to talk about Pauline, about myself, about Fima . . . but I quickly fell silent when I noticed on Solovyova's round and smiling face that same familiar, slightly tense expression Polikarpov used to have when he was trying to suppress a yawn—"Oh, Jews . . ."

Solovyova was in a hurry to go somewhere—after all, she was in charge

* Communist mayor of Dijon, France, and a wartime leader of the Resistance. [Translator]

of the whole cultural life of Moscow. Telpugov and I left the building together, and I asked him in bewilderment what had happened. The secretary of the Central Committee of the Communist Party of the Soviet Union, Demichev, the man responsible for ideology, had said one thing, yet here we had the smiling official, Solovyova, a whole skyscraper lower on the hierarchical ladder, saying something entirely different. Directly opposite.

So what happened?

Telpugov held his hand out for quite a time to make sure that it wasn't beginning to rain. Then he put on a raincoat, a round hat, rather like a pastor's, and finally answered lamely that people were afraid of pouring yet more water on the millwheel.

"Whose millwheel?" I asked angrily, so loudly that the smart and observant militiaman on duty outside the City Committee offices turned to look me up and down.

"On the millwheel of the Zionist elements," said Telpugov, hailing a taxi. Then he leaned over confidentially, with his face close to mine: "There are signs. Some Jews want to leave for . . . Israel. Making out that things here are bad. Then there are the young people. Dancing in the synagogues. For show. And tongues are beginning to wag—people saying that they can't get jobs or university places and so on. The City Committee is watching out for it; your speech was water on the millwheel." Then he slammed the door of his taxi, and through the glass I could see him making a gesture imitating the turning of the wheel.

I asked all my friends and acquaintances to do me a favor—to find me a miller—that is, a Zionist. Or simply a Jewish nationalist, one without any particular philosophical "-isms." Even one who wasn't very literate. But he must dream of going to Israel.

I wanted to understand what the Regional Committee was so scared of. Apparently the Soviet nation, two hundred and twenty million people, was waiting in anticipation, holding its breath. Maybe there was indeed some serious danger?

Recently I had talked with a young woman teacher, who frenziedly maintained that Jews were guilty of bringing about the ideological fall of Lunacharsky.* It had all begun when he married Rosanella, the Jewess. I jotted down a portrait of this woman, and made a note of her manner of speaking. It was a long time since I had met a zoological specimen of an anti-Semite in such a pure strain. But could there possibly be an exact

* Anatoly Lunacharsky (1875–1933), People's Commissar for Education in the first years after the Revolution. He was particularly involved in the theater both as writer and critic. [Translator]

opposite of people like her? In the end, I would have to find one for myself, feel the creature with my own hand. What kind of people could they be? Finally one of my friends hurried in, delighted with himself.

"I've found one! A real one! Alexander Weiner, twenty-nine years old. He's a technician in the street lighting department. I talked about him with the laborers who put the lampposts up. They think he's a little strange in the head. Doesn't drink, doesn't smoke. Blushes when they talk about women. The foreman said, 'I don't know what to make of that Jew. Jews are either in business, or else they're scientists, wise men. And this one? He's just a worker. Spends his days out in the cold. In a faded raincoat. There aren't any Jews like that.' But it's not true. He's got a whole library at home of books about Jews. All he thinks about is Judaism. In a word, he's a full-blown nationalist. He says if they won't let him go to Israel, he'll try to cross the frontier. . . . Shall I bring him in?"

He stopped by the door, turned, and whispered awkwardly, "There's one condition. He'll be absolutely open with you, but he doesn't want any propaganda from you—no trying to re-educate him, no persuasion, nothing like that."

The young man appeared. He looked very young, thin. He introduced himself quietly: "Sasha." He took off his long raincoat, which hung on him as if he were a hanger. He looked down at his feet, at the carpet, and asked for a damp rag. He carefully wiped his boots with it. They were very serious boots, made of coarse leather with a thick molded sole; they looked as if they would never wear out. They were boots for a site foreman, a geologist, an around-the-world walker. A traveler.

He came quietly into the room and sat on the edge of a chair. He was very shy. He didn't know where to put his hands. Sometimes he tried them on his knees, then he got hold of his elbows and hugged himself as if he were cold. His wrists were thin, his fingers knotted, his nails chewed.

The friend who'd brought Sasha along said as he left that Sasha had heard about my speech. That was why he had agreed to come.

"Yes, I heard about it," Sasha confirmed. His voice was very quiet, with a tremor, as if it had only just broken. "Forgive me for being so annoyed about your speech. But you were . . . overexcited. You gave free rein to your feelings. That's no use to anyone."

I must have been gaping with astonishment. So this is the song the millers sing! Overexcited. Annoyed . . . he must work for Solovyova. Part-time. Or do opposites meet?

"Good God!" I finally recovered the power of speech. "Why don't you approve of what I said? You're a confirmed nationalist, or so I've been told. Come on, let's have it straight."

Sasha shuffled his feet under the table, grew red in the face; you could tell he didn't like hurting people's feelings but he was screwing up his courage to tell me where I had gone wrong, and why.

"You're spreading illusions," he said, after a long pause. "Giving people hope. One more speech. One more time. Let's try again. Just one more heave—and we'll push Russia off the sandbanks of anti-Semitism. Why spread illusions? People believe what you say because they want to so desperately. But there is no hope. There *are* no ways. Even if you get clear of one sandbank, there's another one just waiting to catch you again. All the channels are silted up. You won't shift Russia. She's far too firmly seated."

I looked at his anguished face. His curly black hair fell in tight ringlets to his chin, which sported a thin growth of beard. You see quite a few bearded youths in Moscow these days. Beards on twenty-year-olds always look so deliberate, sometimes almost unnatural. In this case, the beard was clearly being worn as a matter of principle. It was his way of crying defiantly, "I am a Jew. You don't like it? Well, that's O.K. by me." The words poured out of him—excited, stubborn, indignant. "Where are you calling people to? Why? You'll just do yourself harm. You'll get such a thrashing, you'll be licking your wounds the rest of your life."

"Why?"

"History." He laughed again, but his burning dark eyes were full of sorrow. They suddenly lost their sharp, youthful shine, and went misty; as if they had clouded over with the grief of ages. "The history of the Question. Even the most recent history. I've studied it. Grigory Perets—he was a Jew who'd been baptized a Christian—was discussing with Pestel, the Decembrist,* a plan for the solution of the Jewish Question. He was sent to Siberia. To the mines. Just for discussing the Question. There were no other charges against him. He was a Jew and he'd discussed the matter. That was enough. But what if Pestel had won? He was a humanist, he wouldn't have sent the Jews to Siberia. He would have expelled them from the Russian Empire altogether. Those were the plans he had. But of course, the humanist didn't win.

"When Nicholas I exiled Perets he resolved the Jewish problem at a stroke. By the Tsarist formula. He 'shaved the heads' of the Jews, on equal terms—twenty-five years each. Twenty-five years of compulsory service in the army. Actually, Jews had an advantage over Russians—they started their service in childhood. As messenger boys. Your great-grandfather was one himself. Remember your Herzen: 'A troop of Jewish children comes past. Eight or nine years old. The officer complains, "A third of them

---

* The Decembrists were a group of noblemen opposed to the autocracy of the Tsars. They were mainly army officers and were led by Pestel, Muravyov, and Ryleev. In December 1825 they rose against the Tsar and were crushed. [Translator]

have been left behind on the road, and half of them won't reach their destination . . . they die like flies; they're frail and puny, and for ten hours a day they have to shuffle through the mud with nothing to eat but crusts." '

"Herzen* only caught a glimpse of this, but he almost fainted in horror. He wrote: 'No brush could ever set out such horror on canvas. I wanted to weep. I felt that I could stand no more.' And later—a year didn't go by without the Jews being given some little gift or other.

"In 1876 the student Sasha Bibertal was sentenced to fifteen years hard labor. Why? For standing outside the Kazan cathedral while a funeral service was going on inside. When the president of the court asked him, 'Why were you arrested if, as you say, there was no reason for it?' Sasha replied, 'Well, you see, my coat is shabby, and I suppose I look a bit like a student.'

"A Jew could be given a sentence for anything—or nothing; so, fifteen years hard labor. 'That'll teach you to stand near cathedrals!'

"In Kiev in 1879, the military prosecutor Strelnikov insisted on the death penalty for Rozovsky, an under-age student. For what? He had been reading a leaflet and refused to say who had given it to him.

"A Jew could be shot. Just like that. Even a boy. Just for refusing to tell tales, to give his friends away. And at that time there weren't even any special laws about Jews. Up till then it was just pure enthusiasm on the part of the officials.

"But then when Alexander III turned up—our benefactor! . . ."

I laughed, thanked Sasha, and said that I'd heard enough about Alexander III.

Sasha looked gloomily at his shoes. He said quietly, unsmiling: "So why, I ask you again, do you deceive people? Give them hope? We shall overcome. We shall break through, and illumine holy Russia with bonfires! That's just the same as whistling to a hungry dog in the street, then when it comes running up expecting food, you slam your door in its face. What are you calling for? To find a common language with those complacent crooks—the Stalinists, the criminals, the betrayers of Christ? What do you expect?"

His face grew hard, and I suddenly believed that he would actually try to cross the border in order to sentence himself to certain death. Indeed he himself brought it up, and it was clear that that was all he lived for. Perhaps that was why he had come to me with his secret hope.

"How can I get away from here? In Israel I'd do anything—carry manure, drain swamps—anything. But I'd be an equal. Right?"

* Alexander Herzen (1812–1870), revolutionary thinker and writer, founded the magazine *Kolokol* ("The Bell") in London. [Translator]

I didn't answer, and he sagged, chewing nervously at his beard.

"Of course, I haven't come to the right place." And then the breath rushed from him in a hissing whisper: "But there isn't any right place to go to. You wander around town like a letter with no address. Until they fling you into the waste bin."

I asked him about his family. His father had been a Bolshevik, but he'd ended up in one of Stalin's camps. Sasha had lived in poverty with his sick mother who struggled on desperately, like a fish trapped under the ice. He had wanted to become a lawyer, to try to understand why under our highly developed system of Socialist legality there was room for so much total and unheeding lawlessness.

"And now I'm a Jew, and only a Jew."

That reminded me of something a wounded pilot once said to me as he was being carried into a hospital after his arm was blown off. He had dreamed of going to an academy. Now, he shouted, "Tell the boys I'm wounded, I'm wounded!"

Sasha laughed bitterly. "Equality! Just imagine a swimming race on such an equal basis. Some swimming just as they are. Others with weights on their legs, from four to thirty pounds if they're Jews. Then you hear the starting gun. On an equal basis. Those are the rights accorded us by Stalin's Constitution. And you can't complain. Complaints, as they say, aren't accepted. Of course. If you live with the wolves, you must learn to like them. . . ."

I hurriedly looked for a copy of Zola on the shelf, found the place I wanted, and read aloud that to account oneself just a Jew, just a German, just a Frenchman, just a Russian was to return to the forests. Atavism. A play unworthy of the twentieth century—a play on primitive fears, mythology, racial conceit. "That's just being a reflector, Sasha, to live from insult to insult. To go from lamppost to lamppost, like someone learning to ride a bicycle who keeps crashing into them full tilt. Then the world narrows down; everything is overshadowed by the posts of gallows and gas chambers, and you don't notice that you're in a deep well. So you're frightened out of your wits. All history shouts that message out loud if you study it properly.

"And here's something about your personal enemies, Sasha! 'To use the people's misery to turn the poor against the Jews as the representatives of capitalism is the work of hypocrites and liars, passing themselves off as Socialists. They must be unmasked and covered with disgrace.' So your nationalism, Sasha, it's not a thought, not a way of life. It's a bruise, it's what's left after a severe blow."

"Excuse me, is that Zola?" asked Sasha with a flash of a grim smile. "Another theorist around my neck!"

I put the book aside and talked about my uncle.

"My uncle worked with Ordzhonikidze. When Ordzhonikidze was shot, my uncle was arrested, and Kaganovich announced in the People's Commissariat of Heavy Industry: 'Svirsky is an international spy. He has been shot.'

"But in 1954 my uncle returned. He was a skeleton—hardly enough body for his soul to live in. He was wearing a jacket that was too tight for him. He had a prisoner's passport* in his pocket, which said where he could and could not go. We sat down at the table, just the two of us. With a bottle of vodka. I asked him what was the worst.

" 'The main thing,' he said, 'is not to get bitter! Not to lose yourself in bitterness. On the one hand, there's a column of political prisoners being beaten up with rifle butts. On the other, the criminal prisoners who shout and sneer, "Hey, Soviet man! Have they chosen a lighter club to beat you with because you're a Soviet?" Don't get bitter. That's all that kept us alive.'

"His comrade in the prison van, the father of the poet Karpekov, threw a note scribbled on a cigarette packet beneath the wheels as they were getting in. What message had he sent his wife? What was his most pressing anxiety in what might be the last days of his life? 'I pray that our children shall not grow up in hatred.' . . .

"Sasha, it seems that your father was one of that breed of revolutionaries. What about you? What have you become?"

I suddenly remembered the policeman in Engels Street who had peered in through our window. "Jews get beaten up whatever happens. So they must be up to something. They're people, not iron." And now—the full completion of the program—the young man ready to fling himself on to the barbed wire, to be shot . . .

"Our fathers—that was another age," Sasha replied quietly.

I picked up from the table a photograph of Pauline taken ten years earlier. She had rosy country cheeks, arched eyebrows; she looked younger than Sasha. I showed him the photograph. "This woman's not much older than you. The Nazis killed her entire family. Father, mother, brother, the old people. Everyone. Then she was refused permission to study for a higher degree at Moscow University, and then she couldn't get work here in Moscow, for the same reason the Nazis murdered her family."

"And what's happened to her?" Sasha breathed rather than asked, hunching his entire body forward and spreading his feet in their heavy shoes wide apart, as if he were about to jump up and go find her.

---

* These passports had a list of exemptions stamped in them indicating places where the holder was not permitted to go. [Translator]

"Since then she's made seventeen major scientific discoveries for her country. She's worked on its defense in dreadful conditions, sometimes so bad she had to wear a gas mask, although no one forced her to."

"Well, then. Give her my congratulations!" he said in a voice that made me want to end the conversation right there and make a quick farewell. I forced myself to sit quiet and calm down. Everything had been knocked out of this boy already. There was no point in my joining in.

One of my friends once told me that national feelings develop more in a concentration camp than anywhere else. There they can become painfully sharp. Once in a camp an Abkhazian prisoner said to my friend, "Your brother's arrived." My friend said he didn't have any brothers.

"How do you mean?" said the Abkhazian prisoner, surprised. "You're a Jew; so's he. For me all Abkhazians are brothers." And he looked scornfully at my friend. "Do you deny your brother?"

Unfortunately, it looks as if there is an equation to be made—national feelings are strongest where persecution is at its worst.

"Do you know how many Yakuts there are in the USSR?" Sasha suddenly asked. "Two hundred and forty thousand. They have twenty-eight newspapers. There are five hundred thousand Mari. They have seventeen newspapers. There are about three million Jews—and there's just one news sheet in Birobidzhan. And what about the Jewish theater?"

"Sasha, let's say they opened one tomorrow, which I agree would be fair. But you wouldn't go to it. You don't know the language."

"I'll learn it. And even if I didn't understand, I'd go to every show. Out of principle. They've taken away my homeland, and in its place they've given me a stepmother who's abused me for years. Finally she's almost torn my head away. And now people point me out in the street and say, 'Look at him, look, he's crop-eared!' Bastards! I'm getting out! Even if I have to walk barefoot through the snow, I'm going."

"Are you going to make a fuss? Are you going to demand to be allowed to go?"

Sasha looked at me the way he might look at a lunatic. "Whom can I demand that from? Whom can I have a fight with? In Toulouse in 1018 it was a custom every Easter that a Jew should be publicly beaten. That was repealed later in the eleventh century. But have they repealed it in Russia? Russia's a disorderly country. They don't have special dates for beating you up. That's the difference. What about respect for human dignity? Recognition of rights? Do you realize how far we're lagging behind? Three hundred years at least! Let's say for the sake of argument that the impossible happens. Let's say you get your equal rights, as they're defined in the Constitution, and a parliament, as in the Constitution. I'll bet you they'll burn down that parliament for the price of a half-liter of vodka. It's just a writer's dream to approach Russia with European standards. 'In the West there is law, in Russia influence.' Who respects the law here? I'm a fitter, I travel around a bit, and I have never in my whole life met anyone who respected the law. So whom are you going to argue with? Our ruffians? The chauvinist thug is nothing but a backside which sits on your face," he said sharply and rapidly; it was clear it wasn't the first time he'd had this argument. "And all you can do with a backside sitting on your face is lick it or bite it. You can't argue with an asshole."

"But, Sasha, forgive me, Russia isn't a backside. If it hadn't been for Stalingrad, Rommel would have run straight through to the Far East with his tank columns. And there would have been no one left to shoot. They say that in Israel there were communes that bought up the supplies of potassium cyanide. . . ."

I kept on trying to convince him, and then suddenly I realized that I was using nothing but arguments from the past. From times long gone.

But for Sasha even the war years were as much ancient history as the times of the Persian emperior Darius, who, if historians are to be believed, treated Jews as people. The Jews had equal rights for a hundred and fifty years. It didn't matter that the same thing had happened here in the twenties. That there was a decade of shaky equality. Of course he hadn't experienced that.

I searched for arguments everywhere I could think of. Arguments from today. But I could find none. And like a man who can't escape the blows falling on him, I covered my head with my hands. What it came down to was that I was blaming him for being young. He didn't have the first idea of what equal rights meant. I attacked him angrily. But my words lacked force. They lacked the irrefutable weight of facts. I had nothing to say to this boy who was so painfully close to me, both in his pride and in his pain.

I wanted only one thing. That he should not perish. That he should not hurl himself onto the barbed wire, as the desperate Jews hurled themselves onto the wire at Auschwitz. For I know what the frontier is like, say near Batumi, where there is a false boundary eighteen kilometers from the real one. How many people like Sasha have been caught there when they thought they had managed to escape?

Sasha sat and listened, biting his nails, then got up abruptly, fastened the zipper of his jacket as a sign that the visit was over. And he said with mocking irony: "Well, carry on then. Attack them, unmask them! You and Zola both. In the name of the future. But I live in the name of the present. After the cremation ovens there *is* no future: there's only ash. Zola was poisoned by carbon monoxide. And no one was to blame. They have different ways of getting rid of us. That's the whole difference. . . ."

I got to my feet, intending to bawl him out before he left for being a child who gives up before he takes his first step. He'd betrayed himself, the little whiner. "There's no hope, no way!" I said firmly. "So that's it, is it? That's all?" And I quoted a line from Mandelstam: " 'The age of the wolf hurls itself onto my shoulders.' "

He raised his eyes, and it seemed that there was some movement in them, some possibility of trust, of discussion. Sounding surprised for some reason, he asked if I liked Mandelstam.

"Yes. You?"

His face lit up, and he looked like a child who had run away from the grownups to the edge of the forest and found himself in full sunlight. Arms spread wide, he declaimed happily:

"What street are we in?
Mandelstam Street.
What a devilish name.
No matter how you turn it about,
It's a name which always sounds oblique, never direct.
There's little in it which is straight—
Not even its morals.
And so this street—
Or rather this abyss—
Is called by the name
Of this Mandelstam."

We both laughed. I felt that at last we had drawn closer together. We had found a common language, now the main thing was not to lose it. . . . We recited Mandelstam to each other in turn. Then I stopped reciting, for the poems he chose and his monosyllabic comments on them told me more about him than everything else.

"Did Mandelstam demand much from life? No more than I do . . .

"A few warm chicken droppings,
A little of the warmth from the silent sheep,
And I will give everything for life—I so need to care,
And a sulphur match could warm me
To stroke the fleece gently, to rustle the straw,
Like a winter apple tree, hungering on its brush matting,
To stretch myself out, to offer my hand to the stranger
with senseless tenderness,
To fumble in the void, and wait patiently."

Sasha fell silent and looked at me. "He wasn't as bitter as I am. The poems he wrote before he died are requests, prayers. And he was ready to endure everything. A saintly man." He waved his hand. Tears came to his eyes. He didn't speak for a long time. He sat with his face hidden from me. When he turned back his eyes were dry and sad.

"And how did it all end?" he asked in a whisper. "Writers! Throughout Jewish history there have always been these enlightened thinkers—pinning their hopes on benevolent rulers. They lived by a dream. Their poems are hopes. Their speeches are illusions. They shouted 'We don't want!' But no matter how loud they shouted, sooner or later the knife came out.

"Yet Mandelstam meant more to Russian poetry than Levitan meant to its painting. So what?" He clenched his fist, his rough workman's fist. "I remember what Anna Akhmatova wrote about Mandelstam's nights in Voronezh: 'And in the room of the disgraced poet, fear and the muse took turns watching.'" Then he banged his fist on his knee. "And now where are his books? What has changed? They killed a great poet, and now they live their lives in terror of him. Almost everything has been forgotten, but they, they remember."

Sasha got up to leave. He had to go to work.

"Do you want to know what I think? Never in the whole history of Russia have Jews been as persecuted as they are now. Never! Not even under Alexander III. Earlier if you were desperate you could at least become a Christian. But now? It's not the priests who decide what's written in a passport. Like the poem about the Jew-priest. 'There the Tsar persecuted for the faith—here the biologists persecute for the blood.' It's an order as strict as any of the Gestapo's. Jews this side, the rest, that side. Incidentally, the new passport system with those points in it made it much easier for the Nazis to sort out the Jews. Did you know that? They helped ensure that all the Jews died. Whoever wasn't betrayed by the neighbors was betrayed by his passport. But getting baptized—well, good luck to them! I'm not a believer. I'd like to dance the 'Freiloch' at the synagogue just to annoy officialdom. But I can't assimilate!"

"But you've already assimilated," I burst out. "You live in the heart of Russian culture. Pushkin, Blok, Mandelstam. Your heart is here."

"I can't assimilate," he replied firmly. "I can recite Blok and Pushkin. All right. I might even go along with Lenin and believe that the way out is via assimilation. But there's a stick beating me around the feet—'Yid, yid!'—to make sure I don't get far along that road. How often have I been turned away because I'm alien? At least under the Tsar there was a percentage quota. Jews knew how many of them were going to be accepted. But now we're completely in the hands of the local anti-Semites. Don't you agree? Yes, I can see you do.

"And the final thing is, we can't have our own culture. No, we can't.

Don't argue. Those crumbs, that literary rubbish that you sometimes find turning yellow in great heaps in the newspaper stands, that's not culture. That doesn't unite anyone. They can't even get around to setting up a theater. Not even a monument at Babi Yar!* As if a monument could unite the ones who survived. The ones left to weep.

"And then there's the pinnacle of police achievement—the apotheosis—everyone locked up! No chance of getting out. *But I want to leave!*" he shouted, raising his hands as if in prayer. "Why do they keep me here? Just to keep the sneering and insults going longer?"

"Have you asked permission to leave?"

"No! Two of my friends tried it, and they lost their jobs immediately. And I have my mother to support. She's sick and unhappy, and she has no income. I can condemn myself to starvation, but not her! And so despite everything, despite common sense, even, you just sit there in chains, not even daring to spit in the face of the person who's torturing you. It's a steel trap. But I'll find a way out. I'm either going to walk on the earth or lie in it. I'm not going to crawl."

He stopped, wrenched his shoulders back as if his arms were being broken, and then burst out again.

"Forgive me for being so direct. . . . But it doesn't matter how noble, or how sincere your speeches are—they're rubbish. They just raise people's hopes. 'Lenin said,' etc. . . . They don't give a damn what Lenin said, even if he shouted it from the top of the Spassky Tower. Can't you see that for yourself? That no one gives a damn? Forgive me, but you're worse than the most rigid Orthodox rabbi who just sits and waits for the Messiah. You won't move either. You're just waiting for the Messiah as well. How many thousands of years are you going to have to wait—when salvation's there, three hours' flying time away, where no one will call you a Jewish swine, or yell, 'Get off to your Israel.' I'll be there already, thank God. You may be right, and sometime there'll be a trial of this age, and the defendants will be everyone who's turned the ideas of internationalism into a urinal where the whole world comes to piss—politicians, philosophers, writers, journalists—anyone who wants. And the trial can be for Stalin, Khrushchev, and all the others.

"But when will it come? The twentieth century turned out to be the age of nationalism. The whole world's on fire with it. Asia is a nightmare—covered in blood. Africa is writhing. All those Tshombes snatching power from one another, selling themselves to anyone who'll help them get it.

---

* The place near Kiev where the Nazis massacred thousands of Jews. Evtushenko wrote a well-known poem entitled "Babi Yar." Plans were announced in 1975 for the erection of a monument on the site. As of January 1976, however, there had been no apparent progress. [Translator]

The Arabs trying to fill Africa with anti-Semitic literature so as to turn the black world against the Jews as well. Don't you think Russia's got something to do with all that?

"People respect the Germans, when they're a nation—they're a people to be reckoned with. But when they're Volga Germans? A national minority. Kick them on a barge, and send them down the Volga. The Ukrainians are free. No one curses them for being Bandera's men—nor should they.* They're a nation—not some kind of fragment.

"And what about the Kalmucks? The Chechens, the Ingush? Russified Greeks and Turks? The Crimean Tartars? The Kurds? National minorities—so, into the truck please, and good-bye.

"I'm sick to death of being a little brother who just comes up to the level of other people's elbows. The elbow moves and I end up with a bloody nose. I want to be a national majority. That's all. In this age of nationalism I want to be a national majority."

He stuck out his hand at me, his hard worker's hand, and went out quickly without looking back. . . .

I sat alone for a long time. I didn't move as the evening grew darker. Pauline came in. She pushed the door open a crack, looked surprised that the room was full of smoke, and went off to slam a few cupboard doors in the kitchen. Why hadn't she come in as usual to tell me about her experiments with Meturin? Unfortunately, I was so preoccupied with my own thoughts that I wasn't as concerned as I should have been.

I didn't stir. All my life I'd written about young people, thought about young people. And now life had brought me face to face with a young man in terrible trouble. In despair . . . What could I do to help? Was there any way of saving him? Even just Sasha? This one?

The illness was so widespread . . . just as a sufferer from a liver complaint has a bitter taste in his mouth, a sufferer from an ulcer a metallic taste, as a man with a heart condition may have a sudden attack, so a man who is forced into a national minority group, insulted like a national minority group, sometimes deprived of food like a national minority group, also has his own distinctive symptoms, an embittered eye looking out at those around him.

Not a Tartar? Not a Ukrainian? Not a Jew? Not an Uzbek? One of ours?

Did our generation ever have such an outlook on life?

I went to school on the very edge of Moscow, where the Sharikopodshipnik factory and the houses around it had only just been built. The other children at school were the children of factory workers and cleaners—

* Stepan Bandera, leader of the Ukrainian Nationalist organization, under whose aegis was established the rebel Ukrainian army which fought against the Red Army. [Translator]

the ragged eager to study!—and we simply didn't know what nationality we all were. It was only after the war when I was told about the tragic fate of some of my classmates that I learned with astonishment that one of them turned out to have been half German, another a Pole. I suppose Misha Ermishev was the only one who everyone remembered wasn't Russian—he had a fighter's biceps and a Caucasian temper. . . .

And now, as I'm writing this book and ought to be indicating for the sake of accuracy that so and so was Russian, and so and so an Armenian or a Jew, I have to make a special effort each time to remember what nationality my friend or enemy was. In the life we led, all manner of things could serve as dividing lines; human characteristics, political views, position on some particular matter, anything you like, but not nationality. And so to this day, even after everything that's happened—including the war with Hitlerism that so shattered our lives—the prewar brotherhood of children has held fast: we developed a staunch immunity. In our youth we had gulped down the air of equality, and we were strong because of that.

But it seems that things can go differently—very differently. What happens to Jewish young people? To a Sasha Weiner, for example?

For a start, why are they described as Jewish? Well, if not that, what then? Jewish-Russian? Intermediate? Halfway? Western scientists who have studied similar questions have introduced the term "marginal man," a person on the frontier between differing national cultures. The marginals have their own complications, their own reasons, their own prejudices. Moreover, knowledge of more than one national culture, as can easily be seen, does not tend to impoverish man, but to enrich him.

But this is another case altogether. Sasha is by no means a marginal man. Bolshevik calls to assimilation have been present in his family for a long time. That was the quarrel of the grandfathers and the great-grandfathers. Lenin and the Bund. The Bund and Lunacharsky, Lunacharsky and C. N. Bialik.* But not Sasha.

Sasha doesn't speak Hebrew. All he knows about Jewish culture is that it's been wiped from the face of the earth. He is a person of Russian culture. He loves Russian culture, and he probably knows it better than our literary Russophiles, who as a rule are mere boors. He, like me, is not first and foremost a Jew by nationality. He, like me, is a Jew by social situation. For the time being . . .

How many blows does a man have to take, how many invisible wounds does he have to suffer, how desperate does he have to become

* The Jewish Socialist Bund was formed in 1897 as part of the revolutionary movement in Eastern Europe. The Russian section participated in the second Congress of Soviets, but dropped out together with the Mensheviks. Chaim Nachman Bialik, 1873–1936, was a Zionist and poet who wrote in Hebrew. [Translator]

to be prepared to turn his face toward an unknown language, a culture he knows nothing of, to a distant and burning sky?

"It is the call of the blood," the nationalists say in such cases.

Yes, blood. Not the blood that flows in your veins, but the blood that spurts out of them. To drive young people whose native language is Russian, who are the most Russian of Russians by tradition, by education, by culture, by their very spirit, into a soulless ghetto—soulless because most of them have no spiritual world other than the Russian one—to drive despairing souls along that road by means of Alexander III's percentage quota in universities, by limitations on military service, by jibes in the press, by violence in the Stalin mold, by callousness, by mockery, by simple disregard, to drive them, like branded cattle into tribal enclosures—that is no mere mistake, that is not official stupidity or official ardor. It is racism.

Racism doesn't cease to be racism because it wears a red coat. Incidentally, if there are any young people in Russia still speaking and thinking in Yiddish—although I have never come across any—if there are any, what right does the Soviet state have to fix its sights on them? After all, for half a century the Soviet state has been proclaiming "a culture national in form and Socialist in content." By what right can people be driven by a mark in their passports into tribal reserves? And not even reserves. There is sky over reserves, and distance. But here . . . Truly, such things have never happened before—never!

We are surprised by the psychic traumas and early heart attacks suffered by our friends who wear the invisible yellow star. The doctors shake their heads as they observe in their patients a catastrophic deterioration of nervous systems and blood vessels—a deterioration which comes at an unreasonably early age. But scientists who have studied the deleterious effect of racism on people have long ceased to be surprised. They know that a categorical refusal of equal rights—say, by the open racist brutality of the old cotton planters—is often easier for a man to bear than indeterminate, half-scornful attitudes. The humiliating existence of a second-class citizen, as scientists from all continents warn, can engender constant inner anxieties and sometimes a feeling of isolation from people: alienation, a feeling that there is no way out. "In its extreme forms," the eminent sociologist Stonquist explains, "this can lead to mental breakdown and suicide."

But who in the high commissions has ever heard of Stonquist and other serious sociologists? Do they even feel they need to know about them? Aren't most of them Jews anyway?

And when was it ever the case that the firing squad was concerned about the health of its victims?

23

All these years I had been frightened for Pauline's health. It was mere chance that the guard with the machine gun had let her through into the very heart of that highly secret military institute in the pogrom year of 1951 when she had been rudely turned away from every other job, even from a wax-melting tank.

Goebbels called the period in Germany when Jews were not being shot but only boycotted the period of the cold pogrom. That was the time when the cold pogrom was loose in Russia, and the hot pogrom seemed to be about to start, or rather to start up again. Yet they took Pauline on. Why?

I was doubly worried when I learned that if you worked for more than five years in that institute, you qualified for your pension ten years early. The workingman gets nothing for free. If he's offered a pension ten years early, how many years of life has he lost? I had the almost physical sensation that I had let Pauline into a cold Auschwitz, where people were exterminated not by the instantaneous Cyclon B but by other poisons which work more slowly.

Once I found on Pauline's desk a translation of an article from a Swiss chemical journal. The article included data about a new substance, a quarter of a glass of which would be enough to poison an entire ocean. A yellow-faced, hollow-cheeked colonel came to collect the article. He told me to take care of my wife. "She's worth more to the defense of the state than several tank divisions."

"Thank you," I said, a little disconcerted. "At last I have some reason to look after her."

When I'd shown him out I stood for a long time at the door, plunged in grief. It seemed that just when our newspapers were baying for the "Jewish poisoners," Pauline and her colleagues were saving their country from the real global poisoners, who were preparing for chemical warfare. And they were saving Russia while ignoring the daily additional dose of poison thrown in their faces by *Pravda*, *Isvestiya*, and the other papers, which she merely glanced at, wrinkling her little nose as if at a bad smell, and then stuffed into the cages of her experimental guinea pigs, who so liked fresh newsprint.

One day there was a phone call: "Come and fetch your wife! Quickly! She's still alive, but . . ."

I waited a long time at the gates, where the guard stood with his machine gun. He was a country lad, and when he discovered who I was he looked at me sympathetically. He even broke standing orders and chatted with me to make the waiting easier.

Pauline was carried out. Her face was swollen up like a balloon, and her eyes and temples were covered in a fine black powder, like coal dust. She looked like a miner dug out after a cave-in and carried to the surface.

What I had feared most of all had happened. Serious poisoning. Fortunately the alarm signal had been given at once. The first-aid service had done a brilliant rescue operation according to all the rules of lifesaving in war. After a time Pauline clawed her way out of danger. My son and I gradually picked the fine dust from her pale cheeks and wiped them with a solution. That was our family occupation on Sundays; Pauline only allowed her loved ones to do it.

Naturally, she left military chemistry. Thank God! She now worked on substances with the romantic name of "urea." They were trying to isolate a herbicide that would kill weeds in cotton fields. Here everything was open even for the unconsecrated eye to see, and if I made the effort even I could understand what she was doing.

I had known before this that Pauline was wholly committed to science. I had told her so, often and sourly, when in the evenings instead of going to the theater or to see friends she would sit down at her desk. But while my wife was living nine-tenths in secrecy from me, I couldn't grasp completely just how deep her devotion to her work was.

Then suddenly I discovered.

In the first week she worked with those fine-sounding ureas, Pauline isolated in its pure form a herbicide she called Meturin, which killed weeds not only in cotton fields but in potato fields as well, while remaining completely harmless to man. The director of the institute solemnly declared that this discovery alone justified the three years of the institute's existence.

Pauline began to receive glossy patent rights documents looking like Tsarist charters, from the Committee for Inventions and Discoveries, with the wax seals of the state and gay silk ribbons. All our southern republics, and many foreign countries, asked for Meturin for trial. Canada sent a million-dollar order. Uzbekistan sent letter after letter. For the Uzbeks an efficient and harmless weedkiller was a matter of life and death. The Uzbeks drink water from the irrigation systems, and so what is on the fields goes into their stomachs.

But Meturin, like any new-born child, remained in its cradle. It wasn't included in the high-level plans. No one was awarded bonuses for it, no one was fired, no one was rebuked. The ministries discouraged the preparation of experimental samples. Profit? Who needs UNPLANNED profit? The Uzbeks? Give them our regards! The whole business was shelved for years. So Pauline put on her rubber boots and set off in the autumn mud to the Shchelkovo Chemical Factory, outside Moscow. There she made a deal with the factory manager and some enthusiastic workers and began to produce an experimental sample of Meturin.

She took her instruments, two empty buckets and a huge saucepan, with her to use for pouring and mixing the solutions. In the train the farm workers tried to guess what this girl was carting about with her or what she was selling. She and her friends and helpers traveled to Shchelkovo for six months. It took three hours in the packed train. Then there were eight hours' work, much of the time wearing a gas mask, as one of the basic ingredients of Meturin made your eyes water. And there was the battle with an officialdom which longed to see her fail.

In Ufa her first experimental sample was burned because of an oversight by a foreman. Pauline nearly killed the chief engineer, bawled out all the idlers and oafs, then sat down and wept. She flew back to Moscow streaming with angry tears. Everything had to begin again—her saucepans dangling from her belt, the crammed train to Shchelkovo, the gas mask which made the skin of her face burn. When she got home she collapsed on the divan and went straight to sleep, while Fima and I took off her wet shoes.

But by early spring she had managed to get her Meturin, although she grew very pale and was ill throughout the summer. From experimental stations in the republics, the Comecon countries, Canada and other countries where the Meturin was sent there came back glowing reports, and at last the statesmen got a grip on themselves. They decided to build chemical factories for the production of Meturin.

But my concern for Pauline didn't relax. One day when she came home from work I was on the phone. When I hung up she said casually that there had been a phone call from the Regional Committee to her institute advising them to keep an eye on her. Her husband was a writer, the caller had said. He made speeches on anti-Semitism. They were slanderous of course—that kind of thing simply didn't happen here. I was about to tell her that exactly the same thing had just happened at our son's school, but I decided against it—why poison her evening any further?

"I wish I could find a substance that would rid the earth of human swine," Pauline said suddenly. "Something that would leave only the good people in the world." She sighed. "My God, what rubbish I'm talking. There'd be all those orphans. The children haven't done anything. Where was your phone call from?"

"From the Party investigator. They want a meeting, since I wouldn't recant."

Pauline was amazed. Whenever some dirty deed was in the wind, her first reaction was always surprise. Even after all those years.

. . . I sat and waited a long time outside the door of the Party investigator, whose name appeared to be Gorevanova. I'd obviously come at the coffee break. People kept passing me with neatly wrapped packets and bags from the buffet. Behind them came an imposing military-looking woman loaded down with oranges and other things. She swept down the corridor and stopped at the door where I was waiting. She looked at me attentively, unlocked the office and disappeared inside. There was a long rustling of stiff paper, and I heard her dial a number. Then a strong woman's voice began to talk about a country house, and about a girl who was to go to school this year and who needed a coach. Twenty minutes passed, during which time she made a great many phone calls, and talked about theater tickets.

Finally I knocked and went in. I stood by the door. The telephone conversation went on as if I hadn't been there. Finally Gorevanova put the receiver down, and said, as a statement, not a question—"Svirsky! You must give me an explanation of this business . . . in connection with your charge of anti-Semitism against Vasily Smirnov, the editor-in-chief of the magazine *Friendship of the Peoples*." Then the telephone rang, and Party investigator Gorevanova began another long conversation about the girl who couldn't start school if she didn't have a coach.

At last! I thought happily. That proves what a little support from a secretary of the Party Central Committee can do. The machinery has finally ground into action. Sometime or other an anti-Semite with a Party membership card is going to be punished. I've managed it!

On a sheet of paper I wrote the names of witnesses who would be able to confirm that Vasily Smirnov was a chauvinist and anti-Semite. I named more than thirty. Too many! I shortened the list, leaving in most of the editorial staff of *Friendship of the Peoples*, headed by the Party organizer Vladimir Alexandrov, the feature editor. Who should know his boss better? I added a few writers and poets to whom Vasily Smirnov had explained his views in person—from the poet Yunna Morits to the prose writer and poet Alexander Yashin, author of the talented novel *Levers*, to whom Smirnov had yelled in front of everyone, "You've sold yourself to the Yids!"

Finally Gorevanova put down the telephone and looked at me as if she couldn't remember who I was.

"I'm Svirsky," I said, almost apologetically. It was clear that I was in her way.

She leaned forward, and slowly, with all her strength, raised her arm and slammed her fist on the desk. "What's all this slander?"

I had once been in a militia post when some young delinquent had been brought in. The militia had set out to frighten him, just to show him they wouldn't stand any messing around.

Gorevanova's hand had turned red. It was clear that she had hurt herself, poor thing.

"Sit down, Comrade Gorevanova," I said quietly and sympathetically. "Blow on your fingers. It must hurt."

She looked at me a little wildly and sat down in her chair uncertainly, a little sideways, as if she herself were being interviewed by the Party investigator. Then she continued completely rationally: "Please write out a full explanation. All right? Ready?"

Within a week my home telephone began to ring constantly. The writers I had named in my list of witnesses began to call. They warned me that something strange was going on. Gorevanova wasn't behaving the way an investigator ought to. Even before she began talking with the witnesses she summoned she would tell them straight out: "Bear in mind that I am not on Svirsky's side!"

To declare whose side you're on, even before you've begun the investigation! That's a strange kind of investigator. I immediately phoned the City Committee and asked them to replace this investigator who was behaving so strangely. It took a long time to sort things out. Several written protests had to be made, and finally I had to send a telegram. There were six "conversations" of many hours' duration. By this time there were two people conducting the investigation. One of them put the questions while the other sat and stared at me, screwing up his eyes.

Finally Gorevanova was replaced by another investigator, an elderly man, pleasant but cautious. And next day . . . there were more phone calls at home. A writer called as a witness told me that first he had been sent to Gorevanova, who screamed and shouted as before, perhaps even more aggressively, and only then was he allowed to see the new investigator, Ivanov. "Your Gorevanova's like a promised bride. You'd need a horse to escape from her."

I had to send another telegram.

Document No. 2
MARCH 11, 1966, 1100 HOURS, MOSCOW, KUIBYSHEV STREET.
TO THE CITY COMMITTEE OF THE PARTY. TO THE CHAIRMAN OF THE PARTY
COMMISSION OF THE MOSCOW CITY COMMITTEE.
Comrade Ryzhukhin.
"In a statement already sent to you I requested the removal of Party investigator Gorevanova from my case, and the Party commission agreed to this. Nevertheless I have learned that initially witnesses are seeing Gorevanova as before, and only after a preliminary conversation with her are they being allowed to see Comrade Ivanov. I must protest against the pressure Gorevanova continues to exert on the witnesses. I demand her complete withdrawal from the case. Has the poet Eduard Mezhelitis been called as a witness? I sent you a telegram about this. I insist that he should be called. Grigory Svirsky."

At first the investigation ground forward very slowly, scraping and groaning, like a freight car being hauled out of a siding. Then it gradually accelerated, like the same freight car rolling downhill, until finally it came off the rails.

The day of trial arrived. Representatives of the Writers' Union and I were summoned to the meeting of the Party commission. Here it became clear that not one of my witnesses had turned up. Not only had they not called the poet Eduard Mezhelitis,* who lived in Vilnius but was staying in Moscow at the time, but not even witnesses who were natives of Moscow were there. Party investigator Ivanov declared officially that he had telephoned this one and that one, and sent a telegram to the other. There had been no response.

The members of the commission shook their head knowledgeably. That sort of thing did happen. Ilf and Petrov once wrote, "Witnesses, give your names here! . . . And the busy crossroads were suddenly deserted." If they say no, that means no. The court can't pull people in by the ears.

But the machinery gave a hiccup in that very first moment. The door opened and a secretary announced rather uncertainly that there was a person called Morits who'd been waiting for an hour saying that she was a witness but no one would let her in or call her to give evidence. Ivanov glanced from beneath his bushy brows at Gorevanova, who was sitting nearby. As if nothing had happened.

I had called Yunna Morits myself. Ivanov had told me the previous day that among other writers he had invited the poet Yunna Morits to

* A well-known Lithuanian poet and a Lenin Prize winner. [Translator]

attend the session. To make doubly sure, I had sent her a telegram. It was a pity I hadn't done the same to everyone.

When Gorevanova heard the name Morits, she stood up. Then she sat down again. Her face was changing color, as if she were right next to a brightly burning bonfire. Indeed, perhaps she was. If no witnesses had been summoned, despite all the promises, that must mean there had been no investigation and none intended. They'd simply lit the fire to burn the heretic. A cosy little *auto-da-fé*. And then suddenly came this annoying and unexpected interruption from downstairs.

There was a dead silence. Just the sound of chairs creaking, like dry logs crackling on a bonfire. Someone suggested doubtfully that it looked as if the whole thing would have to be postponed. So that the witnesses could be there. Had there not perhaps been some irregularity? Ryzhukhin looked somewhere above our heads—and slowly, his face twisting, he not so much said as squeezed out of himself the words that the session was postponed.

It was a month or more before we were called again. It was the beginning of April. And indeed everything that had happened could have been explained as an April Fools' joke.

"What case are you here for?" the secretary of the Party commission asked me.

"The case of Vasily Smirnov."

"There's no such case being heard today."

"What do you mean? I've been called."

"What's your name? . . . Oh—well, you're in the case of Svirsky!"

The case of Svirsky. In other words, even officially I was the accused. So what were they accusing me of? The charge turned out to be slander. Malicious slander against the Russian writer Vasily Smirnov, who for five years had been running the all-union magazine *Friendship of the Peoples*. All the representatives of the Writers' Union let out a simultaneous whistle of disbelief, and looked at each other. . . .

Well, well! So they hadn't managed to start the fire around the stake at the *auto-da-fé*, so they had chosen another method from the arsenal of Ignatius Loyola. . . . The undesirable personage is declared in advance to be a heretic, a witch, a slanderer, a spy, an enemy. . . . He is shown the noose, and then the unfortunate person standing before the Jesuit Fathers has only one concern—to convince them by every method possible, by his own voice, by his tears, that they shouldn't hang him, that he isn't a heretic, a spy, or a slanderer.

Fight!

. . . Yet things weren't quite so bad now. Under Stalin I would simply have been taken away in the night. There wouldn't have been any disturbance. And then there would have been an announcement at the writers' meeting that it had become "officially known" that not only was I a subversive agent, but also an old Anglo-Japanese-German spy. And there'd be no more of this slandering of true Russian people. And it wouldn't be anti-Semitism, of course. How could it be, since anti-Semitism could never exist in our country?

But now they would have to deal with me in the presence of the Party Committee of the Writers' Union.

"Listen, Comrade," I said to the man from the Party commission who was going into the session with his arms full of files—"What about the presumption of innocence?"

"What?"

So much for that!

There were fifteen people seated at a solid table. Three of them were representatives of the Writers' Union Party Committee. At opposite sides of the big table, as if to separate us from each other as much as possible, sat myself and my opponent, Vasily Smirnov, well turned out but dry-looking, like an old bone, gazing at me angrily.

Gorevanova was there as well. When she bumped into me in the corridor she had hastened to assure me that she had nothing to do with all this. After all, there hadn't been such a case in all the forty years' existence of the Moscow City Committee. Nothing. So what could I expect her to do?

The new Party secretary, a quiet-voiced, stolid, phlegmatic man, read something aloud, monotonously and interminably. It was his official conclusion. Each member of the commission had a carbon copy before him, so that he could absorb the text by ear and eye simultaneously.

But what was it exactly that he was saying, this soft-spoken, solid Party investigator? From the evidence that had been given by Boris Yakovlev, the literary critic and specialist in the works of Lenin (evidence of which I shall reproduce in full later), the investigator had taken only the first sentence: "V. A. Smirnov has never had any anti-Semitic conversations with me personally." And as for the other witnesses, they might as well not have turned up at all. There were no further statements in Ivanov's pile of documents.

In the face of this lack of evidence, it was inevitable that the commission should find the editor of *Friendship of the Peoples*, Vasily Smirnov, slandered, libeled, and defamed. When I realized this, I felt like a man falling into a machine. The metal chain dragged me along inexorably, no matter how loud I shouted. I could try to prove whatever I liked, but my shouts would still be those of a man who'd fallen into the meat grinder, nothing more.

The painstaking investigation had dragged on for six months, and at least half of the writers I had named as witnesses had been questioned, plus almost as many more I had not even mentioned. Later, when I was given the right to speak and I opened my file of documents, it took me two hours to set out the facts; and then suddenly there wasn't one witness; they'd all vanished like rain down the gratings in the street. All that was left was my own dossier. But at least I could deal in detail with thirty-one facts, which I set out in the courtroom to the members of the Party commission and to the writers. Since my speech had been in public, I said, many people were awaiting the decision of the Party commission . . . people who wanted to know, once and for all: "Do we punish great-power chauvinism in our multinational country? Or is it permissible to insult the national dignity of a Soviet citizen, and to do it unpunished?"

No one so much as blinked an eye. It was as if I were addressing an audience of the deaf, all equipped with hearing aids. If they wanted to, they could switch on; if they didn't want to hear, they simply switched off. But they didn't even take their hearing aids out of their pockets. Surely it couldn't be true that no lessons at all had been learned from the deaths of millions of people under Stalin? But still they sat there, deaf to everything, with their eyes glazed and stupid. You've got facts? So much the worse for you, as Stalin used to say in similar circumstances.

When I told them about Pauline's personal tragedy, it produced the same lack of reaction as everything else. I thought it was pointless to try and persuade them further. The machine had been programmed. Whatever I said, it would churn out the same old answer. Have I been boring you? Then let the witnesses speak. Fifteen Communist writers—that's more than just one heretic who refused to help himself by admitting that he just made a fool of himself and got overexcited.

I stopped my statement in midsentence and waited for the members of the commission to return from their mental wanderings and focus on what was actually going on. Then I asked that at least some of the evidence given by the writers should be heard.

At this point a fantastic scene began. It was as if neither I nor any of the representatives of the Writers' Union were in the room at all. Ryzhukhin, the chairman of the Party commission, a thin, stern-browed man with an expressionless face, got to his feet. He dismissed all the writers' evidence in one phrase (and the writers included men who had been members of the Communist Party since 1918)—he said, sharply and categorically, "We are not going to read any of that rubbish!"

For six months now I had hung about the doorways of investigators' offices. I had had my share of misery in my conversations with Gorevanova and Ivanov, and I understood that the Party commission wasn't made up exclusively of saints. But that they should dare to say such things about *every* scrap of evidence from the writers! That was the same thing as slapping the entire Soviet Writers' Union in the face, and a hard, stinging slap, at that.

"Excuse me," I said calmly, with my last ounce of strength, "What do you mean by 'rubbish'?"

This question forced him away from the position he had established, and he replied, or rather bellowed—"What I have said is said!"

Next to me was Viktor Telpugov, the singer of spring, a man who could describe in ecstatic terms the life of the camomile plant, or the fluttering of a butterfly. I nudged him with my elbow. "Listen to what's going on here?" Viktor shifted in his chair, moving right to the very edge, as if he really wanted to squat on the ground. I could see that he had grown pale.

Unlike me, Vasily Smirnov had been allowed to call as many witnesses as he wished. He had managed to find one—a one-armed poet of no reputation, who had not long previously been taken on at *Friendship of the Peoples*. The one-armed poet was informed that his hour of glory had come. He rose, and repeated, with minor variations, one single sentence: "Svirsky is muddying the waters."

Everyone looked at him with some astonishment. Was this all he had to say? . . . There were quite a few lightweight poets like that, plus some slow-witted critics. More often than not they were neither poets nor critics. They were barely literate rhymesters, cobblers of words. They were prepared to do anything, even prepared to write verses extolling the virtues of Stalin, if it would help them up the ladder. There wasn't a single person of talent among them. For many years, even more so after 1949, writers like this had been largely helped on their way by the monumental editor of *Ogonyok*, Anatoly Sofronov.

But it seemed that Vasily Smirnov was good for a helping hand as well. For some time now, I had been watching two old women, sitting on either side of the chairman of the commission. One had huge, gleaming, stainless-steel front teeth, like the jaws of an excavator. The other was a neat little person, pleasant-faced, with her blouse darned at the elbows. She looked like an Old Bolshevik, I thought. I wondered who she was. I watched her calmly, sympathetically, until she erupted into action. "You say you're a Russian writer, but your passport says you're a Jew!" she shouted. "How can this be—a Russian writer and a Jew at the same time?"

I turned to the singer of spring, who was sitting with his head hunched into his shoulders. "Vitenka, perhaps you could explain that to them?"

Viktor Telpugov rose and, with a sigh, began a patient explanation of just how such a thing was possible. It had happened many times in the history of Russian culture. He even provided examples so that they would believe what he was saying.

I looked at the pleasant, elderly face, and tried to calm down. Why should I be so surprised? The old woman didn't wrap her words up in smooth scientific jargon, she just spoke straightforward kitchen filth. Why should she know any better? After all, the same view was expressed day and night by Vasily Smirnov, member of the Soviet Writers' Union, who spent his time baying that Russian Jews had no right to be Soviet Russian writers. Engineers?—O.K. Scientists?—fair enough . . . but writers . . .

Of course, he would trust Russian engineers or scientists, but everyone had his own specialty—and literature was his. And naturally he wasn't alone in his views, there were plenty of others who shared them. For instance, if you dug a little deeper you would find the toilers in the Ministry of Culture, headed by Ekaterina Furtseva, who had recently begun tilling the same soil as Vasily Smirnov with all the impressive weight she could muster. Not only did she strike Isaac Babel's play *Sunset* out of the repertory but she allowed herself to express her indignation to the dumbfounded theater director: "Why do you want to do these local interest plays?" Plays like *The Mountain People*, about a tiny Caucasian tribe of little-known hill-dwellers, or plays about Australians, or Negroes, even from the most remote places, are not, of course, "local interest" plays. They run in every theater, and the Ministry of Culture deserves our deep gratitude for showing such a breadth of interest, such internationalism. . . . But if you mention Jews! . . . Or when not only is the author a Jew himself— and sometimes you've got to put up with that—but when also his heroes turn out to be the same, then, well, thank you very much, that's too much!

Non-native heroes had disappeared from prose some time ago, back in Stalin's days, when a Leningrad magazine suddenly stopped printing Yuri German's story about a Jewish doctor.* They'd already brought out half the tale in episodes, with the familiar "to be continued in our next"— but finally there was no "next." "Yuri German's so orthodox he's been circumcised" was Moscow's grim joke. So far as prose went, everything was in order.

But what about the stage? There they were still a menace. And on the screen! The young director Aksolodov had just shot his remarkable film *Commissar*. One of the main heroes—another oversight—was an elderly Jew. But the main thing was the kind of man he was: a good, humane sort of man, who saved a pregnant woman commissar from a gang. And *Commissar*, which had been acknowledged by the most demanding Moscow

* German: Author (b. 1910) of a number of social and historical novels. [Translator]

critics as a work of genius, was not only banned, but was ordered to be destroyed. (That didn't happen even under Stalin.) Only the intervention of the Central Committee Secretary Suslov saved the banned film from immediate destruction—the director had to approach him personally. But that didn't save the director himself, who was banned from ever directing a feature film again. Sometime later he passed out in a subway in Gorky Street and was whisked off to hospital by ambulance. He took it very hard. Served him right! After all, he dared to portray a Jew on the Soviet screen, and a good one at that. What would the movie-goers derive from the film? The idea that Jews, too, were people, and that some of them were actually good people? Anti-Sovietism! Downright anti-Sovietism!

The old woman with the stainless-steel teeth suddenly interjected angrily, "How can you complain about anti-Semitism when seventy-five percent of the members of the Writers' Union are Jews?"

Ah, the "synagogue"! I livened up a little. Khrushchev may have gone, but his ideas live on! Telpugov explained in some alarm that the figures were gigantically exaggerated.

Yet people still thought in terms of the "synagogue." I imagined this old woman in the Writers' Union building, standing by the marble slab which bears the names of Moscow writers who died in the war. She would have run her startled eyes down a long list, where alongside Gaidar she would have found Afinogenov, Altausen, Bagritsky, Gershenson, Gurstein, Zozulya, Ivanter, Kogan, Kopshtein, Rosenfeld, Roskin, Khatsrevin, Utkin . . . and many, many other names famous in Soviet literature. A third of all Moscow writers who fell in the war were Jews. Would that have made her revise her ideas, or just made her angry?

"There is no quota for dying," as General Kidalinsky once said to me. And he knew what he was talking about.

The old woman returned to the attack, and I realized that we had been transported in a time machine back to 1949. The year 1949 stretched its coal-black wings over us, and over the shoulders of those two old women I seemed to see the figure of the pogromist in excelsis, and to hear him declaiming his striking poem, "Those Whom We Can Do Without in Russia . . ."

> They poked about, did all they could,
> To make things go their way.
> And their way is an alien way,
> Against true Russian blood!

It's Jews poking about, of course. But how?

> One dashes off for vodka,
> Another for a herring.

The third shoots off at full speed
To gather in the garlic!

But what do they want, when they've clustered around their half-liter of vodka?

Give us Joyce and Kipling,
Give us Akhmatova,
Give us Pasternak . . .

What odd things they wanted! It would have been a good idea to present the old woman with a copy of that poem, to complete their ideological education. I listened and listened to their penetrating, birdlike voices (Ryzhukhin didn't interrupt them) and I felt queasy, as if I'd been bound hand and foot and tossed into a cellar.

The Constitution of the Party laid down that the "case of Svirsky" must be investigated, even though it began, first of all, in a lower organization where the majority of members were Communists with forty years of Party membership. I reminded Ryzhukhin of this.

"What will you try next?" he rasped.

So the Party Constitution was thrown out the window as well, was it? I stood up, spreading my legs wide, the way one braces oneself on deck in a storm. I was pale with anger, ashamed that such things were possible. All around me the crazy women were raging and shouting that they'd show me, they'd make sure I got what was coming to me.

People like that never get tired, I thought to myself. They're powered by perpetual motion. They were raging around the pyres the heretics were to perish on; they were baying for Dreyfus' blood when the soldiers ripped the officer's insignia from his uniform, they were noisily demonstrating their true loyalty when the gendarmes broke their swords over Chernyshevsky's head;* they were threatening to destroy all Jews as they clustered around the door of the courtroom where Beilis had been reviled and insulted. They were the selfsame kitchen harpies: merchants', salesmen's wives, with contorted minds and just one idea: blood.

In the past, these viragoes had uttered their threats by waving their umbrellas and spitting at their victims from behind a military cordon. But now? How had they broken through the cordon and reached the seats of party judges? How many generations of revolutionaries had had to die or be exiled in order to allow hysterics like these to be accepted by the civil authorities as the real revolutionaries?

* *Chernyshevsky:* Nikolai Chernyshevsky (1828–1889), journalist and democratic revolutionary. One of the editors of the magazine *Sovremennik* and author of the novel *What Is to Be Done?* [Translator]

. . . Ryzhukhin would never have allowed the affidavits of the writers to be read, and I would have been dragged down into the groaning, thundering machine, if Yuri Strekhnin had not got to his feet. Strekhnin was a member of the Writers' Union Party Committee, a large, slow-moving man, who had been an army colonel. He was one of those peaceful, taciturn Siberians whom nothing can move to anger, short of a shameless lie. Strekhnin warmed up slowly, like a Russian stove. But once he was really warm . . . !

His normally red face went purple as he declared that the Party Committee of the Writers' Union knew nothing of the evidence that had been given by the writers and editors. We had been told that it wouldn't cast any light on the case, but as a member of the Party Committee, he demanded that the documents be read.

Someone sitting at the far end of the table muttered uncertainly, "Well, if the Party organization asks . . ."

"No!" Ryzhukhin broke in. "The matter is quite clear."

I got up. "In that case, I shall be forced to read them myself. I've been given the right to speak, and I haven't finished yet."

Ryzhukhin's eyebrows seemed to drop to the bridge of his nose. He and the two old women sitting beside him stared aghast at the papers lying in front of me. They suddenly realized that my files contained copies of actual writers' statements. Then came the real explosion.

"Take those papers away from him!" screamed the stainless-steel teeth.

"What is the meaning of this?" rapped the pleasant-faced woman. "How did he get his hands on our documents?"

Indeed, the commission had implied that the documents did not even exist. They had just been stuffed into the Party commission's safe, and with any luck no one would be the wiser. So they could simply assert that a man was a slanderer, a heretic, maybe even a madman suffering from persecution mania.

The incredible uproar seemed to last for an eternity, until it was drowned by Yuri Strekhnin's booming bass voice, with barely concealed fury.

"In the name of the party organization of the Writers' Union, I demand that the writers' statements be read! What is this disgraceful behavior?"

Not a muscle twitched in Ryzhukhin's face. He looked around at everyone present, and in a strangled voice, as if it were a real effort to pronounce the words, said, "Very well, since the Party organization demands it . . ."

24

Promptly, as if in response to an order, the old Party investigator rose and began to read the statements in a monotonous voice. It turned out that they had been there all the time, in his black file. He read out the two documents on top of the pile:

Document No. 3

TO THE PARTY CONTROL COMMISSION OF THE MOSCOW CITY COMMITTEE OF THE COMMUNIST PARTY OF THE SOVIET UNION

from Weiss, G. L.,
member of the CPSU since 1942.

In connection with the accusations raised by the Communist writer G. Svirsky against the Communist writer V. Smirnov, I can report as follows:

1. I have known V. Smirnov since 1950 in connection with our work together on the magazine Friendship of the Peoples. I did not know him prior to this either professionally or socially, and I had neither antipathy nor sympathy toward him. My relations with G. Svirsky are also of a casual nature. Consequently, everything I consider it my duty to say here is free from all prejudice and is only the result of my own bitter five-year experience of what I have personally seen, heard, or experienced. However, let us take things in order.

2. When it became known in 1960 that V. Smirnov had been appointed editor of the magazine Friendship of the Peoples, this not only caused general indignation in writers' circles, but also, as I saw with my own eyes, depressed and even frightened all the people who worked on the magazine; there were persistent rumors that V. Smirnov was a coarse and malicious man, an open great-power chauvinist and anti-Semite who had clearly demonstrated these traits of character, most of all in his work at the Literary Institute, and later in the secretariat of the Writers' Union.

Soon these rumors began to be confirmed by the way he worked as editor of the magazine. It began with coarse and peremptory orders, insults to human dignity, administrative abuses, and an unwillingness to listen to the views of the collective or to trust his staff. This led to the point where in one of the first open meetings I felt obliged to say, "We seem to be advancing through a mine field, not knowing when or where our editor will explode, nor what losses we may suffer." As a result of this mine field atmosphere that V. Smirnov created, several first-class writers left the journal, including Communist Party members Comrades Lebedeva, Kukinova, and the critic E. Pomerantsev. When they left they said openly that they did not want to work with Smirnov.

Thus the first part of the rumors about V. Smirnov were confirmed. The second part, too, soon showed itself to be true.

3. One of V. Smirnov's first actions after his appointment as editor was his individual (and unsupported) refusal to print in the magazine two novels by the Jewish writers, Comrades Zilberman and Svirsky. These novels had been accepted and approved by the editorial board, and the authors had already received sums of money, amounting by contract to 60 percent of the fees. Despite all this, Smirnov refused to publish. The case was taken to court, and the verdict obviously came down on the side of the law, ordering that the writers be paid the full fees contracted to them. This capricious and personal decision by Smirnov, who refused to be swayed by the decisions of the editorial board or by the contracts signed by his predecessor A. Surkov, cost hundreds of thousands of rubles of public money and began to confirm the worst rumors about him and the fears of the collective.

But things did not end there.

4. At that time, I was in charge of the features department. I immediately began to come up against capriciousness of this kind. V. Smirnov ordered that a feature by Boris Kostyukovsky, already set in type, should be dropped from the current number. I was given no reason for this decision. However, shortly afterward I was forbidden to approach two well-known and talented feature writers who had written for the journal for many years. They were A. Litvak and Ilya Zverev, both now dead; this recurred with the very successful and fine writers Mark Poporsky and Lev Davydov-Lomberg. On this occasion V. Smirnov explained his categorical instruction in the following words: "These are not our authors!" Incidentally, these writers were widely published, and in the past the editorial staff of the journal had been keen to commission them to work for us. So why did V. Smirnov find

them unsatisfactory, and what principle united them in his mind? They were people of different generations, different styles and interests. The only thing they had in common was their Jewish descent; that is why Smirnov regarded them as being not *our* authors on the magazine.

Meanwhile, Smirnov did regard as one of *our* authors the feature writer K. Busovsky, who was expelled from the Writers' Union for his brazenly anti-Semitic attitudes. Despite this, Smirnov, without asking the opinion of the department, immediately sent Busovsky off on two successive research trips, both long and expensive. Until then, no author had ever enjoyed such privileges. Smirnov could not have done this by accident, without thinking: as a demonstration of solidarity it was far too blatant.

5. Obviously Smirnov took care not to let slip any overt anti-Semitic statements in my presence. But over the five-year period there were occasions when his guard dropped, and I became an involuntary witness both of his openly anti-Jewish remarks and his behavior. I need quote only examples. Once when he had noticed that I was standing near the open door of his office, he said to my deputy, the Party member V. Alexandrov, "Watch out that Weiss doesn't turn the department into a feeding trough for Jews. . . ." I could hardly believe my ears, but this was later confirmed by Alexandrov himself, who can give a more circumstantial account of the event himself.

A second occurred when Smirnov, in the presence of Communist Party member Kutorg, dealt crudely and tactlessly with E. Markish, the widow of the Jewish Soviet writer and Communist Party member Perets Markish, who had fallen a victim to Beria's terror. She herself had spent several years in the camps, and when she brought the manuscript of an anti-Fascist novel by her late husband to Friendship of the Peoples, Smirnov said, "Take it to your own magazine. We won't touch it."

Having sent the widow of a Soviet Communist writer of unusual talent to a Jewish journal, Smirnov was unable to explain why Friendship of the Peoples, a magazine which prints contributions from representatives of very small national minorities, had no room for a novel originally written in the Yiddish language. His subsequent references to the fact that he had printed Jewish authors are in no way mitigating, first because this was done under pressure from above, and secondly, because he did not choose the strongest or the most characteristic works from Jewish writing.

On another occasion, when Alexandrov asked Smirnov's permission to send Perets Markish's son on a trip to a kolkhoz in Dagestan, the editor refused, on the grounds that "These Jews don't understand a thing about agriculture."

These are cases in which I myself was a witness. I add here some other incidents that were reported to me.

6. When the Communist Party member Polukhin was turned down on his first application to join the Writers' Union, since the admission committee decided to postpone their final decision, Smirnov met Polukhin afterward, and said, "It's because the selection committee is packed with Yids."

Polukhin told my colleague Alexandrov about this in my presence immediately afterward. He was very angry. Statements of this kind by Smirnov became both more outspoken and more frequent after the famous March meeting of the Party leaders and writers.* Apparently Smirnov now believed that anything was permissible, and began to bang his fist even harder on the table. Every day when he was going home from work to his flat on Lenin Avenue, he gave Z. Kutorg, V. Dmitrieva, and Y. Surovtsev a ride as they lived in the same area. In the car he allowed himself free rein. One day, for example, it became known in the office that the previous evening Smirnov had said, "They've got nothing but Jews on Novy Mir. They're stirring up the literary waters." "Ilya Ehrenburg ought to go off to Israel and stop bothering us." "The Jews have mutilated the Russian literary language." And finally, he once even made a discovery. "You know," he said to the woman traveling with him, "Solzhenitsyn is really Solzhenitser. That explains everything. . . ." It would be too depressing and unpleasant to list any more.

7. Nor did Smirnov attempt to conceal from the collective his great-power chauvinist views and tendencies, which made themselves particularly clear in incidents like the following. In one of his articles, B. Yakovlev referred to Lenin's famous remark about Tsarist Russia being the prison of the nations. At our next meeting, in the presence of the entire staff, Smirnov issued Yakovlev a coarse and impermissably rude rebuke, saying that he had all but slandered Russia, and insulted the Russian people, and hinting that only a man such as Yakovlev would have been capable of such a thing. This conflict had its sequel—there was a special hearing, and Smirnov was obliged to moderate his tone and be more careful in future when dealing with Lenin's classic formulas.

I have had to travel widely in many republics, and everywhere I have found that leading national writers agree in their opinion of Smirnov. They see him as a great-power chauvinist and a nationalist. It was for these very reasons that a number of distinguished writers and poets either left the magazine or refused to publish in it—writers like Mezhelitis, Slucskis, Rasul Gamzatov, Bryl, Bokov, and others. They explained their decision

---

* This meeting took place in March 1963, when Khrushchev criticized a number of Soviet writers to their faces—e.g., Voznesensky, Evtushenko, V. Nekrassov, M. Aliger. [Translator]

by the fact that under Smirnov's editorship the journal had lost its popularity. Its print order shrank. During his tenure there, the old rumors about him were in no way dissipated; on the contrary, they grew and spread far beyond Moscow.

In conclusion there is something I must add:

I have found it difficult and painful to write about all this. I am no longer a young man. In my lifetime I have survived no less than five pogroms—the Black Hundreds, the White Guards, and others. During one of these, my twin sister was brutally murdered, and I only escaped death by a miracle. In 1942 the Fascists shot all my relatives, down to my infant nephews. I shall always know and remember that Soviet power freed us Jews from the horror of the pogroms, as it has saved other downtrodden peoples and nations. And the great Red Army, in which I served for twelve years, including the war, dealt with the German racists. That has always been and will always remain my great pride. Which is why it is so hard and bitter, after all that has happened, for me, a Communist, to accuse another Communist of these things. But to remain silent, especially when the Party commission has asked me to make this statement, would be permitted neither by my conscience, nor the bright memory of those who have perished, nor the years of my personal sufferings.

MOSCOW, FEBRUARY 7, 1966

In complete and even more embarrassed silence, the Party investigator began to read the second document.

Document No. 4

TO THE PARTY COMMISSION OF THE MOSCOW CITY COMMITTEE OF THE CPSU.

Attention Comrade V. N. Ivanov.

In connection with our conversation at the Party commission, I can report the following:

1. V. A. Smirnov has never had any anti-Semitic conversations with me personally, of the kind reported to the commission by Communists from the staff of Friendship of the Peoples, whose honesty I do not doubt.

In my presence Smirnov never plucked up courage to say, for instance, that the Don Cossack Alexander Isayevich Solzhenitsyn was in fact Abram Isaakovich Solzhenitser, that the Yids of the Moscow Writers' organization would never admit Polukhin, and so on. In the years I worked with Smirnov I was obliged on so many occasions to put a sharp stop to his hysterical behavior that naturally he never allowed himself such openness in my presence.

2. I shall, however, refer to an incident which took place in the au-

tumn of 1963. On that day we were discussing issue No. 7 or 8 of the magazine, which began with a poem by the Buryat poet Daldinov; after some lines attacking British imperialism, it included the words, if my memory serves me right: "Always, Russia, you have been different, and for that reason you have become dear to us."

I approved the poem in general, and commended Smirnov for including a work of such point, but I stated that the lines I have just quoted were a contradiction of the historically accurate interpretation of Tsarist Russia as the prison of the nations.

"Indeed," I said. "The Russian Empire was in no way different from the British, and until the October Revolution it remained a colonial power which used brutal force to oppose national liberation movements."

Smirnov immediately shouted that he would "not allow" this sort of blaspheming and slandering against the history of the Russian people.

I insisted that he stop shouting at me, and that we should transfer the quarrel away from the full staff meeting to a meeting of the editorial board. The following day I sent the board a letter in which I quoted not only Lenin's assessment of Tsarism, but also some of Stalin's comments on the same subject. Smirnov was greatly devoted to Stalin, and these quotations enabled me to prove the great-power chauvinistic character of the position Smirnov adopted.

3. I shall quote one more typical incident. On February 25, 1964, when the Secretariat of the Writers' Union of the USSR discussed my statement about E. Chalmaev and A. Bogdanov who had forged a purported reader's letter about Tvardovsky's poem "Tyorkin in the Other World" on Smirnov's direct instruction, Smirnov, trying as usual to discredit anyone who criticized him, said that I, as editor of supplements to the magazine, had palmed off on him a collection of various stories "by various Drapkins and Khapkins."

Smirnov was rebuked by A. A. Surkov, who said that the remark about Drapkins and Khapkins was shameful for an editor of Friendship of the Peoples. I would recall that on this occasion Smirnov was insulting Elizaveta Drabkina, a member of the Communist Party since June 1917, the daughter of S. I. Gusev and the professional Bolshevik revolutionary F. Drabkina. She was secretary to Y. M. Sverdlov, had fought in the Civil War, and had talked more than once with Lenin. She was also the author of an excellent book about the first years of the Revolution—Dry Crusts.

Smirnov's behavior at the Secretariat was, of course, "Black Hundred" in nature, since he was protesting the inclusion of works not "by various Ivanovs and Petrovs," as one would usually say in similar circumstances, but specifically "by various Drapkins and Khapkins," sneering at their Jewish descent.

4. At another open staff meeting, Smirnov persistently referred to the writer G. Baklanov as "Fridman," again deliberately emphasizing the Jewish name. But there is no writer called Fridman, and there is a writer called Baklanov. To ignore this is just as inept as, for instance, stressing that the Central Committee of the Party was once run by Minei Israilevich Gubelman and not Emelyan Mikhailovich Yaroslavaky, or the Central Committee of the Party by Soso Dzhugashvili and not Joseph Stalin.

These are just three of the public performances of Smirnov that I remember. It is not difficult to imagine how far he could go in private conversations.

Knowing V. A. Smirnov as I do from one year working on the magazine with him, during which time things went along more or less normally, until he started to respond with hysterical fury to any critical remark addressed to him, I am afraid that he will dismiss this letter, written AT THE REQUEST OF THE PARTY COMMISSION, as motivated by some personal feeling of enmity toward him, even perhaps of vengeance. But whatever he may think, I value his talent, and even his well-known directness, although I regard many of his views as alien to proletarian internationalism, in whose spirit the Party educated my generation.

The whole trouble, in my view, is that Smirnov understood nothing of the resolutions of the Twentieth and Twenty-second Party Congresses* on Lenin's norms of social life. He recognizes only one method of polemic—violence toward those who do not agree with you, the use of insulting and noisy slogans, and a deafening shower of curses instead of calm reasoning—typical of a man who works through a clique—slanderously and scandalously misusing Party organs.

So this is why, despite the vehemence and perhaps something of a lack of factual documentary proof in G. Svirsky's speech, I think it to have been a bold, honest, and opposite attack on the Black Hundreds, who are unfortunately still present even among writers.

Although Smirnov will probably call me a "Talmudist" and a swindler, yet again I cannot fail to end this letter with the words of Lenin calling on the Party to defend the representatives of national minorities in our country from the "great Russian chauvinist," who is in fact a villain and a tyrant, and who is inside every typical Russian bureaucrat.

Speaking in 1922 against the "chauvinistic greater Russian riff-raff," Lenin warned that "nothing will so much delay the development and strengthening of proletarian class solidarity as national injustice, and 'in-

---

* At the Twentieth Congress in 1956, Khrushchev for the first time denounced the terror and cult of personality of the Stalin era. The Twenty-second Congress went a step further—one of its results was Khrushchev's ordering the removal of Stalin's remains from the Lenin mausoleum. [Translator]

sulted' peoples are sensitive to nothing more than to their feeling of equality and to the disruption of this equality—even if this disruption is caused by carelessness or by a joke—by their proletarian comrades."

Vladimir Ilyich warned more than once "that even the slightest hint of anti-Semitism betrays reactionary inclinations."

I am certain that the Party commission will help V. A. Smirnov to understand the political significance of Lenin's warning and that the same lesson will serve to educate others, who, judging from incidents like those involving M. Bubennov and S. Vasiliev, are unable to repress in themselves feelings remote from internationalism.

B. YAKOVLEV

The "honest old man" sat down and swiftly closed his file, fearing perhaps that I was going to demand the reading of the remaining twelve similar statements. But I did not. What had been read already was quite enough.

The silence grew heavier. Such a silence is found only among passengers who have been traveling several hours toward their destination, only to arrive and find that the bridge has been swept away by the flood. They know they must set off back the way they have come with nothing to show for their pains. Or find a new way around—a very long detour. And they're all tired.

Ryzhukhin's face wasn't dismayed. With a look of deep concern, he asked Vasily Smirnov if he had anything to say in rebuttal. Smirnov didn't help him. He erupted like some filthy volcano. Out of the flood of cursing it was possible to isolate three unforgettable statements which were recorded with stenographic accuracy by the representatives of the Writers' Union. "How can I be an anti-Semite, I've got a brother who's married to a Jewess!" . . . I've always suffered from a lack of restraint." . . . "And it doesn't matter what you say! My views aren't to be found in what I say, but what I write!"

Out of the corner of his eye, Smirnov noticed Ryzhukhin sitting very straight and imperturbable, like the teacher's pet in the front row of the class, with answers ready for any question he might be asked. He knew that they were expecting something of him. But what was he supposed to say? He realized that it was better not to talk about the facts. . . .

Smirnov's voice almost rose to a falsetto as he shouted, "So they say I'm an anti-Semite? Don't you dare repeat any such thing! Just think how they'll use it abroad!"

If I were to create a fictional character like that, no one would believe me. They would say it simply wasn't true to life. Your hero's a downright fool, they'd say. And besides, our Purishkeviches are different now.* They know what's what; they don't have sawed-off shotguns in their hands, they have briefcases, and it's the profit motive they attack at meetings. They don't strangle people with their bare hands anymore. Would your anti-Semite ever give himself away like that? It's not true to life. It's rubbish.

Initially I was surprised as well. Vasily Smirnov was far from being a fool. Judging by his books, he was a man with roots in village life, and not at all untalented. He seemed to be a descendant of that race of cunning peasants who listen more than they speak. His head was screwed on all right. So why was he waving his arms about like a windmill? Far from the facts . . .

It was only later that I realized that the powerful editor of *Friendship of the Peoples*, used to behaving exactly as he wished, simply didn't think it necessary to conceal any of his feelings. He believed that his hour had come. That was also why later, at higher levels, it never occurred to him to change his behavior. Everything was the same. At first there was the unbroken stream of curses, lies, and attempts to blacken the name of the witnesses ("They're all the people I fought because I knew they were ideologically unsound"), and then later, when he'd been taken by the arm like a thief, he produced his last hysterical argument—"Sh-sh. Think what they'll do with this abroad!" although it had been plain for a long time that the appearance of internationalists like Vasily Smirnov armed with bludgeons on the ideological high road was like an injection of bubonic plague for the multinational Soviet Union. Compared with that, anything the foreign press might say about similar things was the merest chill from a damp ocean breeze.

What is the significance, indeed, of ten or so articles in the foreign press about anti-Semitism in Russia compared with such a real problem as the presence of a zoological specimen of an anti-Semite like Vasily Smirnov in the job of editor of a magazine called *Friendship of the Peoples*? Yet Smirnov remains to this day a member of the editorial board of that journal.

Smirnov's bony hands trembled, and I thought, what would happen if he had an automatic pistol in them at this moment? No, no. You could find others to do that. . . . This is the age of civilization—and the division of labor . . . He's wily, Smirnov, he knows it's better to keep his operations within the limits of the COLD POGROM. Here it's perfectly safe to walk upside down, on your hands. As indeed he did. He wasn't shy. . . .

---

* Vladimir Purishkevich (1870–1920): the founder at the beginning of the twentieth century of the anti-Semitic organization known as the "Black Hundreds." [Translator]

Alas, that's no exaggeration. He confidently, even enthusiastically, turned everything upside down.

"You're saying I'm an anti-Semite? That I'm inciting nationalistic discord? In the fiftieth year of Soviet power we have nationalism in the republics? Did I say that? No, that's all Svirsky. He's the one who's doing the inflaming . . . and at an open meeting. He inflamed it all. No one except him said a word about it. He's the one. . . ."

It seemed that Ryzhukhin hadn't expected anything like this. He seemed to thrust his whole body forward, he stretched his neck, he was attention itself. What a wealth of ideas! Who is to blame? Not the pyromaniac who blows on the flame, but the man who is cowering away from the burns. Not the quisling militiaman with the rifle, but the man who's groaning on the floor of the quarry. Not the thief, the racist, the one who hands out the insults, not the murderer but the victim.

That was confirmed from issue to issue by the *Russian Banner*. THE JEW HIMSELF IS GUILTY OF EVERYTHING.

"Think what they'll do with this abroad!"

Purishkevich advised the Jews to stay away from crafts that Christians practiced, and even more so to stay away from Russian literature. If they had cleaned boots from century to century, then there would have been no criticism. That true Russian Vasily Smirnov would even have praised their work. He'd have tossed them ten kopecks, or even, if he'd been feeling generous, fifteen. But instead, they crawled, as another contemporary man of letters wrote:

> . . . with catapults, with bookmarks,
> into science, into philosophy,
> onto the radio, into painting,
> into technology, into sport.

They crawled along and turned into people—you've only got yourselves to blame. True Russians know what they must do. . . . Quietly. Sh! Weep into your pillows. Die quietly. Without moaning. Without inflaming passions.

"What they'll do with this abroad!"

Even Viktor Telpugov, wary as a marmot, couldn't restrain himself, and said to me under his breath: "If you can't think of anything better to say, Smirnov, shut up!"

The commission stayed silent as well. They couldn't recover themselves immediately. They needed time to digest this "new" idea. Ryzhukhin rose slowly, looked over our heads with his customary steady gaze, and said firmly, in the kind of voice you'd use for passing sentence: "We cannot say that the witnesses have lied, but equally we cannot say that they have spoken the truth. . . ."

This led to a certain astonishment even among those members of the Writers' Union who had dreamed of ending the affair by making some convenient deal.

Yuri Strekhnin, stooping over the table, leaning on his huge fists, expressed his surprise with his usual ineradicable directness: "Listen, what year is all this happening in?"

But Comrade Ryzhukhin didn't even look at him. Once the machine had been programmed to give Smirnov a whitewash, then it would give it, even if you attacked with a sledge hammer. That was programming.

"Good," said Ryzhukhin, gazing fixedly over our heads. "So this is the position. We find that Grigory Svirsky is not a slanderer. But Vasily Smirnov is also not a chauvinist. He merely gave grounds for thinking that he *might* be a chauvinist."

Someone laughed nervously. Strekhnin's bass said, "Really?"

But what have emotions to do with all this? The secretary scribbled briefly with her fountain pen, writing down the official conclusions of the months-long inquiry. But still Ryzhukhin didn't feel wholly sure of himself. And as he formulated the final conclusion of the Party commission, he looked across at Solovyova, who until now hadn't uttered a word. It seemed that she was going to have to bear the responsibility for today's "measure." To my surprise she didn't try to come up with some compromise formula. Instead, Solovyova, the official head of the cultural department of the Moscow City Committee of the Party looked at us and said authoritatively, in no way embarrassed: "I support the position of Vasily Smirnov."

There was a deathly hush. Not even a chair squeaked. Just a sigh and a cough. Never before, in all the fifty-year history of Soviet power had a responsible Moscow Party leader allowed him- or herself to state in open, at a public meeting, that he SUPPORTED THE POSITION OF A CHAUVINIST AND PURE-BRED ANTI-SEMITE.* When she had set out her ideological credo, Solovyova glanced at the man who had coughed, who was still coughing, and only then deemed it necessary to develop the theoretical basis of her sensational statement.

Vasily Smirnov's chauvinism, she explained, was revealed only in his words, not in his actions. In what he said rather than in what he did. And we must judge Smirnov as he himself asked—not by his words but by deeds.

* Solovyova was the wife of A. A. Solovyov, assistant director of the Institute of Marxism-Leninism of the Central Committee of the CPSU and the principal guardian of the heritage of V. I. Lenin.

At this point several members of the commission began to stir, "switched themselves on." They even exchanged glances. Hadn't she gone too far this time? Even if you turned a blind eye to the fact that Vasily Smirnov had as you might say chased Jewish writers away with a stick (after all, who hasn't ever scratched out "non-natives" from some list or other?), even if you chose to ignore his direct actions, how did you cope with the views of Vladimir Ilyich Lenin? How did you cope with the position he expressed so clearly and directly as to need no further explanation—"THE WORD IS ALSO THE DEED"?

And that is even truer when the word comes from the mouth of a well-known writer, the editor of *Friendship of the Peoples*. And there were other people here. A lot of them. And when they left the building, what would they write? Lenin and Solovyova seemed to be on opposite sides of the barricades. Were they? It made you wonder. . . .

The members of the commission looked at each other.

. . . We parted in silence. I walked out of the room quite shattered. Not because the City Committee Party commission had protected a pogromist (that came as no real surprise), but because of the casual way in which the head of the City Committee's cultural department, who controlled all the cultural life of Moscow, had defied Lenin himself.

What had they done to Lenin? At least no one spoke out against him from public platforms, in speeches. No one ever rejected him in the open, where people could hear—except sometimes by mistake. This was the first time that a responsible Party leader of the City of Moscow had said from a platform in the presence of Party workers and of writers that as far as she was concerned Lenin's words, to put it mildly, didn't matter a damn.

We said good-bye at the main doors of the City Committee. One of the writers shook his head in amazement; clearly he hadn't been expecting anything like this. He said: "It's like a waxworks show."

Another laughed sadly: "A chimpanzee trial? The main thing was, who was in the dock?"

A taxi bore them away, and I walked through the spring streets of Moscow with the snow turning to slush underfoot, thinking about those people who had sat around that massive, impressive table. Who were they? What did they believe in? What was in their souls?

The inquisitors burned Giordano Bruno and Jan Hus on their bonfires. Fanatics, they believed they were helping a holy cause: they were driving out the devil. The Jacobins chopped off heads and believed that that was in a holy cause as well. "Long live the Revolution!" executioners and victims cried in chorus. And finally Tsarist officers fought for "the one indivisible Russia" and sometimes marched to their deaths at a parade ground pace with a cigarette between their lips; they were fierce enemies of the Soviets—but they were enemies with principles.

But what was in Ryzhukhin's mind? Or Solovyova's? In the minds of the "stainless" old women? Or in the minds of the official silent ones who sat around the table, their brows furrowed with the responsibility of the state?

Were there any ideas in those heads? If there were, they must have marched straight out of the Union of the Russian People by squads and battalions or come from Mikhail Arkhangel* or from the editorial offices of *Russian Banner*!

No. They were all different. One of the members of the commission had been grumbling in the corridor: "Our leaders are getting weaker. They've let them off the hook. In the old days . . ." He sounded word for word like the merchant Bugrov who was afraid about what would happen to all his money and asked Gorky anxiously: "We need to think very seriously about this, Mr. Gorky; what are we going to live on when the terror's passed?" People can't hide this kind of merchant philosophy because they don't even know that it *is* a merchant philosophy.

Others (including Ryzhukhin), when they were alone with their consciences, would convince themselves "I am a soldier of the Party!" "I have its affairs on my mind," or something like that.

And Solovyova? Was she speaking with her own voice? Or was she just a mouthpiece for other people's ideas? Whose ideas?

Or what about the evasive Viktor Telpugov, the singer of spring? He clearly wasn't an anti-Semite. I once said to him that he always seemed to be kowtowing at sessions like this. As if it were some gymnastic exercise, getting down to the level of Solovyova. If Solovyova bowed, Telpugov crouched lower. Telpugov spread his hands wide in embarrassment and said that he found himself in a complex position. "You understand . . ."

I was told about one young man working in television who was told to go through a card index of authors to see if there were any Jews among them. "That was a nasty job," he said with disgust to his friends later when he'd done what he'd been asked.

Someone else came out with a string of false accusations, and the same evening rang the man he'd been slandering: "Please forgive me. There was nothing I could do."

A third, a journalist writing on international affairs, wrote a shrill article, and in the evening, when he'd had a drink or two in the club, told me with a cynical smile of a joke invented by his friends: "There's a new

---

* A well-known anti-Semite around the turn of the century. [Translator]

proof that the earth is round. All the slops we pour over the West come pouring back on us from the East."

Stalin used to drink a toast to the "cogs and screws," the voiceless ones, always obedient, never guilty of any offense, who kept the machine turning. When you talked of them, you moved into a new circle of Dante's Inferno.

Eichmann was not an anti-Semite. That was established by the tribunal that judged the faceless bookkeeper of death, whose job it was to organize the extermination of the Jews. In his businesslike way he managed, with all the efficiency of a well-trained clerk, to dispatch six million Jews to the gas chambers—and during his trial denied angrily that he had ever killed so much as one single solitary Jewish child. With his own hands? Never. Eichmann had always considered himself to be a decent, honest man. And, of course, by no means the greatest murderer of all times and of all nations.

Another who presented himself to the astonished world as being far from an amoral person was the commandant of Auschwitz, Hess, a figure almost comparable with Eichmann. It was explained in his defense that Hess was a good family man, the father of five children, that he loved his wife, and in the letter he wrote before his execution he urged his children to grow up honest. In his book *The Death Trade* about Hess, the French writer Robert Merle observes that Hess was educated at home, at school, in the army, and throughout his whole life in militaristic Germany to be an automaton. Hess would follow his own initiative and his own argument only when the order had already been given.

But an automaton—and there is such a specific psychological type—is a result, not a reason. Many thousands of Hesses also acted deliberately, not just because of their orders. There is a more fundamental basis that supports the order itself. And what is this basis? What force sets the automaton into action? There can only be one answer to that, and I shall put it bluntly: the idea. It is the idea that raises man above the level of beasts, and it's the idea that brings him lower than the beasts, depending on what idea it is. Even today we come across ideas which say that to save humanity, humanity will have to be destroyed in flames.

My family and Pauline's had been pursued with clubs and iron bars in every generation. The pogroms of 1905 chased them with iron hooks. They were fired upon by Cossacks putting down "disorder" in the factories. They were slashed by knives, and hanged, as we have seen, by the Blues, the Whites, the Greens leaping from their horses in the villages. And when those gangs had been crushed and dispersed by the Red Army, the task of persecution passed to safe hands—to the Yagodas, the Yezhovs, the Berias, the Abakumovs, the Ryumins. There is no end to the names, to the satraps of Stalin who opened fire on those who had survived, the more so if they turned out to be not merely Communists but Jews as well. The business was successfully continued by the panzers which burst into Russia, the SS officers and the Ukrainian quisling militia, who hurled the few survivors from the heights of the Inguletsk quarry.

Khrushchev of course did his bit too. And so we were left almost on our own, I, Pauline, and Fima, wedded by our names to those who had been shot, flogged, put to the sword.

What awaits us? We are alive, and naturally we think of the future. What awaits our friends in whose passports the criminal hand of Stalin has drawn the yellow star of Point Five that has never been removed?

Eichmannism needs no extra words, no arguments. The Eichmannites are calm, well-balanced, just as he was. They obey orders. Racial laws, "instructions," directives—and sometimes even quite intangible things—a phone call, a signal, and there is no longer any place for a man's mind, his own heart, his own conscience, or other similar outmoded concepts of humanity. Invisible impulses, like those in a computer, have programmed speeches, arguments, behavior. "The duty of office" although it is such a modern idea, as one author aptly remarked, was the excuse that Pontius Pilate used to justify himself.

People calmly shake you by the hand with every appearance of friendship, chat about the approaching centenary of Lenin, drink to Pauline's health, and tell you whenever the opportunity occurs that they aren't anti-Semitic, heaven forbid. Half of their friends are Jews. But if in the silence of their offices the phone rings, or a "signal" comes, or a secret letter, then they'll throw you out on the street with that selfsame business-like friendliness, leave you to starve, push you into a cattle truck, and say as they wave you good-bye, that you must understand they're in a difficult position. "Don't feel badly about it. You can see for yourself—we're not doing it because we want to."

I walked along, not hurrying. I hadn't the strength to go home to Pauline. I couldn't even telephone. And what was there really to phone about? That the anti-Semites remained unpunished as before, and that our troubles might begin again?

Near the Revolution Square metro station I witnessed a street scene that made me walk even slower. A short lad, a Chinese, with a blue cap and his shirt half open over his chest (he had a briefcase in his hand and looked like a student), was talking to a girl—a Russian girl, blue-eyed and cheerful. They shifted from foot to foot and clearly didn't want to part. Then another Chinese boy came briskly past. He had the same blue cap, the same briefcase. But he was tall and heavily built. Without saying a word he took a lighted cigarette from his mouth and pressed the burning end into the smaller boy's chest. Without haste, absolutely convinced of the rightness of what he was doing, he ground it against the yellow skin: the smaller boy clenched his lips and didn't utter a sound. He went pale, and his face was twisted in pain, but he didn't speak.

I ran up and struck the cigarette away. Both the Chinese immediately disappeared in different directions, leaving the girl in complete confusion.

She moved off a little, and stayed to watch, waiting faithful spirit, in case he came back. A militia officer came up to me in his long dark raincoat. He was a correct, Moscow militiaman who, as it turned out, had been standing close by and had observed the whole episode.

"You're wasting your time, citizen. They're foreigners. That's their business."

I nodded to him. He was probably right. I lost myself in the crowd going into the metro. It was like plunging into a fast-flowing stream. I was swirled down the escalators and onto the train. I moved my feet mechanically, thinking that for six months or more I had had a cigarette pressed into my soul. By our own people, not the Chinese. "That's their business . . ." But this—whose business was this? Whose?

25

Now I had to appear before the powerful secretary of the Moscow Party Committee, Egorychev himself, at the next session of the Bureau of the City Committee.

So there we were again, waiting outside the great doors, I and two emissaries from the Writers' Union, sitting there looking like professional undertakers. Viktor Telpugov's face still told the same story: "It's dreadful, Grisha. But you must understand that I'm in a difficult position." That's the way it was with the Moscow Writers: from that storm-tossed ocean they always selected the quietest, calmest representatives.

Every now and again the massive doors to the lobby opened, and people shot out, their faces red and sweaty, as if they'd come from a bathhouse.

Smirnov—who had "given cause"—had disappeared somewhere. It turned out he had dropped into Solovyova's office for a tranquilizer. Yuri Strekhnin, the honest colonel, wasn't there either. He was probably the only one who would dare to doubt that Egorychev was always right. His absence alarmed me, in the same way that an infantryman is alarmed when he's putting on his steel helmet before a battle, and suddenly hears that the artillery isn't going to be there because it got stuck somewhere. I was the more disturbed because I was also fully unprotected from above, from the high and seemingly cloudless sky. Both my phone calls to Pyotr Demichev, the secretary of the Central Committee, who was presumed never to know what was going on with his underlings, had gone unanswered. Demichev wasn't in town. And as one of his friends had made clear to me, he wouldn't be—not for Svirsky. The infantry was going into battle alone. . . .

Well, it had been the same in Byelorussia in '41 when my bomber had gone up in black smoke and as I was groping my way through the night someone had given me two smooth metal grenades, vintage 1914.

I opened my portfolio and had a look at the "grenades" I'd packed with me. I found one of them. Saltykov-Shchedrin's *Unfinished Conversations*. We had been told that we needed Saltykov-Shchedrin and Gogol.* That was absolutely right. They were grenades that didn't deteriorate with age.

It's interesting that of all the Russian writers, only Saltykov-Shchedrin took a cautious view of Germany, as if he could foresee the evils of the Nazis. "The anti-Semitic movement in Germany shows that even an improvement in the level of education does not bring any demonstrable improvements to the situation."

So what, then, was needed?

". . . what is needed is that mankind should ultimately become humanized. And when will that take place?"

I looked at the dark doors, through which Solovyova had just sidled, and thought anxiously that if she could dismiss Lenin as easily as an automatic potato peeler deals with a potato, Shchedrin would hardly strike her as a vegetable at all.

I could see that the representatives of the Union were beginning to get nervous as well. They were sitting on either side of me, looking at the doors as if they were the Royal Gates in a church. They too seemed to fear that the cherished dream of Shchedrin had not yet come to pass— that we hadn't reached the final stage of complete humanization.

We were called, and we filed quietly into the great, high-ceilinged hall where we sat down at the side, on a wooden bench. It was an astonishing room. There was a wide table of expensive wood, and sitting at it the secretary of the Moscow Committee, Comrade Egorychev. The table was horseshoe-shaped, its ends pointing outward. It looked like a huge industrial magnet. Everyone else was sitting in the body of the hall as if along the lines of force of this magnet, at little movable tables.

Egorychev rose and stood at the microphone. Immediately the little tables moved and settled themselves into orderly lines. Moved, and then stopped dead. It was obviously a powerful magnet. I smiled involuntarily, and several unfriendly faces turned to me. Telpugov leaned over me and repeated in a whisper, like an incantation, "Calm down, Grisha. Calm down! Calm down!"

Egorychev was lean and athletic. He began to talk louder and louder, as if he were warming himself up; his hoarse bass grew steadily deeper, and from the way that Solovyova listened to him from behind one of the little tables, leaning forward, her lips half open, it was obvious that my

* We had been told . . . Gogol: Statement made by Malenkov in 1952, applauding the merits of satirical writers. [Translator]

quarrel wasn't with her directly. Such a correct official from the department would never have made that sensational statement—"I support the position of Vasily Smirnov"—on her own authority.

Egorychev's excited, hoarse voice reminded me of another one—the false witness! The inexplicable false witness in the smoke-filled militia room at the Kursky Vokzal metro station, who'd come to support the drunken anti-Semite. . . . Here again was a hoarse, nervous voice, vibrating with a strange, inexplicable kind of hysteria.

Why? There was no Stalin outside, not even a Khrushchev. Why had Egorychev voluntarily undertaken to run the next lap in this execution relay race? Voluntarily? Who could force him to do so? He was one of the most influential men in the Party. He held so much power in his hands yet his voice was full of hysteria. Why? Could it be that in the depths of his mind he was frightened? Isn't that why all anti-Semitic campaigns invariably sound a hysterical note?

Egorychev was a powerful and intelligent man, an engineer who'd graduated from the best technical school in Moscow, the Bauman Institute, named after the revolutionary Bauman. Of course he understood that the condemnation of history was not an abstract concept. So what was he doing? There was not a single person in the Writers' Union who did not know the kind of person Vasily Smirnov was. And the names of the members who made up the "black dozen." There could be no two opinions about that.

People used to laugh gently about Khrushchev's cry: "We don't have any anti-Semitism here." That was never an argument, just an assertion. Egorychev could not fail to understand, could not fail to sense that he was taking up Khrushchev's role. With his own hands he had hung around his own neck a board bearing the inscription "False Witness."

Egorychev, not long ago you suppressed the case against those highly placed literary officials who had organized a brothel in a country house near Golitsyn. You saved those influential bastards from prison. Now you have thrown a life belt to Vasily Smirnov. It's a well-trodden path. It's not the first time he's had to be rescued. A year ago he was accused of provocation against *Novy Mir* by rank forgery; he published an article signed by a certain author attacking the journal. The author in question never wrote it, as was proved by the Secretariat of the Writers' Union. But despite all that, Smirnov was never removed from his job: that, in the opinion of our home-grown strategists would have meant indirect victory for Tvardovsky.

It doesn't matter if they're slanderers or corrupt swindlers, drunks, even anti-Semites, as long as they're fighters against "sedition"—hands off! They're fine people. The caste of the untouchables. Is that what's behind it, Comrade Egorychev?

Or is it something else? Not long ago one of the most important leaders of industry addressed the writers' meeting. He spoke sadly about the difficulties of the economy, about the rundown machinery, about the lack of money, about difficulties in Comecon. Finally about the bad harvest. He left the hall, and, depressed by this unexpected picture which had been unfurled before us, one of the old famous writers said to me with a sad smile: "I suppose they'll be after you now."

"Who do you mean, us?" I asked, not understanding.

"After the Jews. You heard the man say things are in a mess. And there's no other safety valve."

An ideologue on *Russian Banner* once wrote a pamphlet called "On the Impossibility of Giving the Jews Equal Rights" (St. Petersburg, 1906). "According to information received from the police department, 90 percent of revolutionaries in Russia are Jews, and only the remaining 10 percent are drawn from among the ignorant of other nationalities."

And now, as the writer Amfiteatrov prophesied long ago, are the anti-Semites beginning to turn around and roar that 90 percent of *counter*-revolutionaries are Jews? That all trouble-makers in every country are Jews? That Jews are the greatest danger for Socialism?

But all anti-Semitic hysteria is a drug—a quick-acting one. It can knock you out, but only for a short time. No government has been able to save itself for long by unfurling the banner of anti-Semitism. It's been clear for a long time that people turn to anti-Semitism only out of fear. As a last straw. What are you afraid of, Egorychev? What's in your mind? Go tell all Moscow—"I am a false witness!"

There was silence in the Committee hall. Egorychev was the only one who had spoken, and it looked as if no one else was going to get the chance. When he paused for breath, I asked, "Perhaps I could be allowed to say something?" Just so the other side could be heard!

Egorychev appeared not to hear my request. The next time he paused to gulp air, I said it again, louder: "I hope you are going to let me speak!"

He turned to face me. His eyes were hard and cold as before, and narrowed into slits at the corners.

"How much time would you need?" he asked.

"Seven and a half minutes."

He made a sign to give me permission to speak.

I looked for Ryzhukhin and Solovyova sitting behind their little mobile tables. They were gazing fixedly at Egorychev, the way singers who haven't had much time to learn the tune keep their eye on the choirmaster so as not to get out of time.

Taking out my typewritten text, I began to read. The aphorisms I quoted from Smirnov, "the iron chancellor"—and even the information that he made them publicly—didn't produce any change in the expressions of the faces watching me. "The Jews are everywhere," "He's sold himself to the Jews," or "Go off to Israel!" Nothing new about them—everyone had heard those before.

I looked anxiously at the members of the Bureau of the City Committee. There were forty or fifty white faces listening with cautious attention. Behind them were some older men, perhaps Party members from the time of the Revolution. And in the corner some young workers. Surely I could raise a response from some of them. Suddenly one young lad's eyes lit up in surprise.

". . . when the poetess Yunna Morits," I read, "wrote some excellent verse about Pushkin, Smirnov said to her, 'Why are you writing about Pushkin? He's not *your* writer, he's *our* writer.' "

Now most of them were paying attention. They hadn't heard that one before.

Quickly, so as to fit into the time allowed, I read through the document I had prepared solely on the basis of facts checked by the Party Commission. Even Ryzhukhin had confirmed them. Of course, the document includes things the reader knows already, so forgive me for any repetitions—but it is an official paper.

Document No. 5

The witnesses, members of the staff of Friendship of the Peoples, *quote the names of well-known writers who no longer write for the magazine merely because they are Jews. "These are not our authors," Smirnov said repeatedly and added anxiously, "They're hiding behind pseudonyms. But you ask them their fathers' names—that'll give them away."*

Smirnov was by no means one-sided in his chauvinistic acts against the people of our country. "Georgian prose is not Soviet," Smirnov used to say. He was even more categorical about Estonians, Latvians, and Lithuanians— "Those people are not Soviet."

Gabit Musrepov, chairman of the Writers' Union of Kazakhstan, said at the Secretariat of the Writers' Union of the USSR that "Smirnov's observations were a humiliation to national literature."

Smirnov's deep-rooted amorality resulted in the Russian poet Alexander Surkov, the national poet of Lithuania and Lenin Prize winner Eduard Mezhelitis, and the major Byelorussian writer Yanka Bryl all giv-

ing in their notice and leaving the editorial board of Friendship of the Peoples.

The witnesses summoned by the Party commission of the Moscow Committee, writers and journalists, confirmed thirty-one instances in which Smirnov had made chauvinistic remarks and statements. Of these, seven were made in public. It was no accident that V. Alexandrov, who for five years was the secretary of the Party organization of Friendship of the Peoples and a candidate member of the Frunze Regional Committee, concluded his statement by saying, "I consider that there is no room for Smirnov in the Communist Party."

At the sessions of the Party Committee, Smirnov did not contest the majority of the facts. "Whatever you say," he said; "My view is not contained in what I have said, but what I have written." He only questioned four of the facts we cited.

If we reject not just these four, but fourteen, or even twenty-four, and rely only on four or five, it still remains clear that Smirnov did not leave those sessions with his head held high.

The facts were confirmed by the Party commission. But what were their conclusions? "Svirsky is not a slanderer, but Smirnov is not a chauvinist." Smirnov, as Comrade Ryzhukhin put it, "only gave grounds for thinking . . ." "Only gave grounds . . ." to think of him as a chauvinist.

Smirnov gave those grounds, not to one man only, but to dozens, perhaps hundreds of people. Finally, he gave grounds to a thousand Moscow writers to applaud when from the platform of an open Party meeting he was accused of being a great-power chauvinist. And if we take into account the fact that Smirnov's views have been made available to all the republics of the Union, then it is easy to see the damage caused by his immunity for so many years. That much is clear even from the evidence given to the Party commission by twelve witnesses—writers and journalists.

Comrade Ryzhukhin declared, "We cannot say that the witnesses have lied, but equally we cannot say they have spoken the truth." When you want to close your eyes to the facts, then this is the sort of thing that happens. Statements by twelve worthy, reputable writers, Communists and non-Communists, are rejected, and one man is taken at his word—Smirnov, who has already been twice accused at the Union Secretariat of lies, falsification of facts, and straightforward forgery, Smirnov, who at the famous reception in the Kremlin in the spring of 1963 slandered the entire writers' organization of Moscow.

It has been considered an extenuating circumstance that Smirnov's chauvinism manifested itself only in words and not in deeds. In statements rather than actions. And we must, of course, judge Smirnov by his actions, not his words. Such an argument cannot refute the criticisms, even if we *ignore all the chauvinistic instructions given by the editor-in-chief of Friend-ship of the Peoples, i.e., his direct actions.*

Chauvinism and anti-Semitism (if of course we are not talking about street pogroms) are a manifestation of ideology, in which the weapons are words. Lenin said, "The word is also the deed." And that, let us add, applies even more strongly to the words of a writer—particularly of the editor-in-chief of Friendship of the Peoples.

Three times in recent years at Party meetings writers have raised the question of Smirnov's chauvinism and anti-Semitism. The first to raise the matter was Professor Shukin, a former member of the Cheka, who headed the battle against counterrevolution under Dzerzhinsky. From that very hour he was hounded until he died of a heart attack!

There was a moan from a gray-haired man sitting in front of me. He leaned on his desk, his head in his hands.

It soon became clear that Smirnov's flagrant chauvinism had been discussed at writers' meetings not three times, but seven. Openly and publicly discussed. Later the Old Bolshevik Comrade Voitinskaya appealed to the newly elected Party Committee to "unmask the false face of Smirnov." Finally even the leader of the Moscow Writers' organization, the super-cautious Sergei Mikhalkov, said in public that "Smirnov seemed very remote from Friendship of the Peoples."

The elderly writer Semyon Rodov sent to Egorychev, the secretary of the Moscow Committee and the Central Committee, a special letter in which he wrote that this was very far from the first time Smirnov had been accused of anti-Semitism.

Document No. 6

TO THE FIRST SECRETARY OF THE MOSCOW CITY COMMITTEE OF THE CPSU

Comrade N. G. Egorychev:
. . . I think it necessary to report that this [speech by Svirsky] was not the first public speech to accuse V. Smirnov of anti-Semitism.

Some years ago at a closed Party meeting of Moscow writers the late Professor Shukin made the selfsame allegation. In breach of the existing rules, the personal case of Professor Shukin and Smirnov was not heard at a general meeting of the Moscow branch of the Writers' Union of the USSR, and the accusation that V. A. Smirnov held anti-Semitic views therefore remained without rebuttal.

SEMYON RODOV
Member of the Communist
Party since 1918

April 4, 1966

When I had finished going through these documents, no one was looking at Egorychev anymore, not even Solovyova. There was a heavy, ominous silence, reinforced rather than broken by the occasional rustle or creak from a table. The only time I'd heard a silence like it was on an airfield when a dummy was dropped out of an airplane to demonstrate to us students that parachuting was completely safe—and the dummy's chute failed to open.

Finally, Egorychev's bass voice broke the silence. "So. But you weren't merely talking about Vasily Smirnov. You spoke about anti-Semitism. You were generalizing."

Dozens of eyes turned in my direction. Solovyova had the gloating look of a hunter who sees that his prey is almost in the trap—one more step and . . .

"That is true. I was generalizing," I forced the words out, realizing that it was all about to begin.

Egorychev rose, swaying a little. You could see that he was spreading his feet farther apart. He began to speak in that cheerful, fatherly tone which radio announcers reading stories for children use for Grandmother persuading Little Red Riding Hood not to be afraid. But his voice was very deep, hoarse—not at all like a grandmother.

"Come nearer." He indicated his horseshoe table. "Come over here, please."

I went across to Egorychev and stood by the left hand microphone. I suddenly noticed that two or three of the people sitting at the little movable tables were stretching up—"standing on their tails," as one of the writers described it acidly later. One wide-faced man called out, "I bet you've got a dossier on all of us, not just on Smirnov!" His lips twitched with hatred. Egorychev made a slight movement of his hand, and the man sank back in his seat.

Solovyova's neighbor, a fluffy-haired blonde with a squint in one clouded eye, also suddenly yelled something at me—it sounded poisonous, but I couldn't catch what she said. Egorychev barely flicked his finger, and the blonde turned away as if she couldn't bear to look at me.

An orchestra—and so beautifully trained . . .

"We're listening to you, please carry on," said Egorychev, in the same reassuring tones of encouragement.

I looked for my briefcase. I had left it by the door. "Just one moment," I apologized, and went to get it. Solovyova's round eyes followed me. At first they looked surprised, then alarmed. Surely I wasn't planning to run away, to leave the session?

But I came back. I looked at the microphone, which didn't amplify, but presumably was there just for recording. I took from my briefcase a slim volume in gray covers, which Solovyova eyed nervously, as if the book was something that might blow up. I showed it to everyone. The title was *The Criminal Code of the RSFSR.*

I leafed through and stopped at Article 74. I read it out, not hurrying this time:

> "Propaganda or agitation designed to provoke national or social hatred or antagonism or to lead to direct or indirect limitation of the rights of citizens, or to furnish them with direct or indirect privileges arising from their national or social classification are punishable by deprivation of liberty for a period of from six months to three years or by exile for a period of from two to five years."

I put the code down, and looked at the people sitting in front of me.

Some of them had sneered at Pauline. Or at best they had silently approved when she had been driven out of the personnel departments, weeping, hungry, and ill. And they had struck her off as a "non-native" from the institute's recommendations to the regional appointments commissions. What did they feel now, those powerful Regional Committee secretaries, those personnel officers, those directors of factories? "The voice of the Russian worker should sound loud against national humiliation," Lenin told them. According to Lenin, when these people heard about Vasily Smirnov, there shouldn't be any talk of his Party membership. What Party membership? They should be talking about Article 74 of the Criminal Code. Or had they, like Nikita Khrushchev, decided that Lenin required radical correction? Indeed, how many times had almost all of them participated, albeit silently, in the division and discrimination of their workers, their engineers, into "native" and "also-rans," according to rules laid down by Alexander III? How many times had it happened? How many years had it gone on?

Not one head was lowered. Their faces were impenetrable. Only in Solovyova's glimmering eyes was there a shade of alarm. What else would this little lawyer dig up?

I spoke briefly about my efforts on one occasion to charge racial hatemongers operating in a metro car. And I told them about the People's Court, where there were powerful filters, sieves through which only "clean" cursing passed, unsullied by admixtures of nationalistic poison.

"What is your opinion; is this independent action by those particular militia and judges? Or is it accepted as a quasi-legal norm?" In other words, was it possible in our country to apply Article 74 of the Criminal Code?

I took from my briefcase another volume in a leather-cloth binding and showed it to the members of the Bureau. Its title was A *Scientific and Practical Commentary on the Criminal Code of the RSFSR*; Second edition, Moscow, 1964.

"I don't know whether you are familiar with this? It is the basic reference book of every practicing lawyer. This authoritative commentary explains the meaning of Article 74. Here is what it says: 'Propaganda of racial or nationalist enmity means the distribution in oral, written, printed, or any other form to greater or smaller numbers of people of views or ideas which arouse, or could arouse, a hostile, disdainful, or scornful attitude in those people toward any nationality or race.' Those are the words—'to greater or smaller numbers of people.' Hardly very precise!

"The metro carriage or the trolley car crammed with passengers: Do you regard those as a larger or smaller number of people? And the yard of a multistory block, swarming with children and adolescents—a larger or a smaller number? Perhaps one should use a megaphone to summon people to a pogrom, so that the circle of listeners would be large enough to be recognized by the lawyers as actually being 'large.'

"That's the way juridical imprecision is born—it exists in the codes of some other countries, which is where, no doubt, the RSFSR code found it. But here this imprecision is widened into a hole, a crack, through which illegality can squeeze. Illegality, as you might say, 'legalized.' This time by Khrushchev's law.

"As a rule, judges tend toward precision. And so on the same page of this learned commentary, we are told that actions designed to degrade the honor or dignity of an individual person in connection with his nationality can be dealt with under 'insulting behavior.' And I find it very bitter to tell you that PUBLIC chauvinistic actions are to be dealt with as cases for so-called PRIVATE prosecution. In that trolley car a man shouted, 'Hitler should have finished you off as well!' That was no anti-Soviet talk, no pogrom poison. It was just an ordinary everyday insult.

"And even that is not always the case. There is another clarification of the law which demonstrates how an anti-Semite can escape responsibility under any circumstances. The commentary says: 'The offense under consideration can only be deemed to have been committed if there is direct intent. That is to say that the accused must acknowledge that he inspired in the third person views or ideas which aroused or could arouse a hostile attitude to another nationality or race, and that he wished these consequences to follow.' (*Commentary to the Criminal Code of the RSFSR*, p. 173.) I have never once come across a judge who forced an anti-Semite to that kind of answer: 'So you deliberately, consciously inflamed enmity toward this nationality and hoped to bring about this enmity? You wanted these consequences to happen?' The anti-Semite blinks his eyes, and finally grasps the point: 'What? No, I just said it . . . I didn't want . . . any consequences . . .'

"Just imagine the situation if under other articles of the Criminal Code the accused were fully cleared of responsibility merely by muttering 'I didn't want . . . I didn't intend . . .' For instance, drunken drivers who've killed pedestrians. Thugs who've murdered a passer-by, and who say in court: 'We never wanted to kill him, of course not!'" But for a Great-Russian chauvinist, a boor, an oppressor, to get off scot-free, all he has to do is to say he didn't want to inflame passions. . . .

"As you see, Article 74 of the Criminal Code is a dead letter. To all practical purposes it doesn't exist in Soviet law. So consequently the article in the Soviet Constitution about equal rights of races and nations is a dead letter too—the clause which Article 74 should be there to protect.

"But there is no protection. It's been removed by that special 'explanation' in the commentary. The frontiers are open for Great-Russian chauvinism. Carry on, enjoy yourselves. That is how statistics can falsify, destroy. It is not happening at the highest levels, as it once did in agriculture, when the farm workers were starving and the papers were full of stories that we were gathering in a record harvest. It is happening far down below, in the People's Courts, in local militia posts, and if there is no statistical record of chauvinism, that means that chauvinism does not exist. . . .

"You have now heard these commentaries on the law which effectively destroys the law.* But did you know of the disgusting practices of racism— of the open chauvinists who walk our streets unhindered, who turn up in schools, institutes, wherever they choose?"

. . . I waited to hear what they had to say. There was no answer. They were all staring, as if at a movie screen where some strange man was mouthing at them and they didn't know what he wanted. Oh well, never mind, the lights would soon go up and he'd vanish.

"I did not choose my language, my culture, my customs, any more than I chose my parents. I was born in Russia, I have lived all my life in Moscow. I was brought up in a Russian cultural milieu. I became a

---

* In the new commentary to the Criminal Code of the RSFSR, Moscow, 1971, there is a small alteration. In recent years pogromists in Russia have been given so free a rein that they have begun to beat up Jews, and sometimes to kill them. It became slightly embarrassing to charge them merely with insulting behavior. So the following words have been added to the commentary: "Insolent and cynical behavior in public places can be brought under the heading of malicious hooliganism" (p. 171). So now any act of anti-Semitic slight in the USSR is juridically transferred immediately either to insulting behavior or, if the victim has had his head beaten in, then it becomes malicious hooliganism.

Moscow writer—and even if all that weren't true, there's still another qualification for nationality—blood, spilled for freedom of one's country.

"Like many of my colleagues, I only think of myself as a Jew when someone shouts "Dirty Yid" after me in the street, or when in some way or another it's thrust down my throat. And that sort of thing has been happening more and more often recently. . . ."

"Less and less often!" shouted Egorychev, waving his head and arms about for greater emphasis.

I smiled sadly. I saw things more clearly than he did.

"That is why so many people in Moscow, thousands of people, are waiting to hear your decision. . . . It's easy to see that it's not only about Smirnov! Is a man who doesn't belong to a national majority—is a Jew—protected against discrimination? From national humiliation? Or is he like me—unprotected?"

I tried to fasten my briefcase, but I couldn't. I couldn't see the locks. I shoved the case under my arm and sat down on the side bench, where the representatives of the Writers' Union were waiting anxiously.

26

Slowly, stooping, Egorychev got to his feet and began his speech by muttering something about the "millwheel." As if he had pronounced some magic formula, I almost literally saw Sasha Weiner standing beside him. Sasha Weiner, thin, a mixture of dismay and terrible despair, despair from which there was no escape. And his old mother leaning on his shoulder.

How could I dare compare, almost as equals, the state, this heavy tank lurching along on its tracks, and the child who happened to be in its path? The executioner and the victim.

The clattering tank, blind in its rage, is inescapable. You can't get away from it, can't hide from it, can't burrow into the ground. And what right had I to condemn this terrified boy to face it alone? Shouldn't I rush to help him?

What were they doing to the children? Just what they were doing to me? . . . And it was happening here, in the capital! In the very center of ideological life. Nasim Khikmet once said that when they trim your nails in Moscow, in the provinces they chop your fingers off.

Only recently in the Altai an old theater director was fired just because he'd been discovered with a copy of my public speech about Vasily Smirnov and the "black dozen," which, we thought, had been supported by Demichev, a secretary of the Central Committee of the Party. "You're fired for having Zionist literature," they told him when they sacked him. Why "Zionist"? Well, that's what it is. . . . Why not just take the decent old man and chop his fingers off? After all, he's a Jew, and there's no demand for them!

Should I have stayed silent, a living man, while millions of graves cried out in protest? Cried out, "What are you doing, madmen?" Should I have let the pogrom-makers rage and roar like wild beasts? Let the desperate young people hurl themselves on the frontiers, across the mine fields, onto the barbed wire, where death waits for them—let them go to their prisons, into non-existence—these healthy, strong Russian lads, who were being thrown aside as if they were already dead, down the ravine—should I have stayed silent? If I did, then I was no longer a writer, no longer a man, nothing more than a speck in the galaxy of Eichmannites.

"In vain . . . we must remember . . . arouse . . . attitudes . . . onto whose millwheel?"

Egorychev now looked a tired, stooping figure, who seemed to be carrying out his duties reluctantly. He was speaking without spirit and said as if in passing that we would have had no complaints about me if I had made my speech in a closed session. But to say things like that in public?

Fine, I thought, well-disciplined; next time I'll speak in a closed meeting.

Then suddenly he began to get excited, as he had been at the beginning. He suddenly recalled that Vasily Smirnov, at the meeting with Khrushchev, had slandered the entire Moscow Writers' organization. . . . "At that time you were really throwing oil on the flames!" he yelled.

All his pent-up anger and annoyance flowed out over Vasily Smirnov, who, as Egorychev said, never watched his words, and by his unrestrained, hysterical behavior really did "give grounds . . ."

I listened to the secretary of the Moscow Committee as he laid into the Great-Russian chauvinist if for no other reason than that he couldn't keep his tongue behind his teeth, and I thought of the many things that I might have said. About Sasha Weiner, and about a boy about the same age as Sasha, a fair-haired young soldier, who once got very drunk and told my old mother that if she wouldn't work for him, he might turn nasty. He was the boss, and he might choose to get rid of her, a Jewess.

The Party leaders seemed not to notice how young people were being grimed by all this, how they fell back on the old ways of the Slavophiles.* "Our social life is bankrupt," said the middle-aged prophets, both with and without university degrees. "We must take refuge in nationalism." And they did.

Pravda officially encouraged Canadian nationalism, because that of course was progressive opposed to the "Yankees," and gave its full, unthinking support to black nationalism, even if it emitted the filthiest stench of racism. The wind wasn't blowing toward Russia, of course.

* *Slavophiles:* In the eighteenth and nineteenth centuries, Russian intellectuals were divided into two major factions: those who looked to the West, and those—the Slavophiles—who, in a strongly nationalistic spirit, rejected Western culture and sought out the elements of a new civilization from within Russia itself. [Translator]

But if the wind were to change? It already has changed, more than once. In Ghana, in Indonesia. Try and name a place where it hasn't changed! Lumumba was shot in Leopoldville, and now Communists are being killed by the same people who yesterday swore eternal friendship with Russia.

The forest fires of nationalism are uncontrollable. The wind of history fans the flames to east and west. If the wind changes even a few degrees, the fire from a faithful ally could become a dangerous enemy. How much does the world have to pay in blood on account of the new social-nationalists?

Stalin fanned the flames of the fires of nationalism when he lost faith in international ideas. Perhaps he never believed in them at all. And as a result again and again there are attempts to repress, to corrupt the spirit of the people, including the Russian people, even though in words the Russian people are glorified. How long will the living go on crawling after a corpse on the bloodsoaked tracks of nationalism toward the abyss?

I was distracted from these thoughts by Egorychev's voice, rising higher and higher in anger. By some miracle it seemed that the secretary of the Moscow Committee was goading himself toward some kind of sincerity. He was still yelling at Vasily Smirnov, so violently that when he finally reached his conclusion, and said, exhausted, "Let us limit ourselves to a discussion of this particular question," I knew that Smirnov must feel profoundly relieved.

By nature, I'm easily appeased. I was angry with myself for having tarred Smirnov and Egorychev with the same brush. Still, he's taken a good swing at the "iron chancellor." A lesson to others. They weren't really both out of the same stable. I was quite wrong. But, alas, I wasn't. . . .

Six months later (a deliberate delay to allow the excitement in the Writers' Union to die down) I was summoned to the Regional Committee and shown the following document from the office of the Moscow City Committee, dated April 27, 1966.

Document No. 7

TO INFORM SVIRSKY G. T. THAT HIS POLITICAL ACCUSATIONS AGAINST SMIRNOV V. A. HAD NO FOUNDATION, AND THAT BY HIS INCORRECT CONDUCT SVIRSKY HAS STIRRED UP NATIONAL DISCORD.

Another reversal.

Our literary cripples, men like Smirnov, Shevtsov, Sofronov, were brazen-faced, and at the same time unsure of themselves, like all hooligans. But from now on they had been granted an indulgence—for former pogroms, for present pogroms, and future ones. From Egorychev himself. With the signature of the first secretary and the seal of the Moscow City Committee.

All that needs to be added (especially for the Moscow Institute of Marx-Engels-Lenin of the Central Committee of the CPSU) is this: "The slightest manifestation of anti-Semitism has always been and always will be a convincing proof that a given person or group is reactionary."— V. I. Lenin

I have produced seven official documents from one investigation, from one attempt to call a spade a spade, and to prove that chauvinism is a crime.

Stalin himself is long gone, but the avalanche he started still rumbles on. . . . Where then is the beginning and where the end? When—in our Soviet time—did the first stone begin to roll?

I thought about this for the first time when I was visiting Viktor Granovsky, Pauline's uncle, on that tragic birthday. All his colleagues from work were there, engineers, accountants, with their wives and children. Someone recalled how Granovsky had saved him in 1949 from starvation, and when he had drunk one or two glasses went over to embrace him.

But Granovsky grew gloomy. He too remembered the "feverish forties." He adjusted his white embroidered Russian shirt, belted with a silken cord, and began to talk about conscience.

"We grow, we get richer, and conscience disappears down the drain. There's no one you can rely on. There aren't any decent people left." He looked at us from beneath his black shaggy eyebrows, which covered the old scar over his eye, a personal gift from Petlyura. "The consciences people have nowadays couldn't be found even with a microscope. Why is that?"

The first to respond was Sergei Ivanovich, a withered old man with yellow sunken cheeks. He was an engineer, wearing a shrunken striped suit with shabby elbows. He swayed to and fro like a string of dried mushrooms in the wind. Sergei Ivanovich had been a former commissar with Shchors,* and he had shriveled up in solitary confinement, where he had been held on false evidence for twelve years. As Uncle Vitya said, he had had time to think.

"In India the cow is a sacred animal," he began, and then coughed a characteristic tubercular cough. "Don't kill the cows! A child has to make

---

Shchors: Nikolai Alexandrovich Shchors (1895–1919), Ukrainian Red Army commander and Civil War hero.

do with his mother's milk. If this principle were suddenly to be broken and someone opened fire on the cows with a machine gun, and remained unpunished, that would mean the moral collapse of India! Do you understand?

"Even the incorruptible Robespierre, Robespierre with his guillotine, drew the line at driving out religion. And by that I mean, you understand, the system of moral standards. 'Thou shalt not kill.' 'Thou shalt not steal,' 'Thou shalt not commit adultery.' But what did we do with those standards? We exploded all the moral taboos, like the Church of Christ the Savior. And what did we put in their place—leaving pockmarked Joseph† aside (as if we could)—what did we put in their place? Everything is moral that is useful to the proletariat! Those words have been carved in marble, canonized—for now and ever more. And just who decided what was useful to the proletariat? Joseph? Khrushch? Do you understand?"

Uncle Vitya cried out, as if someone had struck him.

"That sounds as if you're saying Lenin himself back in the twenties cleared the airstrip so that these Jew-hating bastards could take off for the attack. But those were the days when anti-Semitism was tried as counterrevolution. . . ."

"Rubbish! Arguments like that can end up anywhere. . . ."

Just an hour, or more accurately fifty minutes, were left before the knock on the door came, and the search party with their warrant burst into Uncle Vitya's home, and Uncle Vitya died because he couldn't stand the shame. And through all those remaining minutes Uncle Vitya went on arguing that in the twenties "there was nothing like this. . . ."

I listened to his hoarse voice and began to understand just when and where our home-grown racism was conceived . . . when it first moved, as the embryo first stirs and kicks in its mother's womb. Oh, years of the twenties, I look at you now steadily, and in horror. Didn't the sources of our present racist violence stem from you? It may seem madness to say that. In the twenties anti-Semites were indeed tried and condemned as counterrevolutionaries. The Jew-hater was regarded with scorn and derision, as vermin. Surely it couldn't have started then? But the twenties, the years that affirmed the equality of nations, were nevertheless pregnant with anti-Semitism, and the day of its birth was drawing near. They legalized illegality, our much-vaunted twenties. It became customary to look for scapegoats.

Lenin set the task of preserving power, by any means at any price. It was the first time in Russian history—since the pogroms of Ivan the Terrible in Novgorod the Great—that people were killed not for what they

† Nickname for Stalin, on account of his pitted face. [Translator]

themselves had done, but because they belonged to some group or other of "Novgorodites." Whether you actually fired at the Red Guards from your attic or were asleep in bed at the time, it made no difference. You were a Novgorodite, and that was enough.

Whole social classes found themselves tied to the whipping posts. First of all it was the gentry who were dragged out, even if they were descendants of the Decembrists. Then there were the Mensheviks and the Social Revolutionaries—they were transferred from the prisons of the Tsar to those of the Bolsheviks. They were moved from Irkutsk and Orlov to Solovki and Butyrki. Then a little later came the old engineers, then the individual peasants (and not only the rich ones), then there were the "disenfranchised," who included priests and vergers, and widows who had rented out their only spare room to feed their children (unearned income). The government was a little embarrassed by it—they gave the thirty-five-year-old Anna Akhmatova an "old-age pension" on condition she kept quiet. They starved Mandelstam.

Everyone knows what happened during the madness of the thirties! Whole social classes were driven to their deaths to the beat of the newspaper drum. Widows, children, parents were condemned to non-existence. So were their friends and their friends' friends. Finally society was declared to be classless. General equality reigned at last—in the concentration camp huts.

At the beginning of the forties, even if people were talking about "ideological vacillation" or "a hostile onslaught," it was considered unworthy to talk about individual guilt. Even foreign philosophers were cursed by threes—Nietzsche, Bergson, Freud. Later a new grouping came in for attack—Kafka, Joyce, Proust. Almost no one had read their works, but it was considered patriotic to attack them. Three at a time.

Violence became the norm. It became normal to pillory anyone at whom the finger of power had pointed.

And at the end of the forties, the finger pointed at the Jews. Well, Jews are just Jews.

But meanwhile Jews had become different. The Revolution was a gigantic bore-hole. The national riches which had been buried for so long burst forth like a geyser. Former aliens flowed into science and industry, helping to fill the intellectual vacuum left by the Civil War, by emigration, and the extermination of hundreds of thousands of educated people. When the finger stopped at the Jews, they had already managed to produce Landau and Grossman. So much the worse for Landau and Grossman!

"Vacancies coming along," was the whisper in professional offices, in ministries, in editorial offices. It was this thought alone that warmed the hearts of the Egorychevs of 1949, who counted themselves among the intelligentsia and who happily raised the banner of the Russian shopkeepers. They did not merely attack the Jews. They attacked the intelligentsia, to whom they claimed to belong. Of any nationality. It wasn't important what language they thought in—Russian or Tartar . . . they thought!

And if they thought in Yiddish! . . .

That's the Russian paradox. The deep, terrible shadow of the whipping post stretches over it. The shadow of the truly internationalist twenties, the fateful thirties, the heroic and Stalino-fascist forties . . .

It's time for me to stop being surprised. And yet I was struck by the blatant, unceremonious falsification of facts that took place in the office of the Moscow City Committee. In my presence, in the presence of all the other writers and of members of the City Committee, Egorychev said one thing, and then in the quiet and privacy of his office signed something completely different.

But there seemed to be nothing out of the ordinary in this. Stalin proclaimed that violent anti-Semites should be shot, and later organized the anti-Semitic Doctors' Trial and everything else that we already know about, and that made the world shudder. Stalin inspired and wished long life to the Soviet Constitution of 1936, with all its clauses about personal immunity, and similar high-sounding paragraphs, full of sunny humanism. And the next year was 1937, taking millions of innocent people to their graves.

Incidentally, it's worth noticing that *Pravda*'s most vicious editorial, which printed Stalin's words saying that "enemies of the people" will be answered in pools of blood, was a sub-editorial. The leading editorial, printed on the same page, was a joyful account of the heroic performance of our pilots. Stalin concealed his own sins behind the heroism of the people.

This wasn't the first time I had come across the idea of hypocrisy as a style, as an immutable, constant way of life—but still I was surprised.

Normally, if you have a suitcase with a false bottom, you don't tell everyone. It is a secret of secrets. But Khrushchev's times didn't pass unnoticed. Khrushchev did his bit. People began to bare their souls in public! But that didn't go far enough.

At the first Writers' meeting, in the presence of several hundred Moscow writers, I talked about all this. On the presidium were the propaganda secretary of the Moscow City Committee, Shaposhnikova, Egorychev's ideological right arm, and Solovyova, the head of the cultural department, whom we have already met. I spoke about many of the things I have written about here. Even about the "stainless" old women. I said everything I could think of about my meetings with Solovyova.

Her face came out in red blotches, then she hurried off somewhere to telephone someone for advice, and when she came back she sat silently at the presidium table, although several members of the Writers' Union tried to persuade her to answer.

The Moscow City Committee secretary Shaposhnikova said that she had never heard of "the above-mentioned case." The trial of Sinyavsky and Daniel had just ended, and Shaposhnikova began her speech about the Svirsky affair with these words: "As regards Sinyavsky's speech . . ."

The hall burst into laughter. "Oh, mighty Freud!" several voices called out.

What can you do with people like that? She said she'd never heard a word about it, but she'd made the connection properly enough.

At about this time I handed all my materials over to the Party Control Committee of the Central Committee of the CPSU—the highest Party authority. I was protesting against the position Egorychev had adopted. This committee carried out a new and searching examination of the matter. Comrade Gladnev, the Party investigator for the Control Committee, invited me to see him and told me that the case was now finally over; Smirnov was summoned to the Control Committee as well.

"You know, he simply doesn't have a leg to stand on," the investigator said to me. "God knows what he's doing. You had every justification to accuse Smirnov." Then he said, more quietly, with a tone of gentle reproach: "But why make a private fact so public? Was that right? You should have kept yourself within limits." Then he raised his voice again. "We have no complaints about you at all, Comrade Svirsky."

"What do you mean? Pardon me, but what complaints against me could you have? Surely the case isn't against me?"

"Of course it was. We were considering the case of the writer Svirsky!"

As he showed me out, the Party investigator advised me again and again "not to go outside the framework of individual facts." Since then I have tried not to do so. But individual facts keep on heaping up as if poured from a cornucopia.

I left the Party Control Committee, and came out onto the Square of the Revolution. People hurried past me through the snow, their coat collars turned up, clutching bottles. Tomorrow was New Year's Day, 1967. I longed to telephone Pauline immediately to tell her to get ready, buy a bottle of wine and then go off with her to visit Stepan Zlobin or Academician Gudzy . . . to see out the old year.

I stood for a long time, like an abandoned child, until I nearly froze.

All the time a sentence was going around in my mind, that evil sentence which Vasily Smirnov and his kind had now been given the full right to use; no one would pay any attention now, any more than they had in the past. "Pushkin is not your writer . . . not your writer . . . not yours."

That evening, when Pauline asked me what I wanted to do for the New Year, to stay in Moscow or go off somewhere, I burst out: "Let's go. Where? Mikhailovskoye, Trigorskoye. To Pushkin's places, shall we? We've wanted to go for such a long time."

Pauline understood. "Let's go!"

We phoned the station, friends we knew in Mikhailovskoye, and discovered that a whole party of actors and translators were going there for the New Year. We joined them. That night in the train, we sang and quoted poetry. That master performer, Yakov Smolensky, recited quietly:

> "I greet you, deserted village,
> Haven of calm, of work and inspiration."

Again we had plunged headfirst into our native tragedy, and as in a nightmare we saw through the dark windows of the train the "stainless" old women and Egorychev; how many there were like them in Russia, currying favor. Then they disappeared, like evil forces dispersed by Pushkin's sign of the cross.

We went to our sleeping compartments. I tried to sleep, but felt that I couldn't. I was still there. . . . "Pushkin is not your writer . . . not yours . . . not yours. The hell with you." And then, worse still—powerful, like a court sentence:

". . . I support . . . the position . . . of Smirnov."

I support . . . I support . . . I support.

The wheels beat out their rhythm. Then there was a squealing and hissing. The train stopped, and the cars clanged together gently.

"Pskovshchina already," someone muttered sleepily from next door.

I got up and went out into the corridor. The other members of the party were out there still. Actors go to bed late.

I rested my forehead against the cold pane, looking out at the moon-whitened silence of Russia, which curved and swam before my eyes. I didn't hear the others speaking to me. All I could hear was one angry voice: "Oh, these writers! They aren't interested in people. All they want to know about is the landscape!" And the actors went back into their compartment, slamming the door behind them.

. . . Friends! Forgive me! I promise to return to you. But for the time being, the pain is too much. I feel I'm being stretched on the rack. . . .

Early in the morning we went to the Sviatogorsk monastery. It was a quiet Russian morning. The snow crackled beneath our feet. "Frost and sun. A marvelous day!" We sat down in one of the cells, intending first of all to visit Alexander Sergeevich Pushkin's grave. Someone asked us to wait, and I sat by one of the monastery windows alone with my thoughts.

Is Russia cruel? Officialdom has cowered through the ages like Vitya Telpugov, sometimes groveling to Alexander III's drunken stupors, sometimes to Rasputin's stomach convulsions. Sometimes officials have dashed about in panic, fearful of losing their footing, and fallen victim to Stalin's Asiatic viciousness. Others have rushed about in a mucksweat, like Khrushchev in his confrontation with America! That ancient fawning servility before the highest in the land—is that Russia? Court balls and curtseys—is that Russia?

Alas, I'm afraid it is. Her troubles, her tears.

But surely that's not all Russia is? Isn't it also all those people who helped Pauline come through, to survive? Academician Zelinsky, Academician Kazansky, Nesmeyanov, the powerful, taciturn president of the Academy of Science, demanding that he be shown Pauline's diploma work and attacking the racists from the Ministry . . . The old village woman in the starving railroad station of Obiralovka. And the cold-stiffened Moscow militiaman who should have turned Pauline out of a wartime Moscow, but who instead let her go through to the university and gave her money for the fare . . . And the workers at the Ufa chemical plant who gave up their nights to develop Pauline's Meturin, even though they knew they wouldn't get a kopeck for their trouble. Like Pauline herself.

But if we were surrounded by goodwill, by the honesty of most people, by an ineradicable feeling of internationalism, if everyone from peasant woman to academicians blocked the road to baseness, how then could the things that did happen come about? Genocide, the racist campaigns, the silent trolley cars, where baseness rules with the permission of the management, the baseness of the cold pogrom which has lasted for a quarter of a century—how could all this happen, if the inoculation of chauvinism hadn't been effective? *Depite the people?* Yes, *despite the will of the people* . . .

But that is another tragic theme of Russia. An eternal theme, a theme of Pushkin . . .

Pushkin's grave is humble and modest, like the Russian people. A dark marble slab covered by sparkling frost, isolated forever, for eternity.

And protecting the slab, a casing of aircraft plexiglass. As if even here someone wanted to keep Pauline and me away from Pushkin, to protect him from us. In vain!

Just think what our mindless literary cripples would shout about Lermontov, who was proud of the fact that he had a drop of Scottish blood in his veins. What would they have said of him, if he were alive today, with his pride, his incorruptible honor, his implacable resistance to the "servile crowd?"

Or what about Dahl?* His father was a Dane, a foreigner. What would our neo-Slavophiles say about him? Our protectors of racial purity? Or the personnel officers, those unveilers of "half-breeds," what would they say of Dahl, that great protector of our linguistic heritage? A Russian among Russians. Would they put him on the list of "useful Jews"?

We stood side by side around this national monument, and listened to you, Russia. We heard the whistle of the snowstorm and the far-off clatter of a tractor, and in our hearts we heard the words we had taken in with our mother's milk:

> And she calls me with every language in her body—
> Proud descendant of the Slavs, Finns, even the wild Tungus,
> And friend of the Kalmuck from the steppes.

Can Russia be like that, if the proud descendant of the Slavs can scream, "Pushkin is not your writer!"

So suddenly the steppes of the Kalmucks are being turned into a place of exile. And a Finn fired at me, a Muscovite, on the day of my coming of age on the Mannerheim line. . . . These Russophiles are my enemies.

The Russia of Pushkin will live in us and with us. And the Egorychevs will disappear, as the Bührens,† Purishkeviches, Rasputins all disappeared. . . .

The main thing is not to let things get out of perspective. . . . The main thing is to remember that Pushkin is with us. With us who want to live, to think, to bring up our children . . .

And if I should live . . . (I know what things racism is capable of, for I have looked it in the eye), if the old man Gudzy prophesied the truth when he traced the vile line with his finger—"The Boyar was right, and the offenders were punished. But the Boyar was killed later, for another crime"—even if we go back to Tsarist ways, at least I have touched your high, cold grave, Alexander Sergeevich, where you lie buried after Dantès'‡ infamous shot, and by that alone I gained courage, and I have whetted my heart with courage.

Moscow, 1967

---

* Compiler of a major dictionary of the Russian language. [Translator]
† Count Ernst Johann Bühren (1690–1772), favorite of the Empress Anna Ivanovna (1730–1740) who let him and his friends take over the government of the country. [Translator]
‡ Dantès was a trained duelist who was set up to cast aspersions on the morals of Pushkin's wife. In the duel which inevitably followed, Pushkin was killed. [Translator]

EPILOGUE

WHICH CONTAINS UNCONNECTED FACTS

In 1968, the leap year of the tanks, I was summoned as if at an alarm signal. I was taken first to the Regional Committee and then to the City Committee, where my appearance was greeted in the discordant and triumphant tones of a women's choir: "We know *him!*" and "Not for the first time!" (In particular I could make out the voices of Gorevanova and Shaposhnikova.) They had called me of course "for another fault," another speech I had made three months previously at a closed meeting,* which at first had caused no concern. But all this is another story, which I am not going to write now. I am certain that works on the theme of Stalinism and Culture will in due course appear in Russia—unlike this one—but they won't be written by me. Here I want to talk about something else. . . .

In the ill-lit corridor of the Moscow Committee, along the walls, rows of people were standing—summoned, as I had been, to the City Committee office, and I looked along the line to see if I could recognize anyone. There was one man I seemed to know. He had appeared from the other direction and was climbing the stairs. I saw him out of the corner of my eye. The top of his head gleamed as if it had been polished. One ear stuck out, the other was flattened to his head. Kostin? Pauline's Kostin; From Dante's circle of the Eichmannites? It looked like him. . . .

He walked upstairs with a cheerful, bouncy step, the knot of his tie loosened. He looked at me, and then followed my gaze and said with a grin: "Must have seen some of your own people?"

Then he asked the receptionist something, and hustled away the way he had come. I stood by the door, covering my eyes with my hand, staggering as if someone had just hit me in the solar plexus.

. . . On the second day of the war, June 23, 1941, I was standing on a road in Byelorussia, with leaflets flying around me like feathers from a

---

* The speech was about Stalinists censoring writers who had spoken out against the decisions of the Twentieth Congress, and about those who were claiming to save Russia under the banner of anti-Semitism. (The speech was published in full in *Le Monde*, April 28–29, 1968, and in other papers, and in Russian in the *Collected Works of Alexander Solzhenitsyn*, vol. 6, *The Case of Solzhenitsyn*.)

plucked bird. One fell at my feet, and I picked it up and looked at it. Adolf Hitler was making a firm promise to kill me, as a Jew.

I trampled the leaflet underfoot, and began to eat some of the smoked fish my corporal had shoved into my gas mask case to "see me through the war." The fish tasted of gasoline and of burn.

Refugees flowed past me in waves. There were unshaven men carrying suitcases tied up with white string, with bundles made of sheets over their shoulders. There were old men, who sometimes collapsed on the road and pleaded with their relatives not to wait for them, but to keep moving the children along.

As I chewed on my fish, I felt someone looking at me. A huge cart was trundling by, driven by an old man with a long beard, a Jew looking like something straight out of Sholom Aleichem, in a torn tarred canvas cloak and his best hat. The cart was crammed full of children. It looked as though when the gunfire had started the old man from the frontier town had loaded all his neighbors' children onto his cart and had driven this far non-stop. The children could not all fit into the wagon. Some of them were running alongside hanging onto the sides of the cart, and one little girl of about five was crying quietly, "My feet hurt, my feet hurt!" As they drew level, the children began to stare at me silently. The cart squeaked past and the sounds died away, but the children were still following me with their big black eyes.

At last I realized that it wasn't me they were looking at but my fish. They hadn't eaten for days, since the moment the old man had picked them up. I dashed after the cart, which was rumbling into the distance. I remember that my ammunition case flapped open, spraying cartridges all over the road. I caught up with the wagon and dumped everything I had in the gas mask case onto someone's scratched knees.

As I was coming back, gathering up the scattered shells, I heard a hoarse, mocking voice behind me, which I still remember a quarter of a century later. I looked around. The face was beet-red, so swollen that the eyes were hardly visible. There was a scar on the forehead. He was one of those run-of-the-mill bandits, a Zaporozhets Cossack. His battledress blouse didn't meet around his neck and his green corporal's stripes were flapping on his sleeve. He opened his lips, from which dangled a cigar, and said, with a sly smile, "Seen some of your own, have you?"

I didn't manage to reply, or even to understand what he had said.

A wave of Junkers was approaching; there was a green flare and our squadron took off. . . .

Stretched out at the feet of the air gunner, getting my breath back, I looked back along the length of the yellow plexiglass of the cabin. The Junker 87's had passed already and were turning to dive, one after another, to drop their bombs on the airfield we had just left and on the fleeing refugees in the carts. The earth was standing on end.

For me, those children were my own, I thought finally. But not for him? It seemed impossible, inexplicable.

What about the things I've had to see since those days? Babi Yar, Buchenwald, the cosmopolitan campaigns . . .

Yet I remember that incident more often than the others, perhaps because then, on the eve of the bloodiest war in history, it was the first time that I, a mere boy, had come across inhumanity—and because on that occasion inhumanity was wearing a red star in its forage cap.

. . . And now here it was again, that "Seen some of your own?" Is that what he meant? I looked at the faces of the people lining the wall. Indeed, there were a number of people with pale intelligent faces standing there. Two or three of them were unmistakably Jews. They were waiting, a little way away from each other along the wall, like people who had been sentenced to death.

There is nothing more frightening than a crack in metal. It conceals death. Suddenly an aircraft engine blows up in midair. A dock crane keels over on a ship. A bridge breaks under the weight of a train. Nationalism in a multinational country is a crack in the metal. It is a rail that could give way. Things look as if they're in order, and then suddenly the whole country is tumbling downhill.

Poland has always lived with the crack of anti-Semitism. Even in the works of the Catholic scholars of the seventeenth century. In particular, the tract *The Worm of Conscience* states that "Poland is paradise for the Jews, and this noxious tribe must be driven out of the country." The flood of pogrom literature had not even dried up by the beginning of the last war, when that extreme Jew-hater Cardinal Primate Glond issued a special pastoral letter (1938) in which he demanded that there should be an economic boycott against Jews, and that they should be forced out of the country.

Even the social movement divided the Warsaw educated middle class of the twentieth century into "Yids" and "Boors." Yids weren't all Jews by any means but supporters of Russia—including Gomulka. The Boors were Krayov's former army.

The Poles have a saying that when the nobles fight, the serfs get their heads cracked open.

"Hitler should have dealt with you as well!" began to be a common cry in the streets of Warsaw, bawled to the counterpoint of breaking windows. Those whom Hitler had failed to "deal with" were now being flung out of their homes, out of their jobs, driven into the columns of exile and expulsion—old men, women, children.

How the fanatical Catholic author of *The Worm of Conscience* or Cardinal Primate Glond would have rejoiced. The age-old dream of the obscurantists had become reality. The Jews were being driven out of Poland. . . .

Thousands of native Poles suddenly found themselves in Vienna, thrown out of the country of Auschwitz, no less! And as should have been expected, anti-Semitism swiftly turned into anti-Sovietism. One Cracow paper proclaimed that the Jewish leaders had been infiltrated into Poland by the Soviets. They had come in with the Lyudowa Army, which had been raised in Siberia. That's where the attack had come from . . . From Russia.

The Polish press did not have a monopoly on these jibes at the Soviet Union.

"During the investigation of my case, officers of the security service tried to discover even one Jewish name among my family," said Jacek Kuron, a Warsaw University teacher who spoke out against the anti-Semitic hysteria and was tried for it. "When they didn't manage to turn me into a Jew, they decided they'd make me a Ukrainian at least." Similar things became common knowledge. The closing speeches by Jacek Kuron and others at their trials were published by the Communist press, including the Austrian Party's weekly *Tagebuch*, from which I have quoted Kuron's words.

In Poland they began to beat a retreat.

"With regard to the problems of Zionism," wrote *Izvestiya* on May 15, 1966, "W. Gomulka said that the Politburo had appreciated the significance of the events of March 19 of this year, but in practice these were not correctly understood everywhere. There were many extremes to be condemned. Revisionists had been labeled Zionists."

Unlike *Izvestiya*, which published just a short report, on the next day, May 16, 1968, *Pravda* published a detailed, four-column account of the speech Gomulka had made at the plenum of the Central Committee of the Polish Workers' Party. The paragraph about there being many extremes in Poland, and about the fact that the word "Zionist" had been turned into a malicious slogan, a term of abuse, this paragraph, which *Izvestiya* picked out in its short report as the most important and only new thing in Gomulka's speech, was totally omitted from *Pravda*'s much longer version. It had been cut by some farsighted hand.

What extremes? There weren't any extremes. There's no anti-Semitism. Not even in Poland. People had "started to dub the Jews Zionists"—what's extreme about that? Jews had been thrown out of their jobs, and now they were being thrown out of the country. They'd lost their homes, their friends, their native land. But that's not extremism—just the Polish model for solving the problem of nationalities.

Indeed, what humanity! They weren't shooting people with dum-dum bullets in the back of the neck, or flinging them into quarries. Just kicking them in the ass—old men, women, and children; a Polish version of Sergei Vasiliev's poem—"We Know Who We Can Do Without in Russia." But this time it was being put into practice.

. . . There's nothing more frightening than a concealed crack in metal. It spells death. . . .

In the *Pravda* office I chanced to meet Vasily Smirnov. The journalists grinned and said he was going half frantic trying to achieve his moral rehabilitation and recover from the prejudice which had grown up against him. Yet, as if in honor of the fact that the Party Control Committee of the Central Committee of the CPSU had recognized him as a chauvinist, he seemed to be receiving a twenty-four gun salute. He had been praised before, as many writers are, but never with such a tremendous firework display. It was as if someone somewhere had issued an order.

The first shot of the salute came from *Ogonyok*, in the lead as usual. V. Peletin, a critic with a respectable reputation was the writer. Smirnov was praised to the skies in the article immediately following the editorial "The Banner of the Proletarian International Is in Safe Hands!" As you might say, theory and practice at one fell swoop.

Literaturnaya Rossiya didn't lag far behind. The critic and politician Zoya Kedrina* wrote a long article saying that V. Smirnov was "working with new zeal, like a new Gorky. And in *Literaturnaya Gazeta* she wrote that Vasily Smirnov, together with other writers, "had accomplished that which Gorky had had to leave undone!" I wonder what Gorky would make of that!

A year ago Smirnov had been nothing more than "an acute observer of the Yaroslav countryside." Now, on the basis of exactly the same works, he was the reincarnation of Gorky. And they didn't write all that much about Smirnov's books—a book, after all, is only a book. More often—and more outrageously—they praised the "spiritual worth" of "Gorky reincarnated," of V. Smirnov, man and citizen.

Before Kedrina's article appeared, *Literaturnaya Gazeta* rushed out a half-page literary profile of Smirnov, with a big photograph. The critic Smirnov on the prose writer Smirnov. The article itself pulled no punches. "Our friend Vasily Smirnov is a good Party member and, more important, a friend of other nations. Smirnov began his book just after the war when he was already a mature man, a man experienced in Party work, experienced as a journalist, And he underlines the well-established truth that

* Zoya Kedrina was officially appointed the public prosecutor in the case of Sinyavsky and Daniel.

cannot be repeated too often—that no one can build a new world and be a friend of other nations unless he has a feeling of national pride toward his own country." Thanks to *Literaturnaya Gazeta* we now know, finally, what is meant by "national pride," "mature man," and "friend of other nations."

The solemn salute was taken up by other papers. *Pravda* first nodded to the "latter-day Gorky," friend of other nations, in a survey of the literary scene by the Writers' Union leader G. Markov, and later in a special article. This, as in *Ogonyok*, was placed just after the editorial: "Internationalism Is the Source of Our Strength."

The literary journal *Moskva* also took part in this unusually massive triumphal salute. The other journals were still loading their guns. But the applause went on. It was as if a special commemorative medal were about to be struck—"To V. Smirnov, Mature and Wise Friend of Other Nations."

I suddenly began to feel like a city taken by storm, which has been handed over for three days to the frenzied soldiery. "Rape! Rob the infidels! Nothing will happen to you!"

The setting into type of three of my books which were about to be published by the Soviet Writer publishing house was stopped and the type broken up. This was done after the books had been officially approved by Glavlit, something that had never happened before in the history of Soviet publishing. An official document informed me that my contract was dissolved. This applied both to the books under dispute, and to the others which had already been published, like *Leninsky Prospekt* or my stories about the war in the air. I was supposed to leave without looking back.

The publication of any work by me was stopped by all publishing houses. The military publishing house called the Writers' Union in a panic to ask what they should do with a collection of army stories which included one of mine. My contribution, "King of the Pamirs," was physically torn out of the copies of the collection which had already been printed.

When they take it into their minds to shoot a writer, they use a full artillery bombardment. . . .

Throughout all these years Pauline had been my main support. She didn't urge me on, but at the same time she realized that she could not act as a brake on me in matters of conscience. Just occasionally when I was leaving the house, she hugged me as if I were setting off to the wars.

No matter how hard things became for her, she was always calm, full of life, and strong. But one night I was wakened by the sound of her sobbing. She was weeping with her face buried in the pillow, her teeth clenched, so that I should not hear.

I have just had a phone call. Sasha Weiner has committed suicide. So as not to upset the people living in the same house, he went out to the park and hanged himself on the branch of a birch tree.

When I arrived at the morgue his body was covered by a sheet, and all I could see were his heavy thick-soled boots, the boots of a geologist, a builder, a traveler.

Sasha's friends showed me a notebook in which there were some scribbled verses. I don't know whether Sasha had written them himself, or had copied them from somewhere.

> I am sick and tired of reading the book of evil.
> And I have turned all the pages of the book of happiness.
> O Mother Death, take this tiredness from me, and cover
> my thin nakedness in a shroud. . . .

Sasha, caught up in his dream of Israel, rambling about leaving Russia, had been reduced to such a state that he had even left a note for his beloved old mother in which he advised her, if she too became desperate, to take the same course he had taken. . . .

His friends decided not to show his mother this letter but the state attorney who examined the suicide handed it to her. The law is the law.

At Sasha's graveside, the representative of the Party organization from his work said pityingly that Sasha was an honest, quiet, hardworking man. That he loved Russian nature, and poetry . . . Why had he done this?

That day, and the days which followed, *Pravda* and *Izvestiya*, *Komsomolskaya Pravda*, and all the other papers, as usual, printed angry and just protests against racism. The thick type of the headlines screamed "NO! TO RACISM" (in South Africa), "THE LAWFUL DEMANDS OF THE NEGROES" (in the USA), "AN END TO DISCRIMINATION" (in this case the appeal came from Anatoly Sofronov, the hero of the cosmopolitan campaign, and now the main fighter for internationalism on the Soviet Committee for the countries of Asia and Africa), "PORTUGUESE RACISTS! BE TRUE TO LENINISM! DISCRIMINATION AGAINST THE JEWS IN THE USA!" I leafed through the papers out of habit, but behind the type, as if it was transparent, I could see Sasha Weiner's workman's boots sticking out from under the mortuary sheet, those heavy boots with thick soles, in which he, a workingman, should still have been walking the earth.

And I also seemed to see the coldly cautious eye of Egorychev fixed on me, while he said what our local policeman had said: "The Jews are being abused unmercifully. It's about time they did something. After all, these people aren't made of iron."

. . . These people . . . I have always remembered their faces as they left the cemetery. . . . I saw their lips tight with pain and anger, their clenched fists, and I began to understand that the days when Russian Jews would go on taking these blows in the face without answer had passed forever. . . .

A new age had dawned—where would it end? In mindless bomb outrages? In a massive dash to the frontiers—to the land, sea, and air frontiers? Would there be more unnecessary victims? I still don't know the answer, but I understand that the death, or rather the murder of Sasha, and of many other such deaths in every corner of Russia, from Malakhovka to Vorkuta, had become the last straw. . . .

Neither Demichev, nor Sofronov, nor Sergei Vasiliev, nor Gribachov, who figuratively speaking had turned the screws on Sasha Weiner—none of them were waiting to see who the next victim would be. But they were waiting for the "Jewish explosion," which in itself probably wouldn't worry them unless it were to become—which it certainly would—a powerful catalyst for national movements in the Ukraine, in the Baltic States, in Uzbekistan. The future Jewish explosion would have its losses and its victims, who would figure in the literature to come.

At the cemetery where Sasha Weiner was buried I met a demobilized frontier guard. His arm was in a sling. He said that he had been wounded on the Soviet-Chinese frontier, and that two of his friends had been killed.

I was shattered. It was the first time I had heard that blood was being spilled on the Chinese border. There were military funerals again in the villages of Russia.

And in whose direction was the terrible Chinese fire coming? In my lifetime I have had to bury so many of my airmen friends and unknown soldiers that every funeral reminds me of the soft rustle of earth on coffins, of the hard, dry cracking sounds of the waterproof capes, caked in frozen blood, which we used to carry the bodies from the airfields we had just taken by storm.

I have lived with this appalling news for some days now. Judging by the fury of the Chinese Red Guards, their feelings against Russia are being whipped up according to all the rules of Stalinist anti-Semitic hysteria. The Soviets are imperialists and the biggest revisionists of all. It is time to drive them out of Siberia and the Far East, for (the Chinese papers write) the Russians are not the native population.

Almost every nation has its own Jews, its own pariahs. Russians have become Jews for the Chinese. The non-native population. The blood-stained circle of chauvinism has no end.

Several members of the Soviet Writers' Union have been taken to hospitals with serious heart attacks—the prose writers Boris Balter, Vladimir Pomerantsev, Max Bremener, and the literary critic Emil Kardin. The poet Yunna Morits has been sent to a mental hospital, as have the critic Sergei Lvov and Boris Yakovlev, the author of books about Lenin who dared to speak out after me, together with Yunna Morits, against Vasily Smirnov's chauvinism.

Vladimir Pomerantsev was the first man to have the temerity to write in *Novy Mir* about sincerity in literature. He was taken off immediately afterward in an ambulance with a heart attack. And then he had a second. Boris Balter, a brave and direct man, formerly in command of a rifle regiment, much decorated, sent the Central Committee a letter of protest about the arbitrary behavior of the courts. Max Bremener, so quiet and peaceful, never signed anything at all. . . . All of them, apart from Pomerantsev, were under fifty years old. There is no quota for dying. . . .

The writer Leon Toom, the husband of Yunna Morits, committed suicide by throwing himself out of a window. It was said to be an accident. Stella Korytnaya, the film critic, and niece of General Yakir, who was shot, also laid hands on herself. They said it was because she was ill. Boris Falkovich Medvedev, a witty, talented cineaste, hanged himself. He was a good man, absolutely honest, liked by everyone. His death wounded me especially, since it was the third suicide in our circle within a month.

When someone who is mentally disturbed kills himself, it may be the result of freak circumstances. But when, one after another, three literary figures commit suicide, and heart attacks and nervous breakdowns put a whole series of writers out of action—comparatively young men and women at that—then there is no longer any question of coincidence. Then, as the specialists say, we have to look for a social reason.

Perhaps we should look first of all at the history of the Moscow Writers' Party organization. And at the way it was blocked, destroyed, and defamed.

"That filthy organization!" they shouted in Egorychev's City Committee, when a representative of the writers' party tried to defend me. "Filth!" they shouted again later when they were browbeating everyone, like Balter and Kopelev, who dared protest the general arbitrariness. It was the same when Communists tried to defend Solzhenitsyn's *Cancer Ward*, the poetry of Pasternak, Tsvetaeva, Mandelstam, and many other Soviet writers—Russians, Ukrainians, Georgians, Tartars, Jews, Kalmucks. Autocrats have always known since time began that "EVERY POET IS A YID."

Sometimes I visit Sasha Weiner's turf-covered grave in the Jewish cemetery. Was he right? *Is* it stupid to protest, and by the very fact of protesting raise hopes? Hopes of leaving Russia?

In April 1942, when our battered divisions were pulled back from the Western Front, an incident took place which shall serve as my final testimony. Soldiers from various units who were being posted back— wounded men, and those due for leave—were sitting in a freight car in the ruins of Volokolamsk. We stoked up the stove and waited for the train to leave. All kinds of people were there: Cossacks from Pamfilov's division, Uzbek gunners, Russians from Katukov's tank regiment, Cossacks from Dovator's cavalry brigade. The cavalrymen were telling us that only forty men from their regiment had survived—twenty were looking after the horses, and the rest were stretched out in a chain with gaps of seven meters between them. And that was on the main, Moscow sector of the front.

We sat quietly. We realized that this was the truth of the matter. No more soldiers. Not enough of anything anywhere. Huge losses. Suddenly we heard the shrill sound of women's voices: "Katyusha came down to the bank . . ." We looked out of our freight car. They were singing in the train parked alongside. We just sat motionless and stared. They were girls in battledress, carrying rifles.

Someone said dazedly, "Hey, lads, what's going on?"

I dropped the mess tin I was holding. Tears came to my eyes, and I said, "So, it's all over."

"What do you mean, over?" asked the Uzbek, who was squatting on his heels by the stove.

My neighbor, a huge Cossack with a scarred face, ground out the stub of a cigar with his foot and said gloomily, "Russia's finished. No more men left. They're scraping around for anyone they can lay their hands on."

I couldn't restrain myself any longer, and started to cry silently, biting my lips. Never in my life had I felt such an overwhelming sense of despair. How could we go on fighting? The Germans were already almost at the gates of Moscow. . . .

We were all quiet. We all of us realized the gravity of the position— Russians, Uzbeks, Cossacks. We all shared the same fate, the same country. We were silent for a long time. We didn't even stir when the freight car lurched as it was coupled to the train and we finally set off.

Then suddenly someone yelled, "Boys, boys, look!"

We leaped to our feet and saw that in the forests on either side of the tracks there were troops. Camouflaged tanks stood waiting for their moment to come—not camouflaged in white for snow fighting, but in green, bright grass green. Green field kitchens sent up curls of smoke. All the villages, the forests, and the fields from Volokolamsk to Moscow were crammed with soldiers, tanks, and artillery. All in the color of spring. They were the spring reserves. They weren't being given to us. We must run to the end of our winter limits. That was why the line was stretched so thin.

Someone began to bawl out the words of a triumphant folk song at the top of his voice, tapping out the rhythm with his feet, and the whole carload of us began to dance, in a single joyous bound. No, Soviet Russia was not finished. This was not the end. We could go on fighting.

The freight car rattled over the rails, rocking from side to side, and we—a third of us wounded, bandaged, on crutches—laughed and shouted aloud, beside ourselves with joy.

I believe in the spring reserves of Russia.

I finished this book in June 1967, as the Israeli tanks roared into the Sinai desert. A year later, the tracks of Soviet tanks crushed the soil of Prague—and I felt compelled to write an epilogue. This redoubled rumbling of tanks so far apart on the globe drove my persecutors into a frenzy. For the third year running I lived feeling like a man who had been thrown into a grave and was being buried.

"They want the same thing they got in Czechoslovakia," someone shouted at me, as he sat next to Pelshe, a member of the Politburo of the Central Committee of the CPSU, and Pelshe, motionless, white as frost, seemingly frozen Pelshe, listened imperturbably to this ranting. Who were "they"? The writers? The Jews? What did Czechoslovakia have to do with it? There were no explanations.

The sound of the spades rings out. Earth, stones, dung, water shower down on me. I cry out, gasping through the earth and the filth, that I'm alive, that this is murder. That they daren't do it . . . But they dare.

As a writer, I have been struck off the list of the living. Since the day when I dared to challenge our "native" pogrom-makers, not a single word I have written has been printed—and that is six years now.

Every night Pauline weeps silently. There is no hope left. No strength left. Sometimes there isn't money to buy our growing son a pair of trousers; his schoolteacher is surprised that the son of a writer should be going about with holes in his pants. Many people tried to help me. My friends from the front, writers, the Heroine of the Soviet Union Valentina Grizodubova, who during the war delivered weapons to my comrades and me.

But alas, hatred is stronger than goodwill. New Black Hundreds spring up like mushrooms after rain. They bring out books which allege, as in 1949, that Einstein is a figment of Jewish imagination, that the Jews have wildly exaggerated his achievement. Drunken poets roar the hallowed chant of "These Jews are everywhere!" and believe themselves to be patriots. In an abandoned church, quite openly, they hold meetings of the "Fatherland" club, which admits only native Russians—Jews and dogs keep out. They read each other learned papers about the fate of Russia, which was destroyed by the Jewish Bolsheviks, of course, and about Mandelstam, who, they say, was just a Jewish succubus feeding on Tyutchev. ("A Jew can't be a Russian writer," I remember the steel-toothed old woman of the City Committee shouting at me.)

For a long time it was unclear who should be blamed for the collapse of the Soviet economy. Finally, however, they found the culprit: Gosplan, the state planning authority. "That explains it," I heard from a Party official, a Komi by nationality. "It's all because they got that . . . what's his name . . . that Dymshitz there." They couldn't think what term of abuse to nail to the back of the writer Anatoly Kuznetsov, who did not return from a trip to London and stayed in the West. But finally they thought of one—"Jew."

In a similar case, they wouldn't stand on ceremony with me! The sound of the spades rings on. The earth and filth are up to my chest, my throat. Just a few more spadefuls, and I know that I shall suffocate. I had not noticed how the deathly choking of the earth had crept up on me. A despair like that of Sasha Weiner, who saw no way out. Who suddenly felt that he could no longer go on breathing. I felt it particularly sharply, clutching at my heart, when the neighbors banged on our door and told me to switch on the television set.

For years it had sat silently in its corner. Now its screen lit up. . . . First of all there was a voice. A resonant yet curiously dead voice, like the sounds of people in a bathhouse. It was saying that life for Jews in Russia was good. He himself, for instance, was the head of a kolkhoz, a millionaire. . . . Then the picture swam onto the screen, and the hero appeared in a pale blue light. He looked thin, eaten away by disease. His folded arm was twisted as if he were caught in a net and he was struggling vainly to free himself from its meshes.

The kolkhoz chairman disappeared and was replaced by Arkady Raikin. And he—Arkady Raikin*—was tongue-tied. He looked shamefaced, as if he had just been dragged naked into public view. How to explain one's nakedness? He began to make wild faces, to wrinkle his cheeks, to pretend that it wasn't him talking, only one of his characters. But he clearly knew that this time they had managed to capture his very soul. And at this point there was no talking himself out of it, no wriggling off the hook. . . .

The war hero General David Dragunsky had hardly begun to talk

---

* A much-loved Soviet stage comedian. [Translator]

about his big family, all of them killed by the Nazis, when he was interrupted by some invisible person off-screen. He sighed gratefully. Over already! But he'd only just begun. Behind him was a platform, with Maya Plisetskaya, and the magnificent actress Bystritskaya, sitting there like statues. Their shame was solid, tangible, like a mist. It betrayed itself in the nervous gestures, lowered eyes, the tortured stammering of the speakers, and the defensive words of the announcer. What was going on here?

"We are people of Jewish nationality. We protest. We do not have, cannot have, any anti-Semitism in this country." The words reverberated round the room. "We do not have the kind of class roots that could produce anti-Semitism."

Ah. So that's what it's about. Is not and cannot be. Swear to it! And you swear for me, too. And for Sasha Weiner.

. . . The following day the show was the only topic of conversation on the streetcar and buses. I heard one fair-headed broad-faced boy carrying a portfolio say to his friend, "Saw that circus on TV last night. Dymshitz and a troupe of trained Jews."

And there was more.

"So Bystritskaya is a Jew, is she? Who'd have thought it?"

Now they had made it clear. Who, until that memorable day, had ever cared about the nationality of Bystritskaya? We had all seen her on the screen, and that was enough. Probably her most striking role in the cinema was that of Aksinya, Sholokhov's Cossack girl. For the public she was Aksinya, the proud, freedom-loving Russian Cossack. For her colleagues in the film business she was People's Artist of the Russian Federation. Who cared that she was a Jewess?

And what of Plisetskaya? Perhaps she was a soloist with the Jewish ballet? For the Soviet audience she was the best ballerina in the country, whose art had enriched Russian classical ballet. For the whole world she was the pride of the Russian ballet. Who cared that she was a Jewess?

People said that some hooligan had once shouted, "Jew!" at Arkady Raikin from the back of the theater. Not true. It wasn't the audience that shouted at him. Not the public. That was flung at him by the people who had organized this dreadful spectacle, appalling in its stupidity.

"Jew!" . . . learn to dissociate yourself from them!

No one had summoned, say, People's Artist Ivan Kozlovsky; the thought of pushing him forward had never crossed anyone's mind. Or the Bolshoi theater dancer Ivan Petrov. What would be the point of Ivan Kozlovsky or Ivan Petrov? Their Point Five status was all in order.

Arkady Raikin, Bystritskaya, Plisetskaya—Jews! To be cut off from their fellows!

The donkey's ears of Russian anti-Semitism had not twitched so provocatively for a long time. Now they reared over the whole planet, up into the blue sky. In the morning *Pravda* printed a piece about the press conference. The texts of the speeches were so polished that no one would have recognized them as the ones they'd heard the previous day. The deputy chairman of the Executive Committee of Birobidzhan had said on the program, for instance, that they had a national theater which puts on the plays of Sholom Aleichem in the national language. In *Pravda* the words "in the national language" had disappeared. National language indeed! That means in Yiddish.

General Dragunsky had said sadly that twenty-four members of his Jewish family had been killed by the Fascists. *Pravda* corrected the war hero twice. There was no need to go into the fact that Fascists had killed Jews.

"Could you tell us the names of well-known Jewish generals and diplomats?" had been one of the questions put from the hall, in everyone's hearing. In *Pravda*, the word "diplomats" was omitted. Indeed, what Jewish diplomats were there to mention? Uritsky? Volodarsky? People's Commissar for Foreign Affairs Litvinov?* Memories of the past . . .

Egorychev, the former first secretary of the Moscow City Committee of the Party, had just been appointed ambassador to Denmark. And our new ambassador to Algeria, which was becoming the reserve airport for the Arab world, was the courteous, supple, oh-so-military Gruzinov, formerly the first secretary of the Frunze Regional Committee in Moscow, the man who first rapped me over the knuckles. Calmly, as if the whole thing was second nature to him by now. Just so you remember your place, you Jewish bastard!

Now he was being sent abroad as an ambassador plenipotentiary. For some reason all my persecutors seem to become ambassadors. They draw my blood, and receive immediate promotion.

A week later it became clear to everyone why it had been necessary to stage that magic show on television.

Behind the mesmerizing images, a Soviet rocket division had been moving into Egypt. Just a few hours previously it had been disembarking in Alexandria. Russian soldiers were going to war with Israel. . . . Arkady Raikin, Bystritskaya, Plisetskaya—JEWS! You must dissociate yourself from your own people!

The baser elements, stimulated by similar campaigns, and maybe

---

* *Uritsky:* An old Bolshevik, one-time head of the Moscow secret police; *Volodarsky:* an old Bolshevik, one-time Commissar for Propaganda; *Litvinov:* first People's Commissar for Foreign Affairs. All three were Jewish. [Translator]

by other things, too, sprang into renewed life. In a Moscow street the daughter of Mikhoels was attacked and beaten up. A group of young men in raincoats was waiting outside the house she lived in. One of them, the leader, was no youth. He wore a hat with a drooping brim, and when he saw her he whispered authoritatively—"That's her!" She was attacked with an iron bar.

Elsewhere in Moscow, the son of the writer Daniel was beaten up by another bunch of storm troopers. It was as if a flash of lightning suddenly revealed the sum of my experiences. The long line of people who had been decimated over the years glowed before my eyes like the Milky Way in the night sky. Everyone who had killed themselves, been driven to heart attacks, been trampled in the mud . . . Oh God, how many of us are there who wear this target over our hearts! How many of us to be destroyed, how many hostages? . . .

The word "hostages" echoed in my brain. I tried to tell myself that it was nonsense, but what other word could I use, how could I not believe my own eyes when personnel departments in institutes and factories were receiving official documents warning against taking on people belonging to a nationality whose state conducts a hostile policy toward the USSR.

This is why the laws protecting the national dignity of the Jews are dead letters. Juridically, in the eyes of the bosses of the personnel departments, we are already excluded from the Soviet Union. Our state affiliation is not to the USSR but to Israel. The basic differentiation as to whether a man is "ours" or "not ours" depends on "purity of blood." There are even forms which insist on asking both the nationality of the father and of the mother.

"Go to Israel!" is being shouted more often than ever, and not just by drunks in the streets. Reins on newspaper propaganda have been slackened. Now it's government officials who say that to me—people for whom I am "impure." "Go to Israel!" they say to me every day, every hour; they say it by their actions and their contempt, even as they thrust forward their terrified, intimidated spokesmen to affirm the opposite. There may have been worse times, but there have never been more base times.

Hostages, answering with their lives, their children's lives, for the clatter of tanks in the Sinai desert. Where can we go to escape from the whistle of the lash, from the jibes of the racists, from the sea of lies spoken out of sheer terror? How can we save our children?

Hostages!

Some Communists in other countries were baffled and wanted to know what was going on. The answer, when it came, was bawled with a lack of ceremony typical of Khrushchev: "Keep your nose out of our affairs!" Several Western Communist parties inquired what was happening to the intelligentsia? Immediately *Pravda* printed a formula article about the battle against racism that might have been expected in dealings between governments, but that was shameful as regards cooperation between Communist parties. "Let us discuss what brings us closer together, rather than things that might force us apart." As if Communists could vary in their attitudes towards racism, to torture, to persecution of Jews and of the Russian intelligentsia who were being compared with them, or, more accurately, have always stood (or so it seems to the racists) on the same line as the Jews.

"STUDENTS, SOCIALISTS, JEWS!"

"JUDEN UND KOMISSAREN—*Vorwärts Marsch. Schnell!*"

Some Communists grew angry, others were driven away from Marxism altogether. And as in Stalin's time the newspaper campaign produced clouds of dense smoke that formed a curtain of misinformation, black and impenetrable.

An Israeli Phantom dropped a bomb on an Arab school, and *Pravda* angrily and rightly protested against the murder of children. For three weeks our papers printed pictures which evoked sympathy, grief, and anger. They printed the names and ages of the injured and dead. All the literary and artistic unions condemned such murder.

That is only proper in a world inhabited by human beings rather than beasts.

No more than two or three weeks passed and Al Fatah terrorists ambushed an Israeli school bus near the Lebanese border. As they lay by the road holding their Kalashnikov automatic rifles, the Arabs knew that the passengers were all children. They could see whom they were firing at. There could be no mistake. . . . Ten Jewish children were killed instantaneously, and eighteen wounded. The whole world was stunned.

The following day I hastily leafed through *Pravda*. Not a word about the crime. Perhaps they hadn't received the story in time? Perhaps it hadn't been passed? Held over to the next number? But the next day there was nothing either. Not even a passing reference to the cruelty of war . . . no justification. Not a word.

The rest of the world was appalled by *Pravda*'s stony silence, by the silence of *Izvestiya* and the other Soviet papers. But that did not change their policy.

A week later an Al Fatah attack with Katyusha rockets blew a ten-year-old girl into fragments. This time no one was surprised when there wasn't a word printed about it. It is forbidden to kill Russian children, Ukrainian children, Arab children. But it's all right to kill Jewish children— they are children of the enemy.

Never in her wildest dreams did Lyubka Mukhina, the woman who betrayed Fima to the Fascists, imagine how many people would come to think like her in the future.

. . . The bloodsoaked earth fills my throat, I can hardly breathe, hardly go on living . . .

So what can I do? Stay silent like Sasha Weiner? Like Pauline's family? Set fire to myself, like Jan Palach? If only that would help.

In my thoughts I argue with dead Sasha. I argue with murdered Uncle Vitya. How bitterly they would have quarreled between themselves if they had ever met.

But they did meet—in the Jewish cemetery.

Somehow I escaped being killed in the first salvo. I am still looking for a way out. Looking for the truth. I torture myself with the question, "What is to be done?" But the Egorychevs of this world have already decided. They look at me out of cold mocking eyes, and in those eyes I see clearly who I am.

You see me as the rubbish of Russia, the shame of Russia, the trouble of Russia. I really do have curly black hair and a hooked nose. . . . From the point of view of the Sonderkommandos, I am a *Jude*, that's true enough.

Even if I feel myself truly Russian, it doesn't matter; sooner or later, I shall speak out—no, not speak, shout, if all human dignity has not died within me. Shout, "I am a Jew!"

The philosopher Bergson shouted that in occupied Paris. The famous scientist felt himself a Frenchman, he had even become a Catholic, as he often said. But here, under the muzzles of the Fascist machine guns, he found the strength to say, "I am with those who are being persecuted."

I shall say no more, even though all it takes will be more spadefuls and the internationalists will have built a grave mound over me.

"I AM WITH THOSE WHO ARE BEING MURDERED, RUSSIA. I AM WITH THOSE WHO ARE BEING MURDERED."

Moscow, May 1970

WHY*

I am applying for permission to leave Russia to take up permanent residence in Israel. Perhaps no further explanations are needed. The law is on
my side. The law about the reunification of families. But my friends will
remain in Russia, and they have a right to hear about more than my
relatives in Israel. And OVIR† and other official persons, I gather, are
interested not merely in official application forms. They are concerned
about the outburst of national feeling among the Jews. I hope that my
documents, and my explanation, will be read not only by people who
admire the novels of Ivan Shevtsov, or by bureaucrats who, as the Russian
writer put it, have more teeth than brains. So I shall try to be restrained.

What then are the supplementary reasons (let us call them that)
which have forced me, a man of Russian culture, and moreover a Russian
writer and specialist in Russian literature, to declare myself a Jew and
make the irreversible decision to leave with my family for Israel?

First of all I shall give the main evidence, the indisputable facts that
call to be understood by everyone, but that will be more immediately
accessible to those whose profession is the use of language.

Linguistic innovations—neologisms—which are adopted into the
spoken language can document a manifestation more accurately and in-
disputably than any number of pieces of paper. Language is the only
historical document which can never be forged, not even by the most
skillful counterfeiters.

In the Russian language, a formula has appeared and achieved wide
usage despite the fact that at first sight it is incomprehensible: that
formula is "Point Five". It might seem that this bureaucratic jargon does
not in itself have any special meaning. Point Five in the passport form has
for long been the point of nationality. But there can be no one left who
does not understand what is meant when someone is spoken of as "Having

* An open letter to his friends about his reasons for emigrating to Israel. Undated but
not earlier than November 12, 1971. It was reviewed in *Chronicle of Current Events*
(No. 23).
† OVIR (*Otdyel Viz i Registratsii*): Visa and Registration Department, which both
issues visas to Soviet citizens traveling abroad and looks after foreigners resident in
the USSR. [Translator]

Point Five," or "They're using Point Five against him." Russians, Ukrainians, Armenians all know what is involved.

Our great native language! It knows no fear, no hypocrisy, no self-interest. It is eternity captured for us to examine.

POINT FIVE. I have exerted so much mental and physical effort trying to change the circumstances to which the Russian language bears such calm and irrefutable witness for me as a writer. I have tried to act with words. I have been answered with DEEDS.

Here are some documents.

TO THE SECRETARIAT OF THE MOSCOW BRANCH OF THE UNION OF WRITERS OF
THE RSFSR
From Grigory Svirsky   April 28, 1970

Since 1965, after my speech at a writers' meeting, the publication date of books of mine which had already been accepted began to recede each year. Since 1968, all the publishing houses, magazines, and Mosfilm studios with one accord stopped accepting my work—novels, scripts, stories. A little earlier, the Soviet Writer publishing house broke up the type of my novel The State Examination, which had been passed for printing by seven bodies including Glavlit (January 16, 1968).

The military publishing house also stopped the printing in Leipzig of a certain collection of short stories so that four pages written by me could be removed.

Since 1964—seven years ago now—not one single word I have written has been published. I am to all intents and purposes removed from the list of writers.

Almost every leader of the Writers' Union has tried to help me. But hatred, alas, is stronger than goodwill. I would like to believe that the Secretariat of the Moscow branch of the Writers' Union, at its next meeting, will speak out against the slow but deliberate murder of its member Grigory Svirsky and will prevent that murder from proceeding.

There followed immediately two categorical resolutions by the Secretariat of the Writers' Union of the USSR and the Moscow branch of the Writers' Union of the RSFSR (April 29, 1970, and April 30, 1970).

To ask for help for Comrade G. T. Svirsky [In the matter of getting a contract for a new novel].

To delegate to the Secretariat of the Moscow Writers' organization the job of helping him to find work suitable to his talents . . .

To help, to ask, to delegate . . . Hatred, alas, is stronger than goodwill. Six months later, I sent another letter to the leaders of the Writers' Union, S. Mikhalkov and S. Narochatov.

December 10, 1970

Nothing has been done. The resolutions of the Writers' Union have been completely ignored by the workers in the publishing houses to whom I have written. . . .

I do not wish to accept handouts from the Literary Fund. I am not ill; I am a healthy writer, full of creative plans and energy.

If you, leaders of the Writers' Union, are powerless to change anything, please say so openly.

GRIGORY SVIRSKY

Here is another document, sent at the request of the Union of Writers to the prose writers' association of the Moscow branch of the Writers' Union of the RSFSR.

November 12, 1971

In response to your request, I have to tell you that the efforts of the Writers' Union have produced no result. How I shall live in the future I do not know.

Enough of documents. Particularly since they produced a reaction completely opposite to the one I had hoped for. Someone even took the trouble to see that my name was removed from the newly published sixth volume of the *Literary Encyclopedia*. Not a trace of Svirsky must be left in Russian writing.

In Stalin's day there was a practice of depriving writers of "fire and water" for a year or two, to give them ample time to reflect on an empty stomach. I have been separated from my readers, as we see, not just for a year or two. The blockade is now in its seventh year. By this time, however, it is no blockade—it is brazenly illegal persecution. Carried out in broad daylight and intended to be fatal.

Every anti-Zionist campaign has also been understood to be anti-Semitic and has poured oil on the flames. This has angered my fellow writers, but has not surprised them. Indeed, if publishers have allowed themselves three times in recent years to re-issue the pogromist novels of Ivan Shevtsov, which have been officially condemned, or the verses of the young poet Ivan Lystsov, such as "And someone wants to govern his soul,/By jokingly rolling the 'r' in 'Rus'!" or the book *Social Progress* by the philosopher V. Mishin, who welcomes the reduction by one-third in the number of Jews engaged in higher education and thinks the ideal would be a quota, and a lower quota than existed in the days of Alexander III—if publishers have allowed themselves to behave like this, then it is not hard to imagine how they have reacted to Jewish authors, particularly to Jews who protested against anti-Semitism in literature.

"If even my name cannot appear in a newspaper"—I was finally obliged to say recently to the editor-in-chief of *Literaturnaya Gazeta* when two of my articles about the scientists of Norilsk were dropped from a page which had been passed for printing, just because someone rang him up—"if my name is under a strict ban and that ban has lasted seven years, then there can be no doubt that I am either being murdered or driven out of the country." The editor, Alexander Chakovsky, candidate-member of the Central Committee of the Communist Party of the Soviet Union, merely shrugged, figuratively speaking, as earlier the secretary of the Writers' Union of the RSFSR, S. Mikhalkov, the secretary of the Writers' Union of the USSR, S. Sartakov, and before that the secretary of the Moscow branch of the Writers' Union of the RSFSR, V. Ilin, had all shrugged too.

I am being murdered or driven out of the country. . . . I choose the second course.

But perhaps I exaggerate? Have I the right, in official documents, to call the seven-year blockade of a writer "murder"?

Murder is murder.

Have I the right to approach the state prosecutor of the USSR or the chairman of the Presidium of the Supreme Soviet of the USSR, accusing certain persons of murder, and of premeditated murder, at that? To demand an investigation . . . when they still haven't actually managed to kill me?

It's true. But everyone knows of recent precedents where people have been accused of intent to murder—and been convicted. So then what? To demand a trial on the basis of precedent? Year after year? Or at least the admission that I had a right to talk about anti-Semitism?

The highest control organ of the CPSU, the Party Control Committee of the Central Committee of the Communist Party of the Soviet Union, under the chairmanship of Politburo member Comrade Pelshe, officially confirmed that I had every ground for saying in public that the editor-in-chief of the magazine *Friendship of the Peoples*, Vasily Smirnov, was a chauvinist and anti-Semite. And before that the secretary of the Central Committee of the CPSU Comrade Demichev had said (October 27, 1965) in the presence of more than a thousand Moscow writers that Grigory Svirsky had chosen a good time to raise the question of anti-Semitism.

. . . The first person to give way under the years of pressure was my wife, now the only breadwinner in the family. Tortured by the brutal persecution, the lack of money, the inability to buy even necessities, she fell seriously ill. My sixteen-year-old son's eyes were full of grief and pain. He understood what was happening.

I do not want to explain or complain any more. I have nothing more to say about the well-intentioned bureaucrats of the Writers' Union. The road to hell is paved with good intentions. What can be more humiliating than to try to bind to you with love someone who rejects you? You cannot force people to be kind, says the wisdom of the Russian people.

No, I have not changed my convictions. I have not stopped loving the earth for which I have given my blood, nor have I stopped loving my friends, or the Russian language which has been my life and my fate. I am a former soldier of Russia, who fought for four unbroken years. In my diary of 1941, where I kept a record of the missions flown by my old aircraft, I jotted down some lines from the poet Pavel Kogan who was killed, and I came to regard them as my own: "I love the Russian air, the Russian earth."

In those days my family were shot in the back of the neck because they were Jews. The traitors from Free Ukraine turned their neighbors over to the enemy. Lyubka Mukhina lured Fima, my wife's brother, from the house where he had been hiding so that the Germans and the quisling militia could take him too. And they threw the boy into the Inguletsk quarry after his father and mother, grandfather and grandmother. Lyubka Mukhina ran after the wagon taking Fima and my wife's parents to their deaths, shouting, "And they've got a daughter as well, away studying in Moscow—she's in the Komsomol."

Now my son too is called Fima. . . .

I am a Russian writer—I was convinced of my calling. It was as a Russian writer that I was accepted into the USSR Writers' Union. But in 1965, when I began to protest against the anti-Semitism of the editor-in-chief of *Friendship of the Peoples*, Vasily Smirnov, respectable elderly ladies from the official commission lost their last vestiges of dignity and bayed at me: "You say you're a Russian writer but your passport says you're a Jew! How can this be—a Russian writer and a Jew at the same time?" That's what they shouted openly, in the presence of the chairman of the writers' Party Committee, and it came from their hearts.

After the first investigation, I remember that I fled out of the city into the woods to be on my own, and a drunk in the train suddenly attacked me: "You ought to go where you belong—to Israel. Hitler should have dealt with you long ago!" I had already taken people like him six times to the militia, and six times the militia officers had said, "How shall we charge him? Anti-Semitism? We don't have anything like that. Let's say 'public nuisance' or 'insulting behavior.' That'll ensure a conviction."

I am a Russian. Or so I had thought for many years. I had reasons for thinking the way I did. I wasn't the only one who had fought for Russia. My great-grandfather Girsh had been a soldier under Nicholas I, and was wounded nearly one hundred and thirty years ago in the first defense of Sebastopol. He served twenty-five years in the Russian Army, and I was named in his honor.

I thought I was a native Russian. But people looked at me with cold, mocking eyes—people like Solovyova, the "head of culture," who announced for all to hear that she supported "the position of Vasily Smirnov," and I saw in her eyes who I was. . . .

Enough. There is a limit to every man's patience, and I have reached mine. On September 29, 1971, I reached my fiftieth birthday. It is time that I stopped living feeling like a small boy in a crowded bus. The child's nose is at the level of everyone else's elbows, so if anyone moves the boy gets a bloody nose.

I want to be neither the highest among equals, nor the lowest among equals. I want to be equal. And I have had enough of the literary Black Hundreds. I had hoped that militant anti-Semites would disappear with the Smirnov generation. But I do not have time to wait for the Lystsov generation to pass.

I have had enough of the drunken hooligans on the streetcars with their slogans, "Hitler should have dealt with you, too," and "Go to Israel where you belong." They may be only a tiny percentage of the people, you might even say they're atypical. But it's no easier for a man if someone atypical spits in his face. The spit is typical enough. I want to see no more of their self-satisfied faces, full of superiority. I don't want to waste my time, or anyone else's, on them.

"Go to Israel," the drunks shouted and are still shouting.

"Go to Israel," I see in the eyes of the people who say, "How can a Russian writer be a Jew?"

"Go to Israel," like an echo, I have heard in the offices of courteous editors, who for seven years together have not been able, as they put it, to "find room" for my books, my scripts, my articles, my stories. "Go to Israel," I sometimes hear in their respectful, sad good-byes.

Go? Thank you, my friends, I am ready!

So in that case why have they held me back, suppressed my invitation from Israel that is vital for my exit visa? The invitation, sent by my seventy-year-old mother on May 9, 1971, has been received (No. 11600/71). True, not immediately, and in a torn envelope with a hole in the middle, and a little note from the post office, "This letter arrived in a damaged condition." The invitation, which was sent to me, my wife, and my son, took three months to arrive. I was obliged to ask over and over again for invitations which my brother assured me had been sent. Why, to what end, were those invitations held back?

That giant of Jewish literature, Sholom Aleichem, has some lines about a dog caught in a door. The dog is being kicked, beaten with a stick, and shouted at to drive it through the door at the same time that people are leaning against the door so that it can't escape from the blows. The harder the blows, the harder the door is pressed against its maimed body. Sholom Aleichem compared that dog to the Jews in Russia. In my youth the comparison seemed wildly inaccurate. In Aleichem's day, anyone who wished to leave could get a passport and go. Just by calling at the nearest police station. So what did the writer have in mind when he described the door that was crushing the dog? Poverty? The Pale?

Or did he foresee the future?

As far as I am concerned, I want to become an Israeli writer. To reach back and find the sources of the moral health of a nation that has been persecuted for centuries. To immerse myself in a life that can no longer be silenced, no longer be slandered, no longer destroyed. That is why there is no further point in trying to use hunger and oppression to persuade me to go to Israel. I've taken the hint.

Even if I don't know Hebrew, and probably will never be able to learn it well enough to write books in it, even if I always remain a man of Russian culture, with all the symptoms of homesickness known to civilization, I shall say—no, not say, but shout aloud—if I still have any human dignity left, "I am a Jew!"

And I shall remain one, even if those who are now tormenting this writer to death suddenly change their wrath to kindness. The anger and the love of lords are emptier than all our griefs, says the Russian classical proverb.

But enough of metaphor. I shall try to be extremely precise in the expression of my views. I no longer believe in the assimilation of Jews in Russia. At least, of a significant number of Jews.

The reasons for this I have already stated: "Point Five."

How many times have I been marked by that Point? How can marked men be assimilated? Pretense is possible. But pretense is not for me. I am a Jew.

And now that I have decided for myself once and for all, I want, I have the *right*, to live as every one of us lives—Russians, Ukrainians, and so on—without Point Five. Among my own national majority.

APPENDIXES

THE SCHOOL
OF OBSCURANTISM*

Deir Yassin is the Israeli My Lai. On the dawn of April 9, 1948, it was the scene of a bloody massacre. Hordes of Zionists from Irgun Zvai Leumi and the Stern gang burst into the village, burned down all the houses, massacring every Arab inhabitant—women, children, the old people, and the men. . . .

Today we see an extension of the tragedy of Deir Yassin. In the Israeli-held areas of Lebanon, Syria, and Jordan, the Moslems are kept in ghettos and behind the barbed wire of concentration camps. Christians are driven from their homes. Whole villages have been reduced to ruins and ashes. Bakr-el-Bahr, Biram, and Ikrit, Raphiad, Rafid . . . these names have become a symbol for acts of brigandry. The present policy of Tel Aviv is a policy against humanity.

Tel Aviv needs people capable of executing its plans. It needs fanatics who will take on the filthiest and bloodiest tasks without batting an eyelid. And the Zionist is setting about acquiring these people in a business-like way. Israeli schoolchildren, as soon as they have learned to read and write, are taught how to answer the question "What should we do with the Arabs?" Their answer is "We must massacre them!" Savagery begins in the classroom; it is from the schoolbench that the road to Deir Yassin and Bakr-el-Bahr begins.

In Israeli schools the lion's share of time is given over to the study of the scriptures, which "inculcate the feeling of national conscience-ness"—i.e., twenty-four hours a day. So what do these books say, what moral values does the Israeli school offer the young generation?

According to the fundamental conception of these books, in particular the "Shulkhan Arukh": (1) The word should belong to the followers of the powerful God Jehovah, in whose name his worshippers may don any mask. The possessions of non-Jews are theirs only temporarily, just waiting to be taken into the hands of the "chosen people." When the "chosen people" outnumber the other peoples of the world, "God will

* An article that appeared in URSS, a bulletin published by the Soviet Information Bureau (September 22, 1972).

deliver all of them into their hands for the final massacre." (2) These are the concrete rules which determine relations between Jews and all other peoples—"goys," "akums," or "Nazarenes," as they are scornfully termed. (3) Akums are not to be considered as people (Orakh Hayim, 14, 72, 77, 79, 55, 197). (4) "It is strictly forbidden for a Jew to save the life of an Akum with whom he lives in peace." (5) "It is forbidden to look after an Akum even for money, but it is permissible to try the effect of a medicament on him" (Yore Deah, 158). (6) "When a Jew is present at the death of an Akum, he should rejoice in it" (Yore Deah, 719, 5). (7) "To do any kindness for an Akum, or to give him anything, is a sacrilege. It is better to throw a piece of meat to a dog than to give it to a goy" (Hoshen-Mishpat, 156, 3); "but it is permissible to give alms to poor Akums or to visit the sick so that they should think that the Jews are their good friends" (Yore Deah, 151, 12).

Such religious dispositions, which one could go on quoting indefinitely, form the moral code of the Zionist society. The Israeli authorities have established a special department for propaganda of the Torah, the Talmud, and other Zionist ideological materials. This department operates at state level. It is on this "cultural and moral basis" that the "authentic Zionist" acquires his conception of the world. From his childhood he is obliged to learn all these precepts by heart and to recite them in the solemn atmosphere of the "Bar-Mitzvah" (first confirmation) to prove his "ideological maturity."

These repugnant and odious rules of life, and the hatred of other peoples, is inculcated from the very cradle to entire generations of Israelis, who are ordered to (8) "massacre the goys under the vault of heaven" (Orakh-Hayim, 690, 16). These laws of Judaism are embodied in the standing order of the Israeli Army, and any departure from them is punishable under military discipline. They are the very essence of the policy of the Zionist state.

M. ZANDENBERG

THE PARIS TRIBUNAL*

. . . During the trial the Court has taken into consideration the following circumstances of the present case:

The false allegation of the article in the URSS bulletin that Jews do not consider people of other faiths to be human beings is an allegation that disseminates hatred toward the Jewish people and contributes to the exclusion of Jews from the society of others,

the testimony and proofs of the fact that racial slander has repeatedly led to persecution and mass murder,

the statement by René Cassin, Nobel Prize winner, that in 1965 the Soviet Union signed the Declaration of Human Rights and the document subscribing to the battle with discrimination,

the statements by Grigory Svirsky and his proof that the article published in the journal URSS is nothing more than a slightly amended copy of Rossov's pamphlet published in St. Petersburg in 1906 before the start of a series of pogroms, under the title "The Jewish Question,"

the statements by Gaston Monnerville drawing the Court's attention to the fact that the so-called Protocols of Zion (which lie at the base of Rossov's allegations) are a dangerous text which has led to persecution.

Having considered the case from all aspects, the Court pronounces the following ruling:

SENTENCE OF THE PARIS TRIBUNAL

At the final session April 24, 1973:

Bearing in mind that the main point of the trial is the accusation against the journal URSS that it engaged in racial propaganda and that racial hatred is an offense under the law,

and bearing in mind the allegations made in the article in the journal URSS, and the fact that the editor of the above-mentioned journal Robert Leganier has acknowledged to the Court that the printed text was "contentious" and was published "in error,"

and bearing in mind that the article in the journal URSS was not, as it may seem, directed merely against Zionism but was written in such a

* From the official documents of the Paris Tribunal (March–April 1973)

way that the allegations in it were made against all people of Jewish descent,

and bearing in mind that according to the evidence given to the court by Grigory Svirsky and two Rabbis, and according to the evidence of Leon Polyakov, the religious books of Judaism (and in particular the book Shulkhan-Arukh), which were written four hundred years ago, have been distorted by officials of the Tsarist "Okhranka" and by the authors of the so-called Protocols of Zion,

This Court recognizes that the complaint before it is fully justified, despite the counterallegations by the defense that the trial is without foundation.

The Court accordingly finds that Robert Deganier, by allowing the publication of the article in the journal URSS, an article which arouses among its readers a feeling of hatred toward a specific group of people on the grounds of their ethnic or racial descent, and on the basis of their religious belief, is guilty of an offense under the law, and accordingly sentences the accused to pay a fine of fifteen hundred francs and to pay symbolic damages of one franc to the International League Against Racism and Anti-Semitism.

And further the Court rules that the journal URSS must publish in the journal the findings of this court relative to the guilt of its editors in the illegal publication of an appeal to racial hatred, and to do everything within their power to secure the publication of the text of the sentence of the court in six different newspapers.

Moreover, all expenses connected with the conduct of this trial shall be paid by the defense.

SIGNED BY THE JUDGE

A NOTE ABOUT THE AUTHOR

GRIGORY SVIRSKY was born in 1921. During the war he served in the Soviet Air Force, stationed in the Arctic. After the war he had to fight a protracted battle to obtain a place at university as a philology student; his wife, also Jewish, had suffered similar discrimination, and his life from then on was a constant struggle against authority. In 1965 he made a speech at the Writers' Union in the presence of Demichev, secretary of the Communist Party Central Committee, exposing anti-Semitism in high places. But he retained the support of the Writers' Union against his adversaries until in 1968 he spoke out against censorship, as a result of which he was expelled from the Communist Party. No longer able to earn a living in Russia, he succeeded in emigrating to Israel with his wife and son in 1972. In 1973 he was chief prosecution witness in a successful suit for slander brought in Paris against the Soviet embassy by the International League against Racism and Anti-Semitism.

A NOTE ON THE TYPE

The text of this book was set in Electra, a Linotype face designed by W. A. Dwiggins (1880–1956), who was responsible for so much that is good in contemporary book design. Although much of his early work was in advertising and he was the author of the standard volume *Layout in Advertising,* Mr. Dwiggins later devoted his prolific talents to book typography and type design and worked with great distinction in both fields.

Electra cannot be classified as either modern or old-style. It is not based on any historical model, nor does it echo a particular period or style. It avoids the extreme contrast between thick and thin elements that marks most modern faces and attempts to give a feeling of fluidity, power, and speed.

This book was composed by Maryland Linotype Composition Company, Baltimore, Maryland, and printed and bound by The Haddon Craftsmen, Inc., Scranton, Pennsylvania.

The book was designed by Earl Tidwell.